Educating Learners with Dow

For individuals with Down syndrome, the extent of the effect of intellectual disability depends largely on the degree of provision of appropriate support and intervention. In *Educating Learners with Down Syndrome*, editors Rhonda Faragher and Barbara Clarke have brought together a number of expert contributors, whose chapters review recent findings in the field of DS education, highlight promising practices, and identify areas for future research.

While the emphasis is primarily on the school years, links to early intervention and to life post-16 are made, with chapters organized into three parts: conceptual overview of issues in learning and teaching, learning mathematics, and literacy development. The book is also united by the cohesive themes of assessment, evidence-based practice, and inclusive practices.

Educating Learners with Down Syndrome importantly incorporates the voices of individuals with Down syndrome, whose personal narratives add significance to the research mission of the text and demonstrate the authors' inclusive philosophy. Aimed at researchers, teacher educators, higher degree students, and policy makers, this book is the first of its kind to provide a compendium of research on educating learners with Down syndrome.

Dr Rhonda Faragher is a Senior Lecturer in Mathematics Education at Australian Catholic University.

Dr Barbara Clarke is an Associate Professor at Monash University, Victoria, Australia.

Educating Learners with Down Syndrome

Research, theory, and practice with children and adolescents

Edited by Rhonda Faragher and Barbara Clarke

Routledge
Taylor & Francis Group
LONDON AND NEW YORK

First published 2014
by Routledge
2 Park Square, Milton Park, Abingdon, Oxon OX14 4RN

and by Routledge
711 Third Avenue, New York, NY 10017

Routledge is an imprint of the Taylor & Francis Group, an informa business

British Library Cataloguing in Publication Data
A catalogue record for this book is available from the British Library

Library of Congress Cataloging in Publication Data
Educating learners with down syndrome : research, theory and practice with children and adolescents / edited by Rhonda Faragher and Barbara Clarke.
pages cm
1. Children with mental disabilities–Education. 2. Down syndrome–Patients–Education. 3. Developmentally disabled children–Education.
I. Faragher, Rhonda. II. Clarke, Barbara.
LC4601.E26 2013
371.9–dc23

2013017041

ISBN: 978-0-415-81636-6 (hbk)
ISBN: 978-0-415-81637-3 (pbk)
ISBN: 978-1-315-88358-8 (ebk)

Typeset in Galliard
by Wearset Ltd, Boldon, Tyne and Wear

Contents

Illustrations

Figures

Tables

Contributors

Becky Baxter, MRCSLT, is a speech and language therapist specializing in Down syndrome. She has worked on a number of research projects with Down Syndrome Education International. Her current interests include speech and language development and inclusion for children with Down syndrome.

Roy I. Brown, PhD, is Professor Emeritus at the University of Calgary, Canada, and Flinders University, Australia, and Adjunct Professor at several other universities. Through practice, research, writing, and teaching, he has founded and developed programmes in the field of disabilities. His current research and applied writing is in quality and family quality of life. He has written for and edited a series on adults with Down syndrome, is a former trustee of Down Syndrome International, and has consulted to Down syndrome associations in several countries. Currently he serves as the founding director of the IASSIDD Academy and over the years has served on government and regional committees in several countries.

Sue Buckley, PhD, is Emeritus Professor of Developmental Disability, University of Portsmouth, and Director for Science and Research at Down Syndrome Education International. Sue's academic background includes an undergraduate degree in psychology followed by training in clinical psychology. She has been involved in research into the development and education of children with Down syndrome for over 30 years with a focus on language, literacy, and memory. Her current focus is on RCT evaluations of effective interventions. She has an adopted adult daughter with Down syndrome.

Kelly Burgoyne, PhD, is currently working as a Research Associate at University College London. Her research focuses on literacy and language skills and intervention for young children who have language difficulties. She continues to have an interest in working with children with Down syndrome and in furthering research with this group of children.

Barbara Clarke, PhD, is an Associate Professor in mathematics education at Monash University, Victoria, Australia. Her major research focus is supporting young children's learning in mathematics. She has undertaken research on the mathematics learning of children with Down syndrome and has extensive editing experience.

Donna Couzens, PhD, is a researcher with the Down syndrome longitudinal research project in the School of Education at the University of Queensland. Donna's research considers biological and environmental influences on age-related development and learning. Donna became involved with children with Down syndrome through the guiding movement and refined her knowledge and skills as a special education teacher, a researcher, and an educational psychologist. Donna's research spans cognitive development and learning, behaviour change, and communication.

Monica Cuskelly, PhD, is an Associate Professor and educational and developmental psychologist. She heads the Down Syndrome Research Programme at the University of Queensland in Brisbane, Australia. The programme includes a longitudinal study of the cognitive development of individuals with Down syndrome that has been on-going for more than 30 years. Monica's research focuses on two broad areas: the development of individuals with an intellectual disability and the impact on families of having a member with a disability.

Rhonda Faragher, PhD, is Head of Education (Canberra Campus) at the Australian Catholic University. Her major research interests concern inclusive mathematics education and the effects on quality of life. She is a board member of Down Syndrome International and has a teenage daughter with Down syndrome.

Kathleen M. Feeley, PhD, BCBA, is an Associate Professor and Director of the Center for Community Inclusion at Long Island University Post. Kathleen's research focuses on developing communication skills in children with disabilities (Down syndrome and autism) and proactively addressing challenging behaviours. Much of her clinical works focuses on working with educators to provide inclusive opportunities for children with Down syndrome and enhancing families' engagement in the education process.

Linda Gilmore, PhD, is an Associate Professor and educational and developmental psychologist at Queensland University of Technology in Brisbane, Australia. She has undertaken research with children with Down syndrome and their families for more than 20 years, focusing in particular on mastery motivation, self-regulation, and parenting. Her major research focus within the family environment has been on the consequences of maternal support for autonomy for aspects of children's functioning. Linda also has a strong interest in community and professional attitudes towards people with a disability.

Anne Jobling, PhD, is an adjunct Senior Lecturer in the School of Education at the University of Queensland. She has undertaken significant long-term research into intellectual disability, specifically Down syndrome. Her current interests address lifelong aspects of education for individuals with intellectual disabilities in the areas of health and literacy education.

Emily A. Jones, PhD, BCBA-D, is an Assistant Professor in the Department of Psychology at Queens College, City University of New York. Her research involves the development and demonstration of behaviour analytic interventions to address critical areas of impairment in young children with developmental disabilities such as autism and Down syndrome. This research focuses on social communication skills such as requesting and joint attention, as well as early developing cognitive and motor skills and problem behaviour.

Karen B. Moni, PhD, is an Associate Professor in the School of Education at the University of Queensland. She coordinates English curriculum, literacy, and courses in undergraduate and postgraduate programmes, and is the Executive Director of Latch-On, a post-school literacy research and teaching programme for young adults with intellectual disabilities. Her research interests include literacy and young adults with intellectual disabilities, literacy and literature for adolescents, and teaching, learning, and assessment in higher education.

Nicole Neil, MA, BCBA, is an Adjunct Lecturer and Doctoral Student in the Department of Psychology, Queens College, City University of New York. Her research interests are focused on the assessment and treatment of problem behaviour in children with developmental disabilities. Nicole is currently involved in projects investigating applied behaviour analytic assessment and intervention for repetitive and compulsive behaviours and for increasing communication and language skills in young children with Down syndrome.

Rumiati, MEd, has an academic background including undergraduate study in mathematics education at Yogyakarta State University and a Master's degree from Southern Cross University, Australia. She currently works at a centre for development and empowerment of mathematics teachers and educational personnel, PPPPTK Matematika, in Indonesia. Her current research interest is teaching and learning mathematics for students with different abilities. Rumi has a brother with Down syndrome.

Robert J. Wright (Bob), EdD, is an Adjunct Professor in mathematics education at Southern Cross University, Australia. His interests are in assessment, instruction, and teacher development related to early arithmetical learning, and he has published four books and many articles in this field. His work includes the development of the Mathematics Recovery (MR) programme and he has led several projects funded by the Australian Research Council. Bob is currently completing a five-year project focusing on developing specialists in mathematics intervention in the first five years of school.

Foreword

When the children in my study,[1] born in one part of south-east England in the early 1960s, went to school, they were deemed 'ineducable' and none attended a mainstream school. At age 11, three of the most able attended schools for the 'educationally subnormal (moderate)', later termed 'schools for the moderately learning disabled'; all the others went to schools for the 'severely subnormal', or Junior Training Centres (JTC). At that time, nearly 50 years ago, attendance at mainstream schools for children with Down syndrome was almost unheard of, though there may have been a few exceptions. All this began to change. In the USA in 1975, the Education of All Handicapped Children Act made integration a condition of federal funding. In the UK, in 1981, it became mandatory for schools that had previously been called Junior Training Centres to be called schools for children with severe learning disabilities, though one writer gave it as his opinion that 'In practice the organisation of the curriculum and recruitment of pupils to these schools (have) not changed significantly' (Lane, 1985, p. 388).

So children with Down syndrome were now, along with all other children, seen as eligible for education. What then is the purpose of their education? 'The general aims of education are the same … as for anyone else' (Mittler, 1979). So essentially it should be for the benefit of the children themselves, to enable them to enjoy and participate in their society. In the days of JTCs, the major aim was to enable the children to fit in, as unobtrusively as possible, with the wider society, and so there was an emphasis on social skills—toileting, washing, and dressing—and on such socially useful accomplishments as using public transport and shopping. These are undeniably useful skills for any person, but it is also true that the attainment of more academic skills, such as mastering some degree of reading, writing, and number, are of great benefit to children with Down syndrome, as they are to children in the general population; both to enhance their own enjoyment (especially in reading) and in making it possible for them to cope more fully in the everyday world. So there are strong arguments for stressing the importance of these skills for them, and we need to know the best ways to help them learn these skills.

This leads us on to considering how these skills may best be developed in children with Down syndrome, the subject of this book. The old adage, 'Bring him/her up as normal', handed out to and, sometimes, adopted by parents in the absence of any other advice, although worthy enough, is not, we know now, the most useful. The children have particular needs: in the Introduction to this book, Faragher and Clarke point out their well-known difficulties, with short-term verbal memory and with hearing loss as two of particular importance to those learning to read. The adoption of special methods, as set out here, can make all the difference. Some of these indeed—making reading enjoyable, daily practice, starting early in the child's life—would not be out of place for any learner-reader, but take on a special significance for those who find the task less than straight-forward. Other strategies, such as using a multi-sensory approach, forming words in the sand tray or with Play-Doh™, would not be expected to feature routinely in mainstream schools but may further the progress of children with Down syndrome.

Special approaches then are available to help children with Down syndrome progress in reading, and this is to be welcomed. But reading is a relative strength for people with Down syndrome. The same cannot be said about number. In my group, at age 35, of those able to score on the reading test, their mean reading age was over eight years, enough to enable them to read most signs, most instructions, most of many newspapers and many books. In the same group, at the same age, mean number age was almost two and a half years behind reading age and many studies have found number to be a stumbling block for people with Down syndrome. Does this matter? Yes, it does. Numeracy is necessary to them if they are to meet the demands of life, to have greater opportunities for paid work, as an essential for many aspects of independent life, and has been shown to be associated with quality of life (see Chapter 8). Here too help is at hand—with their now well-known preference for visual over verbal media, children with Down syndrome can benefit from working with symbols (the written version of numbers: 6, 3) rather than hearing the words ('six', 'three'). It need not stop there. It appears important not to demand mastery of early number systems before introducing them to some more advanced mathematics, such as algebra, with the additional advantage that they would then be enabled to participate in similar areas of work as that occupying their peers, resulting in their greater motivation and satisfaction. This may be surprising to the general run of educationalists, to the point where they may find it difficult to credit, but the evidence is convincing.

There is available, then, a multiplicity of innovative and useful suggestions for promoting learning for children with Down syndrome, over a wide range of areas, and from the early to secondary school years. Here is where, as a general rule, it stops. In my group, although on leaving school the majority of them attended further education colleges, for very few, less than a third, was there any educational, as opposed to practical or artistic, activities scheduled, and that for no more than an hour a week. Despite this, literacy levels crept up over the years, but to a barely noticeable extent, while numeracy dropped further behind. A strong case can be made, and is made in this book, for education to continue well into the adult life of people with Down syndrome. We can only speculate by how much their lives might be enriched if this were brought about. If it is, it will be due in no small measure to the influence of this book. I whole-heartedly commend it.

Janet Carr
Fellow of the British Psychological Society
Chair of the BPS Welfare Fund
Assistant Editor for the British Association of Behavioural and Cognitive Psychotherapy

Note

1 Carr, J. (2012). Six weeks to 45 years: a longitudinal study of a population with Down Syndrome. *Journal of Applied Research in Intellectual Disabilities, 25*, 1–9.

References

Lane, D. (1985). After school: work and employment for adults and children with Down's Syndrome? In B. Stratford & D. Lane (Eds), *Current approaches to Down's Syndrome*. London: Holt Rheinhart & Winston.

Mittler, P. (1979). *Teaching children with severe learning difficulties*. Second Stanley Segal lecture. Tunbridge Wells, UK: Costello Educational.

Acknowledgements

We would like to acknowledge the support of Sue Buckley and colleagues, specifically for the use of the Sarah Duffin Centre for an initial writing conference. We also thank our fellow authors for their good humour and collegiality through the preparation of the manuscript.

We express our gratitude to Nike Prince, who worked tirelessly on the formatting and editing. Her attention to detail and thorough organization were vital during the final stages of the preparation of the manuscript.

Rhonda Faragher and Barbara Clarke

Book authors at writing conference.

Prologue

This is a book about learners with Down syndrome. To set the scene, we wish to introduce you to some young people with Down syndrome who have provided a brief profile highlighting their experiences as well as their aspirations. In particular, you will read of their experiences with schools and teachers, and suggestions for improvement and future research. In the spirit of 'nothing about us, without us', you will see they provide insights into the range of contexts and experiences through an authentic voice.

Introducing Ruth

My name is Ruth, I am 16, and I live with my mum and dad and older brother in Canberra, the capital city of Australia. My other brother lives in Brisbane. I love my school.

I love being told that I am doing well with my public speaking. It is good to read the notes and then look up to the audience. That's what I do and I am being a confident person. Since I was little I wish—I wanted to do public speaking. Now I can do public speaking because I'm not a kid any more.

I like to teach kids with Down syndrome. When I grow up I can teach them English and a bit of RE [Religious Education]. Students with Down syndrome have to learn RE and English as well.

English is important because you need to learn poetry. You need to read all of the poem. Poetry is important to me because I just love doing poems.

I love tests. People with Down syndrome need help with lots of things. I get a lot of help. Ladies from the learning centre help people with Down syndrome with RE. It is really helpful if I have Miss M [teacher aide]. She helps me with English because I am doing my 'Which Witch' poem and she is helping me.

I like doing Italian. Which is really fun because next year, when I am in year 10, I will go on an Italian trip to Italy. I like to take my camera with me and I can take pictures of Italy—all those interesting things. I will enjoy gelato the best. I love ice cream. Mint is my favourite flavour.

I learn best with music because I can do piano and sometimes my mum teaches me 'Amazing Grace' on the piano. I sing in the youth choir at All Saints Church. I like singing.

In primary school you work really hard in year 5 and you will go to year 6. I do miss my primary school. I miss playing on the playground. I played on the playground before school.

I like school because the teachers are so nice to me. They love teaching me along with the other girls. I love working so hard with my teachers.

Sometimes some kids do the wrong thing like eating in class and using mobile phones.

I love my school. It is a lovely school and we have a new restaurant that is our canteen. I just love talking about school because I like to study harder. I want to finish year 12 and graduate.

What should others know about Down syndrome?

They find things difficult—struggle with maths. They need help.

What is good about having Down syndrome?

It makes you special because your parents love you so much. Brothers and sisters can look after you.

What is hard about having Down syndrome?

Don't give people a hard time with Down syndrome or else they will find it hard. Some people are nice to me.

The future

I'd like to live at Brisbane with my cousins. I will get to work at the child care centre. I love kids. It was my favourite thing.

I want to teach children with Down syndrome in the future.

In my future, because I love boys because they are so enjoyable and they love girls, I would like a boyfriend. I haven't had a chance to have one before because I want one.

Prepared with Barbara Clarke

Introducing Dylan

My name is Dylan Kuehl and I am 29 years old. I'm from Olympia, Washington State. I like doing lots of things, from music, to art, bowling, weightlifting and so on.

At first I started out being mistreated at school. It got better and certain students did become friends. The teachers helped as well. They understand being mistreated and they gave me tools to overcome it.

I went to elementary, junior high to senior high and to community college. I did ABE—that's short for Adult Basic Education. I currently have private tutoring with math and English.

The only thing that helps me to get going in learning was that I gotta make sure that I'm well fed and drink well so I won't lose energy, I learn.

I am self-employed, which means I get to be my own boss. I am artistically talented. I have a new product and that's fused glass. By using my sense of creativity and attention to detail, I now make fused glass necklaces, earrings, rings, pins, decorative tiles, and other glass items. I enjoy this work.

I am a motivational professional speaker. I speak at conferences.

I am a drummer in a band. I do a lot of lifting. [Dylan has won gold medals for weightlifting.]

What should others know about Down syndrome?

Well, all I can think of is we're no different from each other and what I mean is that it's okay to live life with Down syndrome. I love having Down syndrome.

What are your plans for the future?

In the future I want to pass the GED [General Education Diploma]. It is a test that is required to enter college.

I'm planning on building another band that plays kid songs. My mission for the kids' band is to help to heal today's children of the world by teaching. Like, for example, avoiding adult stress and through education. Through the power of learning and also that we should make new friends and keep the old. And also to have the ability to laugh.

Prepared with Roy Brown

Introducing Kathleen

Kathleen is 28 years old and when she was born she needed extensive heart surgery. She was in hospital for a long time and her development was delayed. She has limited oral communication and her mother, Christine, tells her story.

Kathleen attended special school at the primary level in the Northern Territory and secondary school in Canberra. She learns best by being shown something and then being helped to do it. She tries it herself. She can say words and uses Makaton [keyword signing]. Sometimes we have to form her mouth to help her make the sounds and then she tries really hard. Basically it has been a case of show, help do, and then she tries to do it herself. Sometimes she succeeds, sometimes she does not, and we continue to help her by going over it.

When we were in the Northern Territory she went to the special school and it was very, very good. They did physiotherapy exercises and she was in programmes like swimming and horse riding. When we came here, the focus at school was just—come to school and do basic things like learning how to brush your teeth, how to interact with other students, learn some songs, and do some art. There wasn't the outside contact or formal therapy available. We had to figure things out for ourselves.

Kathleen can pick DVDs and tell you what they are. We often wondered whether she was recognising words. At school she wasn't taught to read. No one ever followed up on that even though we spoke to them about it. So we don't know what her full capacity might be. So it is a bit concerning.

Kathleen finished school and basically there was nothing for her to do. The choice was either to give her up and put her in a home or you're on your own and you have to develop your own programmes. So we have carers that come to our home. They come three days a week and she really enjoys their company. She goes to the movies and shopping and her brother and sister take her out and do things when they are home.

But she definitely misses being at school. Because she went from one day having all of her friends, being picked up by the bus, having all the activities and everything, to the next day nothing. We tried to get her into programmes but basically you have to wait till someone dies. So that's why we take care of her in our own way.

She loved school. She loved going. She loved going on the bus. She loved the company of the others and the activities they had, like the concerts and things like that. So it was a real void in her life when there was no more school.

What do you want for her future?

We want her to be happy. That is the most important thing—for her to be safe and to be happy. The carers come to our home because everything she needs is there. She's got her videos because she loves to sing and dance. She loves the music videos with music and dancing and she becomes the main actress and sings and dances. She's got the dogs at home and she enjoys their company. And so she's got the things that she needs. The only thing she misses is the interaction with people outside of that group.

Yesterday her dad took the day off so he could be home with her. We take turns to be with her when needed. Last week the carer got sick so her younger brother took a carer's day off work so he could be with her. So it is all of those kinds of things that we need to do as a family. Her brother and sister take her out, they take her to movies, they take her to shops, and they take her on drives to see things, so she gets to do all of those kinds of things. But not the interaction with other people and she loved that part of school. And that's the one thing I think that I'm not happy about.

Prepared with Rhonda Faragher

Introduction

Barbara Clarke and Rhonda Faragher

Abstract

Down syndrome is one of the most common conditions leading almost universally to intellectual and physical disability and, although a great deal is known about the effects of the syndrome on growth and development, there is much left to understand about the implications for teaching and learning. *Educating Learners with Down Syndrome* brings together current knowledge of Down syndrome of relevance to those professionals involved in the teaching of people with Down syndrome and provides suggestions for further research. In this chapter, we set the scene for this book. We begin with background information about Down syndrome, including historical perspectives, followed by current views on learning and related health matters, acknowledging aspects of living with Down syndrome. The final section focuses on themes that emerge in the light of educating learners. This book is intended for education researchers and practitioners and brings together work from a number of disciplines to aid them in their endeavours.

Introduction

We are at an interesting time in the history of care, support, and education for individuals with Down syndrome. There are still practitioners, researchers, and parents who have been involved in the field since the time of institutional care. In the decades since, there has been a dramatic increase in life expectancy for people with Down syndrome (Torr, Strydom, Patti, & Jokinen, 2010). The anticipation of a long adulthood changes the role of childhood. Parents, teachers, and others involved in the nurture of children with Down syndrome have the task of preparing them for a rewarding adulthood, as would be the case for other members of the community. In the years following institutional care, when children with Down syndrome began to be raised in the family home, initial emphasis was on learning to walk and talk. Guides for practitioners in the fields of physiotherapy and speech pathology began to be available. Many parents are able to recount their experiences from the 1950s and later in Australia and other countries of having to educate their children themselves. Gradually, parents and charities began special education, with groups such as the Subnormal Children's Association in Queensland, Australia, providing some programmes (J. R., 1955). This was followed by government provision of schooling as a right, first in special schools and more recently in inclusive mainstream school settings. Through a remarkable longitudinal study of families including a member with Down syndrome, commencing in

1963 and continuing to the present day, Carr (1988, 1995, 2012) has documented the development of children that have grown up at this critical time in the understanding of Down syndrome.

With the provision of education as a right, and the acknowledgement that people with Down syndrome could indeed be considered 'educable, not just trainable' (Rynders & Horrobin, 1990), attention has moved beyond physical skill development to cognitive skill development. The fields of psychology and education have come to the fore in identifying the needs of learners with Down syndrome.

Background to Down syndrome

Down syndrome has always been a part of the human condition. First depictions appear in art, one attributed to a painting dating from 1515 (Levitas & Reid, 2003). Down syndrome is also present in all racial groups, across socio-economic class lines, and males and females. However, it is only in recent times that the cause of Down syndrome has been known. Writing in medical literature in the 1860s, Dr John Langdon Down first described the characteristics of a group of his patients and residents in his hospital. He named the group of 'Mongolian' type. The physical characteristics were used for many years to determine if a person had the condition and the name 'mongol' became established. This term is considered offensive now; however, Langdon Down's work in the field has been very influential and he was ahead of his time in the support, care, and education of people with Down syndrome (Earl, 2010).

For decades, the presence of a cluster of characteristics was the basis of the diagnosis of Down syndrome. These include the palmar crease on the hand, low muscle tone, epicanthic folds on the eyes, large gap between the big and next toe, small mouth in comparison to the tongue, and gold spots in the iris of the eye. Each of these features is present in the general population but it is only when sufficient characteristics cluster in the one individual that Down syndrome is suspected.

In 1959, Le Jeune identified the chromosomal cause of Down syndrome: the triplication of some or all of chromosome 21. A definitive diagnosis is now possible using a blood test where the chromosomes in the nucleus of cells are separated and counted. Chromosomes are arranged in order of size (chromosome number 21 is actually the smallest of the chromosomes—initially chromosome 22 was thought to be smaller). Each of the 22 chromosomes is in matched pairs, one from each parent. The X and Y chromosomes are called the sex chromosomes, and males have an X and a Y chromosome and females two X chromosomes. Individuals with Down syndrome have additional chromosomal material from triplication of some or all of chromosome 21. The cause of this variation is not known at present, although there is increased incidence with maternal age. Even so, approximately 75 per cent of babies with Down syndrome are born to mothers under 35 years of age. (More women have babies in their twenties and lower thirties.) There are three types of Down syndrome, arising from variations in the time of the error in cell replication: Trisomy 21, Translocation, and Mosaic Down syndrome. The following table (Table I.1) summarises each type. Readers interested in further detail on the genetic basis of Down syndrome are referred to the review by Sherman and colleagues (Sherman, Allen, Bean, & Freeman, 2007).

Chromosomes are composed of genes. Genes have the function of producing proteins from amino acids eaten in food. Additional genetic material from triplication of a

Table I.1 Types of Down syndrome, incidence, and chromosome pattern

Type	*Incidence*	*Chromosome pattern*
Trisomy 21	95%	Three of chromosome 21 in every cell
Translocation	4%	Part of 21 attached to another chromosome in every cell
Mosaicism	1%	Some cells have three of chromosome 21; others are normal (two).

chromosome means an increased dose of protein. This affects the way the body is formed and developed from conception. Advances in genetics in recent times have led to greater understanding of the biochemical effects of Down syndrome. Not all genes produce protein all the time. Environmental triggers, for example, may 'turn a gene on', known as gene expression. It may be possible to prevent a faulty gene working or to interrupt the biochemical processes caused by over-production of proteins. This is the field of epigenetics and may lead to advances in the amelioration of the effects of Down syndrome. At this point, there is no cure for Down syndrome and no treatment.

A common question arising is whether there are degrees of Down syndrome. In Mosaic Down syndrome, the rarest form, there is extensive variability depending on which cells have the additional chromosome. In Translocation and Trisomy 21, accounting for 99 per cent of cases of Down syndrome, variability also occurs. Only one of the 23 pairs of chromosomes has an additional copy and this is the smallest one with the least number of genes. The rest of the genetic information in the cells functions normally (although interactions between genes on other chromosomes can also occur). Variation is a feature of all people across a range of characteristics and is caused by both environmental and genetic factors. This is true for people with Down syndrome as well.

Living with Down syndrome

People with Down syndrome are people first of all, and are more like their family members than like other people with Down syndrome. In the Prologue, people with Down syndrome have been introduced to readers. As authors, we hope you will have the opportunity to meet many people with Down syndrome. In this section, we will discuss issues of family life, including the effects of Down syndrome on health and physical and intellectual development. Readers seeking to understand more of the experience of having Down syndrome or as a family member are referred to Jan Gothard's (2010) book, *Greater Expectations: Living with Down syndrome in the 21st century*. As editors, we came to this field through different roads. Rhonda's began 17 years ago with the birth of her third child—Ruth, with Down syndrome. Barbara is a professional colleague of Rhonda's and has shared a common interest in mathematics education for all. We began our research in this fascinating field together. Below, Rhonda shares her personal story to give a sense of the experiences of parents before they interact with education professionals.

Down syndrome is often diagnosed soon after birth, if not antenatally. The commonly present physical features make this a very recognisable disability and in many countries early intervention begins from a young age. Early diagnosis also enables medical screening for possible health effects. Heart complications are common,

Rhonda's personal story

My daughter was born five-and-a-half weeks early, in a rush in the middle of the night. She was tiny—2.49 kg and under the cut-off for the special care nursery. My husband and I cuddled her for a while before she went to another floor and I to the maternity ward. In the morning, the paediatrician visited to say the triage midwife had noticed signs of Down syndrome—a palmar crease, Brushfield's spots in her eyes, big gap between her toes, and low muscle tone. He told me he 'had sent off for the chromosome test but…' and here I thought he was going to say 'but I don't think she has it'. Instead he said he knew she had Down syndrome and it was just for confirmation. Needless to say it was an awful shock. I was deeply sad—not because I was expecting the perfect baby, as some people assumed. I felt the world was not a nice place for people with Down syndrome. I didn't think she would have the sort of life I would want for my daughter. Since that time, I have worked to make the world a better place for people with Down syndrome and I see that same drive in many other parents.

So far, my daughter's life has been rich and a joy to us. The first couple of weeks were taken up with medical assessments and establishing feeding (a six-month ordeal). She was three weeks old when we were introduced to early intervention. It seems so soon now, but at the time I was so relieved there were wise people around who could help me bring her up. We began with speech pathology to help her swallow. Physiotherapy helped her develop movement patterns to prepare her for walking. Occupational therapy developed fine motor skills. Looking back, I think I was the one who gained most from all this activity. I enjoyed meeting with other parents and many are close friends to this day. At six months, the speech pathology turned to teaching my daughter to use signing. This was great fun and we were absolutely stunned when she used her first sign at 12 months. True to predictions, when she started to speak at about age two, she no longer used the signs for words she could say. She used signing to augment her speech into the primary school years.

As my daughter approached school age, early intervention began to be replaced by community activities. Physiotherapy gave way to gymnastics; occupational therapy to piano lessons; speech pathology to singing in school and church choirs. In common with the experiences of our friends, we have often been struck by how ordinary our family life is! We often forget our daughter has Down syndrome. My initial sadness has given way to joy. My daughter has brought much pride and, like other children, occasional challenges. Down syndrome is a part of her, but just a part.

experienced by up to 50 per cent of babies, and frequently requiring surgery. Sometimes heart conditions need to be monitored during the school years. Other health conditions relevant to educators and other professionals include:

- **Hearing**. Up to 80 per cent of children with Down syndrome experience conductive hearing loss. This condition requires medical intervention and vigilance. Often hearing loss can be missed as it can fluctuate day to day. Conductive hearing loss may occur without ear infections.
- **Sight**. Many children with Down syndrome require glasses from an early age. Cataracts are also common. Strabismus (squint) often requires surgery. Visual acuity may be reduced and this cannot be corrected with glasses. Large fonts and contrast in printed material may assist.

- **Thyroid function**. Hypothyroidism (low thyroid function) is an easily treated condition. Low thyroid function causes symptoms that can affect learning, such as lack of energy, failure to thrive, and changes in cognition.
- **Atlanto-axial instability**. Instability of the first two neck bones at the top of the spine can lead to damage of the spinal cord. X-ray screening is no longer considered predictive of potential risk (Bull, 2011) and should not prevent participation in sport, considered a greater health risk. However, parents and teachers should be aware of early signs of complications, including neck pain, restricted neck movement, changes in gait, loss of bladder or bowel control, and loss of previous fine-motor skills (Selikowitz, 1997). These symptoms can develop gradually and vigilance is required.
- **Low muscle tone**. Muscle tone refers to the tension in the muscle at rest, not strength. If the tone is too high, the result is spasticity. If the tone is too low, the muscles take more work to move them. Children with low muscle tone find it difficult to maintain a body position and to change positions. Good postural support, including appropriate furniture and writing equipment, is important.
- **Respiratory infections and low immunity**. Upper respiratory tract infections, including the common cold, may not be more common in children with Down syndrome than other children. However, relatively narrow air passages may cause the symptoms to be worse (Selikowitz, 1997). As children grow, there is reduced incidence of runny noses with the widening of the nasal passages, as well as improved ability to blow their noses. Interventions should be investigated to minimise exclusion from educational settings due to the symptoms of upper respiratory tract infections.

A focus on possible medical problems can give a distorted impression. Most children with Down syndrome enjoy good health.

People with Down syndrome can experience unrelated medical and other conditions. These include mental illness (Dykens, 2007) and other disabilities. Dual diagnosis of Down syndrome and autism spectrum disorder is evident in perhaps 10 per cent of people with Down syndrome (Ji, Capone, & Kaufmann, 2011). This adds complexity into educational decisions. In this book, we will be focusing on Down syndrome alone.

Down syndrome affects the development of the brain and related cognitive function. Intellectual impairment is almost universal (Silverman, 2007); however, questions are still open as to whether cognitive development is merely delayed or follows a different process altogether (Wishart, 2002). Research continues apace in this area and advancements in understanding the processes may lead to improved outcomes. Effects relevant to the education of learners with Down syndrome include:

- learned helplessness—avoidant learning styles (Wishart, 1993, 1996)
- memory function (Baddeley, 2003; Buckley & Bird, 2001)
- communication—delayed development and difficulties with grammar (Chapman, 1995)
- gross motor impairments, including the appearance of clumsy movements. These can be traced to cognitive impairments where movement patterns differ in individuals with Down syndrome (Virji-Babul, Jobling, Elliot, & Weeks, 2011).

So far we have discussed some of the known impacts of Down syndrome that may affect the education of the individual. As we have seen in the Prologue, learners with Down syndrome are not all the same: they enjoy different talents and have different expectations of life and different needs. As stated earlier, people with Down syndrome are more like their family members than like other people with Down syndrome. Even so, understanding the effects of Down syndrome does offer insight into how we can meet the needs of learners and make accommodations so they can make the most of opportunities in the learning environment. Most of the intellectual and physical ramifications of Down syndrome have resonances in the chapters of the book to follow and we turn now to outline what is to come.

Educating learners with Down syndrome

As we move to focus on the intent of the book, there are a number of themes that play a vital role in the education of learners with Down syndrome and on the decisions that parents, teachers, and other caregivers need to make. This initial discussion is intended to set the scene for the reader, frame the discussion for individual chapters and will be returned to along with further emerging themes in the conclusion.

Inclusive practices

Inclusive practices are encouraged by researchers, educational systems, and policy makers but can be challenging to implement. While inclusion can have different models, Rafferty, Boettcher, and Griffin (2001) refer to it as 'the process of educating children with disabilities in the regular education classrooms of their neighbourhood schools—the schools they would attend if they do not have a disability—providing them with the necessary services and support' (p. 266). The major components of the challenge include willingness of school personnel to embrace inclusive practices, the identification and provision of appropriate services, the focusing of support, and the knowledge of classroom teachers to ensure that these are used effectively. 'The importance of adequately resourcing schools to support teachers in the implementation of an inclusive environment is … second in importance to teacher attitudes to inclusion' (Boyle, Scriven, Durning, & Downes, 2011, p. 72).

In the Australian context, learning support often takes the form of a teacher assistant who may or may not have qualifications or relevant expertise in learning support. Additional support may be available, such as visiting advisory teachers and resources including technology. Inclusion is based on the premise of the rights of the child to best practice approaches to education. Research over many decades has indicated the efficacy of this approach (Buckley, Bird, Sacks, & Archer, 2006; Jackson, 2008) but will only be effective if the corresponding responsibilities of the system and other stakeholders are practised and the needs of the child fore-grounded. On-going debates continue in the literature about different interpretations of inclusion (Ravet, 2011) as well as different philosophical perspectives. It is not our intention to review such debates but to acknowledge the complexities of educating children with diverse needs in the regular classroom.

In most Western countries, inclusion of children with Down syndrome in the regular classroom is increasingly the norm. However, we are still learning to do this effectively. In a recent review of empirical research, de Boer, Pijl, and Minnaert (2011) found that the majority of teachers hold neutral or negative attitudes towards the inclusion of children with special needs into regular classrooms and do not feel confident or competent to teach children with various types of special needs, particularly those with intellectual disabilities and challenging behaviours. As many children with Down syndrome tend to exhibit each of these characteristics, it is vital to identify appropriate inclusive practices as well as educational provisions and strategies that will meet specific needs.

For learners with Down syndrome, what might be the most appropriate support to ensure effective inclusion? What is known from research and practice that can inform this process? What role do methodologies and practices based on mental age have when chronological age is the basis of socially inclusive practices? What is the place of exclusive or targeted practices? Is there a place for special pedagogies? How do we ensure the dignity of the learner's actual age—their place in the world?

Assessment

Assessment can take a range of forms, serves different purposes and is used to inform pivotal educational decisions. Specialist practitioners provide data on individuals that are often used to determine funding for care and support, particularly in school systems, where such information provides a measure of need. While such data are valued for their reliability, they may be of limited use to the classroom or special education teacher.

In the context of the classroom, typically teachers use both formal and informal forms of assessment and these are important for on-going measures of progress and effectiveness. They are more often related to specific content, such as literacy or mathematics. Such measures, tools or techniques can compromise reliability but may have validity for the student or context. Parents are often expected or required to engage in decision-making based on the results of assessment. Difficulties in this process can lead to increased disadvantage for those who are less informed or empowered to advocate.

Researchers develop and use assessment tools, some of which may also have applicability for those directly involved in the on-going education of learners with Down syndrome. Concern has been expressed regarding the overuse in the past of IQ as a measure for comparative studies involving children or adults with Down syndrome (Wishart & Duffy, 1990). However, comparative studies provide important evidence and support our developing understanding. Other bases may be needed for learners with Down syndrome.

There is a need to provide teachers and school administrators with appropriate, valid, and reliable assessment methods that can be used to inform educational decisions. It is encouraging that more varied and nuanced measures are being utilised and provide increased validity for these purposes. Such research will be referenced and discussed in a number of the chapters in this book.

Appropriate assessment tools and how these are used and by whom are a feature of the discussion in a number of chapters. The multiple purposes and stakeholders need to be acknowledged in this process. What is valid evidence for the different purposes that we have to negotiate as educators of learners with Down syndrome?

Evidence-based practice

Evidence-based practice is encouraged across all areas of education and clearly linked to the forms of assessment we use. Our evidence must be robust and valid and our knowledge as practitioners sufficient to support the necessary interpretation and subsequent action. In particular, teachers are being encouraged to use evidence to inform their planning and other instructional decisions. This also links to the discussions around inclusive practices as we consider difference and the differentiation of instruction.

The evidence base for teachers relates to general understandings of student development but also to the specific information about individual learners. In the context of classrooms where students with Down syndrome are included, the teacher needs to understand both general aspects relating to appropriate instructional practices and also knowledge of the child and syndrome in relation to curriculum and related aspects. It is a complex environment where many forms of knowledge are informing decisions.

In focusing on evidence, we want to acknowledge that there is a role for practice-based evidence. That does not mean that we are advocating arbitrary or uninformed decisions but that there are often insights into individuals and effective practices that emerge from informed and reflective practitioners. It must also be acknowledged that the education of learners with significant intellectual disability can be complicated by multiple data sets and conflicting needs and requirements where the educator has to make a professional decision and manage that multitude of data and other evidence they have. The reporting of such experiences can represent valid research to help our collective understanding.

Implications of cognitive profile

What impact do specific cognitive impairments have for learning, including the role of memory, relative difficulties with oral language and the relative strength of the visual for learners with Down syndrome? Couzens and Cuskelly's chapter provides extensive discussion on cognitive strengths and weaknesses, and these aspects are also explored in relation to cognitive development within specific learner areas, particularly literacy and mathematics. For example, the role of oral language in child development is critical across all aspects of learning but particularly in the area of literacy. This might appear to suggest that there is much repetition across chapters; however, we would argue that it provides different and important ways of looking at these cognitive challenges, providing multiple insights into how we teach to strengths while supporting the overall development of each learner.

One source of evidence proving to provide an important perspective—sometimes confirming, sometimes adding new knowledge—is research on *brain function*. It is having significant impacts in educational research and particularly in the study of intellectual disability. The use of brain imaging while undertaking specific cognitive tasks is helping us to understand cognitive processing as well as cognitive differences. Discernment of which specific findings are relevant and how they can inform our educational practices productively is beginning to emerge and will be discussed.

Expectations

Ensuring expectations are realistic and open-ended is key to ensuring opportunities are available for learners with Down syndrome. While it is important to be mindful of the impact of the cognitive impairments and differences, these should not be seen as barriers. What are the possibilities for learning? What can we do to move away from deficit models that are self-fulfilling? How can we ensure that the learner's expectations are positive—that they don't learn not to learn?

The structure of the book

There are three main Parts in this book. The first provides the research basis for aspects and issues that are relevant to teaching and learning: the importance of considering learning as lifelong, cognitive strengths and weaknesses, promoting and sustaining interest, and behaviours that enhance learning. The second Part focuses on research on the learning of mathematics. This has been an area of limited literature but some is emerging and this provides an important opportunity to review and present current research. The third Part focuses on literacy development, including both oral and written language. This has a stronger literature base and the chapters review this, as well as providing new insights. There is an additional chapter that was considered to make important contributions to the field. Chapter 11 is important as it acknowledges that the vast majority of the research is conducted in developed countries and the developing world has different needs and challenges.

The conclusions and summative implications (although part of each chapter) are drawn together and embellished at the end of the book. This could be an important place for researchers in this field to identify gaps and areas of need.

This book focuses on different ways of knowing—different research methodologies are important to gain insights into learners with Down syndrome. A challenge for the educational researcher is that we are working across methodologies to provide research for practice. Research and practice in the field of Down syndrome brings together a range of professional and practical disciplines, such as medicine, biochemistry, genetics, psychology, education, speech pathology, occupational therapy, physiotherapy, and sociology. Each of these disciplines has developed research methodologies and standards for evidence. For example, double-blind trials are considered the gold standard in medical fields and randomised control trials in psychology. These forms of research are rarely used in education, with the complexities of social interactions in the learning process requiring particular techniques and strategies. At times, lack of understanding of these differences has been an impediment to building an integrated corpus of knowledge in the field of Down syndrome. Understanding the merging of fields has become the subject of research in its own right. Akkerman and Bakker (2011) have reviewed the literature that focuses on 'boundary crossing' and argue that boundaries between fields provide opportunities for learning. In this book, there are chapters from researchers and practitioners from a variety of domains.

We hope that you enjoy the journey this book will provide into the research and potential of children with Down syndrome.

References

Akkerman, S. F., & Bakker, A. (2011). Boundary crossing and boundary objects. *Review of Educational Research, 81*, 132–169. doi: 10.3102/0034654311404435.

Baddeley, A. D. (2003). Working memory: Looking back and looking forward. *Nature Reviews. Neuroscience, 4*, 829–839.

Boyle, C., Scriven, B., Durning, S., & Downes, C. (2011). Facilitating the learning of all students: The 'professional positive' of inclusive practice in Australian primary schools. *Support for Learning, 26*, 72–78.

Buckley, S., & Bird, G. (2001). *Memory development for individuals with Down syndrome*. Hampshire, UK: Down Syndrome Educational Trust.

Buckley, S., Bird, G., Sacks, B., & Archer, T. (2006). A comparison of mainstream and special education for teenagers with Down syndrome: Implications for parents and teachers. *Down Syndrome Research and Practice, 9*, 54–67.

Bull, M. J. (2011). Health supervision for children with Down syndrome. *Pediatrics, 128*, 393–406.

Carr, J. (1988). Six weeks to twenty-one years old: A longitudinal study of children with Down's syndrome and their families. *Journal of Child Psychology and Psychiatry, 29*, 407–431.

Carr, J. (1995). *Down's syndrome: Children growing up*. Cambridge: Cambridge University Press.

Carr, J. (2012). Six weeks to 45 years: A longitudinal study of a population with Down syndrome. *Journal of Applied Research in Intellectual Disabilities, 25*, 414–422.

Chapman, R. S. (1995). Language development in children and adults with Down syndrome. In P. Fletcher & B. MacWhinney (Eds), *Handbook of child language* (pp. 641–663). Oxford: Blackwell Scientific.

de Boer, A., Pijl, S. J., & Minnaert, A. (2011). Regular primary schoolteachers' attitudes towards inclusive education: A review of the literature. *International Journal of Inclusive Education, 15*, 331–353.

Dykens, E. M. (2007). Psychiatric and behavioral disorders in persons with Down syndrome. *Mental Retardation and Developmental Disabilities Research Reviews, 13*, 272–278.

Earl, J. (2010). *Dr Langdon Down's Normansfield Theatre*. Occasional Paper No. 6 (2nd edn). Borough of Twickenham Local History Society. London: Down's Syndrome Association.

Gothard, J. (2010). *Greater expectations. Living with Down syndrome in the 21st century*. Fremantle, Western Australia: Fremantle Press.

Jackson, R. (2008). *Inclusion or segregation for children with an intellectual impairment: What does the research say?* Salisbury, Queensland: Queensland Parents for People with a Disability. Retrieved on 21 February 2012 from www.qppd.org/images/docs/jackson_literature_review.pdf.

Ji, N., Capone, G., & Kaufmann, W. (2011). Autism spectrum disorder in Down syndrome: Cluster analysis of Aberrant Behaviour Checklist data supports diagnosis. *Journal of Intellectual Disability Research, 55*, 1064–1077.

J. R. (Ed.). (1955). Editorial. *The Slow Learning Child, 1*, 94–95. doi: 10.1080/0156655540010301.

Levitas, A. S., & Reid, C. S. (2003). An angel with Down syndrome in a sixteenth century Flemish Nativity painting. *American Journal of Medical Genetics, 116*, 399–405. doi: 10.1002/ajmg.a.10043.

Rafferty, Y., Boettcher, C., & Griffin, K. W. (2001). Benefits and risks of reverse inclusion for preschoolers with and without disabilities: Parents' perspectives. *Journal of Early Intervention, 24*, 266–286.

Ravet, J. (2011). Inclusive/exclusive? Contradictory perspectives on autism and inclusion: The case for an integrative position. *International Journal of Inclusive Education, 15*, 667–682.

Rynders, J., & Horrobin, J. (1990). Always trainable? Never educable? Updating educational expectations concerning children with Down's syndrome. *American Journal on Mental Retardation, 95*, 77–83.

Selikowitz, M. (1997). *Down syndrome: The facts* (2nd edn). London: Oxford University Press.
Sherman, S. L., Allen, E. G., Bean, L. H., & Freeman, S. B. (2007). Epidemiology of Down syndrome. *Mental Retardation and Developmental Disabilities Research Reviews, 13*, 221–227.
Silverman, W. (2007). Down syndrome: Cognitive phenotype. *Mental Retardation and Developmental Disabilities Research Reviews, 13*, 228–236.
Torr, J., Strydom, A., Patti, P., & Jokinen, N. (2010). Aging in Down syndrome: Morbidity and mortality. *Journal of Policy and Practice in Intellectual Disabilities, 7*, 70–81.
Virji-Babul, N., Jobling, A., Elliot, D., & Weeks, D. (2011). Aspects of motor development in Down syndrome. In J.-A. Rondal, J. Perera, & D. Spiker (Eds), *Neurocognitive rehabilitation of Down syndrome: Early years* (pp. 153–163). Cambridge: Cambridge University Press.
Wishart, J. G. (1993). Learning the hard way: Avoidance strategies in young children with Down's syndrome. *Down Syndrome Research and Practice, 1*, 47–55.
Wishart, J. G. (1996). Avoidant learning styles and cognitive development in young children. In B. Stratford & P. Gunn (Eds), *New approaches to Down syndrome* (pp. 173–205). London, UK: Cassell.
Wishart, J. G. (2002). Learning in young children with Down syndrome: Public perceptions, empirical evidence. In M. Cuskelly, A. Jobling, & S. Buckley (Eds), *Down syndrome across the lifespan* (pp. 18–27). London: Whurr.
Wishart, J. G., & Duffy, L. (1990). Instability of performance on cognitive tests in infants and young children with Down's syndrome. *British Journal of Educational Psychology, 60*, 10–22.

Part I

Issues in learning and teaching

Chapter 1

A lifespan approach to learning in the context of quality of life

Roy I. Brown

Abstract

The education of children with Down syndrome needs to be re-examined in the context of changing philosophies, research, and practice. This re-examination includes the relevance of quality of life to education, community, and home living, how concepts and principles of quality of life can be put together to promote and influence the lives of people with Down syndrome in education and society, and how family quality of life is involved and can influence education and development. The relationship of the concepts and principles to professional behaviour of educational personnel is considered and finally linked to the ways in which quality of life research can contribute to the education and overall development of children with Down syndrome.

Introduction

This chapter is about *quality of life* (QoL) and Down syndrome as it applies to education. QoL is not an issue that has been significantly researched in the field of Down syndrome, and few studies have been concerned with education and quality of life. However, there is considerable literature in intellectual and developmental disabilities and some of the studies have included people with Down syndrome (see review by Cunningham & Brown, in press). Timmons (1993) noted this in relation to schooling and intellectual disabilities and since then little progress of this aspect of quality of life research and applications has been made (see also Timmons & Brown, 1997).

In this chapter, it is argued that QoL is a useful model or approach to educating learners with Down syndrome, not least because it encourages us to look at Down syndrome in a rather different light (Brown, 1994). Quality of life is about "being, belonging, and becoming". It provides an opportunity to see education from the perspective of lifespan. This is critical because the current outcomes for people with Down syndrome are highly varied and differences that occur are partly the result of genetics but also of environment, and a large part of the environment in developing years is education. It is this aspect with which this chapter is particularly concerned and, unless research and then practice takes a lifespan view, the goals of education for people with Down syndrome are likely to be negatively skewed by lack of possibilities.

Why be concerned?

Why should we be concerned with education of people with Down syndrome? In addition to reasons of family love, and ethical responsibilities associated with bringing a child into the world and enabling them, in many cases, to survive the very early years through medical intervention and parental care and support, there are other reasons. Having started with care and support, there is a need to carry this across the lifespan. That is true for everyone, but some individuals need more specialized support and care that entails particularly effective education and teaching.

Children with Down syndrome survive in the developed world a lot longer than they used to, though it is generally agreed that life expectancy may be greater or less depending on the environment in which the child is raised. From a life expectancy of 11 years on average at the beginning of the twentieth century in the economically advantaged world, to an average span of between 55 and 60 years now (Baird & Sadovnick, 1987; Torr, Strydom, Patti, & Jokinen, 2010), society is faced with either traditional care, as in the first three-quarters of the twentieth century, or providing learning and preparation for a full life over a long lifespan. The implications are enormous. People who can support themselves, in part or whole, reduce the stresses on others. Indeed, they can enhance the lives of others through social and economic contributions. Although we provide more inclusive education than we used to, effective preparation for an adult quality of life is urgently required to avoid the challenges of care and support being placed on to the shoulders of ageing family members.

How do we respond to these challenges?

One way to respond to the challenges of preparation for a long adulthood is to consider not only the well-being of the individual but also family members, and frontline professionals. Any broadly based and effective learning and development process, where specific challenges are involved, must be based on a collaborative approach. Part of that approach relates to research and the involvement of colleagues who work together to carry out research. This includes the links between policy and practice, and evaluation of the needs and support provided in the education of people with Down syndrome.

In terms of educators, Mitchell (2009, p. 422) made this point very clearly:

> Educators are increasingly expected to be responsible not only for helping learners to achieve the best possible outcomes, but also for using the most scientifically valid methods to achieve this. In the United States, the No Child Left Behind law requires teachers to use "scientific, research-based programs". In other words, teaching is increasingly being expected to become an evidence-based profession.

One of the essential features of education is that it needs to support and provide for quality of life over the lifespan, which requires teachers and others to imagine what life can be like for people with Down syndrome in their adult years. The features of quality of life, as portrayed in the research and practice literature, can help provide an effective framework for such development. It is conceptual, formalized, and structured with a lifespan approach. Yet education, and particularly education directed towards children with Down syndrome, often does not make use of such a framework on an assessed, planned, programmed, and evaluated basis, with both present and future goals in mind.

In this chapter, the various concepts and principles of quality of life are described and illustrated through vignettes and research that have the potential to bridge the gap in and between formal education, social aspects of learning, emotional and informal aspects of family experiences, and long-term needs.

From an educational and community perspective, there are two aspects which are conceptually related to value systems and motivation. First is the need to have an image of the future that people with Down syndrome may attain, recognizing that many are capable of reaching competent standards of performance in a wide range of activities (see Brown [Ed.], *Adults with Down Syndrome* series, 2004–2008 examples—see addendum to the series). The examples cover adolescent and adult activities for the most part but illustrate the types of growth and development that can continue well in to adult life and could be fostered much earlier in the developmental cycle. Second, it is essential to recognize that, since the 1960s, considerable variation of demonstrated ability and attainment amongst people with Down syndrome has been noted (for example, see Gibson, 1978).

There is some indication that ability and attainment levels of people with Down syndrome may be rising and no doubt improvement in health and education are important in this context. Borthwick-Duffey (1996) has argued that environmental factors for people with Down syndrome, such as social attitudes and medical intervention, can play an important part in the development of intelligence and therefore it is reasonable to expect the possibility of increasing cognitive abilities if support and intervention continue to improve. The issues of social intelligence as argued by Sternberg (cited in Kaufman & Grigorenko, 2009) are relevant in this context because the accent on social skill development in many programmes, both for children and for adults, may have a major payoff in terms of cognitive development, particularly if a quality of life approach is applied consistently within educational and social programmes.

The majority of children with Down syndrome can do more than most teachers and other professionals expect. Indeed, this is what parents in the various Down syndrome associations have demonstrated. The 40-year (and on-going) longitudinal study by Carr (2009) illustrates that children's largely positive progress over the years seems to have surprised many professionals. The connection and collaboration between education, parent experience and parent-developed schools (such as "experimental" schools), and research development and refinement become critical in this context. Underestimation of people with Down syndrome affects how we intervene, how we help children view their future, and how we ensure that education and various supports bring about improved self-image and performance for quality of life over the lifespan.

It is recognized that people with Down syndrome vary, with some who are remarkably able or with the potential to develop further, and others who are less so. Potential is often seen as what a child is able to do given the right circumstances. An analogy might be that potential is like a tank for water but unless the water (the person's environment) is fed into it, the potential or fulfilment is not achieved. But it is now appropriate to look at potential in a new way because research shows that the brain itself modifies if the appropriate environment is provided (see Doidge, 2007).

This aspect of brain development applies to social enrichment, such as friendship networks, which underscore the importance of social inclusion over the lifespan (Bennett, Schneider, Tang, Arnold, & Wilson, 2006).

Issues of methodology

The methodology for research in quality of life is diverse but, like the early stages of research in any science, observation, recording, and forming hypotheses and questions are critical. There are major differences in carrying out applied research for samples are generally not random but convenience samples. Variables are multiple and need to be teased out and, for this, strategies such as triangulation need to be employed. But ideally this does not rely just on replication because getting the same results through replication may simply be because the same errors are involved. Triangulation needs to come from different approaches to asking the same or similar questions. Both quantitative and qualitative studies are employed and a combination of approaches leads to not only numerical data and analysis, but also commentary, which gives depth to an understanding of the numerical results and enhances the process of question and hypothesis generation. Further, as we shall see as we examine quality of life, the approach requires linking the research to practice framework to policy development, which in some instances may lead to radical changes in both direction and focus (Schalock & Verdugo, 2012).

Quality of life research not only uses traditional means of measurement and exploration but also requires additional and innovative approaches to explore the move from purely objective assessment to concerns about individual perception and thinking amongst individuals with Down syndrome.

> Quality of life, if it is to fulfil its potential, has to bridge the gap from traditional science, with its accent on measurement, including reliability and validity, along with a rigorous accounting of error, to the newer paradigms of science which accent individual variability and personal expression, and individual accounts of personal experience of disability, and lead through model building to a more measured approach to the field.... It can be argued that quality of life structures reflect the development of science from observation through model building with pragmatic definition to measurement in social behavioural terms.
>
> (adapted from Brown, 1997, p. 7)

A QoL model looks at personal internal processes and in so doing suggests the importance of what some call a subjective field of endeavour (Schalock *et al.*, 2002; Cummins, 1997). I now prefer to refer to this as perceptual, which can be recorded, measured, and interpreted. A field of endeavour which until recently was frequently not seen as part of science. In the field of Down syndrome and intellectual disabilities, this has opened up the "black box" as we can begin to explore, using research methodology, the personal thinking, aspiration, choices, and mental imagery of people with Down syndrome (see Brown & Bullitis, 2006). Further, people with Down syndrome become partners in research and at times have their names recorded as co-authors if they so wish. This is an ethical issue, and an important one, since it provides dignity, status, and a voice for their developing self-image.

Quality of life: its conceptualization and principles

Quality of life includes a blend of qualitative and quantitative methodologies set in a range of concepts and principles, which sees a person with intellectual or developmental disability as an equal member of society with the potential for development under appropriate circumstances. The question is, in each instance, what are the appropriate circumstances?

Over the past 30 years or so, quality of life has become an increasingly important and focusing approach to support intervention for people with intellectual impairment. More recently, there has been the development of the concept of family quality of life. Although a number of demonstration projects and conceptual studies have been developed in both areas, it is only in recent times that quality of life has been practised within services and agencies to any large degree and very little in the field of education. Unfortunately, the concepts and principles involved in quality of life have often been misunderstood and have not been entirely supported in the field of education, nor has the educational research field applied an holistic QoL model. There is often a gap between policy, management, and frontline teacher intervention and support, which has led to some rough patches in terms of the realistic development of quality of life.

It is important at the outset to indicate that quality of life should be regarded as a sensitizing concept (Taylor, 1994), which enables educators to modify the approaches they make towards persons with disability. The QoL model has followed but also has arisen out of other concepts and practices, such as normalization and inclusion. However, there are a number of very important differences—for example, the importance of individual choices at times may conflict with tenets of normalization. Specialized facilities for children with extreme social and behavioural challenges may be required, for both the child and the family. That is, quality of life should not be mission-oriented but should recognize that individual choices and needs may be more important than inclusion at all costs.

What is quality of life?

Over the years, a variety of definitions of quality of life have been put forward, along with a number of overarching concepts. The definitions of quality of life are many, though they all have much in common and add to the breadth of the concept. All seem relevant to Down syndrome. Quality of life is:

- The social well-being enjoyed by people, communities and their society (Bach & Rioux, 1996)
- Both objective and subjective, involving material well-being, health, productivity, intimacy, safety, community, and emotional well-being (Cummins, 1997)
- Experienced when a person's basic needs are met and when he or she has the opportunity to pursue and achieve goals in major life settings (Goode, 1994)
- The discrepancy between a person's unmet needs and desires. Referring to the subjective or perceived as well as objective assessment, it relates to all life domains and recognizes interaction between the individual and environment (Brown, Bayer, & Macfarlane, 1989)

The major components of quality of life are expressed in Box 1.1 and direct us to the life of the individual, in this case the person with Down syndrome.

Quality of life
BEING
How people with Down syndrome feel and see themselves
BELONGING
How people with Down syndrome see themselves as part of a family, school, community, employment
BECOMING
What people with Down syndrome think they want to be or achieve

Box 1.1 Quality of life (adapted from Renwick & Brown, 1996).

Quality of life recognizes the importance of individual thinking and learning, which requires passing much of the control within the developmental context to the person with Down syndrome. The person has to be in the driving seat. There may be an instructor and passengers but, as far as possible, the driving has to be turned over to the person with a disability. Research and practice indicate that this is possible to a much greater extent than most people, including professionals and parents, may think possible. Further, it is recognized that quality of life needs to be measured, but that it cannot always be measured entirely by objective (external) and numerical procedures.

The principles involved are fundamental to a model of quality of life and these are shown in Box 1.2.

Much of this and other material has been consolidated in the research and applied literature (see Brown, Bayer, & Brown, 1992; Schalock *et al.*, 2002; Goode, 1994; Renwick, Brown, & Nagler, 1996). For a recent summary, see the special issue of the *Journal of Policy and Practice in Intellectual Disabilities*, edited by Brown, Schalock, and Brown (2009), and Brown and Brown (2003).

Research and demonstration frequently do not get into local service systems very quickly and the research-to-practice gap is extensive. This is markedly the case in terms of the field of Down syndrome.

Personal, Professional and Policy Values
Life Domains
Perception
Lifespan
Holism
Choice
Personal Control
Self Image
Empowerment
Inter and Intra Personal Variability
Duty of Care and Risk

Box 1.2 Specific concepts and principles embedded in a quality of life approach.

Values

Values and attitudes have been the subject of recent study in the field of intellectual and developmental disabilities but again the accent has been on adults. The research and application question is now: To what extent do such policy and practice recommendations apply to the education of children and adults with Down syndrome (see Schalock & Verdugo, 2012)?

Life domains

The most important issues or concepts and principles in quality of life involve a number of life domains that represent functioning areas (e.g. education, physical, material, social, emotional), which are diversely experienced by most people. However, not everyone with Down syndrome has the opportunity to participate fully. This is a challenge for teachers and research personnel who need to explore ways of rectifying such situations. If individuals have the ability or interest in a particular domain or area, it is likely that they will more readily practise the skills required, resulting in improvement. Some data collected during the 1980s (Brown *et al.*, 1992) suggest that following a route that provides support and intervention in areas in which individuals like to perform results in improvement in a wide range of other activities, including those in which they do not receive support and practice. This may have been because improvement in an area which one enjoys raises one's self-image and a sense of self-worth, which in turn can cause a rise in overall confidence and increased motivation. This may lead to individuals becoming more interested or ready to try new activities with the prospect of success.

Perception

Perceptual (personal thoughts) or subjective components are critical as they represent the views held by individuals and these drive behaviour (Andrews, 1974; Andrews & Whithey, 1976). For example, a father felt at one point that his daughter with Down syndrome would never be able to marry or partner. Later, after becoming aware of changes that are taking place, he said, "I should leave the options open and see how she develops." Whether or not the statement agrees with any independent measures is not the point. The point is that these statements are likely to be a reflection of how he feels about his daughter at particular points in time, which, to some degree, directs the behaviour the father shows and indirectly affects how his daughter and others behave.

External objective and perceptual assessments do not necessarily match one another, nor is there a demand that they should do so. Objective measures are external and important but perceptual measures are internal and critical from a behavioural perspective as they play a major role in driving behaviour. Seeing one's teacher as unsupportive affects how a child views the situation and that perception influences learning or learning potential. These same perceptual processes apply to those carrying out research. The reader may have pondered why new approaches to reading or mathematics seem to work better in the hands of their creator. One possible explanation is that the enthusiasm of the creator is imparted to the learner; that is the learner's perception is that he will now be able to master the skill. In other words part of a quality of life approach must take into account the teacher–child dynamic—a field which from a quality of life perspective has not been adequately researched. What then is the effect if the teacher does not really like a child, even though professionally he or she knows this should be overcome? In other words, the attitude and values of the teacher or researcher influence the results obtained, and the view and values of the person being taught influence the outcome. That suggests that, in research involving quality of life issues, we need to take this into account.

Lifespan

Lifespan is an important concept not only because it helps us and families to envisage the future, but because it is critical in terms of the well-being of the person with Down syndrome. How individuals develop in childhood and the opportunities and choices they are provided with on the way are likely to determine in a major way how they will perform as adults, and we now know that adult life is still a time for learning. The question is: Has childhood education provided the appropriate building blocks for adult life, including old age? Many adults with Down syndrome experience some inclusion as children but find the system fails them as adults. The question is: What responsibilities do educators have after the individual has entered adulthood? Unfortunately, there is increasing evidence in some countries that, during the adult years, stimulation decreases. Bertoli *et al.* (2011) indicate this quite clearly. This study was set in Rome, where there is full educational inclusion. It shows that young adults with Down syndrome, having completed inclusive schooling, spend their day attending workshops or remain at home, with only a few going to work. This is in contrast to peers without Down syndrome. This adds challenges to family life as parents need to provide care and support, while the individuals with Down syndrome face a decline in social and allied skills and activity level decreases. The study illustrates why full-life planning, including post-school educational options, is necessary. We will see later that these aspects can critically affect not just the child's economic and social survival, but also those of their parents and of their siblings.

Holism

Holism refers to the integration of approaches and the fact that intervention and support in one domain frequently impacts other domains. It gives educators and others the opportunity to intervene in different ways and to have more wide-reaching results. In quality of life, challenges need to be viewed in an holistic manner with the idea that success or failure in one domain significantly influences success or failure in other domains. This is very important because it suggests that intervention and support can be carried out through a variety of these areas. Someone in poor health may receive medical treatment in terms of pharmacological intervention that improves physical health but that also may improve psychological well-being. Could we make the same claim for the impact of education? Careful selection of activities should enable us to posit what impacts a specific activity might have on the domain and how there might be generalization to other domains. For example, the teaching of and opportunity for physical education and recreation can improve general health and fitness, depending on the activities undertaken, and in doing so increase motivation. But there is another effect of holism. What is learnt while we are young can affect many of our activities and learning when older. The learning of mathematics may improve some concrete skills but can positively affect brain activity, which probably has further payoff down the line, which is particularly relevant to longevity.

Choice

Another important principle is choice, which is important because it can allow people to have control over what they do (see also Chapter 4). At times, this has been seen as providing freedom to everybody to do what he or she may wish. It is not always recognized that choice is a very complex psychological and social concept. For example, choice does not mean doing just what an individual decides, but rather being provided with choice in a developmental and exploratory context. There are now conceptual and pragmatic models of and tests for choice (e.g. Stancliffe & Parmenter, 1999). We can ask people whether they like to carry out an activity, or we can provide alternatives. As Brown and Brown (2009) have pointed out, it is important that choice is within a conceptual framework. Asking questions of people in such a way that they can only give "yes" or "no" answers does not provide adequate opportunities for language to develop, and therefore conceptualization to take place. Choice must be related to development and environmental experience. It also needs to develop from simple choices to complex alternatives (see Brown & Brown, 2009). It may well be that people decide what is best for the individuals concerned because they think they know what the individual thinks or needs. However, the evidence suggests that proxy interpretations of what a person would choose are frequently different from those perceived by the individual (Cummins, 2002). Choice involves 1 : 1 exploration with an individual, which includes exposure to different environments and activities with support. Discussion and counselling are generally required in varying degrees until a suitable path is devised for carrying out a choice. This may include modification of the choice or abandoning the choice (for the time being), with the individual substituting an alternative. Sometimes people with Down syndrome are accused of changing their mind. We all do this as we explore, and time needs to be allowed for personal consideration, which may involve the individual dealing with anxiety because the situation is new and unfamiliar.

Self-image

One of the important impacts of perception and choice is the effect that it has on self-image. Feeling positive about oneself is important because it can enable one to improve performance and become further involved. Note that these two principles—a person's perception and their self-image—are inter-related. Once again it means that we should provide support in different areas in different ways, and it is the job of professionals and support personnel or co-workers to discover the best ways for particular individuals, and this is an important area for research. This is best done through unbiased observation of behaviour, by taking note of what individuals say, and by observing carefully what they do (Brown & Brown, 2003).

Empowerment

Empowerment is the practice of enabling individuals to take control of their lives and promoting the feeling they are in control and contributing. Elsewhere, I have indicated that this is associated with being in the "driver's seat" even when there is an instructor and supporter present. To provide an image of being able to read at a time when the individual is finding reading difficult is very empowering. The author had an opportunity to set up reading clinics many years ago and developed a tape programme which physically tracked written sentences with the result that, when the individual reader became stuck, the tape provided the correct response. For many individuals, this gave the impression of reading, improved motivation, and promoted more effective reading (Brown & Bookbinder, 1968).

Duty of care and risk

Obviously there is an issue of duty of care, and one should not provide opportunities for activities which have high risk without appropriate support (Brown, 2007). However, individuals who do not have Down syndrome are often able to take risks and chances, which will often be considered dangerous and unwise. Some might argue society, particularly for very young people and older people, is moving to more control of the environment, which may be limiting choice and therefore learning, thus making people more vulnerable and leading to greater "institutional" care rather than support. There is also likely to be increased anxiety in unfamiliar situations that inhibits behaviour and therefore further learning. This is a critical issue that needs to be examined very carefully, particularly into the limits of risk taking, the need for care and support, and an understanding where physical control leads to loss of behavioural control. Turnbull III (in press) have written about the relevance of dignity for people with intellectual disabilities, such as Down syndrome, and this includes the dignity of risk, which can enhance self-image, empowerment, and performance. It is a component which has to form part of an ethical approach to education.

Further concepts in quality of life

Imaging the future

The quality of life approach, because of concern for an individual's thoughts and interests, naturally leads to an expansion of issues relating to the individual's future.

It is extremely important that teachers and research students try to imagine the potential future of people with Down syndrome in a positive and encouraging manner. For example, the author conducted a diploma course for teachers who had been teaching people with Down syndrome. One of the aspects of this course was to look at what actually happened to people with Down syndrome as they aged, and also to demonstrate the techniques and strategies that could be employed. The author put together a discussion group made up of adults with Down syndrome from the educational district. Although he did not yet know this, a number of the teachers had taught people with Down syndrome during their primary and middle years, and some even during the secondary years. Now these former students were young adults. The discussion resulted in very clear descriptions of what individuals could now do, and what individuals wanted to do. Afterwards, several teachers came forward and said, "I never believed these people could do so well." The fact is that people with Down syndrome often do much better than expected and it is critical to get this information out to teachers, parents, and others. Some of these young adults were going to college; some were looking for work; some were taking training so that they could work in the leisure and recreation areas of motels. Some were highly proficient in the arts; others at leisure and recreation in terms of their sports abilities and spoke of their achievements with gold and silver medals in the Special Olympics. Many of them travelled around the world, sometimes without parents. The author is not suggesting that such success happens to everyone with Down syndrome. Down syndrome involves a very wide spread of abilities. However, appropriate education and experience enhance the likelihood of success.

It is also critical that peers without Down syndrome understand this information as it is a vital part of friendship and communication. Hughson and Uditsky (2007) indicate from their Canadian experience working with colleges and universities that issues such as inclusion, friendship, and peer support, as well as acceptance of new ways to support people with disabilities are often more easily dealt with at the tertiary education level than at the secondary level. There may be many reasons for this, such as selection and later maturation and development, but the point does have relevance to prior education in terms of values and attitudes. The above authors indicate that peer mentorship, receptive lecturers, and access to a tertiary social life in college or university have very positive implications for people with disabilities, including Down syndrome, and parents view the changes very positively.

Exclusion to inclusion

When exclusion and inclusion are interpreted through the principles and concepts of quality of life, the issue of sensitizing those involved becomes essential. For example, it seems doubtful whether we can really come to grips with inclusion if we are not aware of the nuances of exclusion. People with Down syndrome, whatever their ability level, frequently face issues of exclusion over choices during the normal lifespan, including opportunities in a variety of educational, social, and developmental experiences.

Inclusion has been put forward as an important characteristic of the normalization process but it is now recognized, particularly where there is inadequate support or in communities which are non-supportive, that the local environment, including home, school, and community, can become exclusive, particularly if issues of behaviour are involved—for example, in instances of dual diagnosis (e.g. Down syndrome and autism). In such circumstances, there are often major issues of exclusion, though physically the child is at home living in the local community (see Brown, Geider, Primrose, & Jokinen, 2011). In a quality of life approach, it is essential to look at the processes of exclusion and who is affected by this, why they are affected, and how to remediate the loss or lack of inclusion. This aspect of exclusion, though the child is in the parental home and in an integrated school, needs to be researched in greater depth (Box 1.3).

Very often, exclusion is caused by minor aspects of the environment, including the behaviour of others. Unless people understand exclusion, the detailed dynamics and practice of inclusion are often misunderstood and over-looked. In an educational system, it is critically important that teachers, principals, and other related professional personnel, including government personnel responsible for the development of education, should examine how these principles apply. Brown and Shearer (2004) gave some examples, and their article represents one of the few articles (others include Timmons & Brown, 1997) that have looked at the application of quality of life in the educational field.

Person
Individual with Down syndrome (examples of potential exclusion)

- Lack of experience
- Lack of opportunity
- Low motivation
- Anxiety
- Inappropriate behaviour

Other persons who can be sources of exclusion or inclusion

- Parent
- Other family members
- Neighbours
- Teachers
- Friends
- Authorities (e.g. school principal)
- Shopkeeper
- Members Board of Education or Governing Body

Places where exclusion or inclusion can exist

- School
- Local neighbourhood
- Home
- Shopping malls and other centres (e.g. banks, post offices)
- Religious and recreational organizations
- Support agency

Box 1.3 Examples of sources of exclusion or inclusion.

Exclusion can be the lack of opportunities to learn and carry out activities that other children are provided with at school, at home, and in the community. Any particular child may not be seen as ready for certain experiences—for example, to go downtown on their own, even though they are 15 years old, take the family dog for a walk, go to bed as late as other children of the same age, wear age-appropriate clothing, or listen to music enjoyed by age-peer groups. Although progress has been made since Denholm underscored these social and educational needs at a conference in 1991, and such needs have been underscored since (Timmons, 1993; Timmons & Brown, 1997), there remain many parts of the world where such changes have not taken place. Although many children with Down syndrome are now involved in extensive recreation and leisure activities, and some have been given considerable encouragement in the field of the fine arts (Warren, 1997), such changes are still awaited in many places, particularly in less developed and low-income countries (see McConkey & Timmons, 2006). These aspects of education are part of a normalization and a quality of life or well-being that give people with Down syndrome the opportunities to express and develop recreational, cultural, and spiritual awareness and to meet their personal needs in this regard. These are important and holistic aspects of having a quality life.

It is important to explore opportunities with support to see what the person can do, and how environmental modifications can be made to ensure they are included and have the same experiences as their age peers. For example, in learning about money, they should have the opportunities to have their own bank account and learn how to place those funds within a bank. Other examples include opportunity to choose and to buy their own clothes, and ride the local transit system, with support if necessary. These opportunities may lead to positive outcomes, such as increasing motivation, learning ability, and social knowledge, and not least the ability to choose, decide, and make decisions oneself.

Possible negative outcomes, such as inappropriate talking to strangers, are the very issues that need resolution and should be dealt with within the education process. This requires individualized support because such experiences generally need to be tailored to individual needs. Indeed quality of life and intellectual disability provide good models for individualizing education.

Inclusion involves a host of minor items that can result in major impacts on other aspects of an individual's quality of life, such as self-image, self-worth, and empowerment, and therefore the ability to function effectively at school and in society. These include being regarded as equally valued in a classroom in terms of rights, opportunities, and attention. Much of the change from exclusion to inclusion involves minimal cost. It requires that we make adjustments to how we teach and where we teach—for example, making greater use of home and community.

The research questions in these areas abound. Although the following may not fit stereotypical views of inclusion, the exclusion–inclusion principles do not seem to me to imply that the same opportunities are used at the same time for everyone, though they should be available in any society on the basis of equality. This is the macro level of inclusion. Inclusion at this level means being in environments which are normal for a child of his or her age, having access to the same places, equipment, and opportunities, being able to mix, play, and study with other children, to be able to make friends. This then leads to the micro level of inclusion and provides opportunity for the introduction of procedures which fit the child's approach to learning. This is a difficult decision at times because perceived lack of readiness or ability by parents or teachers can be used as an excuse for not providing opportunities. This is why effective and recorded assessment is necessary. There can be a case made for setting up an agreement with a parent or other responsible adult where general or specific opportunities can be provided for intervention and support along with appropriate assessment. This could be part of the Individual Educational Plan. There are ready guidelines available that include requests and wishes of a child, the results of discussion with a child, and opportunities with support to explore environments.

At the micro level—that is, daily intervention and support—the methods have to take into account individual needs and include processes such as choice, learning styles, and motivation. Quality of life in the context of inclusion requires, at this level, an individualized approach which is expansive, detailed, precise, and flexible.

Effective relationships

In developing and understanding personal relationships, it is important to consider emotional development, independence, the development of friendship, physical maturity, and increasing ability to understand oneself, as well as the developmental processes which are occurring as people mature. Indeed, many people with Down syndrome can have warm and affectionate relationships, and this may involve sexual activity.

The opportunity and ability to have more adult relationships, including emotional and sexual involvement, have an impact on quality of life. Because of varying social mores, those relationships will be encouraged or discouraged by family. Families need to know what impact these experiences are likely to have and if family patterns negate some opportunities, it is critical that stimulating alternatives are found which can promote adult behaviour. The improvement amongst people with Down syndrome in the Western world indicates the importance of exposure and involvement across the same broad range of activities now accepted in Western society.

It is news to many that people with Down syndrome wish to and sometimes can partner or marry. At least this is the author's impression (Brown, 1996), having interviewed a number of people with Down syndrome who have married. Very often forming relationships is a process that accelerates abilities in a way that earlier education has not. For example, the issue of friendship is a critical one for many youngsters with Down syndrome (McVilly, 2006; McVilly, Stancliffe, Parmenter, & Burton-Smith, 2006). If there is partnership or marriage, this can increase dramatically the range of friendships and therefore the range of language that is used, along with increased motivation to integrate normally in society. Research, to date, at this level is largely observational—finding out and seeing how partners operate, or by interviewing the parties concerned. Individual interviews carried out by the author with those who were married or partnered suggest, in most cases, strong motivation, a feeling of "oneness" with those around them, including siblings who are also married, and a sense of enthusiasm for what they want to do and be. They often seem to be the epitome of "Being, Belonging, and Becoming" (Renwick *et al.*, 1996). What we do not know is whether these young partnered adults are the exceptions because of genetics or/and social environment. Wider studies, involving countries where such marriage or partnership is allowed and reasonably well accepted, are necessary.

People with Down syndrome may need more education and support in forming social relationships than others. Further, it is critically important that these are not developed just as specific programmes in sexual knowledge or physical involvement, but rather embedded appropriately in a variety of situations. This, too, is part of holistic and lifespan education. If teaching is appropriate and supportive, and guidance is provided, then effective relationships are likely to take place.

Many parents worry about whether their children will be exploited, and this can result in over-protection. We tend, at least in Western society, to allow older children who "don't have disabilities" to do what they choose, even though we may suggest a range of behaviours which are acceptable or not acceptable. We tend to allow them more exploratory behaviour than we do for people with Down syndrome. However, in a developmentally progressive system, it is necessary to allow opportunities which will, at times, result in error. People who are married and have Down syndrome have sometimes divorced. That is not a reason for not encouraging such relationships. Occasionally people with Down syndrome will be abused within a sexual relationship. But this also occurs in the general population. Children may become lost if shopping downtown. The author is not suggesting that there are no safeguards or supports, but that the supports are of a type which promotes gradual development and understanding. There has grown up in the field of disabilities, particularly intellectual disabilities, a real dilemma between the duty of care, on the one hand, and the opportunity provided by choice on the other. We need to allow choices.

The possibilities: adult life

Despite Down syndrome being a genetic condition, there is great room left for the impact of the genome as a whole and the interplay with environment, as noted earlier. A number of people with Down syndrome as young adults have considerable artistic skills and sell their paintings and sculptures. One young man introduced to readers in the Prologue of this book, Dylan Kuehl, travels around the world, with support, to learn more about art and also to show and sell his art. So he has a small business of his own. In such instances, I am interested in the role of the mother in the process, often going against the "folk" beliefs that more normal development is not possible. In the field of Down syndrome and other disabilities, the role of parents seems critical to progress. There appears to be a correlation between intensity of support and success, and the effects appear to be long term. This, however, may come with other costs in the family, and that is a subject for further discussion (see Cuskelly, Brown, Shearer, & Singh, 2006).

These aspects of success need much further research through evaluation studies, which also includes the nature of individual parents and overall family support patterns over the long term. Studies by Brown *et al.* (1992) indicated that offspring of parents who were keen on their young adults receiving individualized support, based on their offspring's choices, improve more over a three-year period than those who received no intervention. Those individuals whose families rejected such intervention frequently on the grounds that they believed their children could not improve remained the same or deteriorated. A few youngsters with Down syndrome were in these two groups. Were the parents making a correct assumption or setting up a self-fulfilling prophesy?

Employment

Preparing people for some form of employment is relevant for many individuals with Down syndrome and this may range from traditional types of work in restaurants, fast food outlets, factories, motels, through to more sophisticated employment, including self-employment. Opportunities for open employment have often been associated with active parents, particularly mothers, and sometimes school teachers. But we have to make these opportunities available to all in the educational system (see Capie, Contardi, & Doehring, 2006).

Conceptually and practically, this means changing how we deal with later adolescent years for people with Down syndrome. Giving them extra help and support outside normal teaching hours is important because these are often the times when new learning is likely to be lost. Lack of activity is associated with a decline in motivation. So it becomes important to provide supports so those children become more active and more employable. Frequently the individual with Down syndrome appears to have a clear understanding of what they want to do and what they wish to try, and many have a good idea of their current limitations (Grantley, Brown, & Thornley, 2001).

Measurement

Measuring quality of life has proved challenging. Many questionnaires and surveys have been developed for assessment of individuals with intellectual and developmental disabilities, which are suitable for use with people with Down syndrome, but most are for adolescents and adults. There is a shortage of high-quality children's QoL instruments and particularly in the educational field, as noted by Timmons and Brown (1997), but such assessment tests are emerging. The literature to date stresses the importance of the individual reporting on his or her own quality of life. There have been challenges to the idea that young children, and particularly those with disabilities, can give valid and reliable accounts of their quality of life. But then, as indicated earlier, it is important to gain their perceptions of aspects of their life, which may differ from those of the external evaluator. Assessing an individual's own perception is critical to understanding a child's behaviour and motivation. Two studies with schoolchildren were by Timmons (1993) and Shearer (2011), the latter being a small study based on a qualitative model which looked at the quality of life of children and noted the relevance of the results to a QoL framework, as discussed in this chapter. There were five children in the study, aged 9–12 years, four of whom had Down syndrome. A further study by Faragher (2010) also looked at numeracy in the context of quality of life.

A comprehensive list with annotation is provided through the Australian Centre on Quality of Life (2011). A framework for student well-being involving many of the concepts of quality of life is important and can be a useful guide in the field of Down syndrome and education, which calls for a system of measurement in the education domain with recognition of values, choices perception, and allied quality of life concepts as a vital contribution (DEEWR, 2008). This makes reference to several tests for children. Best of all, it provides a useful background to some of the challenges in the area discussed by Zekovic and Renwick (2003). These authors discuss some of the challenges in the area using qualitative methodology in relation to children aged 3–12 years and their families using a modified grounded theory approach. The results underscore the quality of life principles raised earlier in the chapter and importantly note how quality of life needs for children of different ages change (e.g. the importance of peer relationships for 12 year olds compared to three year olds). They also note the relevance and interrelationship between school, home, and community. Lyons (2005) has advocated careful and close observation and recording of children's behaviour, particularly if the person has no or little language. His life satisfaction matrix, an instrument for assessing subjective quality of life, is important in terms of people with profound disabilities. These are major areas for future research as evaluation of the impact of quality of life approaches is important to future development.

Family quality of life

Education and other services and systems need to be very responsive to negative quality of life issues affecting the family. If this is not done, we are faced with further family deterioration and malfunctioning or, alternatively, the possibility of the child being removed from schooling and possibly the family home for periods of time. With support, families can often adapt effectively, and it is important that education systems play a major role in this area.

Increasingly, there has been an interest in family quality of life and this is of considerable relevance to education since the home life of a child is critical to development and education (Brown & Brown, in press). A number of researchers and practitioners have paid attention, particularly over the last 10 years, to issues related to the family and how all members of the family may experience a loss of quality of life when disability is involved (Turnbull, Brown, & Turnbull, 2004). When supporting a person with Down syndrome, it is important to recognize the impact that this may have on the family, and the extent to which the issues are interactive, preventing the family members performing effectively. Lack of support can have an impact on the child's attendance at school, the ability to manage a child's behaviour, and the skills required by parents to be able to support what is going on in the educational setting. For these reasons, there must be a change in how we respond to families, linking education to social requirements for support of the family. This is a high priority for research.

The other side of the quality of life coin

Having described a quality of life approach and briefly described some of the research studies, which could prove valuable in this context, another question needs to be asked. Given we know the concepts and principles of QoL and have some means of measuring change in quality of life for individuals and families, what sort of impact does education have on individual quality of life?

Much research has gone into the education of children with Down syndrome in terms of reading, writing, and social skills, with some research into mathematics. The question arises: How do these interventions improve the quality of life of the individual and the quality of life of families? There are many qualitative comments about this, but little in the way of formal quality of life research. To know the answer to the above question would provide valuable feedback to all parties concerned and, if the outcome showed improvement in quality of life, this would result in valuable feedback regarding method and outcome and would be essential for any informed educational process. With such an approach, specific areas can be targeted. For example, does visual, non-verbal instruction in a particular educational subject produce results which not only enable the individual to progress in a particular area but help him or her perform more effectively, for example, through reducing anxiety and increasing self-image? Some educational bodies and teachers do not become aware of the changing outcome in terms of quality of life issues for children with Down syndrome who leave school and live in the community (see, for example, Bertoli *et al.*, 2011). But change is both possible and necessary (see, for example, Brown, 2004; Velde & Emes, 2006).

Concluding remarks

One of the advantages of any approach or model based on scientific principles is that it gives rise to further questions. The approach discussed here moves from external or objective aspects to subjective or perceptual attributes. It should not be thought that quality of life is just a set of principles and concepts to be simply applied in education or other areas, though the principles have considerable relevance in this context. The other side of the coin concerns what effective subject education can do for the quality of life of people with Down syndrome, and this aspect is also important for research. Quality of life as an approach promotes active, and supported, learning. How well that education takes effect and improves the quality of life of a person with Down syndrome may well depend on how well the content is designed and applied. The development of policy using the quality of life approach is gradually being recognized.

It provides for a pragmatic and diversified approach with a "bottom up" structure involving policy that reflects the needs of children, including those with disabilities for lifelong community living. To be successful, this needs effective and on-going evaluation for helpful feedback. Scientific investigation in this field requires a research-to-practice framework to policy development, which in some instances may lead to radical changes in both direction and focus. However, it must be remembered that not all aspects of inclusive education can easily be measured. This is a challenge but not a reason to sideline such aspects of education as, for example, the role of music or fine arts, which can raise immeasurably many aspects of development and quality of life.

Acknowledgement

Roy Brown would like to thank Dr Robin Jackson and Floris Books for permission to make use of, and adapt from, his chapter: Brown R. I. (2011). Quality of life: Dimensions, perceptions and practice. In R. Jackson (Ed.), *Discovering Camphill: New perspectives, research and development* (pp. 255–263). Edinburgh, Scotland: Floris Books.

References

Andrews, F. M. (1974). Social indicators of perceived life quality. *Social Indicators Research, 1*, 279–299.

Andrews, F. M., & Whithey, S. B. (1976). *Social indicators of well-being: Americans' perception of life quality*. New York: Plenum Press.

Australian Centre on Quality of Life. (updated 2011). *Instruments*. Accessed on 30 March 2013 from www.deakin.edu.au/research/acqol/instruments/instrument.php.

Bach, M., & Rioux, M. H. (1996). Social well-being: A framework for quality of life research. In R. Renwick, I. Brown, & M. Nagler (Eds), *Quality of life in health promotion and rehabilitation* (pp. 63–74). Thousand Oaks: Sage.

Baird, P. A., & Sadovnik, P. D. (1987). Life expectancy in Down syndrome. *Journal of Paediatrics, 110*, 849–854.

Bennett, D. A., Schneider, J. A., Tang, Y., Arnold, S. E., & Wilson, R. S. (2006). The effect of social networks on the relation between Alzheimer's disease pathology and level of cognitive function in old people: A longitudinal cohort study. *Lancet Neurology, 5*, 406–412.

Bertoli, M., Biasini, G., Calignano, M. T., Celani, G., De Grossi, G., Digilo, M. C., & Zuccalà, G. (2011). Needs and challenges of daily life for people with Down syndrome residing in the city of Rome, Italy. *Journal of Intellectual Disability Research, 55*, 801–820.

Borthwick-Duffey, C. (1996). Racism, IQ and Down's syndrome. *Disability & Society, 11*, 403–410.

Brown, I., & Brown, R. (2003). *Quality of life and disability: An approach for community practitioners*. London: Jessica Kingsley.

Brown, I., & Brown, R. I. (2009). Choice as an aspect of quality of life for people with intellectual disabilities. *Journal of Policy and Practice in Intellectual Disabilities, 6*, 11–18.

Brown, R. I. (1994). Down syndrome and quality of life: Some challenges for future practice. *Down Syndrome Research and Practice, 2*, 19–30.

Brown, R. I. (1996). Partnership and marriage in Down syndrome. *Down Syndrome Research and Practice, 4*, 96–99.

Brown, R. I. (1997). Quality of life: The development of an idea. In R. I. Brown (Ed.), *Quality of Life for people with disabilities: Models, research and practice* (pp. 3–7). Cheltenham: Stanley Thornes.

Brown, R. I. (Ed.). (2004–2008). *Adults with Down syndrome*. 11 volumes. Portsmouth, UK: Down Syndrome Educational Trust.

Brown R. I. (2007). Roles, education, training and professional values of disability personnel. In I. Brown & M. Percy, *A comprehensive guide to intellectual and developmental disabilities* (pp. 415–432). Baltimore, MD: Paul H. Brookes.

Brown, R. I., & Bookbinder, G. E. (1968). *Clifton Audio-Visual Reading Programme*. Harlow, UK: Educational Supply Association Limited.

Brown, R. I., & Brown, I. (in press). Family quality of life. In A. C. Michalos (Ed.), *Encyclopedia of Quality of Life Research*. Dordrecht: Springer.

Brown, R. I., & Bullitis, E. (2006). The process of mental imagery in persons with or without intellectual disability: An exploratory project. *Journal on Developmental Disabilities, 12*(1), Suppl. 2, 1–18.

Brown, R. I., & Shearer, J. (2004). Challenges for inclusion within a quality of life model for the 21st century. In D. Mitchell (Ed.), *Special educational needs and inclusive education: Major themes in education. Vol. 2.* (pp. 139–156). London and New York: Routledge Falmer.

Brown, R. I., Bayer, M. B., & Brown, P. M. (1992). *Empowerment and developmental handicaps: Choices and quality of life.* Toronto: Captus Press, and London: Chapman & Hall.

Brown, R. I., Bayer, M. B., & MacFarlane, C. (1989). *Rehabilitation programmes: Performance and quality of life of adults with developmental handicaps*. Toronto: Lugus Productions Ltd.

Brown, R. I., Geider, S., Primrose, A., & Jokinen, N. (2011). Family life and the impact of previous and present residential and day care support for children with major cognitive and behavioural challenges: A dilemma for services and policy. *Journal of Intellectual Disability Research, 55*, 914–917.

Brown, R. I., Schalock, R., & Brown, I. (2009). Quality of life: Its application to persons with intellectual disabilities and their families—Introduction and overview. *Journal of Policy and Practice in Intellectual Disabilities, 6*, 2–5.

Capie, A., Contardi, A., & Doehring, D. (2006). *Transition to employment.* Portsmouth, UK: The Down Syndrome Educational Trust.

Carr, J. (2009). 40 years of life with Down syndrome. *Down Syndrome Quarterly, 11*, 19–25.

Cummins, R. (1997). Assessing quality of life. In R. I. Brown (Ed.), *Quality of life for people with disabilities: Models, research and practice* (pp. 116–150). Cheltenham, UK: Stanley Thornes.

Cummins, R. A. (2002). Proxy responding for subjective well-being: A review. *International Review of Research in Mental Retardation, 25*, 183–207.

Cunningham, C., & Brown, R. I. (in press). Down Syndrome. In A. C. Michalos (Ed.), *Encyclopedia of Quality of Life Research.* Dordrecht: Springer.

Cuskelly, M., Brown, I., Shearer, J., & Singh, B. (2006). *Families of adults with Down syndrome.* Portsmouth, UK: The Down Syndrome Educational Trust.

DEEWR. (2008). *Scoping study into approaches to student wellbeing: Final report.* Australian Catholic University. Gladesville, NSW: Eribus International.

Denholm, C. (1991). The adolescent with Down syndrome. In Down East 91: Learning together. *Proceedings Canadian Down Syndrome Society*: Halifax, pp. 21–23.

Doidge, N. (2007). *The brain that changes itself.* New York: Viking.

Faragher, R. M. (2010). Developing numeracy to enhance quality of life. In R. Kober (Ed.), *Enhancing the quality of life of people with intellectual disability: From theory to practice* (pp. 401–411). Dordrecht: Springer Science + Business Media B.V.

Gibson, D. (1978). *Down syndrome: The psychology of Mongolism*. Cambridge, UK: Cambridge University Press.

Goode, D. A. (Ed.). (1994). *Quality of life for persons with disabilities: International perspectives and issues*. Boston: Brookline Books.

Grantley, J., Brown, R. I., & Thornley, J. (2001). Challenges to employment: Perceptions and barriers as seen by people with Down syndrome and their parents. *International Journal of Practical Approaches to Disability, 25*, 29–35.

Hughson, E. A., & Uditsky, B. (2007). *Inclusive post-secondary education for adults with Down syndrome and other developmental disabilities: A promising path to an inclusive life*. Portsmouth, UK: The Down Syndrome Educational Trust.

Kaufman, J. C., & Grigorenko, E. L. (Eds). (2009). *The essential Sternberg: Essays on intelligence, psychology, and education*. New York: Springer Publishing Company.

Lyons, G. (2005). The life satisfaction matrix: An instrument and procedure for assessing the subjective quality of life of individuals with profound multiple disabilities. *Journal of Intellectual Disability Research, 49*, 766–769.

McConkey, R., & Timmons, V. (2006). *International and cultural aspects of Down syndrome*. Portsmouth, UK: The Down Syndrome Educational Trust.

McVilly, K., (2006). When family and quality services are not enough. *Learning Links,* 1–3.

McVilly, K., Stancliffe, R., Parmenter, T., & Burton-Smith, R. (2006). "I get by with a little help from my friends": Adults with intellectual disability discuss loneliness. *Journal of Applied Research in Intellectual Disabilities, 19*, 191–203.

Mitchell, D. (2009). An evidenced-based approach to teaching learners with special educational needs. Paper presented at 2009 International Forum on Special Education, Beijing, October, P1.

Renwick, R., & Brown, I. (1996). The Centre for Health Promotion's conceptual approach to quality of life: Being, belonging, and becoming. In R. Renwick & I. Brown (Eds), *Quality of life in health promotion and rehabilitation: Conceptual approaches, issues, and applications* (pp. 75–86). Thousand Oaks, CA: Sage Publications, Inc.

Renwick, R., Brown, I., & Nagler, M. (Eds). (1996). *Quality of Life in health promotion and rehabilitation: Conceptualizations, research and applications*. Thousand Oaks, CA: Sage.

Schalock, R. L., & Verdugo, M. A. (2012). *A leadership guide for today's disabilities organizations. Overcoming challenges and making change happen*. Baltimore, MD: Brookes.

Schalock, R., Brown, I., Brown, R. I., Cummins, R. A., Felce, D., Matikka, L., Keith, K. D., & Parmenter, T. (2002). Conceptualization, measurement, and application of quality of life for persons with intellectual disabilities: Report of an international panel of experts. *Mental Retardation, 40*, 457–470.

Shearer, J. (2011). Aspects of Quality of Life for children with a disability in inclusive schools. In R. Kober (Ed.), *Enhancing the quality of life of people with intellectual disability: From theory to practice* (pp. 205–221). Dordrecht: Springer.

Stancliffe, R., & Parmenter, T. (1999). The choice questionnaire: A scale to assess choices by adults with intellectual disability. *Journal of Intellectual & Developmental Disability, 24*, 107–132.

Taylor, S. J. (1994). In support of research of quality of life, but against QoL. In D. Goode (Ed.), *Quality of Life for persons with disabilities: International perspectives and issues* (pp. 260–265). Cambridge, MA: Brookline Books.

Timmons, V. (1993). *Quality of life of teenagers with special needs*. Unpublished doctoral thesis, University of Calgary, Canada.

Timmons, V., & Brown, R. I. (1997). Quality of life: Issues for children with handicaps. In R. Brown (Ed.), *Quality of life for people with disabilities: Models, research and practice* (2nd edn). Cheltenham: Stanley Thornes.

Torr, J., Strydom, A., Patti, P., & Jokinen, N. (2010). Aging in Down syndrome: Morbidity and mortality. *Journal of Policy and Practice in Intellectual Disabilities, 7*, 70–81.

Turnbull, A. P., Brown, I., & Turnbull, H. R. (Eds). (2004). *Families and people with mental retardation and quality of life: International perspectives*. Washington, DC: American Association on Mental Retardation (AAMR).

Turnbull III, H. R. (in press). Foreword. In R. I. Brown & R. M. Faragher (Eds), *Challenges for Quality of Life: Applications in education and other social contexts*. New York: Nova Science.

Velde, V., & Emes, C. (2006). *Recreation and adults with Down syndrome*. Portsmouth, UK: The Down Syndrome Educational Trust.

Warren, B. (1997). Change and necessity: Creative activity, well-being and the quality of life for persons with a disability. In R. I. Brown (Ed.), *Quality of life for people with disabilities: Models, research and practice* (pp. 270–291). Cheltenham, Stanley Thornes.

Zekovic, B., & Renwick, R. (2003). Quality of life for children and adolescents with developmental disabilities: Review of conceptual and methodological issues relevant to public policy. *Disability & Society, 18*, 19–34.

Chapter 2

Cognitive strengths and weaknesses for informing educational practice

Donna Couzens and Monica Cuskelly

Abstract

This chapter describes our current understanding of the cognitive strengths and weaknesses that are associated with Down syndrome. The chapter begins with a discussion of some of the difficulties of establishing cognitive profiles associated with Down syndrome. We then present the research that has investigated cognitive functions in those with Down syndrome and consider the implications of this research for learning and teaching. We conclude with some suggestions regarding the priorities for future research.

Introduction

This chapter describes our current understanding of the cognitive strengths and weaknesses that are associated with Down syndrome. The chapter begins with a discussion of some of the difficulties of establishing cognitive profiles related to Down syndrome. We then present the research that has investigated cognitive functions in those with Down syndrome and consider the implications of this research for learning and teaching. We conclude with some suggestions regarding the priorities for future research.

Influences on behaviour, which are considered to have a genetic basis but are not directly observable, have been termed endophenotypes. Endophenotypes refer to a range of biologically based influences on behaviour that may be neurochemical, endocrinological, neuroanatomical, or neuropsychological, and, while considered to be more directly influenced by genetics than are behaviours, can have complex relationships with observed behaviours (see Kendler & Neale, 2010). The cognitive characteristics that we explore within this chapter are not directly observable but rather are inferred through the analysis of individuals' task performance.

Approaches to and difficulties in identifying a cognitive profile

The process of establishing a profile of cognitive strengths and weaknesses relies on information about the cognitive profile of those who are developing typically and what can be considered to be normal variation from that typical profile. This information then provides one of the comparisons used in the search for the cognitive profile of those who are developing atypically, such as individuals with Down syndrome. Another approach is to compare those with Down syndrome with others with an intellectual disability from a range of causes—this may help determine what is specific to Down syndrome rather than what is a product of intellectual disability. Finally, the comparison of those with Down syndrome with those who have an intellectual disability with a specific aetiology, such as Williams syndrome, is another commonly adopted method for identifying specific strengths and weaknesses in cognitive processes.

Tasks used to establish cognitive profiles

Intelligence tests and other cognitive assessments are used as the basis for understanding cognitive functioning generally and for establishing relative strengths and weaknesses in cognitive processes. These assessments comprise a series of tasks (collected with like items and labelled a test) and each test is allocated to a broad ability type (e.g. verbal, spatial, sequential processing) on the basis of theoretical and research-based models of cognitive processes which underpin the assessment instrument. In reality, however, tasks that measure a single cognitive process cannot be identified as all tasks rely on visual, auditory, and/or physical abilities for understanding and performance. Individuals with Down syndrome are vulnerable to visual, hearing, and motor problems and so poor performance on their part may not always be due to difficulties with the cognitive function being assessed but may be a product of their difficulties in these other areas of functioning.

Comparison groups

Most studies have compared mean scores that have been aggregated from groups of individuals with Down syndrome against mean scores similarly aggregated for the selected comparison group(s). Where statistically significant and meaningful differences have been identified between the groups, a strength or weakness associated with Down syndrome is often proposed. If a small number of individuals with Down syndrome perform exceptionally well or poorly on a task, the aggregated score could be inflated or suppressed relative to the comparison group. This may result in the identification of a specific cognitive strength or weakness for the group when the difference actually applies only to a minority in the group. An example of data fitting this pattern with respect to certain visual processing tasks has been reported by Couzens, Cuskelly, and Haynes (2011).

Comparison groups of children developing typically and selected on the basis that their chronological ages (CA) match the assessed mental ages (MA) within the group with Down syndrome are frequently used to determine specific strengths or weaknesses of individuals with Down syndrome relative to their mental age. This approach is based on the understanding that CA = MA in children who are developing typically, i.e. that children's mental abilities are appropriate for their age. So, to establish MA in those with atypical development, we take their score and determine at which CA this score would be the average score. This comparison, however, does not account for life experiences, particularly when assessing adolescents and adults with Down syndrome, whose substantially longer life experience may affect how they perceive and approach problems relative to the younger comparison group (for example, see discussion of motivation by Gilmore & Cuskelly, Chapter 3). Also, the development of certain accumulated or learnt knowledge may be influenced by time or experience for specific cognitive abilities. This comparison also does not separate differences that may be specific to Down syndrome from differences related more generally to intellectual disability. These are important distinctions as abilities that develop via the same sequences but at a slower rate will require different approaches from abilities that do not develop effectively or develop using different mechanisms or processes than typically expected. Matching by MA generally assumes that the tasks used to assess intelligence work in the same way for those with Down syndrome as for individuals who are typically developing, but this may not be the case (Couzens, Cuskelly, & Jobling, 2004).

Individuals with intellectual disability but without Down syndrome, matched by both CA and MA, are frequently used for comparison. This research design accommodates differences that may occur with time and those that may be associated with intellectual disability generally. As noted above, in some cases, researchers will recruit a group with mixed causes of intellectual disability, and in others, a group with a specific aetiology will be used for comparison. Some researchers have matched the comparison group using particular areas of ability—for example, reading age (Verucci, Menghini, & Vicari, 2006) or face processing (Williams, Wishart, Pitcairn, & Willis, 2005). Frequently, researchers will use several groups for comparison and this allows us to build and revise hypotheses as understanding of each influence is refined. Systematic differences in the comparison group can both magnify and mask cognitive differences that may be associated with Down syndrome.

Changes with age

Development is a continuous process affected by maturation, environmental factors, and the transactions that occur between the person and his/her environment. Cognitive strengths and weaknesses may not be static, so a cognitive profile based on individuals in their early school years may not apply to adults. In addition, the way in which various cognitive functions develop and the variables that influence this development need to be understood. Differences in development of cognitive abilities have not been captured effectively in much of the research undertaken to identify a common profile associated with Down syndrome.

Most cognitive theories and assessments are based on the premise that certain abilities are related and will develop concurrently (synchronously). For example, Piagetian theory posits that the emergence of representational intelligence enables the development of deferred imitation (repeating the actions of another person at a later time), and object permanence (understanding the continued existence of an object when it goes out of sight) (Wright, Lewis, & Collis, 2006). Other abilities are expected to develop sequentially, with development of one enabling the development of another. For example, a certain level of motor development may need to be established before a child is able to effectively solve certain spatial problems (Funk, Brugger, & Wilkening, 2005).

Only longitudinal research, following the same individuals over time, can assist us to understand differences associated with the sequence of development. Longitudinal studies are rare, however, as they are difficult to sustain. Most of our current knowledge is based on cross-sectional research where different groups of individuals have been assessed for each age group represented. Hypotheses about development are sometimes made using these data or static differences are proposed without the associated understanding of how these differences might have developed.

Memory abilities

Memory deficits have been hypothesized to underpin many difficulties experienced by those with Down syndrome and, for this reason, our discussion begins with research on memory differences. Baddeley's working memory model (Allen, Baddeley, & Hitch, 2006; Baddeley, 2000) has been adopted by most researchers to address questions of memory strengths and weaknesses in individuals with Down syndrome. While this model is central to the current discussion as it has provided the theoretical framework for most research in this area, it is important to understand that the model does not address all questions regarding memory and that certain higher-order processes may be better represented by other models. One of these models is considered later when we discuss specific processing or problem-solving abilities. Our view is that, at this time, both working memory and long-term memory of those with Down syndrome is best understood using the model developed by Baddeley.

Baddeley's (2000) working memory model proposes four inter-related components involved in the storage and manipulation of information: the central executive, phonological loop, visuospatial scratchpad, and episodic buffer. The central executive provides the voluntary and conscious control of subsidiary systems. Subsidiary systems include the phonological loop and the visuospatial scratchpad, which provide temporary storage of auditory and visual information, respectively, and the episodic buffer temporarily stores bound multimodal information from both short-term memory and long-term memory in preparation for long-term storage. Auditory information, typically sequential, appears to decay in seconds unless articulatory rehearsal of this information occurs in the phonological loop. The capturing of visual and spatial information is the responsibility of the visuospatial scratchpad. The binding of visual features (a simultaneous process) and spatial features (a sequential process), while dis-associated, are hypothesized to occur automatically in this subsystem (Allen *et al.*, 2006; Baddeley, 2012). Auditory and visual information are thought to decay quickly within both these subsidiary systems unless the central executive provides the attentional resources required to bind information into meaningful chunks (Allen *et al.*, 2006; Baddeley, 2012).

Baddeley's model has proven effective in explaining temporary storage of visual and verbal information, capacity limitations, manipulation of information, and the binding and integration of information for long-term storage. While the terms 'working memory' and 'short-term memory' are often used interchangeably, we follow the definitions of Baddeley (2012), using 'short-term memory' when considering temporary storage and 'working memory' when referring to the 'combination of storage and manipulation' (Baddeley, 2012, p. 4).

Verbal memory

Verbal memory appears to be a significant weakness for individuals with Down syndrome, even individuals who demonstrate relatively advanced expressive verbal abilities. Recent analysis of age-related change in subdomain scores of the Stanford-Binet (4th edn) (Thorndike, Hagen, & Sattler, 1986) indicated that variation between individuals with Down syndrome on verbal memory was very limited, suggesting less scope for external influences on this ability than for any of the other cognitive domains of the assessment (Couzens *et al.*, 2011).The phonological loop is hypothesized to be responsible for the major difficulties individuals with Down syndrome demonstrate in certain areas of language development (see Brock & Jarrold, 2005; Jarrold & Baddeley, 2001; Jarrold, Baddley, & Hewes, 2000; Purser & Jarrold, 2005). It has also been suggested that the 'central executive' of Baddeley and Hitch's model may be implicated in the verbal short-term memory difficulties experienced (see Vicari & Carlesimo, 2006).

Verbal working memory deficits are greater than would be expected in relation to overall cognitive delay and weaker than working memory for visual-spatial information (e.g. Jarrold & Baddeley, 2001; Purser & Jarrold, 2005). Jarrold, Baddeley, and Phillips (1999) replaced the verbal recall task of a memory assessment with a serial recognition task with no positive effect on performance, demonstrating that the verbal memory difficulty was not an artefact of the sequential nature of most of these tasks. It had also been hypothesized that slower speech may result in poorer retention; however, speech rate was excluded as a cause for short-term memory difficulties as individuals with Down syndrome were found to have faster speech production but poorer recall than a comparison group matched for mean length of utterance (Seung & Chapman, 2000).

Many hypotheses have been tested and ruled out as explanations for poor verbal working memory. As verbal rehearsal is typically not used as a memory strategy until age eight years, this cannot explain poor performance relative to those matched using MA (Jarrold *et al.*, 2000). Purser and Jarrold (2005) ruled out rapid forgetting as an explanatory factor for poor verbal working memory by assessing memory for items that were presented in different serial positions. These researchers also adjusted the rate of presentation to assess the rapid forgetting hypothesis. Neither of these manipulations had an effect on recall for the individuals with Down syndrome greater than that of the comparison group. While a capacity limitation in verbal working memory is strongly supported by research, an understanding of exactly how this capacity is limited remains obscure (Purser & Jarrold, 2005).

Visual-spatial working memory

Individuals with Down syndrome appear to rely on using their visual-spatial memory when it can be used in place of verbal memory (Conners, Rosenquist, Arnett, Moore, & Hume, 2008). This evidence provides some indirect support for the possibility that visual-spatial working memory is a relative strength for this population. Strength in spatial memory (memory for locations) has been indicated because groups with Down syndrome have performed at or above the level of groups matched by receptive language on a task requiring the recall of a sequence for tapping wooden blocks (Jarrold, Baddeley, & Phillips, 2002; Laws, 2002) and on a spatial reconstruction computer task, where individuals remembered the path of a frog across lily pads (Brock & Jarrold, 2005). When spatially presented information is presented simultaneously (rather than sequentially), however, the spatial memory strength disappears (Lanfranchi, Carretti, Spano, & Cornoldi, 2009).

Static visual short-term memory for colours (Laws, 2002), pictures, or objects (Vicari, Bellucci, & Carlesimo, 2005) may not be strong, although poor perceptual analysis of visually presented information may cause or contribute to visual-object memory difficulties rather than specific short-term memory processes being the sole contributor (Vicari & Carlesimo, 2006). Research investigating processing that uses the visuospatial scratchpad is still in its infancy compared to research on the phonological loop. This imbalance in focus is true both for the general population and for those with Down syndrome.

Long-term memory

Long-term memory in people with Down syndrome has been the subject of less research than working memory; however, there is some evidence that the verbal memory difficulties identified above are not reflected in long-term memory. Jarrold, Baddeley, and Phillips (2007) determined that, once material had been learnt, rate of forgetting appeared to mirror that expected for MA measured using both receptive vocabulary and non-verbal visual analysis tasks. An exception to this involved a visual memory task that required the learners to recall, rather than recognize, visual shapes. The authors suggested that poorer performance on the recall task may have been associated with motivational factors rather than memory.

Implications of research on memory for learning and teaching

Memory abilities in general appear to develop in parallel with cognitive age. The exception is verbal working memory, which seems to be an area of difficulty for most individuals with Down syndrome. In the one study to provide data on this, minimal change was observed in the majority over the school years. Causal mechanisms of these verbal working memory difficulties have not yet been identified. Visual memory appears to be the default memory strategy used, and, at the group level, those with Down syndrome have been shown to remember more items when they are visually presented. The development of reading may support memory span through the use of visual representation (Laws, MacDonald, Buckley, & Broadley, 1995).

While training in verbal recoding has been shown to improve recall of both verbally and visually presented material (see Conners *et al.*, 2008; Laws, MacDonald, & Buckley, 1996, for training examples), use of the strategy tends not to be maintained in the long term (Laws *et al.*, 1995) and generalization of its use to untaught situations has not been observed (Broadley, MacDonald, & Buckley, 1994; Conners *et al.*, 2008).

Spatial memory has been observed to be a strength relative to visual memory for objects; however, uncertainty remains as to whether poor visual working memory for objects may be more related to perceptual weaknesses when attending to an object rather than a specific memory issue. Further research is required before we fully understand differences in performance on the visual and spatial memory tasks. Long-term memory, while less researched than working memory, appears to be largely unaffected by having Down syndrome.

In the verbal domain, individuals with Down syndrome may be able to retain the main semantic elements of a story but not the detail of the actual words used or the grammatical aspects. This reflects what is being attended to and methods used to process and assimilate the information with phonological and semantic information in long-term memory. There is evidence that individuals with Down syndrome benefit from access to more contextual information. They may rely more heavily on heuristic understanding or chunked information to integrate their knowledge and generate the big idea from a story. While the big picture is retained, the details appear to be ignored or lost.

Verbal processing abilities

Group data indicate language difficulties substantially greater than expected in relation to MA for those with Down syndrome (Abbeduto *et al.*, 2001; Chapman & Hesketh, 2000). Language profiles are typically uneven, with certain areas proving more difficult than others.

While first words and two-word combinations are consistent with general cognitive development, vocabulary and syntax development appear to become increasingly delayed with age (Chapman & Hesketh, 2000). Phonological and morphosyntactic problems also become increasingly evident with age. Phonological problems reflect difficulty in distinguishing and manipulating small units of sound within the language system and morphosyntactic problems relate to the understanding and use of small words and word parts with abstract grammatical meaning. Function words, articles, prepositions, pronouns, and the bound morphemes or the elements of meaning added to the beginning (e.g. un-, pre-) and ends of words (e.g. -ed, -s, and -ing) have been indicated as the most pronounced areas of difficulty for those with Down syndrome. Relative to language production, comprehension of concepts has been shown to increase and vocabulary is generally more advanced than grammatical knowledge (Caselli *et al.*, 1998; Chapman & Hesketh, 2000). Strengths in receptive vocabulary relative to MA occur alongside substantially poorer understanding and production of grammatical morphemes than would be expected by MA (Abbeduto *et al.*, 2001).

While aggregated data demonstrate the trends described for the group, the nature of language difficulty changes substantially from one individual to the next. Some individuals with Down syndrome remain largely non-verbal and a proportion do not progress beyond one- or two-word utterances, while several individuals with exceptional language abilities have been identified (for example, see Papagno & Vallar, 2001). The number of words an individual will typically express in a single exchange changes in relation to their age and also relative to the communication style and skill of their conversation partner (Miles, Chapman, & Sindberg, 2006). While understanding typically precedes expressive abilities, this imbalance is larger for those with Down syndrome relative to children developing typically (Chapman, 1997; Chapman, Schwartz, & Kay-Raining Bird, 1991).

Speech may follow a different, rather than slower, developmental trajectory for children with Down syndrome. Important differences, for example, have been found in the development of phonology relative to children developing typically and children whose development of phonology is delayed. Dodd and Thompson (2001) found that children with Down syndrome were more likely to use inconsistent pronunciations for words each time they were used rather than the consistent pronunciation errors typically related to phonological difficulties. While speech intelligibility and hearing problems have been related to difficulties in the language domain (Dodd & Thompson, 2001), they have not been sufficient for explaining all the cognitive difficulties demonstrated within language for this population (Laws, 2004; Laws & Gunn, 2004).

Research investigating the three primary areas of language—semantics (the meaning of words), pragmatics (the use of language), and syntax or grammar (rules governing the order and structure of sentences)—indicates an almost universal difficulty with syntax (Chapman & Hesketh, 2001; Grela, 2002). Both comprehension and production delays have been demonstrated for syntax when compared with comprehension of vocabulary and what is expected for MA.

Investigations into grammatical difficulties have demonstrated a lack of function word use, including articles, prepositions, and pronouns, while verb use and speech length have been found by some researchers to equal or surpass comparison groups (Grela, 2002; Hesketh & Chapman, 1998). Children with Down syndrome were shown to produce a larger variety of verbs (Grela, 2002; Hesketh & Chapman, 1998) and used verbs as frequently as children matched for mean length of utterance or linguistic level (Grela, 2002). Morphosyntactic development represents a specific area of weakness, while lexical and syntactic domains can follow development expected for MA (Caselli *et al.*, 1998). Matches based on non-verbal intelligence, with children developing typically, indicate reduced speech in relation to the variety, volume, and length of utterances produced (Chapman, Hye-Kyeung, Schwartz, & Kay-Raining Bird, 1998).

Working memory influences on expressive and receptive language abilities

The relationship between verbal abilities and working memory is of particular interest to researchers of development in Down syndrome. While there is an association between language production and verbal working memory in this group (Seung & Chapman, 2000), the mechanisms responsible for this relationship remain uncertain. Chapman, Hesketh, and Kistler (2002) used data collected longitudinally to assess whether language production and comprehension abilities of individuals with Down syndrome could be predicted by verbal and visual memory ability. They found that, together, verbal and visual memory explained approximately 90 per cent of the variation between individuals on language assessments at the start of the study. When grammatical comprehension and production skills were assessed at the end of the six-year study, 79 per cent of the change in scores was accounted for by verbal and visual memory ability. This research indicated the important role of both types of working memory in the development of expressive and receptive language abilities for learners with Down syndrome.

Verbal tasks can be supported by accumulated knowledge of language in addition to memory. Sentence imitation tasks, for example, differ from word span and number repetition tasks because semantic and syntactic knowledge supports retention. Seung and Chapman (2000) found that, while the individuals with Down syndrome in their study had a mean digit span of four, their mean syllable span in a sentence memory task was six. This advantage of semantic and syntactic knowledge, however, was larger for the control group who were matched by MA. The mean digit span for this comparison group was six and mean syllable span was ten. Sentence imitation tasks measure both phonological memory and linguistic, particularly grammatical, knowledge, both of which are areas of significant weakness for individuals with Down syndrome.

Implications of research on verbal processing abilities for learning and teaching

While the verbal domain has been heavily emphasized in the literature as an area of weakness for those with Down syndrome, this weakness is not uniform across all aspects of the verbal domain. Perception of the smallest units of sound is frequently poor, and unstable, idiosyncratic pronunciations occur frequently. Use and understanding of grammatical morphology presents the other major challenge persisting into adulthood. It should be noted, however, that, although rare, individuals with Down syndrome whose grammatical abilities are largely consonant with age have been identified. Less rare is the development of large receptive vocabularies relative to general cognitive ability and good general understanding of semantic concepts from verbally presented material. Further research is required to understand the factors that contribute to the large variation in both verbal expression and understanding within this group. Working memory, both verbal and visual, has been found to be strongly and independently associated with the development of both receptive and expressive abilities; however, more research is required to understand the mechanisms underpinning these relationships.

Explicit teaching techniques have been shown to be helpful, at least in the short term, for teaching grammar (Hewitt, Hinkle, & Miccio, 2005) and phonemic awareness (Kennedy & Flynn, 2003) to learners with Down syndrome. Hewitt *et al.*, for example, taught adult learners grammar in a group conversational setting. The researchers generated language samples by introducing conversation topics and using photographs to elicit contributions of their personal experiences from the learners. A specific grammatical structure was identified for each learner based on the expected magnitude of improvement in clarity of expression for that particular individual. The researchers modelled and provided prompts to support imitation of the targeted grammatical sentence structure and broke the structure into smaller components when necessary. All three adult learners in the study increased in the targeted grammatical structure and generalized their learning to other communication partners.

Picture-based supports and storybooks without words have been found effective for individuals with Down syndrome, specifically for increasing speech (Miles *et al.*, 2006). Understanding of story content demonstrated by adolescents with Down syndrome has exceeded the understanding of children developing typically and matched on grammatical usage (Miles & Chapman, 2002). Because recall of stories relies more heavily on general and syntactic knowledge than on verbal working memory, it can be an area of relative strength for those with Down syndrome (Seung & Chapman, 2003).

Enhanced verbal environments that build semantic and syntactic knowledge are hypothesized to support the development of verbal abilities. Rich and targeted language environments prior to school and during the schooling years are associated with higher vocabulary and comprehension and functional receptive and expressive communication outcomes.

Visual-spatial processing

It has been proposed that visual-spatial processing may be a relative strength for individuals with Down syndrome (Jarrold, Baddeley, & Hewes, 1999; Klein & Mervis,

1999). Interpreting research findings to infer an all-inclusive visual processing advantage, however, may be inaccurate. Visual processing encompasses a range of tasks, including visual memory tasks presented either sequentially or simultaneously, visual-motor integration tasks which include imitation, visual-constructive tasks such as pattern construction, holistic visual perception tasks such as visual closure, judgment of line orientation, object recognition and face recognition, and visual analogical reasoning tasks.

As a group, those with Down syndrome are more effective imitators of visual models (a strength in visual-motor integration) than comparison groups with intellectual disability matched by MA and CA. This visual-motor integration strength has been demonstrated across a range of tasks (see, for example, Hodapp *et al.*, 1992; Kanno & Ikeda, 2002; Zoia, Pelamattib, & Rumiati, 2004).

In our longitudinal study (Couzens *et al.*, 2011), we found that ability on the Pattern Analysis task of the Stanford-Binet (4th ed.) increased across adolescence and adulthood, relative to general cognitive ability. The task required the copying of patterns using marked blocks. While the task represented a strength for some, not all participants demonstrated higher than expected performance. It is possible that other personal characteristics, such as self-regulation or persistence, account for some of the performance increases seen on this task (Couzens, Haynes, & Cuskelly, 2012). Strong imitation ability may not always be a useful characteristic. Wright *et al.* (2006) found that imitation appeared to interfere with problem solving, as others' modelling in novel problem-solving tasks overly influenced the children with Down syndrome. It may be that imitation abilities are simply the first representational abilities to emerge for children with Down syndrome but they may also interfere with the development of other cognitive components of representational thought.

The comparison of verbal and visual abilities is often made on the basis of sequential tasks. Individuals with Down syndrome, as a group, have been shown to perform significantly better on sequential visual-motor integration tasks (e.g. repeating hand movement sequences) than sequential auditory imitation tasks (repeating word sequences) (Hodapp *et al.*, 1992; Hodapp & Ricci, 2002). An important caveat to understand when considering these data is that not all individuals will necessarily process visual and spatial tasks in the same way (see Gunn & Jarrold, 2004; Karmiloff-Smith *et al.*, 2004; Zoia *et al.*, 2004). Individuals with strong verbal abilities, for example, may be able to use these verbal abilities to mediate certain visual processing tasks and this strategy may result in improved outcomes (Karmiloff-Smith *et al.*, 2004). This is sometimes referred to as verbal recoding. Tasks that cannot be processed via semantic processing (naming the visually presented material or verbally recoding it) may have to be processed through a 'direct visual route to actions' (Zoia *et al.*, 2004, p. 9), advantaging some learners. The bead memory task of the Stanford–Binet (4th ed.) requires examinees to remake previously observed patterns of beads that vary in shape and colour. This task is well suited to verbal recoding and may advantage those who use this strategy. Other abilities and knowledge can also assist performance on tasks differentially; for example, the visual aspect and the physical manipulation in the bead memory task may support attention to the stimuli, while there is a lack of physical manipulation with sentence memory tasks.

Visual and spatial processing abilities are frequently considered in combination. These abilities, however, disassociate in visual-spatial working memory (Baddeley, 2012). Individuals with Down syndrome appear to have a specific weakness in long-term memory for visual-object learning and a relative strength for visual-spatial information (Vicari *et al.*, 2005). Vicari and colleagues' (2005) study involved a visual object and a visual-spatial learning task, followed by a long-term memory recognition task. The visual object memory task required participants to recognize a picture seen previously, selecting from a group of four different pictures of the same item type (to block the use of naming or verbal recoding—for example, to recall one particular saucepan from pictures of four saucepans); the visual-spatial memory task required the child to show, using a blank, four-quadrant matrix, the position of the object as presented during learning trials. Individuals with Down syndrome demonstrated significant improvement over time on the visual-spatial memory task but not on the visual object memory task. This pattern was opposite to that observed for a group with Williams syndrome, who showed learning on the object task but not the spatial task. Both were in contrast to typically developing children matched on MA, who demonstrated significant improvement on both memory tasks.

Disassociations have also been indicated within spatial working memory. Lanfranchi *et al.* (2009) found that, when sequential processing of spatial information was required (e.g. replicating a frog's journey on a grid), those with Down syndrome performed at an equivalent level to children developing typically and matched by receptive vocabulary. When the task required simultaneous processing of spatially presented information, however (e.g. remembering the location of all green squares on a grid), those with Down syndrome performed significantly worse than the matched controls. The number of dimensions to be processed simultaneously (location versus location and object) was put forward as one explanation of why those with Down syndrome, as a group, tend not to improve with age on simultaneous spatial tasks as do children who are developing typically (Lanfranchi *et al.*, 2009).

Visual-spatial strengths of individuals with Down syndrome may have been exaggerated in research (see, for example, Fidler, Hepburn, & Rogers, 2006) because of early contrasts with the visual-construction abilities of those individuals with Williams syndrome (e.g. Wang & Bellugi, 1994). The juxtaposition of these two groups exaggerates verbal and spatial ability differences due to differing profile patterns on visual-spatial and verbal tasks.

Within the visual processing domain, individuals with Down syndrome have demonstrated strengths in global processing, or processing the gestalt or overall picture, and a relative weakness in local processing or processing of constituent parts (Bellugi, Sabo, & Vaid, 1988; Zoia *et al.*, 2004). Strengths in the area of global processing have been associated with simultaneous processing, which includes higher-order processing through the integration and synthesis of constituent parts into a unified whole (Naglieri, Das, & Jarman, 1990); however, simultaneous processing strengths in spatial presentation and strengths in gestalt processing of objects may also, or instead, reflect general attention to an overarching message and poor attention to detail.

Implications of research on visual-spatial ability for learning and teaching

Of the multiple aspects of visual processing, evidence of endophenotypic characteristics exist only in relation to (1) relative strengths for visual-motor imitation tasks and holistic visual perception tasks and (2) weakness on visual memory for objects relative to spatial position and visual-spatial tasks displayed simultaneously relative to those presented sequentially.

Imitation abilities have been consistently better than would be expected based on general cognitive ability. Strengths in visual imitation, coupled with increased attention to social models and high levels of social understanding relative to other areas of skill (see, for example, Wishart, Willis, Cebula, & Pitcairn, 2007; Wright *et al.*, 2006) suggest that cooperative learning situations may be useful for learners with Down syndrome. It may be, however, that attention to social models (peers) will also interfere with learning (Wright *et al.*, 2006).

Wright and colleagues' (2006) data explore only the representational period; however, extrapolation beyond this stage of development posits questions about imitation in other situations. Might these learners use social information and imitation in place of other sources of information and cognitive processing (Wright *et al.*, 2006)? If so, this could have implications for the use of group response formats and cooperative-learning strategies used in classrooms. While imitation strengths might increase active engagement of students with Down syndrome in cooperative learning, and group response formats may support task success and social engagement for the learner with Down syndrome, additional strategies may be required to support these learners to engage with the key cognitive aspects of the learning tasks being imitated. The consolidation of learning supported through imitation strategies has not been empirically assessed.

Sequential visual abilities have the potential for developing beyond levels expected on the basis of general cognitive ability, although not everyone with Down syndrome achieves this. Global visual processing, acquisition of the big picture or main idea, is stronger for the group than analysis of the constituent parts of visually presented material. As will be discussed in the section following, however, relational processing requirements in visual tasks, as with other modes, will affect success. Where visually presented tasks require higher-level simultaneous processing, as occurs in the analogical processing required to complete the Raven's Progressive Matrices (Raven, Court, & Raven, 1990), as an example, the default position may be to revert to solving the task at a lower level of complexity, leading to mistakes that reflect processing-level difficulties rather than difficulties in attending to details. Finally, memory for a sequence of spatial positions has been demonstrated to be a strength relative to visual memory for objects on both working memory and long-term memory tasks. Weakness in object memory performance, however, may be more indicative of poor attention to visual details required for object but not spatial memory tasks.

It has been suggested that educators should draw on visual memory and visual-motor integration, particularly imitation (Davis, 2008), which are strong relative to verbal abilities. While the use of drama, for example, has been recommended for supporting explicit memory of prose and narratives (Lifshitz, Shtein, Weiss, & Svisrsky, 2011), empirical evidence supporting this theory-to-practice translation is currently unavailable. A study by Lecas and colleagues (Lecas, Mazaud, Reibel, & Rey, 2010) is suggestive, however. These researchers found that explicitly teaching an adolescent boy with Down syndrome to visually represent verbal information using computer drawing software increased his verbal comprehension for stories and successfully generalized to his use of mental imagery, thus removing the need for technology at follow-up.

Visually based input and output scaffolds, such as pictures or written cues, are generally insufficient for improving short-term memory difficulties; but, when integrated with spatial supports (e.g. when the material to be remembered is placed into a grid), short-term memory spans have reached equivalent levels as those of MA matched controls (Duarte, Covre, Braga, & de Macedo, 2011). The memory span of individuals with Down syndrome reached a median of four when presentation and recognition assessment used a grid format, while simple verbal and visual presentations and outputs resulted in a median span of two (Duarte *et al.*, 2011). Lifshitz and colleagues (2011) suggested that flowcharts might be useful for encouraging deep learning based on visual-spatial strengths for sequentially presented material. Again, this idea for promoting deep learning has not been empirically tested for those with Down syndrome. It remains unclear how stronger spatial short-term memory may be effectively used in the classroom to enhance learning.

As well as assisting memory, visual supports may be useful for increasing sustained and selective attention (Kay-Raining Bird, Gaskell, Babineau, & MacDonald, 2000; Trezise, Gray, & Sheppard, 2008). Speech accompanied with gesture has been associated with improved learning generally (Cook, Mitchell, & Goldin-Meadow, 2008) and the learning of new vocabulary is enhanced when signs accompany speech for children with Down syndrome (Kay-Raining Bird *et al.*, 2000). Teacher use of gesture improves learner comprehension and is hypothesized to be especially important for children with Down syndrome due to their specific weakness with verbal short-term memory and associated difficulties learning new vocabulary forms (Jarrold, Thorn, & Stephens, 2009). While there is evidence that gesture, when explicitly used in teaching, enhances the performance of learners generally (Goldin-Meadow, 2010), the extent to which this advantage may be seen for learners with Down syndrome in the classroom remains an area for research.

Visual scaffolds such as photos and pictures have successfully increased the speech of individuals with Down syndrome (Miles *et al.*, 2006). Gesture, manual signing, and pictures have been shown to be effective in assisting the development of expressive and receptive speech (Kay-Raining Bird *et al.*, 2000; Lecas *et al.*, 2010; Miles *et al.*, 2006).

Problem solving and higher-level processing

The processing of any information, whether verbal, visual, kinaesthetic, or tactile, relies not only on attention to, and retention of, different pieces of the information, but also on integration of the information with other known or presented information. Sometimes processing can occur sequentially, with each piece of information processed and connected to the next. More often, however, two or more pieces of information have to be processed in parallel before connecting sequentially with other information. Examples include the integration of syntactic and semantic information to deduce meaning from grammatical structures, integration of information on speed and distance to make timing decisions, and assessments of container height and depth to make volume judgments. Problems using these sorts of relational processing tasks have been used to measure processing difficulty (see, Halford, Wilson, & Phillips, 1998). Most research specific to Down syndrome that discusses 'simultaneous processing' has not analysed the relational complexity of the processing decisions at each step of the task and ignores the possibility that sequential processing may be used to solve the problem.

Halford *et al.* (1998) proposed that cognitive difficulty is best captured by tasks that require simultaneous processing of two, three, and four variables, without the means of breaking the complexity into component parts able to be solved sequentially. The cognitive difficulty, they argued, should be assessed on the single most difficult step of any task sequence. These researchers have proposed that cognitive difficulty should be assessed by calculating the greatest number of pieces of information to be *processed in parallel* in a single step of the task. Each additional piece of information to be processed in one single step increases the cognitive complexity of the task exponentially (Halford *et al.*, 1998). Andrews (1997) assessed typically developing children aged 4–8 years, using tasks at binary (requiring the processing of two variables in parallel) and ternary (three variables) levels of complexity. The binary and ternary levels of each task required identical content knowledge and response sets, differing only in the processing level required to complete the task. Children were typically able to process at the binary level of complexity at about two years of age and to process at the ternary level of complexity at a mean age of five years. This increase in processing capacity is hypothesized to be enabled through maturation of the prefrontal cortex (Halford *et al.*, 1998). The development of processing capacity represents an important but largely unexplored area of developmental research for individuals with Down syndrome. The contemporary working memory model developed by Oberauer (2009) incorporates relational reasoning and may assist researchers to understand capacity in relation to higher levels of reasoning (see, for example, Halford, Wilson, & Phillips, 2010). There is some evidence, in research specific to Down syndrome, that relational complexity may offer a useful framework for understanding the development of problem-solving abilities, as explained below.

Abstract reasoning has been investigated for individuals with Down syndrome through analogical reasoning tasks, such as the Raven's Coloured Progressive Matrices (CPM; Raven *et al.*, 1990). Natsopoulos, Christou, Koutselini, Raftopoulos, and Karefillidou (2002) used structural equation modelling to demonstrate that the scores of adults with Down syndrome were related to other measures of verbal and non-verbal reasoning in the same way as for a group of typically developing children matched by MA. A more nuanced analysis of error patterns on the Raven's CPM tasks (Gunn & Jarrold, 2004) indicated that, despite similarities in overall scores, the specific error patterns of children with Down syndrome (9–17 years) differed from those of children developing typically matched by MA *and* those of children with moderate intellectual disability matched by CA. Error patterns of children with moderate intellectual disabilities were very similar to the group of children developing typically. Children with Down syndrome demonstrated more 'difference errors' than the two comparison groups. They were more likely to select a piece with no relevance to the target pattern; they chose pieces with irrelevancies or incomplete patterns, and they demonstrated significantly fewer errors of the type that arose from choosing pieces that were identical to the pieces that were next to the missing piece. The errors were similar to those of much younger children than indicated by the overall achievement level of the individuals with Down syndrome on the assessment.

The immature error patterns for Raven's CPM may be explained through differences in the development of relational processing capacity. Increases in performance for the children with Down syndrome could be explained by their development of sequential processing ability, while immature error patterns may be explained by their inability to process in parallel at the same level as the other children matched by MA. This hypothesis is consistent, in part, to comments by Gunn and Jarrold (2004) who suggested that the 'individuals with Down syndrome [were] only able to successfully focus on one feature of the pattern at a time in this task' (p. 453). Alternate explanations were also provided by Gunn and Jarrold, including possible visual acuity difficulties and poorer motivational patterns that have been hypothesized for this group (see, for example, Wishart, 1996).

Implications of research on higher-level processing for learning and teaching

Early claims of a successive processing weakness have not been substantiated and studies of simultaneous processing for this population do not appear to capture current conceptions of simultaneous processing. Higher-order processing is a new and potentially important research area for this population as it could inform our understanding of development in relation to problem solving and the major aspects of task difficulty. Analysis of task error patterns can inform researchers (and teachers) about the strategies being used by individuals to solve different problems. There appears to be some support for the hypothesis that those with Down syndrome may have a greater delay than MA matched peers with respect to processing ternary relations. Perhaps alternative strategies for solving ternary-level processing tasks, such as chunking and sequential processing of the information presented, can explain the immature error patterns on certain processing tasks relative to unusual levels of success.

Conclusion

One aim of this chapter has been to stimulate educators and researchers to work together to develop an understanding of the links between theory of cognitive development and educational practice and to inform advances in education for individuals with Down syndrome. A research agenda engaging teachers with education research represents one important avenue to advance this aim.

Our understanding of cognitive and learning difficulties associated with Down syndrome has become increasingly refined since phenotype research progressed into the field of education. This research base provides educators and researchers with direction for assessments, frameworks for interpreting results, and promising areas of practice. Phenotype research does not remove the requirement for individual assessment but can assist with interpretation of these assessments. As research methodologies improve, data are increasingly informing us about group trends, individual variation within these trends, and the environmental and individual characteristics that contribute to the variation. There is now strong evidence that Down syndrome is associated with poor verbal short-term memory as well as morphosyntactic and phonological problems. There is weaker evidence indicating that Down syndrome is associated with superior learning of spatial information relative to visual object information. There is also evidence that a number of cognitive abilities, including long-term memory and certain visual processes, are unaffected by Down syndrome but appear to be related to cognitive development generally and that other abilities such as vocabulary and imitation abilities can surpass general cognitive level for a substantial minority of individuals. There remains considerable work ahead to understand how knowledge of the cognitive patterns described can inform effective educational interventions and supports. Research is required to understand whether generic programmes for slower learners are effective or may be improved in relation to a Down syndrome-specific learning profile.

While we have considerable research identifying a number of important areas of cognitive strength and weakness related to Down syndrome, this research does not translate directly into supports or approaches for teaching and learning. The intervention research targeting Down syndrome specifically is segmented and based on small sample sizes. There has been insufficient replication of findings by different researchers for us to be confident that results are stable and/or transferable to other contexts. Rigorous applied research is required to assess interventions and supports that may appear intuitive, based on the cognitive differences discussed.

References

Abbeduto, L., Pavetto, M., Kesin, E., Weissman, M. D., Karadottir, S., O'Brien, A., & Cawthon, S. (2001). The linguistic and cognitive profile of Down syndrome: Evidence from a comparison with fragile X syndrome. *Down Syndrome Research and Practice, 7*, 9–15. doi: 10.3104/reports.109.

Allen, R. J., Baddeley, A. D., & Hitch, G. J. (2006). Is the binding of visual features in working memory resource-demanding? *Journal of Experimental Psychology—General, 135*, 298–313. doi: 10.1037/0096–3445.135.2.298.

Andrews, G. (1997). *Relational complexity as a capacity construct in cognitive development.* Unpublished PhD thesis, University of Queensland, Brisbane.

Baddeley, A. D. (2000). The episodic buffer: A new component of working memory. *Trends in Cognitive Sciences, 4*, 417–423. doi: 10.1016/s1364–6613(00)01538–2.

Baddeley, A. D. (2012). Working memory: Theories, models, and controversies. *Annual Review of Psychology, 63*, 1–29. doi: 10.1146/annurev-psych-120710–100422.

Bellugi, U., Sabo, H., & Vaid, J. (1988). Spatial deficits in children with Williams syndrome. In J. Stiles-Davis, M. Kritchevsky, & U. Bellugi (Eds), *Spatial cognition: Brain bases and development* (pp. 273–298). Hillsdale, NJ: Erlbaum Associates.

Broadley, I., MacDonald, J., & Buckley, S. (1994). Are children with Down syndrome able to maintain skills learned from a short-term memory training programme? *Down's Syndrome: Research and Practice, 2*, 116–122. doi: 10.3104/reports.41.

Brock, J., & Jarrold, C. (2005). Serial order reconstruction in Down syndrome: Evidence for a selective deficit in verbal short-term memory. *Journal of Child Psychology and Psychiatry, 46*, 304–316. doi: 10.1111/j.1469–7610.2004.00352.x.

Caselli, M. C., Vicari, S., Longobardi, E., Lami, L., Pizzoli, C., & Giacomo, S. (1998). Gestures and words in early development of children with Down syndrome. *Journal of Speech, Language and Hearing Research, 41*, 1125–1135.

Chapman, R. S. (1997). Language development in children and adolescents with Down syndrome. *Mental Retardation and Developmental Disabilities Research Reviews, 3*, 307–312. doi: 10.1002/(SICI)1098–2779(1997)3:4<303::AID-MRDD5>3.0.CO:2-K.

Chapman, R. S., & Hesketh, L. J. (2000). Behavioral phenotype of individuals with Down syndrome. *Mental Retardation and Developmental Disabilities Research Reviews, 6*, 84–95. doi: 10.1002/1098–2779(2000)6:2<84::AID-MRDD2>3.0.CO:2-P.

Chapman, R. S., & Hesketh, L. J. (2001). Language, cognition, and short-term memory in individuals with Down syndrome. *Down Syndrome: Research and Practice, 7*, 1–7. doi: 10.3104/reports.108.

Chapman, R. S., Hesketh, L. J., & Kistler, D. J. (2002). Predicting longitudinal change in language production and comprehension in individuals with Down syndrome: Hierarchical linear modeling. *Journal of Speech, Language, and Hearing Research, 45*, 902–915. doi: 10.1044/1092–4388(2002/073).

Chapman, R. S., Hye-Kyeung, S., Schwartz, S. E., & Kay-Raining Bird, E. (1998). Language skills of children and adolescents with Down syndrome: II. Production deficits. *Journal of Speech, Language, and Hearing Research, 41*, 861–873.

Chapman, R. S., Schwartz, S. E., & Kay-Raining Bird, E. (1991). Language skills of children and adolescents with Down syndrome: I: Comprehension. *Journal of Speech and Hearing Research, 34*, 1106–1120.

Conners, F. A., Rosenquist, C. J., Arnett, L. A., Moore, M. S., & Hume, L. E. (2008). Improving memory span in children with Down syndrome. *Journal of Intellectual Disability Research, 52*, 244–255. doi: 10.111/j.1365–2788.2007.01015.x.

Cook, S. W., Mitchell, Z., & Goldin-Meadow, S. (2008). Gesturing makes learning last. *Cognition, 106*, 1047–1058. doi: 10.1016/j.cognition.2007.04.010.

Couzens, D., Cuskelly, M., & Haynes, M. (2011). Cognitive development and Down syndrome: Age related change on the Stanford Binet Test (4th ed.). *American Journal on Intellectual and Developmental Disabilities, 116*, 181–204. doi: 10.1352/1944–7558.116.3.181.

Couzens, D., Cuskelly, M., & Jobling, A. (2004). The Stanford Binet: Fourth Edition and its use with individuals with Down syndrome: Cautions for clinicians. *International Journal of Disability, Development and Education, 51*, 39–56. doi: 10.1080/1034912042000189193.

Couzens, D., Haynes, M., & Cuskelly, M. (2012). Individual and environmental characteristics associated with cognitive development in Down syndrome: A longitudinal study. *Journal of Applied Research in Intellectual Disabilities, 25*, 396–413. doi: 10.1111/j.1468–3148.2011.00673.x.

Davis, A. S. (2008). Children with Down syndrome: Implications for assessment and intervention in the school. *School Psychology Quarterly, 23*, 271–281. doi: 10.1037/1045–3830.23.2.271.

Dodd, B., & Thompson, L. (2001). Speech disorder in children with Down syndrome. *Journal of Intellectual Disability Research, 45*, 308–316. doi: 10.1046/j.1365–2788.2001.00327.x.

Duarte, P. C., Covre, P., Braga, A. C., & de Macedo, E. C. (2011). Visuospatial support for verbal short-term memory in individuals with Down syndrome. *Research in Developmental Disabilities, 32*, 1918–1923. doi: 10.1016/j.ridd.2011.03.024.

Fidler, D., Hepburn, S., & Rogers, S. (2006). Early learning and adaptive behaviour in toddlers with Down syndrome: Evidence for an emerging behavioural phenotype? *Down Syndrome Research and Practice, 9*, 37–44. doi: 10.3104/reports.297.

Funk, M., Brugger, P., & Wilkening, F. (2005). Motor processes in children's imagery: The case of mental rotation of hands. *Developmental Science, 8*, 402–408. doi: 10.111/j.1467–7687.2005.00428.x.

Goldin-Meadow, S. (2010). When gesture does and does not promote learning. *Language and Cognition, 2*, 1–19. doi: 10.1515/LANGCOG.2010.001.

Grela, B. G. (2002). Lexical verb diversity in children with Down syndrome. *Clinical Linguistics and Phonetics, 16*, 251–263. doi: 10.1080/02699200210131987.

Gunn, D. M., & Jarrold, C. (2004). Raven's matrices performance in Down syndrome: Evidence of unusual errors. *Research in Developmental Disabilities, 25*, 443–457. doi: 10.1016/j.ridd.2003.07.004.

Halford, G. S., Wilson, W. H., & Phillips, S. (1998). Processing capacity defined by relational complexity: Implications for comparative, developmental and cognitive psychology. *Behavioral and Brain Sciences, 21*, 803–864. doi: 10.1017/S0140525X98001769.

Halford, G. S., Wilson, W. H., & Phillips, S. (2010). Relational knowledge: The foundation of higher cognition. *Trends in Cognitive Sciences, 14*, 497–505. doi: 10.1016/j.tics.2010.08.005.

Hesketh, L. J., & Chapman, R. S. (1998). Verb use by individuals with Down syndrome. *American Journal on Mental Retardation, 103*, 288–304. doi: 10.1352/0895–8017(1998)103<0288:VUBIWD>2.0.CO:2.

Hewitt, L. E., Hinkle, A. S., & Miccio, A. W. (2005). Intervention to improve expressive grammar for adults with Down syndrome. *Communication Disorders Quarterly, 26*, 144–155. doi: 10.1177/15257401050260030301.

Hodapp, R. M., Leckman, J. F., Dykens, E. M., Sparrow, S. S., Zelinsky, D. G., & Ort, S. I. (1992). K-ABC profiles in children with fragile X syndrome, Down syndrome, and non-specific mental retardation. *American Journal on Mental Retardation, 97*, 39–46.

Hodapp, R. M., & Ricci, L. A. (2002). Behavioural phenotypes and educational practice: The unrealised connection. In G. O'Brien (Ed.), *Behavioural phenotypes in clinical practice* (pp. 137–151). London: Mac Keith Press.

Jarrold, C., & Baddeley, A. D. (2001). Short-term memory in Down syndrome: Applying the working memory model. *Down Syndrome: Research and Practice, 7*, 17–23. doi: 10.3104/reviews.110.

Jarrold, C., Baddeley, A. D., & Hewes, A. K. (1999). Genetically dissociated components of working memory: Evidence from Down and Williams syndrome. *Neuropsychologia, 37*, 637–651. doi: 10.1016/S0028-3932(98)00128-6.

Jarrold, C., Baddeley, A. D., & Hewes, A. K. (2000). Verbal short-term memory deficits in Down syndrome: A consequence of problems in rehearsal? *Journal of Child Psychology and Psychiatry and Allied Disciplines, 41*, 233–244. doi: 10.1111/1469-7610.0064.

Jarrold, C., Baddeley, A. D., & Phillips, C. E. (1999). Down syndrome and the phonological loop: The evidence for, and importance of, a specific verbal short-term memory deficit. *Down Syndrome: Research and Practice, 6*, 61–75. doi: 10.3104/reviews.97.

Jarrold, C., Baddeley, A. D., & Phillips, C. E. (2002). Verbal short-term memory in Down syndrome: A problem of memory, audition, or speech? *Journal of Speech, Language, and Hearing Research, 45*, 531–544. doi: 10.1044/1092-4388(2002/042).

Jarrold, C., Baddeley, A. D., & Phillips, C. (2007). Long-term memory for verbal and visual information in Down syndrome and Williams syndrome: Performance on the Doors and People Test. *Cortex, 43*, 233–247. doi: 10.1016/S0010-9452(08)70478-7.

Jarrold, C., Thorn, A. S. C., & Stephens, E. (2009). The relationships among verbal short-term memory, phonological awareness, and new word learning: Evidence from typical development and Down syndrome. *Journal of Experimental Child Psychology, 102*, 196–218. doi: 10.1016/j.jecp. 2008.07.001.

Kanno, K., & Ikeda, Y. (2002). Short-term memory for verbal and visuospatial information in youth with Down syndrome. *Japanese Journal of Special Education, 39*, 57–63.

Karmiloff-Smith, A., Thomas, M., Annaz, D., Humphreys, K., Ewing, S., Brace, N., … Campbell, R. (2004). Exploring the Williams syndrome face-processing debate: The importance of building developmental trajectories. *Journal of Child Psychology and Psychiatry, 45*, 1258–1274. doi: 10.1111/l.1469-7610.2004.00322.x.

Kay-Raining Bird, E., Gaskell, A., Babineau, M. D., & MacDonald, S. (2000). Novel word acquisition in children with Down syndrome: Does modality make a difference? *Journal of Communication Disorders, 33*, 241–266. doi: 10.1016/S0021-9924(00)00022-8.

Kendler, K. S., & Neale, M. C. (2010). Endophenotype: A conceptual analysis. *Molecular Psychiatry, 15*, 789–797. doi: 10.1038/mp. 2010.8.

Kennedy, E. J., & Flynn, M. C. (2003). Training phonological awareness skills in children with Down syndrome. *Research in Developmental Disabilities, 24*, 44–57. doi: 10.1016/S0891-4222(02)00168-3.

Klein, B. P., & Mervis, C. B. (1999). Contrasting patterns of cognitive abilities of 9- and 10-year-olds with Williams syndrome or Down syndrome. *Developmental Neuropsychology, 16*, 177–196. doi: 10.1207/S15326942DN1602_3.

Lanfranchi, S., Carretti, B., Spano, G., & Cornoldi, C. (2009). A specific deficit in visuospatial simultaneous working memory in Down syndrome. *Journal of Intellectual Disability Research, 53*, 474–483. doi: 10.1111/j.1365-2788.2009.01165.x.

Laws, G. (2002). Working memory in children and adolescents with Down syndrome: Evidence from a colour memory experiment. *Journal of Child Psychology and Psychiatry and Allied Disciplines, 43*, 353–364. doi: 10.1111/1469-7610.00026.

Laws, G. (2004). Contributions of phonological memory, language comprehension and hearing to the expressive language of adolescence and young adults with Down syndrome. *Journal of Child Psychology and Psychiatry, 45*, 1085–1095. doi: 10.1111/1469-7610.2004.t01-1-00302.x.

Laws, G., & Gunn, D. (2004). Phonological memory as a predictor of language comprehension in Down syndrome: A five-year follow-up study. *Journal of Child Psychology and Psychiatry, 45*, 326–337. doi: 10.1111/1469-7610.2004.00223.x.

Laws, G., MacDonald, J., & Buckley, S. (1996). The effects of a short training in the use of a rehearsal strategy on memory for words and pictures in children with Down syndrome. *Down Syndrome: Research and Practice, 4*, 70–78.

Laws, G., MacDonald, J., Buckley, S., & Broadley, I. (1995). Long-term maintenance of memory skills taught to children with Down's syndrome. *Down's Syndrome: Research & Practice, 3*, 103–109.

Lecas, J.-F., Mazaud, A.-M., Reibel, E., & Rey, A. (2010). Using visual strategies to support verbal comprehension in an adolescent with Down syndrome. *Child Language Teaching and Therapy, 27*, 84–96. doi: 10.1177/0265659010371564.

Lifshitz, H., Shtein, S., Weiss, I., & Svisrsky, N. (2011). Explicit memory among individuals with mild and moderate intellectual disability: Educational implications. *European Journal of Special Needs Education, 26*, 113–124. doi: 10.1080/08856257.2011.543536.

Miles, S., & Chapman, R. S. (2002). Narrative content as described by individuals with Down syndrome and typically developing children. *Journal of Speech, Language and Hearing Research, 45*, 175–189. doi: 10.1044/1092-4388(2002/013).

Miles, S., Chapman, R. S., & Sindberg, H. A. (2006). Sampling context affects MLU in the language of adolescents with Down syndrome. *Journal of Speech, Language, and Hearing Research, 49*, 325–337.

Naglieri, J. A., Das, J. P., & Jarman, R. F. (1990). Planning, attention, simultaneous, and successive cognitive processes as a model for assessment. *School Psychology Review, 19*, 423–442.

Natsopoulos, D., Christou, C., Koutselini, M., Raftopoulos, A., & Karefillidou, C. (2002). Structure and coherence of reasoning ability in Down syndrome adults and typically developing children. *Research in Developmental Disabilities, 23*, 297–307. doi: 10.1016/S0891-4222(02)00088-4.

Oberauer, K. (2009). Design for a working memory. In B. H. Ross (Ed.), *The psychology of learning and motivation: Advances in research and theory* (Vol. 51, pp. 45–100). San Diego, CA: Elsevier Academic Press.

Papagno, C., & Vallar, G. (2001). Understanding metaphors and idioms: A single-case neuropsychological study in a person with Down syndrome. *Journal of the International Neuropsychological Society, 7*, 516–528. doi: 10.1017/S1355617701744086.

Purser, H. R. M., & Jarrold, C. (2005). Impaired verbal short-term memory in Down syndrome reflects a capacity limitation rather than atypically rapid forgetting. *Journal of Experimental Child Psychology, 91*, 1–23. doi: 10.1016/j.jecp. 2005.01.002.

Raven, J. C., Court, J. H., & Raven, J. (1990). *Manual for Raven's Coloured Progressive Matrices*. Oxford: Oxford Psychologists Press.

Seung, H.-K., & Chapman, R. S. (2000). Digit span in individuals with Down syndrome and in typically developing children: Temporal aspects. *Journal of Speech, Language, and Hearing Research, 43*, 609–620.

Seung, H.-K., & Chapman, R. S. (2003). The effect of story presentation rates on story retelling by individuals with Down syndrome. *Applied Psycholinguistics, 24*, 603–620. doi: 0.1017/S0142716403000304.

Thorndike, R. L., Hagen, E. P., & Sattler, J. M. (1986). *Stanford-Binet Intelligence Scale: Fourth Edition*. Chicago: Riverside Publishing Company.

Trezise, K. L., Gray, K. M., & Sheppard, D. M. (2008). Attention and vigilance in children with Down syndrome. *Journal of Applied Research in Intellectual Disabilities, 21*, 502–508. doi: 10.1111/j.1468-3148.2008.00421.x.

Verucci, L. Menghini, D., & Vicari, S. (2006). Reading skills and phonological awareness acquisition in Down syndrome. *Journal of Intellectual Disability Research, 50*, 477–491. doi: 1 0.1111/j.1365-2788.2006.00793.x.

Vicari, S., Bellucci, S., & Carlesimo, G. A. (2005). Visual and spatial long-term memory: Differential pattern of impairments in Williams and Down syndromes. *Developmental Medicine & Child Neurology, 47*, 305–311. doi: 10.1017/S0012162205000599.

Vicari, S., & Carlesimo, G. A. (2006). Short-term memory deficits are not uniform in Down and Williams syndromes. *Neuropsychology Review, 16*, 87–94. doi: 10.1007/s11065-006-9008-4.

Wang, P. P., & Bellugi, U. (1994). Evidence from two genetic syndromes for a dissociation between verbal and visual-spatial short-term memory. *Journal of Clinical and Experimental Neuropsychology, 16*(2), 317–322. doi: 10.1080/01688639408402641.

Williams, K. R., Wishart, J. G., Pitcairn, T. K., & Willis, D. S. (2005). Emotion recognition by children with Down syndrome: Investigation of specific impairments and error patterns. *American Journal on Mental Retardation, 110*, 378–392. doi: 10.1352/0895-8017(2005)110[378:ERBCWD]2.0.CO;2.

Wishart, J. G. (1996). Avoidant learning styles and cognitive development in young children. In B. Stratford & P. Gunn (Eds), *New approaches to Down syndrome* (pp. 173–205). London: Cassell.

Wishart, J. G., Willis, D. S., Cebula, K. R., & Pitcairn, T. K. (2007). Collaborative learning: Comparison of outcomes for typically developing children and children with intellectual disabilities. *American Journal on Mental Retardation, 112*, 361–374. doi: 10.1111/j.1741-1130.2010.00246.x.

Wright, I., Lewis, V., & Collis, G. M. (2006). Imitation and representational development in young children with Down syndrome. *British Journal of Developmental Psychology, 24*, 429–450. doi: 10.1348/026151005X51257.

Zoia, S., Pelamattib, G., & Rumiati, R. I. (2004). Praxic skills in Down and mentally retarded adults: Evidence for multiple action routes. *Brain and Cognition, 54*, 7–17. doi: 10.1016/S0278-2626(03)00055-1.

Chapter 3

Mastery motivation in children with Down syndrome

Promoting and sustaining interest in learning

Linda Gilmore and Monica Cuskelly

Abstract

Using the framework of mastery motivation, this chapter introduces the complex construct of motivation and highlights its importance for children's learning. As demonstrated for typically developing children, mastery motivation has been shown to be an important predictor of academic outcomes for children with Down syndrome. Although deficits in motivation are sometimes presumed to be part of the learning and behavioural profile of Down syndrome, most of the empirical evidence shows no differences in mastery motivation when children with Down syndrome are compared to typically developing children of the same developmental level. By contrast, parent reports consistently suggest that children with Down syndrome have difficulties with motivation, possibly because parents are making comparisons with their child's same-age peers rather than with children of similar developmental levels. Drawing on a wider research base, the chapter considers the child and environmental characteristics that influence mastery motivation. Children with Down syndrome and other developmental disabilities experience a range of health, sensory, and motor difficulties that may interfere with their motivation for mastery. Children's beliefs about their own ability, the attributions they make for success and failure, and their expectancy about future success are all likely to impact on approaches to learning tasks. In addition, the difficulties many children with Down syndrome have in relation to self-regulating their attention, learning, and behaviour are likely to undermine their mastery motivation. Although some of these individual characteristics are intrinsic to the child, many are influenced or modified by the contexts in which children live and learn. Within these contexts, of particular importance is giving children the opportunity to engage with cognitively stimulating activities. Other important environmental influences on motivation are adult attitudes and expectations, structure, positive reinforcement, and support for child autonomy. The chapter concludes with strategies for promoting and sustaining children's interest in learning, and recommendations for future research.

Introduction

Motivation is central to children's learning. Without persistent effort, especially in the face of failure, and an eagerness to engage in challenging tasks, individuals are unlikely to learn as effectively as they might. Because of their cognitive impairments, children with Down syndrome will almost certainly have difficulties with learning. These difficulties will be ameliorated somewhat by strong engagement with learning activities, whereas problems with motivation are likely to further jeopardise their academic progress as well as potentially limit achievements in other areas of life.

In this chapter, we begin with a general overview of motivation. Using the framework of mastery motivation, we review the relatively small amount of research about children with Down syndrome. We identify the individual characteristics and features of children's environments that are likely to be related to lower or higher levels of mastery motivation. In the final section, we consider implications for educators and then draw together the findings to provide a set of recommendations for future research.

Motivation: an overview

Motivation is the force that energises, directs, and sustains goal-directed behaviour (Morgan, Harmon, & Maslin-Cole, 1990; Pintrich & Schunk, 2002). Stipek (1997) described motivated learners as those who are

> willingly engaged in the learning process, self-confident in their ability to learn and to complete school tasks, persistent in the face of difficulty, oriented towards developing, understanding and mastering skills, enthusiastic and optimistic about learning, and proud of their accomplishments.
>
> (Stipek, 1997, p. 77)

The concept of motivation thus incorporates behaviours such as engagement and persistence with challenging tasks, cognitions including beliefs and attributions about one's own competence, and emotional responses like enthusiasm and pride in achievement.

Motivation is a very complex construct and there are a number of overlapping theories that have guided research. One of the most common distinctions is between intrinsic and extrinsic motivation. When intrinsically motivated, people engage in tasks that are inherently enjoyable and rewarding, whereas extrinsic motivation involves engagement for external rewards or consequences. This dichotomy is a matter of some debate, with theorists having different approaches to the meanings of both intrinsic (to the person or the activity) and extrinsic motivation (a single construct versus a continuum of distinguishable approaches). Research with typically developing children has demonstrated the ways in which willingness to engage is influenced by children's beliefs about their own competence (self-efficacy theory), their expectations of success and the extent to which they value achievement of a particular task (expectancy-value theory), their goals of either achieving mastery or performance recognition (goal theory), their reasoning about the causes of their successes and failures (attribution theory), and the consequences of reinforcers or punishment (operant theory).

Drawing on these different theoretical perspectives, a considerable amount of research has been undertaken, with a particular focus on understanding why some children are more strongly motivated for school learning while others are less motivated, and the ways in which children's academic performance and social-emotional well-being might be enhanced through particular teaching practices and interventions that promote motivation. There is a notable scarcity of research about motivation in children with intellectual disability; however, some researchers have concluded that these children have particular problems with motivation. In a frequently cited study,

Harter and Zigler (1974) found that children and adolescents with intellectual disability displayed lower levels of motivation than typically developing children of the same mental age. None of the children in their sample had Down syndrome or any other organic aetiology. Other reports of motivational difficulties for children with intellectual disability have been published (see, for example, Jacobs, 1972; Switzky, 1997; Wong, 1980) but, in most cases, this research comes from a time when children with intellectual disability experienced exclusion from many educational opportunities as well as a range of other sources of discrimination that may have negatively affected their motivation to engage in learning activities and their capacity to be successful in their interactions with the world.

More recently, Fidler (2006) has argued that deficits in motivation are part of the learning and behavioural profile (i.e. the behavioural phenotype) of Down syndrome. As we discuss later, however, most of the empirical evidence does not support the notion of motivation difficulties for children with Down syndrome when they are compared with typically developing children at the same developmental level. Furthermore, differences between children with Down syndrome and those whose intellectual disability is related to other causes have not been demonstrated as would be expected if there were a phenotypic effect. This is not to say that motivation is not a concern. Within any group of learners, there are some who are poorly motivated and, as we discuss later in this chapter, certain aspects of the environments in which children with Down syndrome develop and learn are likely to impact negatively on their motivation.

Although many theories may be relevant to understanding motivation in children with Down syndrome, mastery motivation is the only framework to have been applied in any systematic way with this population. In the following section, we describe mastery motivation and its measurement, and then review research that has been conducted with children with Down syndrome. We also include several relevant studies that have examined children's motivation without being embedded in any particular theoretical framework.

Mastery motivation

Mastery motivation was originally defined by Morgan *et al.* (1990) as a "psychological force that stimulates an individual to attempt independently, in a focused and persistent manner, to solve a problem or master a skill or task which is at least moderately challenging for him or her" (p. 319). The essential elements of this definition are the requirement for *persistent* effort with respect to a *challenging* task for that *individual* (Busch-Rossnagel & Morgan, 2013). Inherent to the definition is the view that mastery itself is the motivating force—the behaviour is not pursued with the view to extrinsic reward. Rather, the basis for mastery motivation is understood to be the intrinsic need to achieve competence in the world (Piaget, 1952; White, 1959); so, for example, mastery motivation is implicated in the move from crawling to walking in infancy. Following success, the drive towards competence is strengthened by feelings of satisfaction and pleasure, which, in turn, motivate further mastery attempts. This affective element of pleasure during engagement or following success with challenging tasks has been incorporated into the definition of mastery motivation (see Barrett & Morgan, 1995). More recently, preference for challenging tasks has been added to the definition (see Gilmore & Cuskelly, 2009), reflecting work by Dweck and colleagues (Smiley & Dweck, 1994).

Most research studies have focused on object-related mastery motivation; that is, attempts to master cognitive problem-solving challenges. Fewer researchers have focused on the dimension of social mastery motivation, the motivation to generate and sustain social interactions, which was recognised in White's (1959) original conceptualisation. Children generally have different levels of motivation for mastery in each domain (Morgan & Yang, 1995) and there is some evidence that object and social motivation may be opposing dimensions of mastery motivation. Wachs and Combs (1995), for instance, found that children high on object mastery motivation were less motivated to master their social environments, while socially motivated children were lower on object motivation, and a third group appeared to use object mastery to gain adult approval. This distinction may have particular relevance for individuals with Down syndrome, and will be taken up later in our discussion.

In infants and young children, the intrinsic motivation to explore and become competent appears to be spontaneous, undifferentiated, and inherent to the individual (White, 1959), but in later childhood and adulthood, intrinsic motivation becomes more dependent on the feelings of competence and enjoyment associated with specific activities themselves. Although it is presumed that all children are born with an inherent motivation to master their environments, as their experiences of success and failure accumulate, and they develop increasing self-knowledge of their strengths and interests, they become differentially motivated for different types of tasks (Guay *et al.*, 2010). Not surprisingly, children tend to display greater persistence and enjoyment of challenge when they are tackling areas of interest in which they feel relatively competent. Few are similarly motivated across all domains of learning. Some children may be particularly interested in mathematics or languages, while others will be driven by their talents in sports or music.

Early research on the construct of mastery motivation found that motivation in infants (aged five-and-a-half months) was a significant predictor of intelligence test scores at three-and-a-half years, and was in fact a better predictor than scores on an infant test of cognitive development (Yarrow, Klein, Lomonaco, & Morgan, 1975; Messer *et al.*, 1986). The importance of motivation for later competence has been a consistent finding of the field (Hrncir, Speller, & West, 1985; Jennings, Yarrow, & Martin, 1984), although relationships appear to be stronger for girls than boys (Gilmore, Cuskelly & Purdie, 2003; Messer *et al.*, 1986; Yarrow *et al.*, 1975).

Moderate stability has been demonstrated in mastery motivation but most studies have been restricted to relatively brief periods across the early childhood years. Establishing continuity from early to middle childhood tends to be more difficult because developmental transformations in the way mastery motivation is displayed make measurement more complex. Some researchers have identified discontinuities (e.g. Maslin-Cole, Bretherton, & Morgan, 1993), while others have shown more stability (e.g. Gilmore *et al.*, 2003).

Mastery motivation would appear to be the precursor to achievement motivation (Busch-Rossnagel & Morgan, 2013), a construct that is familiar to educators. Achievement motivation comprises two elements: mastery orientation refers to the focus on *developing* competence, while performance orientation refers to the *demonstration* of competence (Senko, Durik, & Harackiewicz, 2008). It seems likely that, as children accumulate mastery experiences, they become more influenced by social acknowledgement of their performance. For some, this may result in greater importance being placed on performance, at least in certain areas of activity, than on actual mastery.

For others, mastery continues to be their primary goal in learning tasks. While these hypotheses make sound theoretical sense, the links have yet to be established empirically.

Measurement

Three main methods have been developed for measuring mastery motivation in childhood: observations of free play, structured tasks, and questionnaires that are usually completed by parents or teachers. In free play situations, measures include sustained behaviour, duration, and complexity of exploratory play (Jennings, Connors, & Stegman, 1988). However, behaviours observed during free play may be ambiguous reflections of mastery motivation (McCall, 1995), and it can be difficult to determine whether they are motivated by a desire for mastery over the environment, which is the critical component of mastery motivation, or simply by exploration and curiosity (Morgan *et al.*, 1990). In addition, children tend to display fewer mastery attempts and less persistence during free play sessions than when they are presented with structured activities (Busch-Rossnagel & Morgan, 2013), perhaps because structured tasks make the challenge of mastery more salient.

Structured tasks offer advantages for the assessment of mastery motivation: they provide precise scoring procedures and can be individualised to ensure that children are assessed with tasks that are optimally challenging (Busch-Rossnagel & Morgan, 2013). Their limitations include the fact that they require a degree of compliance from children, and only a relatively narrow range of behaviours are recognised as representative of mastery motivation (MacTurk, Morgan, & Jennings, 1995).

Various structured tasks have been used to assess mastery motivation, including mazes (Dichter-Blancher, Busch-Rossnagel, & Knauf-Jensen, 1997), lock boards (Maslin-Cole *et al.*, 1993), shape cards (Lütkenhaus, 1984), curiosity boxes (Jennings, Connors, Stegman, Sankaranarayan, & Mendelsohn, 1985), and impossible tasks (Gilmore & Cuskelly, 2011; Gilmore *et al.*, 2003). For infants and young children, mastery motivation is frequently operationalised as persistence with a developmentally appropriate sequence of tasks. The importance of optimal challenge for the display of mastery motivation is recognised in the method of assessment devised by Morgan and colleagues for children aged 15–36 months (Morgan, Busch-Rossnagel, Maslin-Cole, & Harmon, 1992). This method incorporates structured tasks (puzzles, shape-sorters, and cause–effect toys), each with six levels of difficulty to ensure that a child is presented with a level that is optimally challenging for him/her. For a task to be optimally challenging, it needs to be difficult enough that the child cannot complete it without some effort but easy enough that some success can be achieved.

Observations during structured mastery tasks can provide information about task-directed persistence and positive affect after success. Measuring the affective aspect of mastery motivation has proven to be more difficult than persistence, mainly because overt expressions of pleasure are relatively infrequent and often fleeting when they do occur. Several researchers have developed tasks that provide information about children's preference for challenge (see Gilmore & Cuskelly, 2009; Jennings *et al.*, 1984; Smiley & Dweck, 1994). The methods typically provide both success and failure experiences (often artificially created) and then give children opportunities to choose again from these tasks. Children who consistently select a difficult task are judged to prefer challenge.

Persistence and preference for challenge tasks are currently available only for children aged up to approximately eight years. These tasks are suitable for older children with Down syndrome when mental age is being considered; however, there is a need for appropriate measures for older children and adults, as well as a wider range of tasks. At the current time, instruments for observing mastery behaviours have been developed only for mastery with cognitive problem-solving tasks, and these tend to require spatial and physical skills (e.g. puzzles, shape-sorters, fishing tasks) that some children may find difficult or uninteresting.

Mastery motivation can also be measured using questionnaires. Morgan and his colleagues developed the Dimensions of Mastery Questionnaire (DMQ) (Morgan, Busch-Rossnagel, Barrett, & Wang, 2009) to assess the various aspects of mastery motivation, including physical and social mastery motivation, for which there are currently no observational measures. The DMQ can be completed by a child's parent or teacher, or, if the child is old enough, by the child him/herself. The difficulties of self-report by individuals with intellectual disability (Cuskelly & Gordon, 2011) mean, however, that research with children with Down syndrome has used only parent and teacher versions of the DMQ. An important difference between observational and questionnaire measures is the fact that structured tasks and free play assessments are usually derived from observations at a single session, whereas questionnaire ratings are likely to be based on observations of children's behaviour in a variety of contexts and on many different occasions. Although the use of different methods in combination seems appealing, task observations and parent report are generally correlated only weakly at best (Morgan *et al.*, 1990; Morgan, Wang, Liao, & Xu, 2013; Ruskin, Mundy, Kasari, & Sigman, 1994).

Mastery motivation research: children with Down syndrome

Relatively little research has investigated motivation either in children with Down syndrome or in those with intellectual disability more generally. However, a recent study demonstrated the importance of mastery motivation for later learning in a sample of children with Down syndrome. Gilmore and Cuskelly (2009) found that persistence measured in the preschool years was significantly related to academic performance in reading and mathematics at adolescence, even when the effects of cognitive ability were taken into account. This finding demonstrates that motivation is an important predictor of outcomes for children with Down syndrome and is in line with the conclusions of studies with typically developing children (see, for example, Gilmore *et al.*, 2003; Hustinx, Kuyper, & van der Werf, 2009).

Observational research

Studies undertaken over the past two decades have focused mainly on comparing young children with Down syndrome to typically developing children of the same developmental age. In most studies, children with Down syndrome have been found to display similar levels of persistent, goal-directed behaviour (Gilmore, Cuskelly, & Hayes, 2003a; Glenn, Dayus, Cunningham, & Horgan, 2001; MacTurk, Vietze, McCarthy, McQuiston, & Yarrow, 1985; Ruskin *et al.*, 1994). While Ruskin *et al.* identified no differences at the overall level of mastery motivation, a more fine-grained analysis revealed some differences that we discuss later.

The research mentioned above was all conducted with infants and young children. In a recent study of school-aged children, Gilmore and Cuskelly (2011) investigated motivation in 10–15-year-old children with Down syndrome and a comparison group of typically developing children matched for mental age (3–8 years). There were no significant group differences on observational measures of curiosity, persistence, and preference for challenge. In a recent extension of this work, we found no differences between children with Down syndrome and those with either mild intellectual disability or moderate intellectual disability associated with aetiologies other than Down syndrome (Gilmore, Cuskelly, & Browning, unpublished data).

By contrast with the above studies, some researchers using other approaches for observing motivation have identified differences between children with Down syndrome and typically developing children. Wishart and Duffy (1990) reported that, when offered tasks which were just beyond their level of competence, children with Down syndrome often refused even to attempt them. Instead, they used social strategies to divert the examiner's focus. Such avoidant behaviours, observed both in infants (Wishart, 1991) and in older children (Duffy & Wishart, 1987; Pitcairn & Wishart, 1994) may at times be related to task difficulty (or perceived task difficulty) rather than to lack of interest. However, Wishart's consistent findings of counterproductive behaviours, such as refusals to attempt tasks, lack of persistence with difficult tasks, and unstable performance over time, led her to conclude that the development of motivation is not only delayed but "fundamentally different" for children with Down syndrome (Wishart, 1999, p. 497). Gilmore, Cuskelly, and Hayes (2003b) also found that children with Down syndrome aged 4–6 years were more likely to disengage from a problem-solving activity than were a comparison group of 2–3-year-old typically developing children.

These studies differ from those using the mastery motivation paradigm in that the tasks are not individualised with respect to difficulty. This means that children's motivation is being measured on tasks that are not necessarily optimally challenging, a fact that may account for their disengagement.

Parent report

Parents of children with Down syndrome consistently give lower ratings to behaviours such as persistence and enjoyment of challenge than do parents of typically developing children (Gilmore *et al.*, 2003a; Gilmore & Cuskelly, 2011; Glenn *et al.*, 2001; Ruskin *et al.*, 1994). It is possible that parent ratings, being derived from observations of a greater number and wider range of child behaviours, are more reflective of motivational orientation than are codings of children's task behaviour observed in the laboratory. It is likely that parent ratings are based on comparisons of their child against his or her same-age peers, rather than against children of a similar developmental level or mental age. Another factor that may contribute to the lower ratings parents assign to mastery motivation is that they rarely see their children working on optimally challenging tasks that elicit mastery behaviours. Many of the day-to-day experiences of children with intellectual disability will involve activities that are either too hard or too easy.

Adult perceptions of mastery motivation may also be influenced by aspects of the behaviour of the child with Down syndrome—in particular, their relative slowness to respond. This slowness may be interpreted as reflecting problems with motivation.

However, as Goodman and Linn (2003) have argued so compellingly, presumptions that slowness and passivity indicate low levels of interest are questionable, given the fact that individuals with intellectual disability require more time to process information and formulate their responses. Apparent passivity may thus reflect slower processing, rather than low levels of interest in learning tasks.

In summary, observational studies of persistence and preference for challenge have shown no differences in mastery motivation for children with Down syndrome when they are compared with typically developing children of the same mental age. Parent reports consistently tell a different story, however, and some research outside the mastery motivation paradigm has shown that young children with Down syndrome display avoidant and counter-productive approaches in problem-solving situations.

Individual differences in motivation

It is not difficult to find examples of individuals with Down syndrome who are highly motivated. Across a range of domains, we find cases of persistent effort, engagement with challenge, and pride in achievement. Li, Liu, Lok, and Lee (2006), for example, described 10 young people with Down syndrome who demonstrated high levels of motivation and perseverance in activities such as academic tasks, sport, dance, and volunteering. There are numerous other examples of outstanding achievement by people with Down syndrome in areas that include music, art, and acting (see, for example, Farag, 2008).

Irrespective of whether or not, as a group, children with Down syndrome are less motivated for mastery compared to their typically developing peers, it is clear that within any group there are those with higher and lower levels of mastery motivation. Understanding what contributes to these differences among individuals will help us to develop appropriate strategies for enhancing or maintaining children's mastery motivation. Unfortunately, there is little research that specifically addresses individual differences with respect to children with Down syndrome, or even those with intellectual disability more generally, so we have drawn on a wider research base and a broader range of conceptualisations of motivation in this next section. We can divide influences on motivation into those aspects that are considered to be characteristics of the person and those that are features of the environment. This is an arbitrary division for the ease of organising the literature, however, as the two are intimately interconnected and reciprocally influencing.

Child characteristics

Many personal characteristics influence mastery motivation. The most obvious, yet sometimes overlooked, explanations for low motivation involve aspects of physical and mental health. Vision and hearing problems, attention difficulties, anxiety, and depression are all likely to interfere to some extent with motivation for learning unless they are recognised and appropriate supports are provided; however, such problems are not always easily identified and parents or teachers might instead attribute children's lack of interest in learning to laziness or lack of motivation (see, for example, Gilmore & Boulton-Lewis, 2009). A high proportion of children with Down syndrome have difficulties with vision and hearing (Roizen, 2003); many have problems with fine motor skills that can make completion of school tasks such as writing more difficult

(Bruni, 2006); some have respiratory problems and sleep apnoea that can result in general drowsiness and subsequent lack of engagement in the classroom (Pandit & Fitzgerald, 2012); others may have problems with their weight and energy levels (Murray & Ryan-Krause, 2010). Additional common health problems that may affect motivation for learning in children with Down syndrome include thyroid disease, epilepsy, diabetes, and middle-ear infections (Määttä *et al.*, 2011).

The personal characteristic that has been the focus of most research with respect to mastery motivation is a disability, such as Down syndrome or cerebral palsy, or a condition that poses risk to optimum development, such as prematurity. It is likely that some disabilities will have more impact on the development of mastery motivation than others; for example, significant motor problems are likely to interfere with a child's ability to explore the environment, thus reducing the *capacity* for mastery, and potentially undermining the *motivation* to strive for mastery. Disabilities such as Down syndrome, which involve intellectual impairment, may affect motivation more indirectly—for example, because of frequent failure experiences or limited opportunities for mastery. We focus on these aspects in the next section of our chapter.

More important than actual ability, the beliefs that a person holds about his or her own capabilities appear to have important implications for motivation. According to Dweck, Hong, and Chiu (1993), children tend to see ability as either fixed (that is, they hold an "entity" theory of ability) or as changeable and thus capable of increasing or improving (an "incremental" theory). Those who view ability as innate and unchangeable have been shown to prefer easy tasks that limit the risk of failure, whereas children who hold an incremental view are more likely to seek challenge and to persist because they believe performance can improve with effort (Dweck & Leggett, 1988). Children may hold contrasting beliefs about their ability in different domains such as reading and mathematics and, not surprisingly, those who see themselves as competent in an activity are more likely to engage in that activity (Rosenberg, Jarus, Bart, & Ratzon, 2011). Students with intellectual disability tend to have fewer experiences of success, and may consequently feel less confident about their own ability. If they also believe that ability is fixed and cannot be improved, they will be more likely to avoid challenge and less willing to keep trying after failure. Very few studies have investigated self-perceptions about success and ability by questioning children with intellectual disability themselves. In one such study, however, no differences were found for expectations of success on a challenging motor task (Kozub, 2002).

In addition to beliefs about competence, the attributions children make for their successes and failures also have implications for subsequent motivation. Explaining failure as the result of insufficient effort is considered to be adaptive and likely to be associated with an increased striving towards success, whereas attributing failure to other causes, such as low ability or luck, may result in decreased motivation because these factors are not seen as controllable and persistence may thus be seen as pointless. Koestner, Aube, Ruttner, and Breed (1995) found that, compared with typically developing children, those with mild intellectual disability were less likely to attribute their failures to insufficient effort, suggesting that they held entity views of ability. In a second stage of Koestner *et al.*'s study, they found that, when tasks were presented as able to be learned, all children, including those with intellectual disability, responded in more motivated ways.

Self-regulation is another child characteristic that contributes to the behaviours identified as indicative of motivation (Cuskelly, Gilmore, & Carroll, 2013). Children need to be able to resist distraction in order to work persistently on a task. They need self-regulatory skills, such as the ability to monitor their own progress and change their approach if necessary. Children with Down syndrome do appear to have difficulty with self-regulation, in comparison to their mental-age matched peers (Cuskelly & Stubbins, 2006; Cuskelly, Zhang, & Hayes, 2003), and this difficulty may account for some of the identified differences in performance on motivation tasks we discussed earlier. Tasks that have little inherent structure require a higher level of self-regulation in order to maintain engagement, and it seems that children with Down syndrome are less able to stay focused in unstructured situations (Gilmore *et al.*, 2003b). This may account for reports of lower levels of engagement in free play conditions.

The study mentioned earlier by Ruskin *et al.* (1994) found that children with Down syndrome displayed similar levels of task persistence to typically developing children of the same mental age when persistence was assessed by the most commonly used method (that is, ratings of the predominant task behaviour in each 15-second interval). Yet, a second coding method provided a somewhat different perspective. Ruskin *et al.* calculated the length of uninterrupted strings of task-focused behaviour, and found that children with Down syndrome stayed on task for shorter periods than the typically developing children. The meaning of these breaks in attention is unclear. They may be interpreted as lack of engagement; however, Goodman and Linn (2003) suggested that such breaks may be necessary for children with intellectual disability to process information effectively.

The issue of children's interest in others also needs to be considered as a potential contributor to motivation in learning contexts. A number of researchers have identified social cognition/sociability as a strength for those with Down syndrome (e.g. Fidler, Most, Booth-LaForce, & Kelly, 2008). However, social interactions may interfere in children's engagement with learning tasks if they prefer to engage with others at the expense of cognitively challenging tasks (Wishart, 2007). Not all research supports the view that social competence is a strength for this group. While children with Down syndrome may have a stronger desire for social interaction, they do not necessarily have the social skills that are required for effective interaction (Guralnick, Connor, & Johnson, 2009; Wishart, 2007).

Children's perceptions about their "place" within the classroom may be another important contributor to their engagement with learning activities. Deci and Ryan's (1985) theory of self-determination identifies relatedness as an important contributor to motivated behaviour. While there has been little direct investigation of this construct in comparison to other aspects of the theory, some work has indicated its relevance, particularly within the school context. Children's feelings of school-connectedness (Fredricks, Blumenfeld, & Paris, 2004; Furrer & Skinner, 2003) appear to account for differences in motivation in samples of typically developing children, possibly because individuals who feel well connected are more confident about taking risks when failure is a potential outcome. There is little evidence about feelings of school connectedness for children with Down syndrome but studies of students with illnesses or learning disabilities have demonstrated lower school connectedness compared with their peers (e.g. Svavarsdottir, 2008).

In summary, students with Down syndrome and other developmental disabilities may experience a range of health, sensory, and motor difficulties that interfere with their motivation for mastery. Children's beliefs about their own ability, the attributions they make for success and failure, and their expectancy about future success are all likely to impact on approaches to learning tasks. In addition, the difficulties many children with Down syndrome have in relation to self-regulating their attention, learning, and behaviour are likely to undermine their mastery motivation. The desire for social interaction with others may be distracting, and low levels of social connectedness to peers and school will also have potential consequences for motivation. Although some of these individual characteristics are intrinsic to the person, many are influenced by environmental factors or can be modified by appropriate home and school interventions. The contexts in which children are living and learning have important implications for their motivation, and we turn now to a consideration of these environmental influences.

Environmental characteristics

A substantial body of evidence has documented the relationship of various contextual factors with children's motivation, although this research focuses almost entirely on children who are developing typically. As well as examining the research that has been undertaken with children with intellectual disability, we also include relevant material from this broader literature.

Cognitively stimulating environments are important for children's motivation and learning. In one of the earliest studies of mastery motivation, six-month-old typically developing infants whose home environments were stimulating and responsive displayed greater persistence and competence at 13 months of age (Yarrow, Morgan, Jennings, Harmon, & Gaiter, 1982). In particular, it was the *variety* of cognitively stimulating activities that predicted children's subsequent mastery motivation. More recent research has produced similar findings about the importance of the home environment and opportunities to engage with challenging activities (Gottfried, Fleming, & Gottfried, 1998; NICHD Early Child Care Research Network, 2005; Wang, Hwang, Liao, Chen, & Hsieh, 2011). This relationship has been found to apply to children who are at risk developmentally (Coscia *et al.*, 2001; Treyvaud *et al.*, 2012) as well as those who are developing typically.

As made clear in our earlier discussion, mastery motivation is most likely to be stimulated when tasks are optimally challenging. Children with Down syndrome will often be in classrooms where their level of understanding differs substantially from that of many of their classmates. The emphasis on developing differentiated curricula and providing learning tasks and opportunities appropriate to each individual in the class is laudable; however, it is difficult to achieve this goal in practice. When work is too difficult or too easy, typically developing children may be able to find ways to stay on task (for example, by reminding themselves about the usefulness of the current task to their future goals), but such self-regulatory strategies are difficult for students with intellectual disability. Thus, the match between the demands of a task and the child's ability is likely to be an important influence on the motivation of a child with Down syndrome.

There is evidence that maternal (Majnemer, Shevell, & Law, 2010; Sparks, Hunter, Backman, Morgan, & Ross, 2012) and teacher (Pakarinen, Kiuru, & Lerkkanen, 2010) stress negatively affects children's motivation. It is reasonable to suppose that adults who are experiencing stress have difficulty in providing structured and stimulating environments, as well as quality adult–child interactions. Various studies have focused on the quality of parent–child interactions in relation to children's mastery motivation. Yarrow *et al.* (1982) found that maternal responsiveness was a significant predictor of mastery motivation in typically developing infants. Similarly, in a sample of children who were at risk because of prematurity or developmental delays, Young and Hauser-Cram (2006) found that maternal responsiveness to child distress (i.e. maternal sensitivity) was significantly related to concurrent child persistence.

Inherent to definitions of mastery motivation is the notion of autonomy. It is the child's independent autonomous efforts towards mastery that reflect mastery motivation. In literature about typically developing children, sensitive parent or teacher support for children's autonomy has been linked to higher levels of task persistence and a range of positive social and academic outcomes (Joussemet, Koestner, Lekes, & Landry, 2005; Matte-Gagne & Bernier, 2011; Ryan, Deci, Grolnick, & La Guardia, 2006). On the other hand, poorer child outcomes have been associated with more directive and controlling adult interactions. Similar effects have been observed for children with Down syndrome. Gilmore, Cuskelly, Jobling, and Hayes (2009) found that higher levels of maternal support for autonomy during a shared problem-solving activity were related to greater child persistence on an independent task; children whose mothers behaved more directively were less persistent. Interestingly, this relationship was apparent only for children with Down syndrome, not for typically developing children in the study, suggesting that children with Down syndrome may be more vulnerable to the influence of maternal behaviours.

Although in our own work we have found no differences in directiveness between mothers of children with Down syndrome and mothers of typically developing children (Gilmore *et al.*, 2009), parents and teachers of children with developmental disabilities such as Down syndrome are often observed to be more directive and controlling (Glenn *et al.*, 2001; Ockjean & Hupp, 2005). The reasons for higher levels of directiveness and control are unclear, but a number of hypotheses present themselves: some related to child characteristics (or perceived child characteristics) such as slowness, passivity, or inability to successfully complete a task independently; others that focus on adult beliefs about the importance of control, adult views of the incremental or entity nature of ability, and adult attributions regarding child success or failure. Cultural issues should not be overlooked, with respect to both home and school environments. Different cultural groups may hold different views about disability and about motivation (see Ly, 2008, for an example).

Definitions of autonomy support include a focus on the way in which feedback is conveyed to the child, with positive and sensitive feedback predicting subsequent child persistence and preference for challenge (Kelley, Brownell, & Campbell, 2000). In the motivation literature, considerable attention has been given to the motivational advantages and disadvantages of various reinforcement strategies. Positive reinforcement in the form of praise or rewards (e.g. stickers, tokens, or food treats) is commonly used as a strategy for encouraging children's interest in learning, for motivating them to strive for particular goals, and for managing their behaviour. While there is controversy over the role that external rewards may play in intrinsic motivation (for a review, see Akin-Little & Little, 2009), there is agreement that positive reinforcement, i.e. the application of a desired consequence after a behaviour, will lead to increased persistence of that behaviour. Many tasks that children are asked to complete at school are not intrinsically motivating, they are not freely chosen, and yet they are important. The literature on the use of operant techniques is extensive and cannot be adequately summarised here, but there is no doubt that these techniques are effective in assisting children to learn new skills and to remain engaged in tasks that are not inherently interesting to them.

In summary, it is clear that environments play a crucial role in promoting and sustaining children's mastery motivation. Likely to be of particular importance is giving children the opportunity to engage with cognitively stimulating activities, especially those that are optimally challenging for an individual child. The provision of such opportunities will be influenced by the attitudes and expectations of adults in the child's home or school, as well as by the level of stress and structure within those environments. The judicious use of appropriate types of positive reinforcement and a focus on supporting the child's autonomy in learning situations are also likely to be important for mastery motivation.

From the research evidence, we can draw particular implications for promoting and sustaining mastery motivation in educational contexts. Although not empirically proven to work for children with Down syndrome, the following strategies are based on the best available evidence. Intervention studies with children with Down syndrome and other disabilities are needed to provide a stronger evidence base for practice, and we highlight this and other directions for future research in the final section of our chapter.

Implications for educators

Motivation for learning will be strong in some children with Down syndrome, while other children will behave in ways that suggest they are not engaged in the tasks presented to them in the classroom. Although mastery motivation is understood to be a personal characteristic, it is clearly influenced very substantially by experience and environment. These elements, external to the child, are open to manipulation and so are the focus of this next section.

Before deciding that a child's difficulty in the classroom is motivational, teachers and parents need to eliminate other explanations. The most obvious of these are sensory or other health difficulties that may be interfering with the child's capacity to attend to, and participate in, learning activities. Once these issues have been addressed, other aspects of the classroom may need to be considered. Of central concern is the level of challenge in the work being provided for the student with Down syndrome.

Children are most likely to be motivated when the level of skill required by a task is just slightly above their current level of competence, or within the "zone of proximal development" (Vygotsky, 1986). In order to achieve the best match between demands and abilities, tasks should ideally be individualised so that they contain an optimum degree of challenge for each child. If demands are too high, children will have no recourse but to ask for assistance, a behaviour that is likely to build dependence if it occurs constantly (Egilson & Traustadottir, 2009). On the other hand, if demands are too low, disengagement is likely.

If teachers are to provide tasks at this optimal level of challenge, they need to have a strong understanding of the child's abilities. With this understanding, they can support the development of competence through the provision of well-scaffolded learning experiences that are built upon a clear understanding of current knowledge. Small, integrated steps will allow children to develop their level of skill. As all children are likely to engage more fully and to experience greater satisfaction from activities they are intrinsically interested in, it is valuable for parents and teachers to be aware of and to nurture each child's strengths, interests, curiosities, and talents. While students will have individual areas of interest and strength, Couzens and Cuskelly (Chapter 2) provide information about areas of cognitive strength and weakness for those with Down syndrome as a group.

Children with Down syndrome inevitably experience more failures in learning than do their typically developing peers. Over time, the accumulation of failure experiences has the potential to undermine motivation for learning. Successful experiences, on the other hand, are not only motivating but also contribute to children's feelings of self-efficacy and well-being. Thus, it is important to provide all children with opportunities to experience success and feel competent. If caregiver expectations are low, children may not be offered tasks with an appropriate level of challenge. Or if slowness and passivity are interpreted as disengagement or lack of interest, tasks may be withdrawn before a child has time to engage with them. As a result, there may be continual stimulation with a series of activities but insufficient opportunity to achieve success with any of them.

The need to experience success does not mean that learning should be organised so that failure never occurs. Failure is an inevitable part of life and, of course, persistence in the face of initial failure is essential for learning. Children need to learn to respond to failure adaptively. An adaptive response is one where persistent effort is applied and, where necessary, new approaches are tried with the problem. Children may need to be explicitly taught to continue to try after initial failure. Tasks that are presented in a way that makes explicit the view that they are able to be learned or mastered with effort are more likely to stimulate continued engagement than those which students may interpret as requiring some innate talent for success.

As for all children, classrooms that avoid competition between learners and encourage mastery of material will support the motivation of children with Down syndrome. Cooperative learning approaches have been shown to result in a range of positive student outcomes, including improved thinking and problem-solving skills (Gillies, 2008). These approaches are likely to benefit children with Down syndrome also. It may be that group work which does not have the separate, inter-dependent roles that characterise cooperative learning tasks will not be as effective. If social motivations are stronger for students with Down syndrome than are those related to mastery of cognitive tasks, it is possible that children's energies will be diverted into the social realm. Group work may also provide a context that allows imitation rather than independent problem solving. Teachers who use group work as a regular practice in their classroom should not assume this will be ineffective for a student with Down syndrome, but should observe a child's engagement in tasks before making a decision about its usefulness for the particular student. As mentioned by Couzens and Cuskelly (Chapter 2), group work does carry some hazards for children with Down syndrome that need to be considered.

For all children, engagement in the classroom requires self-regulatory skills, such as goal setting, management of attention, initiation, flexibility, and resisting distraction, as examples. Even in young children, behaviours directed at achieving mastery require them to inhibit impulsive behaviours and to self-manage emotions such as frustration. Older children need to be able to think ahead and plan a course of action, as well as delay gratification of smaller goals while working towards a larger, more distant goal. Many children with Down syndrome have difficulty with these skills (Cuskelly *et al.*, 2003), making it harder for them to deal with classroom situations requiring self-management.

There is some evidence to suggest that self-regulatory skills such as setting goals and developing a plan for achieving those goals can be taught successfully to students with intellectual disability (Harris, Graham, & Mason, 2003; Palmer, Wehmeyer, Gipson, & Agran, 2004). Direct teaching of skills is important because young children generally are not aware of strategies that could assist them to regulate their learning and behaviour (Cooper & Corpus, 2009) and the self-regulatory skills that older children tend to acquire instinctively may not develop without assistance for children with Down syndrome. These include cognitive and metacognitive strategies, such as self-administering rewards, using positive mastery-focused self-talk, transforming a boring task into a game, adapting the environment in some way, or understanding the contribution mastery of a task will make to achieving one's goals, all of which can be used to foster effort, persistence, self-efficacy, and achievement.

Self-talk is often used as a strategy for regulating thinking and behaviour. Children can learn to use positive self-talk that guides their efforts and helps to maintain their persistence with an activity. Phrases such as "I can do it, yes I can" or "Try, try again" may be useful to sustain motivation (Day & Burns, 2011). Such positive self-talk has been linked to mastery orientations (Chiu & Alexander, 2000) and contrasts with more helpless approaches that are reflected in self-talk statements such as "This is too hard" or "I can't do it". Self-talk that is spoken aloud may be distracting to other students; however, it should not be discouraged as it is likely to be a necessary mechanism of self-regulation (Vygotsky, 1986). It may be helpful to teach students to use self-talk more quietly.

An important environmental influence on motivation is the support parents and teachers provide for children's autonomy in learning (Ratelle, Guay, Larose, & Senecal, 2004; Reeve, Bolt, & Cai, 1999). Support for autonomy is defined as the degree to which parents and teachers "value and use techniques that encourage choice, self-initiation, and participation in making decisions" (Grolnick, Deci, & Ryan, 1997, p. 148). There are several ways in which parents and teachers can support children with Down syndrome to experience as much autonomy as possible. Listening carefully, actively encouraging them to express their opinions, and accepting their views (even those that are negative) as valid are all respectful ways of communicating that encourage autonomy (see Cuskelly & Poulsen, 2013). In addition to the quality of communication between adult and child, the amount and pacing are also important. Adults and peers may tend to speak too quickly or not wait long enough for the child to respond, thus denying them opportunities to participate in the conversation.

Providing choice is an important element of an autonomy-supportive context. True choice enhances feelings of control, and children are more likely to engage and persist with a task that they have chosen. A recent review of research about the impact of choice on intrinsic motivation (Patall, Cooper, & Robinson, 2008) showed that choice enhanced effort, task performance, and feelings of competence. In an intervention with children with autism, Koegel, Singh, and Koegel (2010) incorporated choice and appropriate reinforcers in order to improve children's interest in learning. The intervention was effective in encouraging children to begin working on school tasks and improved their level of interest as well as their performance. There were also decreases in disruptive behaviour. Teachers need to be conscious of the cognitive load involved in making choices. If there are too many options to choose from, or if the child is being required to make too many choices, then the experience may be overwhelming and stressful. Initially, it may be necessary to assist children to consider each option, with a view to developing their capacity for choice making.

Another way in which adults may support the development of children's autonomy is through the provision of clear and informative feedback that focuses on improvement and mastery. Feedback should offer encouragement and, for those with Down syndrome, needs to be offered at a pace that is appropriate for their slower processing. Timing is an important aspect of effective feedback. If it occurs too soon, it may interfere with the child's independent problem-solving; if it occurs too frequently, it may undermine the child's sense of mastery.

Educators have used positive reinforcement, including praise, effectively for many years (Hester, Hendrickson, & Gable, 2009; Stormont, Smith, & Lewis, 2007). The provision of feedback related to effort and successful processes (as opposed to merely successful outcomes) will contribute to children's motivation for further mastery attempts. Feedback that provides information which is useful to the child is likely to enhance motivation through the support for autonomy associated with this interaction. In general, specific praise is preferable to generic comments. When children are given praise that is specific to the task and their effort (e.g. "You wrote that story very carefully"), they tend to have higher subsequent motivation, whereas those who are offered generic praise (e.g. "You are such a good writer") display lower levels of persistence and preference for challenge (Cimpian, 2010; Zentall & Morris, 2010). Generic praise suggests that the child's performance can be attributed to a stable ability, "good writer", whereas praise for the specific task or way of working suggests that success is related to effort and provides specific feedback that the child can transfer to other situations.

Although research has focused only on the effects of praise for typically developing children, it is likely that there are similar influences on motivation for children with disabilities such as Down syndrome. For all children, as well as reinforcing performance and effort, praise that is provided promptly with clear explanations generally will be more effective. However, praise should be judiciously used—avoid too much praise, or praise that is undeserved, such as when the child succeeds on a very easy task or with little effort, and avoid lavish or exaggerated praise.

Future research

The current review has made clear that there is very little research specific to Down syndrome, and the existing evidence base comes almost entirely from one theoretical framework, mastery motivation. There are a number of other theoretical approaches that have made substantial contributions to our understanding of motivation for learning in typically developing children, and it is likely that these could further enhance our understanding of appropriate approaches for engaging students with Down syndrome.

Using the mastery motivation framework, in the laboratory under controlled conditions, children with Down syndrome are as capable of demonstrating persistence as typically developing children of the same mental age. Unlike the experimental research laboratory, the classroom is replete with distractions and includes the availability of models to provide guidance for behaviour. In addition, children's behaviour in the classroom may reflect emotional responses related to past experiences and teacher expectations are more likely to be based on chronological, rather than mental, age expectations. We need to include research in these real-world contexts if we are to expand our understanding of motivation and to develop effective methods for supporting those with Down syndrome.

It has been hypothesised that social and cognitive motivations are competing and that, in children with Down syndrome, the motivation to engage socially is more pressing than the motivation to engage with challenging cognitive tasks. To date, this hypothesis has not been tested explicitly, but it clearly has important implications for classroom practice and would thus be a useful focus for future research.

There are a number of other methodological challenges to be addressed in future research. These include the need for an expanded set of measurement techniques that encompass all of the dimensions of mastery motivation (including social motivation), that can be applied in real-world contexts, and that capture mastery motivation in its more mature form in older children and adolescents. It is important that these measurement techniques incorporate strategies that do not depend on self-report so that they are applicable to individuals with intellectual disability. Such methodological advancements would allow longitudinal investigations of individual and group trajectories, and the influences on these, including classroom and educational practices.

References

Akin-Little, A., & Little, S. G. (2009). The true effects of extrinsic reinforcement on "intrinsic" motivation. In A. Akin-Little, S. G. Little, M. A. Bray, & T. J. Kehle (Eds), *Behavioural interventions in schools: Evidence-based positive strategies* (pp. 73–91). Washington, DC: American Psychological Association.

Barrett, K. C., & Morgan, G. A. (1995). Continuities and discontinuities in mastery motivation during infancy and toddlerhood: A conceptualization and review. In R. H. MacTurk & G. A. Morgan (Eds), *Mastery motivation: Origins, conceptualizations, and applications* (pp. 57–93). Norwood, NJ: Ablex Publishing Corporation.

Bruni, M. (2006). *Fine motor skills in children with Down syndrome: A guide for parents and professionals* (2nd edn). Bethesda, MD: Woodbine House.

Busch-Rossnagel, N. A., & Morgan, G. A. (2013). Introduction to Section Three: Overview and analysis. In K. C. Barrett, N. A. Fox, G. A. Morgan, D. J. Fidler, & L. A. Daunhauer (Eds), *Handbook of self-regulatory processes in development: New directions and international perspectives* (pp. 247–264). New York: Psychology Press.

Chiu, S., & Alexander, P. A. (2000). The motivational function of preschoolers' private speech. *Discourse Processes, 30*, 133–152.

Cimpian, A. (2010). The impact of generic language about ability on children's achievement motivation. *Developmental Psychology, 46*, 1333–1340.

Cooper, C. A., & Corpus, J. H. (2009). Learners' developing knowledge of strategies for regulating motivation. *Journal of Applied Developmental Psychology, 30*, 525–536.

Coscia, J. M., Christensen, B. K., Henry, R. R., Wallston, K. R., Radcliffe, J., & Rutstein, R. (2001). Effects of home environment, socioeconomic status, and health status on cognitive functioning in children with HIV-1 infection. *Journal of Pediatric Psychology, 26*, 321–329.

Cuskelly, M., Gilmore, L., & Carroll, A. (2013). Self-regulation and individuals with developmental disabilities: Barriers, supports and strategies. In K. C. Barrett, N. A. Fox, G. A. Morgan, D. J. Fidler, & L. A. Daunhauer (Eds), *Handbook of self-regulatory processes in development: New directions and international perspectives* (pp. 381–402). New York: Psychology Press.

Cuskelly, M., & Gordon, K. (2011). Social comparisons: Associations with psychosocial functioning in individuals with Down syndrome. *Down Syndrome Quarterly, 13*, 20–28.
Cuskelly, M., & Poulsen, A. A. (2013). Children's understanding of purpose: A matter of choice. In J. Ziviani, A. A. Poulsen, & M. Cuskelly (Eds), *The art and science of motivation: A therapist's guide to working with children* (pp. 59–90). London: Jessica Kingsley.
Cuskelly, M., & Stubbins, P. (2006). Self-imposed delay of gratification in adolescents with Down syndrome. *Journal on Developmental Disabilities, 12*, 19–28.
Cuskelly, M., Zhang, A., & Hayes, A. (2003). A mental age-matched comparison study of delay of gratification in children with Down syndrome. *International Journal of Disability, Development and Education, 50*, 239–251.
Day, C. A., & Burns, B. M. (2011). Characterizing the achievement motivation orientation of children from low- and middle-income families. *Early Education and Development, 22*, 105–127.
Deci, E. L., & Ryan, R. M. (1985). *Intrinsic motivation and self-determination in human behaviour*. New York: Plenum Press.
Dichter-Blancher, T. B., Busch-Rossnagel, N. A., & Knauf-Jensen, D. E. (1997). Mastery motivation: Appropriate tasks for toddlers. *Infant Behavior and Development, 20*, 545–548.
Duffy, L., & Wishart, J. (1987). A comparison of two procedures for teaching discrimination to Down's syndrome and normal children. *British Journal of Educational Psychology, 57*, 265–278.
Dweck, C. S., Hong, Y.-Y., & Chiu, C.-Y. (1993). Implicit theories: Individual differences in the likelihood and meaning of dispositional inference. *Personality and Social Psychology Bulletin, 19*, 644–656.
Dweck, C. S., & Leggett, E. L. (1988). A social-cognitive approach to motivation and personality. *Psychological Review, 95*, 256–273.
Egilson, S. T., & Traustadottir, R. (2009). Assistance to pupils with physical disabilities in regular schools: Promoting inclusion or creating dependency: *European Journal of Special Needs Education, 24*, 21–36.
Farag, T. I. (2008). Lessons from celebrities with Down syndrome, *Ambassadors Online Magazine, 11*, http://ambassadors.net/archives/issue24/educators.htm.
Fidler, D. J. (2006). The emergence of a syndrome-specific personality profile in young children with Down syndrome. *Down Syndrome Research and Practice, 10*, 53–60.
Fidler, D. J., Most, D. E., Booth-LaForce, C., & Kelly, J. F. (2008). Emerging social strengths in young children with Down syndrome. *Infants & Young Children, 21*, 207–220.
Fredricks, J. A., Blumenfeld, P. C., & Paris, A. H. (2004). School engagement: Potential of the concept, state of the evidence. *Review of Educational Research, 74*, 59–109.
Furrer, C., & Skinner, E. (2003). Sense of relatedness as a factor in children's academic engagement and performance. *Journal of Educational Psychology, 95*, 148–162.
Gillies, R. M. (2008). The effects of cooperative learning on junior high school students' behaviours, discourse and learning during a science-based learning activity. *School Psychology International, 29*, 328–347.
Gilmore, L., & Boulton-Lewis, G. (2009). "Just try harder and you will shine": A study of 20 lazy children. *Australian Journal of Guidance and Counselling, 19*, 95–103.
Gilmore, L., & Cuskelly, M. (2009). A longitudinal study of motivation and competence in children with Down syndrome: Early childhood to early adolescence. *Journal of Intellectual Disability Research, 53*, 484–492.
Gilmore, L., & Cuskelly, M. (2011). Observational assessment and maternal reports of motivation in children and adolescents with Down syndrome. *American Journal of Intellectual and Developmental Disabilities, 116*, 153–164.
Gilmore, L., Cuskelly, M., & Hayes, A. (2003a). A comparative study of mastery motivation in young children with Down's syndrome: Similar outcomes, different processes? *Journal of Intellectual Disability Research, 47*, 181–190.
Gilmore, L., Cuskelly, M., & Hayes, A. (2003b). Self-regulatory behaviours in children with

Down syndrome and typically developing children measured using the Goodman Lock Box. *Research in Developmental Disabilities, 24*, 95–108.
Gilmore, L., Cuskelly, M., Jobling, A., & Hayes, A. (2009). Maternal support for autonomy: Relationships with persistence for children with Down syndrome and typically developing children. *Research in Developmental Disabilities, 30*, 1023–1033.
Gilmore, L., Cuskelly, M., & Purdie, N. (2003). Mastery motivation: Stability and predictive validity from ages two to eight. *Early Education & Development, 14*, 411–424.
Glenn, S., Dayus, B., Cunningham, C., & Horgan, M. (2001). Mastery motivation in children with Down syndrome. *Down Syndrome Research and Practice, 7*, 52–59.
Goodman, J. F., & Linn, M. I. (2003). "Maladaptive" behaviours in the young child with intellectual disabilities: A reconsideration. *International Journal of Disability, Development and Education, 50*, 137–148.
Gottfried, A. E., Fleming, J. S., & Gottfried, A. W. (1998). Role of cognitively stimulating home environment in children's academic intrinsic motivation: A longitudinal study. *Child Development, 69*, 1448–1460.
Grolnick, W. S., Deci, E. L., & Ryan, R. M. (1997). Internalization within the family: The self-determination theory perspective. In J. E. Grusec & L. Kuczynski (Eds), *Parenting and children's internalization of values: A handbook of contemporary theory* (pp. 135–161). New York: Wiley.
Guay, F., Chanel, J., Ratelle, C. F., Marsh, H. W., Larose, S., & Boivin, M. (2010). Intrinsic, identified, and controlled types of motivation for school subjects in young elementary school children. *Journal of Educational Psychology, 80*, 711–735.
Guralnick, M. J., Connor, R. T., & Johnson, L. C. (2009). Home-based peer social networks of young children with Down syndrome: A developmental perspective. *American Journal on Intellectual and Developmental Disabilities, 114*, 340–355.
Harris, K. R., Graham, S., & Mason, L. (2003). Self-regulated strategy development in the classroom: Part of a balanced approach to writing instruction for students with disabilities. *Focus on Exceptional Children, 35*, 2–16.
Harter, S., & Zigler, E. (1974). The assessment of effectance motivation in normal and retarded children. *Developmental Psychology, 10*, 169–180.
Hester, P. P., Hendrickson, J. M., & Gable, R. A. (2009). Forty years later—The value of praise, ignoring, and rules for preschoolers at risk for behavioral disorders. *Education and Treatment of Children, 32*, 513–535.
Hrncir, E. J., Speller, G. M., & West, M. (1985). What are we testing? *Developmental Psychology, 21*, 226–232.
Hustinx, P. W. J., Kuyper, H., & van der Werf, M. P. C. (2009). Achievement motivation revisited: New longitudinal data to demonstrate its predictive power. *Educational Psychology, 29*, 561–582.
Jacobs, S. U. (1972). Acquisition of achievement motive among mentally retarded boys. *Sociology of Education, 45*, 223–232.
Jennings, K. D., Connors, R. F., & Stegman, C. E. (1988). Does a physical handicap alter the development of mastery motivation during the preschool years? *Journal of the American Academy of Child and Adolescent Psychiatry, 27*, 312–317.
Jennings, K. D., Connors, R. F., Stegman, C. E., Sankaranarayan, P., & Mendelsohn, S. (1985). Mastery motivation in young pre-schoolers: Effect of a physical handicap and implications for educational programming. *Journal of the Division for Early Childhood, 9*, 162–169.
Jennings, K. D., Yarrow, L. J., & Martin, P. P. (1984). Mastery motivation and cognitive development: A longitudinal study from infancy to 3½ years of age. *International Journal of Behavioral Development, 7*, 441–461.
Joussemet, M., Koestner, R., Lekes, N., & Landry, R. (2005). A longitudinal study of the relationship of maternal autonomy support to children's adjustment and achievement in school. *Journal of Personality, 73*, 1215–1235.

Kelley, S. A., Brownell, C. A., & Campbell, S. B. (2000). Mastery motivation and self-evaluative affect in toddlers: Longitudinal relations with maternal behaviour. *Child Development, 71*, 1061–1071.

Koegel, L. K., Singh, A. K., & Koegel, R. L. (2010). Improving motivation for academics in children with autism. *Journal of Autism and Developmental Disorders, 40*, 1057–1066.

Koestner, R., Aube, J., Ruttner, J., & Breed, S. (1995). Theories of ability and the pursuit of challenge among adolescents with mild mental retardation. *Journal of Intellectual Disability Research, 39*, 57–65.

Kozub, F. M. (2002). Expectations, task persistence, and attributions in children with mental retardation during integrated physical education. *Adapted Physical Activity Quarterly, 19*, 334–350.

Li, E. P.-Y., Liu, Y.-M., Lok, N. C.-Y., & Lee, V. W.-K. (2006). Successful experience of people with Down syndrome. *Journal of Intellectual Disabilities, 10*, 143–154.

Lütkenhaus, P. (1984). Pleasure derived from mastery in three-year olds: Its function for persistence and the influence of maternal behaviour. *International Journal of Behavioral Development, 7*, 343–358.

Ly, T. M. (2008). Asian American parents' attributions of children with Down syndrome: Connections with child characteristics and culture. *Intellectual and Developmental Disabilities, 46*, 129–140.

Määttä, T., Määttä, J., Tervo-Määttä, T., Taanila, A., Kaski, M., & Iivanainen, M. (2011). Healthcare and guidelines: A population-based survey of recorded medical problems and health surveillance for people with Down syndrome. *Journal of Intellectual & Developmental Disability, 36*, 118–126.

MacTurk, R. H., Morgan, G. A., & Jennings, K. D. (1995). The assessment of mastery motivation in infants and young children. In R. H. MacTurk & G. A. Morgan (Eds), *Mastery motivation: Origins, conceptualizations and applications* (pp. 19–56). Norwood, NJ: Ablex Publishing Corporation.

MacTurk, R. H., Vietze, P. M., McCarthy, M. E., McQuiston, S., & Yarrow, L. J. (1985). The organization of exploratory behaviour in Down syndrome and nondelayed infants. *Child Development, 56*, 573–581.

Majnemer, A., Shevell, M., & Law, M. (2010). Level of motivation in mastering challenging tasks in children with cerebral palsy. *Developmental Medicine and Child Neurology, 52*, 1120–1126.

Maslin-Cole, C., Bretherton, I., & Morgan, G. A. (1993). Toddler mastery motivation and competence: Links with attachment security, maternal scaffolding and family climate. In D. Messer (Ed.), *Mastery motivation in early childhood: Development, measurement, and social processes* (pp. 205–229). London: Routledge.

Matte-Gagne, C., & Bernier, A. (2011). Prospective relations between maternal autonomy support and child executive functioning: Investigating the mediating role of child language ability. *Journal of Experimental Child Psychology, 110*, 611–625.

McCall, R. B. (1995). On definitions and measures of mastery motivation. In R. H. MacTurk & G. A. Morgan (Eds), *Mastery motivation: Origins, conceptualizations and applications* (pp. 273–292). Norwood, NJ: Ablex Publishing Corporation.

Messer, D. J., McCarthy, M. E., McQuiston, S., MacTurk, R. H., Yarrow, L. J., & Vietze, P. M. (1986). Relation between mastery behaviour in infancy and competence in early childhood. *Developmental Psychology, 22*, 366–372.

Morgan, G. A., Busch-Rossnagel, N. A., Barrett, K. C., & Wang, J. (2009). *The Dimensions of Mastery Questionnaire (DMQ): A manual about its development, psychometrics, and use*. Fort Collins, CO: Colorado State University.

Morgan, G. A., Busch-Rossnagel, N. A., Maslin-Cole, C. A., & Harmon, R. J. (1992). *Individualized assessment of mastery motivation: Manual for 15 to 36 month old children*. Bronx, NY: Fordham University.

Morgan, G. A., Harmon, R. J., & Maslin-Cole, C. A. (1990). Mastery motivation: Definition and measurement. *Early Education and Development, 1*, 318–339.

Morgan, G. A., Wang, J., Liao, H.-F., & Xu, Q. (2013). Using the Dimensions of Mastery Questionnaire (DMQ) to assess mastery motivation of English- and Chinese-speaking children: Psychometrics and implications for self-regulation. In K. C. Barrett, N. A. Fox, G. A. Morgan, D. J. Fidler, & L. A. Daunhauer (Eds), *Handbook of self-regulatory processes in development: New directions and international perspectives* (pp. 305–335). New York: Psychology Press.

Morgan, G. A., & Yang, R. K. (1995). Toward a multifaceted conceptualization of mastery motivation: An organized summary of research. In R. H. MacTurk & G. A. Morgan (Eds), *Mastery motivation: Origins, conceptualizations, and applications* (pp. 317–337). Norwood, NJ: Ablex Publishing Corporation.

Murray, J., & Ryan-Krause, P. (2010). Obesity in children with Down syndrome: Background and recommendations for management. *Pediatric Nursing, 36*, 314–319.

NICHD Early Child Care Research Network (2005). Predicting individual differences in attention, memory, and planning in first graders from experiences at home, child care, and school. *Developmental Psychology, 41*, 99–114.

Ockjean, K., & Hupp, S. C. (2005). Teacher interaction styles and task engagement of elementary students with cognitive disabilities. *Education and Training in Developmental Disabilities, 40*, 293–308.

Pakarinen, E., Kiuru, N., & Lerkkanen, M.-K. (2010). Classroom organization and teacher stress predict learning motivation in kindergarten children. *European Journal of Psychology of Education, 25*, 281–300.

Palmer, S. B., Wehmeyer, M. L., Gipson, K., & Agran, M. (2004). Promoting access to the general curriculum by teaching self-determination skills. *Exceptional Children, 70*, 427–439.

Pandit, C., & Fitzgerald, D. A. (2012). Respiratory problems in children with Down syndrome. *Journal of Paediatrics & Child Health, 48*, E147–152. doi: 10.1111/j.1440-1754.2011.02077.x.

Patall, E. A., Cooper, H., & Robinson, J. C. (2008). The effects of choice on intrinsic motivation and related outcomes: A meta-analysis of research findings. *Psychological Bulletin, 134*, 270–300.

Piaget, J. (1952). *The origins of intelligence in children.* New York: International Universities Press.

Pintrich, P. R., & Schunk, D. H. (2002). *Motivation in education: Theory, research and applications* (2nd edn). Upper Saddle River, NJ: Merrill Prentice Hall.

Pitcairn, T. K., & Wishart, J. G. (1994). Reactions of young children with Down's syndrome to an impossible task. *British Journal of Developmental Psychology, 12*, 485–490.

Ratelle, C. F., Guay, F., Larose, S., & Senecal, C. (2004). Family correlates of trajectories of academic motivation during a school transition. *Journal of Educational Psychology, 96*, 743–754.

Reeve, J., Bolt, E., & Cai, Y. (1999). Autonomy-supportive teachers: How they teach and motivate students. *Journal of Educational Psychology, 91*, 537–548.

Roizen, N. J. (2003). The early interventionist and the medical problems of the child with Down syndrome. *Infants and Young Children, 16*, 88–95.

Rosenberg, L., Jarus, T., Bart, O., & Ratzon, N. Z. (2011). Can personal and environmental factors explain dimensions of child participation? *Child: Care, Health and Development, 37*, 266–275.

Ruskin, E. M., Mundy, P., Kasari, C., & Sigman, M. (1994). Object mastery motivation of children with Down syndrome. *American Journal on Mental Retardation, 98*, 499–509.

Ryan, R. M., Deci, E. L., Grolnick, W. S., & La Guardia, J. G. (2006). The significance of autonomy and autonomy support in psychological development and psychopathology. In D.

Cicchetti & D. J. Cohen (Eds), *Developmental psychopathology: Theory and method* (2nd edn) (pp. 795–849). Hoboken, NJ: John Wiley & Sons.
Senko, C., Durik, A., & Harackiewicz, J. (2008). Historical perspectives and new directions in achievement goal theory. In J. Shah & W. Gardner (Eds), *Handbook of motivation science* (pp. 100–113). New York: Guilford Press.
Smiley, P. A., & Dweck, C. S. (1994). Individual differences in achievement goals among young children. *Child Development, 65*, 1723–1743.
Sparks, T. A., Hunter, S. K., Backman, T. L., Morgan, G. A., & Ross, R. G. (2012). Maternal parenting stress and mothers' reports of their infants' mastery motivation. *Infant Behavior and Development, 35*, 167–173.
Stipek, D. J. (1997). Success in school—for a head start in life. In S. S. Luthar, J. A. Burack, D. Cicchetti, & J. R. Weisz (Eds), *Developmental psychopathology: Perspectives on adjustment, risk, and disorder* (pp. 75–92). Cambridge: Cambridge University Press.
Stormont, M. A., Smith, S. C., & Lewis, T. J. (2007). Teacher implementation of precorrection and praise statements in Head Start classrooms as a component of a program-wide system of positive behavior support. *Journal of Behavioral Education, 16*, 280–290.
Svavarsdottir, E. K. (2008). Connectedness, belonging and feelings about school among healthy and chronically ill Icelandic schoolchildren. *Scandinavian Journal of Caring Sciences, 22*, 463–471.
Switzky, H. N. (1997). The educational meaning of mental retardation: Toward a more helpful construct. Mental retardation and the neglected construct of motivation. Paper presented at the Annual Convention of the Council for Exceptional Children, Salt Lake City, UT.
Treyvaud, K., Inder, T. E., Lee, K. J., Northam, E. A., Doyle, L. W., & Anderson, P. J. (2012). Can the home environment promote resilience for children born very preterm in the context of social and medical risk? *Journal of Experimental Child Psychology, 112*, 326–337.
Vygotsky, L. S. (1986). *Thought and language*. Cambridge, MA: MIT Press.
Wachs, T. D., & Combs, T. T. (1995). The domains of infant mastery motivation. In R. H. MacTurk & G. A. Morgan (Eds), *Mastery motivation: Origins, conceptualizations, and applications* (pp. 147–164). Norwood, NJ: Ablex Publishing Corporation.
Wang, P.-J. Hwang, A.-W., Liao, H.-F., Chen, P.-C., & Hsieh, W.-S. (2011). The stability of mastery motivation and its relationship with home environment in infants and toddlers. *Infant Behavior and Development, 34*, 434–442.
White. R. W. (1959). Motivation reconsidered: The concept of competence. *Psychological Review, 66*, 297–333.
Wishart, J. G. (1991). Taking the initiative in learning: A developmental investigation of infants with Down syndrome. *International Journal of Disability, Development and Education, 38*, 27–44.
Wishart, J. G. (1999). Learning and development in children with Down's syndrome. In A. Slater & D. Muir (Eds), *The Blackwell reader in developmental psychology* (pp. 493–508). Oxford: Blackwell.
Wishart, J. G. (2007). Socio-cognitive understanding: A strength or weakness in Down's syndrome? *Journal of Intellectual Disability Research, 51*, 996–1005.
Wishart, J. G., & Duffy, L. (1990). Instability of performance on cognitive tests in infants and young children with Down's syndrome. *British Journal of Educational Psychology, 60*, 10–22.
Wong, B. Y. (1980). Motivation for learning in mildly handicapped adolescents and young adults: A review of related theories. *Exceptional Education Quarterly, 1*, 37–45.
Yarrow, L. J., Klein, R. P, Lomonaco, S., & Morgan, G. A. (1975). Cognitive and motivational development in early childhood. *Exceptional Infant, 3*, 491–502.
Yarrow, L. J., Morgan, G. A., Jennings, K. D., Harmon, R. J., & Gaiter, L. J. (1982). Infants' persistence at tasks: Relationships to cognitive functioning and early experience. *Infant Behavior and Development, 5*, 131–141.

Young, J., & Hauser-Cram, P. (2006). Mother–child interaction as a predictor of mastery motivation in children with disabilities born preterm. *Journal of Early Intervention, 28*, 252–263.

Zentall, S. R., & Morris, B. J. (2010). "Good job, you're so smart": The effects of inconsistency of praise type on young children's motivation. *Journal of Experimental Child Psychology, 107*, 155–163.

Chapter 4

Enhancing learning for children with Down syndrome

Emily A. Jones, Nicole Neil, and Kathleen M. Feeley

Abstract

The descriptive literature on people with Down syndrome shows a behavioural phenotype characterized by both strengths and weaknesses. Relative strengths include visual processing and social development, both of which can be capitalized on to design classroom interventions that enhance learning. Demonstrated weaknesses include expressive communication, short-term memory, and some aspects of motor development, along with decreased task persistence and avoidance of difficult tasks. These weaknesses are of critical concern because corresponding impairments are likely to negatively impact learning from a young age. Developing ways to ensure learners are motivated to engage in instruction, acquire pivotal skills, and have opportunities that build upon strengths are key to ensuring optimal outcomes.

The science of applied behaviour analysis (Carr *et al.*, 1999; National Autism Center, 2009) provides a starting point to integrate an understanding of behavioural phenotype with evidence-based interventions, an approach that may significantly improve learning and long-term outcomes. This integration of fields had occurred for learners with autism and had been suggested specifically in relation to challenging behaviour (Robinson Joy, 2009) and for learners with Down syndrome (Fidler, Most, & Philofsky, 2008). In this chapter, we consider behaviours that interfere with classroom performance, pivotal skills, and strengths that may enhance classroom performance, as well as the role of intervention intensity. We review related interventions, suggest applications with learners with Down syndrome, and provide directions for future research.

Addressing behaviours that interfere with classroom performance

To optimize educational experiences, it is important to understand what motivates learners to engage in inappropriate behaviours or behaviours that would be considered challenging and interfere with classroom performance. Doss and Reichle (1991) define challenging behaviour as behaviour that results "... in self-injury or injury of others, causes damage to the physical environment, interferes with the acquisition of new skills, and/or socially isolates the learner" (p. 215). Although rates of significant psychopathology may be lower in children with Down syndrome compared to those with other disorders (Dykens, 2007), children with Down syndrome engage in challenging behaviour at higher rates than their typical peers, showing more externalizing behaviour, such as stubborn and oppositional behaviour, attention difficulties, and impulsivity (Pueschel, Myers, & Sustrova, 1996). Compared to a normative sample, van Gameren-Oosterom *et al.* (2011) found significantly higher scores, falling in the clinical range, for somatic complaints, social, thought, and attention problems in a sample of eight-year-old children with Down syndrome. Children with Down syndrome also show high rates of overlapping attention deficit hyperactivity disorder and conduct disorder diagnoses (Coe *et al.*, 1999; Myers & Pueschel, 1991). With increasing age, there appears to be an increasing incidence of internalizing behaviour problems, such as anxiety and social withdrawal (Dykens, Shah, Sagun, Beck, & King, 2002).

Early in life, children with Down syndrome engage in behaviours that may not seem challenging, but that interfere with learning and, over time, may become quite significant. Wishart and colleagues demonstrated that, in the first year of life, infants with Down syndrome already show a pattern of behaviour to escape/avoid or "opt out" of learning (Wishart, 1993, 1998). In studies of object concept development, Wishart found that infants with Down syndrome showed a propensity to engage in social behaviour with the tester (e.g. waving, clapping) (Wishart, 1993). At the same time, the infants refused to continue to engage in the task (e.g. sliding under the table) (Wishart, 1993). This pattern of behaviour was noted during difficult tasks and even during easy tasks. Pitcairn and Wishart (1994) also found this pattern of behaviour in preschool children with Down syndrome during an impossible task (putting a puzzle piece in a puzzle with no corresponding spot). The children with Down syndrome showed more distracting behaviours to end this task than the age-matched children, specifically, orienting towards the experimenter, making eye contact and vocalizing, and engaging in "party tricks" (e.g. clapping hands or banging the table). Kasari and Freeman (2001) noted similar patterns of social behaviours and asking for help in 5–12-year-olds with Down syndrome compared to typical children and those with intellectual disabilities. Furthermore, children with Down syndrome took longer to complete tasks, indicating decreased task persistence. Wishart (1993) expressed concern about this pattern shown by children with Down syndrome, who use "socially-based strategies to get out of participating in difficult learning" (p. 54).

Wishart's (1993, 1998) research suggests that, when a child with Down syndrome faces a task, he/she is likely to engage in behaviour that not only recruits social attention, but also results in escape/avoidance of task demands. Caregivers (including service providers) may inadvertently *reinforce* such behaviour by providing attention and escape from demands. The child learns that cute, engaging behaviour results in attention and getting out of difficult tasks: this has the potential to interfere with instruction.

What emerges is the relative social strength in conjunction with a propensity to avoid difficult tasks, characterizes the Down syndrome behavioural phenotype, and negatively impacts the demonstration of and, perhaps, acquisition of critical skills. This highlights the need to consider characteristics of Down syndrome in examining challenging behaviour and implement strategies to prevent seemingly benign behaviours from interfering with instructional activities and worse, escalating into more serious behaviours that impact personal satisfaction and well-being, or quality of life.

There is relatively little research examining interventions for challenging behaviour, specifically in learners with Down syndrome. There is, however, extensive research with other populations of learners as well as research that includes one or a few learners with Down syndrome. Positive behaviour interventions and supports, based on the science of applied behaviour analysis, provides an approach to understanding challenging behaviour in terms of its relation to environmental events. The focus is on developing interventions to change environmental events and teach new skills (Carr *et al.*, 1999; Carr *et al.*, 2002), with promise for addressing the needs of this population (Jones & Feeley, 2011).

Foundation of intervention: functions of behaviour

Given descriptions of challenging behaviour emerging from the Down syndrome literature, even the slightest indication a learner is engaging in behaviour that interferes with, or has the potential to interfere with, skill acquisition (in or outside of the classroom) should result in assessment of that behaviour and intervention. Wishart's (1993, 1998) work suggested a function or purpose for behaviour; as described, the behaviour served to escape/avoid difficult or very easy activities while at the same time resulting in attention for the child. The function of challenging behaviour refers to the consequence the learner obtains as a result of engaging in that behaviour (what happens after the occurrence of challenging behaviour). The crux of intervention to decrease challenging behaviour is in understanding the function of that behaviour.

In behaviour analytic terms, the *escape/avoidance* behaviour described by Wishart (1993) means the learner engages in behaviour that results in him/her discontinuing the activity or avoiding the activity altogether. For example, Joe, a middle-school student, whines and fidgets with the workbook presented by his teacher. As a result, he does not complete it, only managing to write his name by the end of the lesson. A few studies show that challenging behaviour for some children with Down syndrome serves an escape function (e.g. Hall, Neuharth-Pritchett, & Belfiore, 1997; Oliver, Hall, & Nixon, 1999). Hall *et al.* examined the function of aggressive behaviour in a nine-year-old with Down syndrome. Observing and manipulating what happened before (antecedents) and what happened after (consequences) the behaviour showed the behaviour functioned to escape from long periods of instruction on the same activity (i.e. to escape task demands).

The function of challenging behaviour may also be to gain access to something. For example, during story time, Sally, a kindergartener, repeatedly interrupts the teacher by asking to hold the book. The teacher often responds by handing Sally the book. In this case, the challenging behaviour functions to provide Sally with *access to an object/item* (i.e. the book). Marcus and Vollmer (1996) addressed challenging behaviour that served the function of gaining access to an object in three participants, one of whom was a five-year-old girl with Down syndrome. The child with Down syndrome engaged in self-injurious behaviour, including hitting her head or hands on a wall, floor, or table, and aggression towards others in order to access an object.

Learners may also engage in challenging behaviour to gain *attention*. For example, during small group lessons in her third grade class, Vanessa nudges the child next to her and makes faces and silly comments. The other children repeatedly tell her, "Stop," but giggle at the comments, providing Vanessa with attention for inappropriate behaviours. The function of obtaining attention is often alluded to in the descriptions of the Down syndrome behavioural phenotype (e.g. Fidler, 2005; Wishart, 1993, 1998, 2007). In a study with adolescents, Shaw and Simms (2009) found the challenging behaviour (screaming and swearing) of two participants with Down syndrome served to access attention. Millichap *et al.* (2003) found adults with Down syndrome and Alzheimer's disease showed increased problem behaviour (talking to self or stereotypic behaviour) in situations in which there was no contact with staff, suggesting a function to obtain attention.

Thus far, the functions we described are mediated by others. However, some behaviours serve a function that is *not* mediated by the social environment: rather the function involves internal stimulation. Challenging behaviour might serve to gain, or even escape/avoid, internal stimulation or sensory feedback, referred to as *automatic reinforcement*. For example, Renee grinds her teeth when unoccupied, resulting in automatic auditory and tactile stimulation thought to make her "feel good." Thompson, Iwata, Conners, and Roscoe (1999) examined the function of and intervention for self-injurious behaviour in four adults, one of whom had Down syndrome. To determine the function of challenging behaviour, Thompson *et al.* manipulated antecedents and consequences for challenging behaviour by providing attention, escape from demands, and free access to activities following challenging behaviour, as well as leaving the participant alone. The participant with Down syndrome showed the highest rates of hitting her head when left alone, suggesting the behaviour served an automatic reinforcement function.

The same topography (i.e. form) of challenging behaviour (e.g. throwing materials, hitting, crawling under a desk, etc.) may serve different functions for different learners and even different functions for the same learner. For example, continuously asking for an item may result in access to that item in one situation (story time), but may result in gaining a great deal of attention within another situation (e.g. the music instructor stops and explains at length why the child needs to "wait" for the item, thus providing attention). One behaviour may also serve multiple functions at the same time (e.g. teeth grinding may provide internal stimulation and also result in attention as the teacher tries to "interrupt" the child's teeth grinding).

Determining function involves examining the context in which the behaviour occurs, including consequences, as described (Carr *et al.*, 1994), and antecedents (variables that occur prior to challenging behaviour), some of which are "cues" or "triggers" for challenging behaviour. For example, a particular peer may provide a great deal of attention (e.g. laughing, encouraging silly comments, etc.), more so than other peers. As a result, his/her presence indicates a greater likelihood that challenging behaviour will result in reinforcement. Similar to consequences, antecedents also provide information about what learners may be getting, or getting away from, by engaging in challenging behaviour.

Some antecedent variables have broader influences on the likelihood a learner will engage in either challenging or appropriate behaviour (Horner, Vaughn, Day, & Ard, 1996). These are referred to as contextual variables, setting events, setting factors, and motivating operations. We will refer to them as setting events. Setting events include aspects of the social, physical, and biological setting. Recall Vanessa, who nudges and makes jokes with her peers during small group lessons. If these lessons occur after a period of individual work (social setting event), then Vanessa will not have had attention and the value of attention as a reinforcer increases; thus, she is more likely to engage in challenging behaviour to obtain attention. McComas, Thompson, and Johnson (2003) evaluated the effects of providing pre-sessions of attention on challenging behaviour serving attention or escape functions. Two of the five participants had Down syndrome (Dan, 11, and Ari, 12 years old). Examination of antecedents and consequences showed Dan's behaviour served an attention-seeking function and Ari's behaviour served an escape function. To examine the effect of the setting event of attention on challenging behaviour, 10-minute pre-sessions involved either no attention from an adult or continuous social interaction. Dan (whose behaviour served to access attention) engaged in much higher rates of challenging behaviour when the adult did *not* interact with him prior to the activity and low rates after pre-sessions of attention. For learners who engaged in escape behaviour, pre-sessions of attention did not affect rates of challenging behaviour. McComas *et al.* (2003) showed how social setting events influence behaviour and also how the function of challenging behaviour influences the effectiveness of intervention with respect to setting events.

The physical setting might also increase the likelihood of challenging behaviour. For example, recall Joe, who whines and fidgets in the presence of task demands. When there are different group lessons occurring simultaneously in his classroom, the noise level rises (physical setting event) and Joe is more likely to whine and fidget when asked to complete a task than when the room is quiet.

Biological conditions may also operate as setting events. There is an association between challenging behaviour and pain and physical illness in individuals with developmental disabilities (Carr & Owen-DeSchryver, 2007; Carr, Smith, Giacin, Whelan, & Pancari, 1993). Carr *et al.* (1993) demonstrated how task demands (the trigger/cue) presented when the participant was in pain from menses (biological setting event) were associated with challenging behaviour in four women with intellectual disabilities.

There are a number of biological conditions, including medical issues, that may function as setting events for challenging behaviour in learners with Down syndrome. Ear infections and upper respiratory infections are common in learners with Down syndrome (Roizen, 1996) and are associated with increased challenging behaviour (e.g. Carr & Owen-DeSchryver, 2007; Kennedy & Meyer, 1996). Poor sleep has been shown to function as a setting event for challenging behaviour (e.g. Kennedy & Meyer, 1996; O'Reilly, 1995); sleep deprivation associated with sleep apnoea or other sleep disturbances is also common in learners with Down syndrome (Cotton & Richdale, 2010). We have encountered several cases in which sleep served as a setting event for challenging behaviour, one of which we reported in Feeley and Jones (2008). Nathan, a five-year-old boy with Down syndrome, tended to stay up late and wake early in the morning. Observation and parent reports about sleep showed an increase in noncompliant behaviour during academic tasks on days following poor sleep.

Setting events are often thought of as temporary conditions that have the effect of momentarily changing the value of consequences and rate of related challenging behaviour. McGill (1999) suggested that more enduring biological conditions may also be setting events. Autism may be a biological setting event with the effect of decreasing the value of social consequences; as a result, behaviour associated with social interaction would (and does) occur at very low rates. Prader-Willi syndrome results from an abnormality on the fifteenth chromosome and is associated with learning difficulties and social and motor impairments, along with increased appetite and weight control issues. Prader-Willi syndrome may be a biological setting event with the effect of increasing the reinforcing value of food; as a result, behaviour associated with gaining food would (and does) occur at very high rates. Robinson (2012) described further how characteristics of disorders may be part of the context for challenging behaviour. Some characteristics of a disorder may overlap with medical conditions, while others may be characteristics of the behavioural phenotype associated with the disorder. Focusing on Down syndrome specifically, Feeley and Jones (2006) suggested the context for challenging behaviour in learners with Down syndrome may be difficult tasks and availability of social partners. Down syndrome may be a setting event with the effect of changing the value of certain consequences; specifically, the effect is that attention is highly valued while task-related consequences are less valuable, resulting in increased likelihood of challenging behaviour to escape/avoid difficult tasks and access attention.

Model for understanding challenging behaviour in learners with Down syndrome

Environmental variables along with characteristics of the Down syndrome behavioural phenotype are influences on challenging behaviour that form a model we can use for understanding challenging behaviour. Figure 4.1 outlines this model, including setting events, antecedents, and consequences in relation to characteristics of the Down syndrome behavioural phenotype as part of setting events for challenging behaviour. Specifically, characteristics such as poor task persistence and impaired requesting may decrease the value of task-related consequences and increase the value of escape/avoidance of difficult tasks. In addition, associated medical issues (e.g. upper respiratory infections and sleep difficulties) may be common biological setting events, increasing the likelihood of challenging behaviour. Then, in the presence of antecedents, such as requests to begin a difficult task, the learner may engage in challenging behaviour. A pattern that seems to emerge in the literature is a topography (form) of behaviour that is also overly social and engaging. The challenging aspect is not related to what the child does (e.g. clapping hands and asking questions); rather it is the frequency, intensity, or the context in which the behaviour occurs that makes it challenging. Finally, consequences in the literature relate to escaping/avoiding demands and obtaining attention. Figure 4.2 illustrates this model with Vanessa, who demonstrates challenging behaviour in the form of nudging her peers and making silly comments and faces to access peer attention. This model combines behaviour analysis with research on the Down syndrome behavioural phenotype and suggests the need to consider these variables in assessment and development of intervention.

This model suggests that knowing the characteristics of the corresponding behavioural phenotype for Down syndrome can help guide understanding of the functions of challenging behaviour. The function of challenging behaviour is identified through functional behaviour assessment (FBA) (Cooper, Heron, & Heward, 2007). The reader is referred to Carr *et al.* (1994) and O'Neill *et al.* (1997) for more information about FBA. An FBA involves evaluation of events that occur prior to and following challenging behaviour via an interview process with teachers, parents, and other caregivers, as well as direct observation and sometimes examination of the behaviour within carefully contrived situations in which antecedents and consequences are manipulated (functional analysis).

Recognizing the potential for increased escape and attention-seeking behaviour as well as biological conditions such as illness and poor sleep helps narrow the field of antecedents, consequences, and functions to examine in an FBA for a learner with Down syndrome. However, the scant functional assessment and intervention literature involving participants with Down syndrome does not provide enough information to

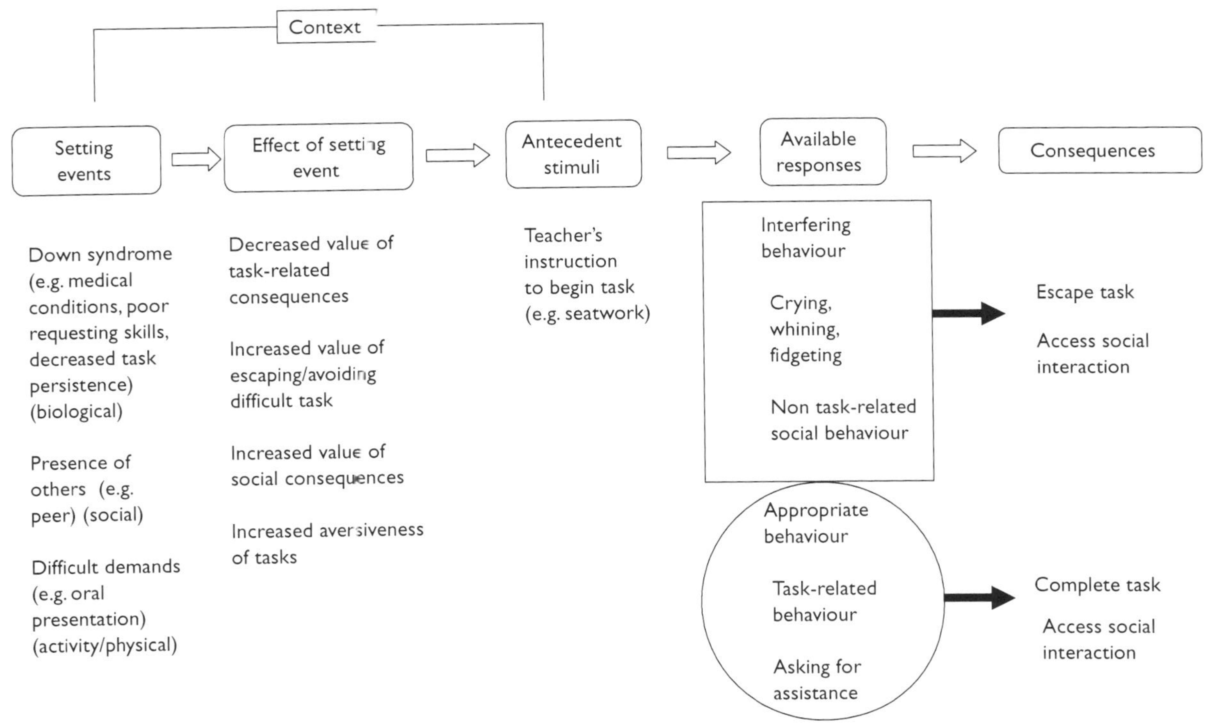

Figure 4.1 Model for understanding the roles and characteristics of the behavioural phenotype and environmental events, including setting events, antecedent triggers, and consequences related to challenging behaviour in learners with Down syndrome.

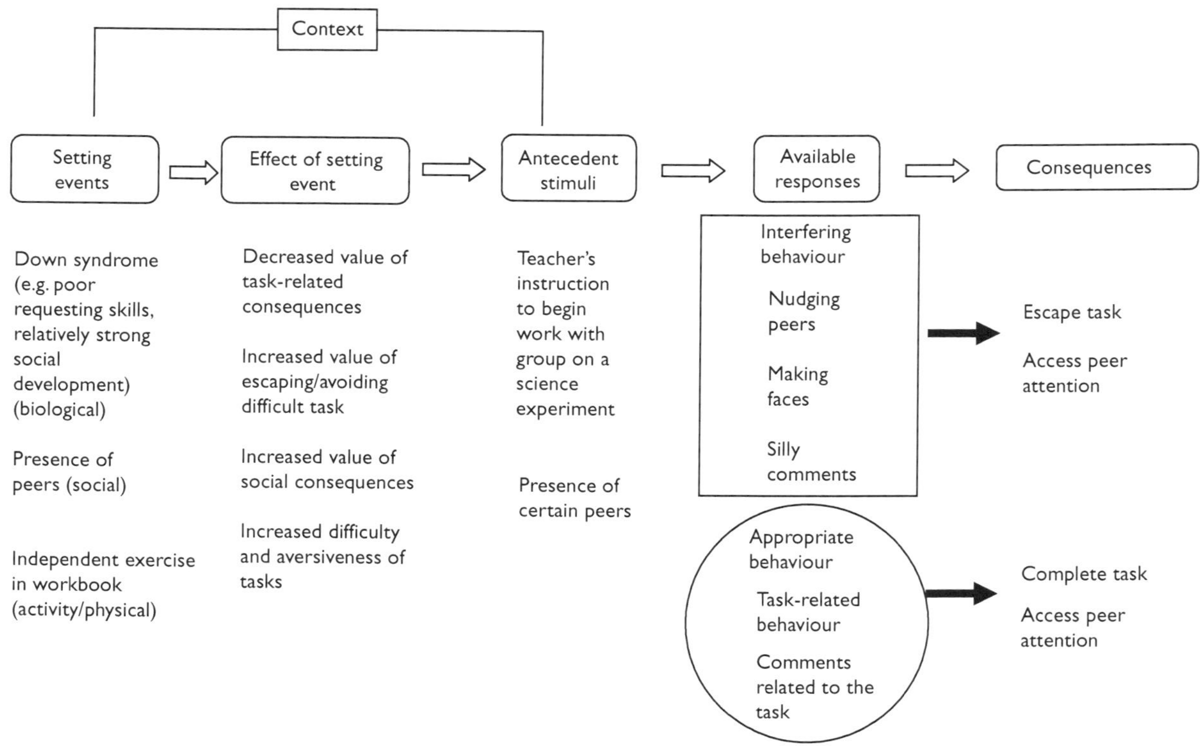

Figure 4.2 Model for understanding the roles and characteristics of the behavioural phenotype and environmental events, including setting events, antecedent triggers, and consequences related to Vanessa's challenging behaviour.

confirm increased rates of escape or attention functions or other contextual variables related to problem behaviour. A comparative approach involving learners with Down syndrome and those with other disorders would help demonstrate differences in functions and contexts. In addition, there is no literature linking behavioural phenotype to the FBA process or the idea of Down syndrome as a setting event. In a study with children with autism and children with Fragile X syndrome (a result of a mutation in a gene on the X chromosome and associated with intellectual disability, challenging behaviour, social anxiety, and communication impairments), Robinson Joy (2009) compared rates of challenging behaviour in situations identified as behaviourally phenotypic situations associated with challenging behaviour to a control condition. For learners with Fragile X syndrome, she examined situations commonly associated with social anxiety, specifically those involving novel people and environments. Results showed much higher rates of challenging behaviour in the situations with novel people/environments than in a similar situation that did not involve novel people or environments, demonstrating that behavioural phenotype may serve as a contextual variable. Robinson Joy went on to demonstrate the effectiveness of an intervention based upon this functional assessment. It is possible to take a similar approach with learners with Down syndrome, recognizing how characteristics associated with the behavioural phenotype interact with environmental variables to influence performance in the classroom. This approach could be used to examine the utility of combining information about behavioural phenotype with evidence-based assessment of challenging behaviour to better understand factors related to challenging behaviour in Down syndrome. This knowledge could be used to develop interventions.

Intervention to enhance motivation to engage in instructional activities

Basing intervention on an FBA results in greater likelihood of success (than not assessing the function of behaviour) (Carr *et al.*, 1999). Interventions may focus on changing antecedents (immediate and/or setting events), teaching appropriate behaviour, and/or changing consequences (for both challenging and appropriate behaviour). Often intervention involves several strategies that focus on all of these aspects; however, much of the research isolates one or two strategies to demonstrate their effectiveness. Although there is extensive research supporting the effectiveness of this approach, only a small portion of the studies involve learners with Down syndrome.

The model presented in Figure 4.1 and exemplified in Figure 4.2 illustrates the influence of multiple variables relevant to Down syndrome that should be considered during an FBA and in the design of interventions. In this section, we will discuss intervention strategies to address these influences, with an eye towards the specific aspects relevant to Down syndrome. We will discuss a few illustrative studies focusing on escape and attention functions because of the potential relation to behavioural phenotype and relevance to classroom performance.

Intervention strategies that involve manipulating setting events and immediate antecedents result in decreases in challenging behaviour (Luiselli, 2008). In our case study of Nathan (Feeley & Jones, 2008), we found that he engaged in escape-motivated challenging behaviour when he had not slept well. On school days when Nathan's parents reported he had not slept well the night before, Nathan's teachers modified the antecedents by decreasing academic demands associated with challenging behaviour and increased available reinforcement by having Nathan engage in more preferred activities. Nathan's challenging behaviour decreased.

Other setting events may include aspects of the physical setting or activity such as task difficulty, a variable related to challenging behaviour in children with Down syndrome. A *high probability request sequence* may be particularly useful for challenging behaviour serving an escape function in the presence of difficult demands. A high probability request sequence involves the presentation of several instructions or requests to which the learner is highly likely to comply or respond appropriately. Immediately after the appropriate response, the interventionist provides reinforcement. After a few high probability requests, the interventionist presents the instruction to which the learner has previously responded with challenging behaviour (the low probability request), resulting in an increased likelihood that the learner will comply. High probability requests may reduce the value of escape and, in turn, result in a decrease in challenging behaviour associated with the low probability request. Mace *et al.* (1988) examined a high probability request sequence in a series of experiments, two of which involved learners with Down syndrome (both adult males). In both cases, introduction of the high probability request sequence intervention resulted in improved compliance and even the amount of time it took for one of those participants to respond (response latency).

Romaniuk *et al.* (2002) examined *choices* (amongst instructional assignments) as an antecedent intervention for challenging behaviour in several participants with developmental disabilities, one of whom, a nine-year-old girl, had Down syndrome. For three participants, challenging behaviour served an escape function; for the other three, including the participant with Down syndrome, challenging behaviour served an attention-seeking function. Choice was only effective for the participants whose behaviour served an escape function. For participants whose challenging behaviour served an attention-seeking function, intervention involved changing the consequences for challenging behaviour and appropriate behaviour using *extinction* and *differential reinforcement of alternative behaviour* (DRA). Extinction involves no longer providing reinforcement for a behaviour; for example, if screaming always resulted in the learner getting a cookie, extinction would involve no longer providing a cookie when the learner screamed. In Romaniuk *et al.* (2002), extinction was implemented by the interventionists no longer providing attention contingent on challenging behaviour. Interventionists also implemented DRA by providing frequent praise for engaging in the task. Thus, DRA involves reinforcing an alternative behaviour (in this case, task engagement) to challenging behaviour as a way to decrease the occurrence of challenging behaviour. This two-component intervention resulted in reductions in challenging behaviour for the participants whose behaviour served an attention-seeking function. Romaniuk *et al.* clearly illustrate the importance of matching intervention strategies to the function of the learner's behaviour.

When the alternative behaviour in a DRA procedure is a communicative behaviour that serves the same function as the challenging behaviour, the intervention is referred to as *functional communication training* (FCT) (Carr & Durand, 1985). For example, teaching the learner to ask to take a break from a task or to begin a conversation provides the learner with a more appropriate behaviour that should result in access to the same consequences. In Hetzroni and Roth (2003), one of five participants had Down syndrome. The 19-year-old man's challenging behaviour served to escape from work tasks in his classroom. Part of the intervention involved FCT in which the man was taught to use a speech-generating device programmed with a series of messages related to the work tasks. When the antecedent triggers for challenging behaviour occurred, but before the participant engaged in challenging behaviour, the teacher prompted him to use the speech-generating device (appropriate communicative behaviour). Prompting involved verbal instruction, gesturing to the device, and/or physical assistance. The teacher provided natural consequences consisting of whatever the learner requested (e.g. if he communicated, "No more," then the teacher ended the task, providing a break). Intervention resulted in decreases in challenging behaviour for all participants.

In Hetzroni and Roth (2003), intervention involved teaching appropriate communication skills as well as ensuring the appropriate communicative behaviour resulted in the participant accessing reinforcers related to the function of the challenging behaviour. Specifically, if the participant communicated "No more," the teacher ended the task (escape function). Lalli, Browder, Mace, and Brown (1993) also changed the consequences for challenging and appropriate behaviour for three participants. One participant, Bob, a 10-year-old boy with Down syndrome, engaged in aggressive behaviour serving an attention-seeking function. Bob was taught to wave his hand and give his teacher an object to initiate social interaction (FCT), which resulted in his teacher providing attention. The teacher also withheld attention following challenging behaviour (i.e. extinction). Each participant's challenging behaviour decreased and appropriate behaviour increased.

Considering that a disorder in itself may change the value of certain consequences suggests those consequences may be particularly effective in changing behaviour. Engagement with and/or completion of task demands, for example, may not provide sufficient reinforcement in the face of difficult tasks for a student with Down syndrome; attention and interaction may be much more valuable. In setting up contingencies within intervention, this should be considered so that appropriate task behaviour results in highly valuable consequences (i.e. social interaction), building on the social strength characteristic of learners with Down syndrome. Although not discussed in relation to the Down syndrome behavioural phenotype, Repp and Karsh (1994) used attention and social interaction as a reinforcer for more appropriate behaviour to decrease challenging behaviour serving an escape function in a nine-year-old girl with Down syndrome. Intervention involved extinction (i.e. no longer providing attention following challenging behaviour) and DRA (in this case, providing social interaction in the form of praise and pats on the back when the learner engaged in the tasks). At the end of a task during which the participant did not engage in challenging behaviour, teachers interacted with the participant for several minutes. Thus, social interaction was used to prevent challenging behaviour by providing it throughout the task and as a reinforcer contingent on appropriate behaviour.

Vollmer, Iwata, Zarcone, Smith, and Mazaleski (1993) examined challenging behaviour in three adult women, one of whom had Down syndrome. Her self-injurious behaviour functioned to obtain attention. Vollmer *et al.* compared an intervention in which attention was provided following periods of time during which the learner did not engage in self-injurious behaviour (*differential reinforcement of other behaviour*—DRO) to an intervention in which attention was provided at regular intervals of time regardless of the participant's behaviour (*noncontingent reinforcement*—NCR). For all three participants, both interventions resulted in decreases in challenging behaviour.

For the participant with Down syndrome, NCR resulted in greater decreases in challenging behaviour initially.

When Shaw and Simms (2009) addressed the challenging behaviour (screaming and swearing) that served to access attention for the two adolescents with Down syndrome, intervention involved ***differential reinforcement of lower rates of behaviour*** (DRL). During DRL, reinforcement occurred at the end of a period of time during which the number of responses did not exceed a predetermined criterion. The criterion decreased as the participant successfully reduced engagement in challenging behaviour. In addition, teachers used a system of marking the occurrence of challenging behaviour with a verbal warning followed by a token (a visual representation). The verbal warning reminded the participant of the behaviour in which he should engage to earn the reinforcer (e.g. hand-raising to obtain the teacher's attention). If the participants had less than a predetermined number of tokens, they earned a reinforcer. At the same time, appropriate attention-seeking behaviour (raising hand) was acknowledged and reinforced with praise. Challenging behaviour decreased for all participants.

This sample of literature demonstrates that there are evidence-based strategies that can be used to address challenging behaviour that severely affects classroom performance in learners with Down syndrome. Future research, specifically with learners with Down syndrome, would allow for greater incorporation of behavioural phenotype characteristics into the FBA and intervention development processes. Using the model presented in Figure 4.1 provides greater opportunity to prevent challenging behaviour through increased attention to early patterns, a streamlined assessment of common variables associated with challenging behaviour in learners with Down syndrome, and the use of strengths in intervention. Doing so may maximize the effectiveness and efficiency of intervention, significantly improving outcomes in terms of challenging behaviour, classroom performance, and overall quality of life. Challenging behaviour is just one area that may impact classroom performance.

Addressing pivotal skills

Several of the skill areas identified as weaknesses that are part of the Down syndrome behavioural phenotype are critical to classroom performance. These weaknesses may be "pivotal" skill areas that, once addressed, result in collateral changes in a range of related areas of development (Koegel, Koegel, Harrower, & Carter, 1999). This cascade of effect maximizes outcomes. In autism, there are several demonstrations of interventions to address pivotal skills with improvements in a broad range of outcome measures. For example, joint attention refers to social communication, involving two people sharing attention on an object or event (Bakeman & Adamson, 1984). Joint attention is significantly impaired in learners with autism (Mundy, Sigman, Ungerer, & Sherman, 1986) and appears to be a pivotal skill (Mundy & Crowson, 1997) in that the corresponding interventions also result in collateral changes in language and social development (Bono, Daley, & Sigman, 2004; Loveland & Landry, 1986; Smith, Mirenda, & Zaidman-Zait, 2007). Thus, the identification of an impairment as a pivotal skill has resulted in the design and demonstration of effective intervention strategies that improve outcomes for this population of learners.

The absence of pivotal skills in a learner's repertoire significantly limits learning and development; in contrast, their acquisition opens doors for opportunity and growth. In this section, we will discuss impairments that are part of the Down syndrome behavioural phenotype that may be pivotal skills. In addition, we will discuss the application of many intervention strategies discussed earlier in the chapter to teach other behaviours, including attention to task and communication.

Attending to and engaging in instructional tasks

To benefit from instructional opportunities in the classroom, a learner's attention should be directed towards the task—that is, instructional stimuli (i.e. the person presenting instruction [referred to as interventionist], instructions/cues presented by the interventionist, and the materials). For many children with Down syndrome, attending to tasks can be particularly difficult. For some, difficulty attending to tasks may be related to comorbid diagnoses, such as an attention deficit hyperactivity disorder, for which children with Down syndrome are at increased risk (Ekstein, Blick, Weill, Kay, & Berger, 2011). Attending to a task, though, also reflects a pattern of responding in children with Down syndrome that is different than that seen in many other learners with and without intellectual disability. For example, Kasari and Freeman (2001) found children with Down syndrome took longer to begin a task, looked to an adult and requested help more frequently, and took longer to complete tasks than a comparison group of children with intellectual disability as well as typically developing children matched on mental age. Because attention directly impacts level of academic attainment during the school years (Turner, Alborz, & Gayle, 2008), it is likely a pivotal skill warranting intervention.

Antecedent intervention strategies focus on changing the *way* in which teaching opportunities are presented to increase the likelihood that the learner will perform the desired response (Cooper *et al.*, 2007). Providing *choices* is one way of presenting instructional opportunities that can enhance attention to a task (Cole & Levinson, 2002). Choices (discussed earlier in this chapter in relation to challenging behaviour) may be offered about the actual tasks to be completed, the order in which to complete them, how to complete tasks (e.g. on the computer or in pencil), or even where to complete tasks (e.g. at the learner's desk or a group table). Providing learners with a choice results in increases in compliance to requests and decreases in challenging behaviour, as well as increased time on task (Ramsey, DaShaunda, Patterson, & Kennedy, 2010). Merely changing from a verbal direction (i.e. "Put the sheet in the front of the folder") to a choice question ("Do you want to put the sheet in the front or back of the folder?") resulted in more steps of a task being completed prior to challenging behaviour in learners with intellectual disabilities, one of whom had Down syndrome (Cole & Levinson, 2002).

Another strategy that modifies *how* instructional opportunities are presented involves interspersing easier tasks with more challenging tasks. This might involve using a *high probability task sequence* (discussed earlier in this chapter with respect to escape-motivated challenging behaviour). A high probability request sequence improves the performance of social communication (Sanchez-Fort, Brady, & Davis, 1995) and self-care skills (Mace & Belfiore, 1990; Mace *et al.*, 1988), as well as academic tasks. For example, a high probability request sequence resulted in a decrease in the latency to initiate non-preferred mathematics tasks (Belfiore, Lee, Vargas, & Skinner, 1997; Belfiore, Lee, Scheeler, & Klein, 2002), an increase in the rate of mathematical items completed (Hutchinson & Belfiore, 1998), and enhanced performance during handwriting and journal writing tasks (Lee, Belfiore, Scheeler, Hua,

& Smith, 2004; Lee & Laspe, 2003). Although this research involved learners with disabilities other than Down syndrome, the application of a high probability request sequence with learners with Down syndrome may be particularly promising with respect to improving attention to (and subsequent participation in) academic tasks.

Inherent in the application of a high probability request sequence is reinforcement for completion of high probability requests that in turn increases the likelihood of continued responding (to access reinforcement) to the low probability request (Cooper *et al.*, 2007). In some studies of high probability requests within academic tasks, the learner independently progressed through the tasks, with the familiarity of the tasks and the likelihood of the learner getting the high probability task items correct, believed to function as a reinforcing event (Belfiore *et al.*, 1997). However, familiarity of the requests and their completion may not function as reinforcers for many learners with Down syndrome. Demonstrations of the effectiveness of high probability request sequences with learners with Down syndrome all involved social interaction in response to the high probability requests (e.g. Mace *et al.*, 1988; Davis, Brady, Williams, & Hamilton, 1992). Comparative studies to determine whether high probability request sequences with social consequences are more effective for learners with Down syndrome remain to be conducted.

Another antecedent strategy for enhancing a learner's attention to and performance during instruction entails carefully considering a learner's *preferences* when choosing and/or developing instructional materials. As Foster-Johnson, Ferro, and Dunlap (1994) demonstrated, learners with developmental disabilities (without Down syndrome) between nine and 14 years of age exhibited fewer challenging behaviours and an increase in the target task behaviours (i.e. coin identification, tracing numbers) when engaged with highly preferred instructional materials. To assess preference, learners were exposed to a series of materials that contained the target task (coin identification). Preference was assessed by how often the learner approached the different materials, the extent to which the learner interacted with the materials, and the level of resistance to having the materials removed. The task was then presented in two conditions, one with high-preference materials and the other with low-preference materials. For two of the three learners, high-preference materials resulted in a decrease in challenging behaviour and an increase in desirable behaviour, such as appropriate vocalizations/verbalizations, following directions, and touching/manipulating materials.

Again, drawing upon research related to the Down syndrome behavioural phenotype provides us with information regarding activity preferences of children with Down syndrome. Sellinger, Hodapp, and Dykens (2006) examined activity preferences in children with Down syndrome compared to children with Williams syndrome (syndrome caused by the deletion of genes on chromosome 7, which is characterized by medical problems and intellectual disability, but strong language abilities), Prader-Willi syndrome, and children with intellectual disabilities of unknown origin. Sellinger *et al.* found children with Down syndrome showed a preference for activities related to music (not playing an instrument, but listening or dancing to music). Thus, music-related activities may be more likely to be preferred and could be used to increase attention to tasks. The social strengths also suggest the likelihood that making tasks more social may increase attention to those tasks; the learner may be more likely to approach the task because the reinforcing value of engaging in the task is increased. For example, a writing task can involve social aspects, such as writing a letter to a friend or family member, that may increase the learner's motivation to engage in the task.

It is important to note that antecedent strategies may be used in isolation or in combination to form a package intervention. For example, Dunlap, Kern-Dunlap, Clarke, and Robbins (1991) decreased the length of instructional sessions, interspersed easy and more difficult tasks, arranged activities so that the content was of interest to the student, and provided choice among activities/materials. Intervention led to near zero (only one occurrence) levels of challenging behaviour as well as substantial increases in on-task behaviour for a 12-year-old student with severe disabilities.

Thus far, we have focused on antecedent strategies (addressing the presentation of tasks) to improve attention to task. Attention to tasks can also be enhanced by systematically providing the learner with reinforcing consequences for approaching/completing a task. Brooks, Todd, Tofflemoyer, and Horner (2003) demonstrated the use of social reinforcement to increase attention to task for Hannah, a 10-year-old girl with Down syndrome. Hannah's functional assessment indicated she engaged in high rates of attention-motivated behaviour in the form of off-task behaviour (e.g. making faces at peers, drawing, playing, and refusing to work) during independent work and group instruction. Hannah was taught a self-management system consisting of a cassette player that signalled her to note on a self-monitoring card a "+" or "0" reflecting whether she was academically engaged for the time interval that passed between signals. Hannah was also taught a more appropriate response for recruiting attention; specifically, she was taught to raise her hand to recruit her teacher's attention. Although the amount of time Hannah engaged in academic tasks did not increase during group work activities, her academic engagement increased during seatwork in her fourth grade classroom and the resource room.

Brooks *et al.*'s (2003) intervention included reinforcement as a critical component to increase attention to task. We have suggested that social consequences and escape/avoidance of difficult tasks may be of particularly high value as consequences for learners with Down syndrome. Both types of consequences can be used contingent on more appropriate behaviour—in this case, attention to task. For example, engagement in instructional activities can result in earned time with a favourite peer, a phone call/email to a family member, or engagement in another academic task with someone's assistance. Attending to task for some period of time can also result in removal of additional difficult task demands; in this case, using escape contingencies but to increase attention to task. Even consequences in the form of social praise delivered to the learner's peers have been demonstrated to enhance attending skills within classroom settings (referred to as vicarious reinforcement) (Kazdin, 1973).

Equally important as delivering reinforcing consequences for attending to instructional activities is withholding them when the learner's attention is diverted to noninstructional stimuli. Often we react when a child stops attending to the instructional task (i.e. "plays" with instructional materials or diverts his/her attention). Keeping in mind the likelihood of behaviour of a learner with Down syndrome being reinforced by social interaction, approaching, speaking, or even establishing eye contact is likely to result in an increase in the behaviours (desirable or undesirable) that preceded the interaction. Even verbal encouragement ("Please write your name") or scolding ("Big boys should write their name") can serve to increase the likelihood that the learner will show poor attention. Alternatively, the interventionist can withhold attention or react in a way that purposefully removes access to social interaction when the learner does not attend, thus decreasing the future likelihood of poor attention. Drash, Raver, Murrin, and Tudor (1989) removed attention using visual screening and light dimming following incorrect responses. Combined with positive reinforcement, this increased vocal responding in preschoolers with Down syndrome. Within classroom situations, this can be done by having the teacher just turn his/her head in a different direction following inattentive behaviour that functions to obtain attention. Merely withholding social interaction when the learner *does not* attend to the task and interacting with the learner when she/he *does* attend to the desired task can improve attention to task and in turn has the potential to enhance performance.

Expressive communication

There are a number of areas of expressive language, including verbal imitation, requesting, conversation, vocabulary, and grammar, in which learners with Down syndrome show impairments. Impairments in expressive language have extensive repercussions within the classroom. Poor verbal imitation limits opportunities for expanding a learner's expressive repertoire through modelling more sophisticated expressive language. With a limited communicative repertoire, interaction with peers is negatively affected. Impairments in expressive language mean learners may not have a socially acceptable communicative response to have their needs met and may engage in challenging behaviour. Expressive impairments also limit a learner's ability to respond to teacher questions, contribute to class discussions, and participate in group lessons, and may mask abilities because a learner cannot readily share his/her knowledge. Because of its importance as a foundation of expressive language, we will begin by considering verbal imitation.

Verbal imitation

Imitation requires a learner to first attend to the model that should be imitated and then engage in the same or an approximation of the behaviour modelled. A learner can imitate either what is heard or what is seen. Visually (what is seen) based imitation is a relative strength in learners with Down syndrome (Hodapp *et al.*, 1992; Rast & Meltzoff, 1995). Imitation of auditory stimuli, particularly verbal imitation, is a relative weakness (Mahoney, Glover, & Finger, 1981; Rondal, 1980; Rondal, Lambert, & Sohier, 1981). Impairment in auditory imitation directly impacts the ability of the child with Down syndrome to benefit from verbal models to expand his/her expressive language. Providing a model is a common instructional strategy used in both natural settings and intervention settings. To illustrate, a parent takes syrup from the cupboard, shows it to the child and says, "This is syrup. Can you say syrup? Say 'syrup'." Most children respond readily to such requests, emitting closer and closer approximations of the modelled word or sound. Lack of imitation can prevent the learner with Down syndrome from benefiting from naturally occurring opportunities to learn expressive language. It also prevents the learner from reaping the benefits of several speech and language interventions dependent on the learner imitating verbal models (i.e. peer modelling, video modelling, milieu language training).

An evidence-based behaviour analytic strategy to teach verbal imitation involves modelling a behaviour for the child to imitate and providing reinforcement for closer approximations to the model (Ross & Greer, 2003). Once taught, imitation maintains over time and learners generalize imitation to conditions not present during instruction (e.g. across individuals) and begin to imitate different sounds/words (i.e. begin to imitate targets that were not specifically taught) (Eikeseth & Nesset, 2003; Garcia, Baer, & Firestone, 1971; Lovaas, Berberich, Perloff, & Schaeffer, 1966; Schroeder & Baer, 1972). In our work with very young children with Down syndrome (Feeley, Jones, Blackburn, & Bauer, 2011), we systematically taught toddlers who did not imitate to imitate vocal models and found some generalization to new sounds. Importantly, having taught verbal imitation, we then used models to prompt vocal responses during requesting situations.

Taking this approach, it is important to determine if the child is able to imitate visual models. If not, instruction can begin by teaching the child to imitate visual models and then proceed by teaching the child to imitate verbal models (Baer & Sherman, 1964; Sherman, 1965). This strategy may be particularly effective for learners with Down syndrome in light of their relative strengths in visual imitation. Another advantage to first teaching imitation of a visual model is that it is easier to prompt the correct response. For example, the interventionist can provide the visual model (e.g. tapping the table) while simultaneously prompting the learner to perform the behaviour (i.e. the interventionist can tap the table with one hand and physically prompt the learner to tap the table using his/her other hand). The correct response would then be followed by the delivery of reinforcement. This can result in the establishment of an imitative repertoire from which verbal imitation instruction can proceed. Although not systematically examined in Feeley *et al.* (2011), that is the approach we have taken. Intervention began with ensuring learners readily imitated visual models such as gross and fine motor movements as well as actions on objects (e.g. pushing a car). Once children readily imitated visual models, the interventionist introduced opportunities to imitate verbal models.

Requesting

Learners with Down syndrome show specific impairments in requesting, with greater impairment within situations that involve instrumental requests (i.e. requests for objects, requests for assistance to access objects) compared to social requests (requests for social interaction with an adult) (Fidler, Philofsky, Hepburn, & Rogers, 2005). There are several demonstrations of interventions to teach appropriate requests to heterogeneous groups of participants, some of whom have Down syndrome, to replace challenging behaviour (Hetzroni & Roth, 2003; Lalli *et al.*, 1993). Hemmeter, Ault, Collins, and Meyer (1996) used specific prompts and reinforcement to increase expressive vocabulary (e.g. requests) in elementary school students with developmental disabilities, some of whom had Down syndrome.

Infants with Down syndrome fail to demonstrate gaze shifting between an object and adult, pointing and vocalizing to request. Naturalistic teaching strategies (e.g. prelinguistic milieu teaching) show mixed results (Yoder & Warren, 2002; Fey *et al.*, 2006). Jones, Feeley, and colleagues took a behaviour analytic approach to addressing requesting that also considered how to incorporate areas of strength in intervention. To address impairments in instrumental requests, beginning intervention with more social requests (for which children with Down syndrome do not show as much impairment) may provide a foundation on which to progress to more instrumental requests. In addition, pairing social consequences (likely reinforcers) with the natural object consequences (which may not function as reinforcers initially) for instrumental requests during early phases of intervention may result in the natural object consequences beginning to function as reinforcers. We took this approach with very young children with Down syndrome who were taught to request continued social interaction with an object and then instrumental requests involving assistance accessing an object (Feeley *et al.*, 2011; Jones, Feeley, & Blackburn, 2010).

Extending this approach to school-aged learners, instrumental requesting opportunities can be created with a built-in social component to begin to address this area of impairment. For example, place a game (that the learner has to play with someone else—the social component) or a book (that the child would like to have read aloud—the social component) in a sealed container or on a high shelf. The form of request taught will vary with learner age and other abilities. If the learner imitates verbal models, a verbal prompt can be delivered (e.g. the interventionist says, "Say 'help, please'"). Alternatively, a verbal learner can be prompted via a textual prompt consisting of a card with the message "help, please" written on it (textual prompts will be discussed at length later in this chapter). However, for learners with a limited verbal repertoire, the learner may use a gesture (e.g. sign) or a symbol (e.g. line-drawn picture or photograph) to communicate the message. The application of this approach to school-age learners with Down syndrome requires empirical investigation.

Conversational exchanges

Expressive impairments in Down syndrome may begin with verbal imitation and requesting, but, with age, extend into conversation skills that involve initiating conversations, answering and asking questions, and engaging in reciprocal commenting (responding to a partner's comment with a similar comment). It is important that the learner has a foundation of verbal imitation. If the vocabulary to participate in conversation has already been taught in imitation, then imitative prompts can be used to assist the learner to use that vocabulary to participate in conversations. For example, having been taught to imitate the name of the town in which the learner lives, "Stony Brook," interventionists can now ask the question, "Where do you live?" and provide a model of the appropriate response.

We have relied on this strategy, building on verbal imitation to teach question answering (Bauer, Jones, & Feeley, in press) and spontaneous utterances (Feeley & Jones, 2008). This approach provides a way to prompt words within functional conversational situations. The foundation in verbal imitation also ensures that responses are clearly articulated, increasing the likelihood of successful interactions and addressing poor intelligibility associated with Down syndrome (Kumin, 1994).

Communication and attention to task are just two areas of impairment that affect classroom performance and for which we can take a behaviour analytic approach to intervention that also incorporates attention to characteristics of the behavioural phenotype. Expanding this approach to other areas of weakness that are also likely to impact classroom performance, such as short-term memory and problem solving, can only continue to improve interventions for learners with Down syndrome.

Building on strengths during classroom instruction

In the preceding discussion about interventions to address pivotal skills, we suggested ways that intervention might incorporate learner strengths as part of intervention. Similarly, we can draw on strengths, including visual processing and social interest to support learners with Down syndrome in the classroom in a variety of other ways.

Visual strengths

Strengths in visual processing have long been described as characteristic of learners with Down syndrome. Intervention can capitalize on this strength by incorporating the use of stimulus prompts which involve manipulating environmental features or adding stimuli to the environment to increase the likelihood of correct responding (Cooper *et al.*, 2007). Picture or textual prompts are one type of stimulus prompt that may capitalize on the visual processing strengths associated with Down syndrome. Picture prompts entail placing a photograph or line drawing that illustrates the desired behaviour (e.g. a photo of a student raising his hand) visible within the learner's environment (e.g. on learner's desk) (Krantz & McClannahan, 1993). Textual prompts entail placing written words in the learner's environment indicating the response that should be performed (e.g. a list of things to complete during independent seatwork placed on the front of the learner's work notebook).

Classroom performance can also be enhanced through the use of technology, which can be used to present visual or textual prompts. In our clinical work, we have incorporated visual prompts into academic instruction through the use of PowerPoint™ slides. For example, a particular topic of study is illustrated within a PowerPoint™ presentation and the learner independently reviews each PowerPoint™ slide. For example, when studying the history of Native Americans in eighth grade social studies, Mark's teacher made a PowerPoint™ highlighting the concepts Mark was responsible for sharing in a class presentation (e.g. Native Americans' housing, wardrobe, and strategies for hunting). Mark independently reviewed the slides so he could then describe each of the concepts illustrated in the PowerPoint™ to the class.

There are several advantages to using stimulus prompts within classroom environments. Specifically, simply pointing to a photo or written instruction allows the interventionist to discretely indicate to the learner what she/he should be doing versus interrupting the activity to give verbal directions. This can certainly be less stigmatizing within classroom settings, as the prompt is more likely to go unnoticed by other students. Another advantage is that, over time, the interventionist may be able to fade his/her presence and the visual prompt alone may control the learner's behaviour (i.e. the learner refers to the visual prompt posted on his desk, responding independently to the teacher's instructions presented to the entire class from the front of the classroom).

A visually based prompting strategy used to help learners navigate a school day and/or academic activity is a visual or activity schedule (Brown, 1991; Mesibov, Browder, & Kirkland, 2002). A visual schedule can illustrate for the learner a chain of tasks that need to be completed upon entering the classroom in the morning. A visual schedule may consist of a display of photographs illustrating each of the tasks; the schedule is posted in a location that the learner with Down syndrome can clearly see. Initially, interventionists may prompt the learner to check the visual schedule (e.g. the interventionist points to the schedule) and provide frequent reinforcement (e.g. for each item the learner completes within the chain of tasks). However, systematic fading of cues and reinforcement can lead to independent use of the visual schedule on the part of the learner (Anderson, Sherman, Sheldon, & McAdam, 1997; Pierce & Schreibman, 1994). Visual schedules can be used across a variety of activities, including preparing for an academic lesson (e.g. steps to follow to get science materials ready), within an academic lesson (e.g. tasks to be followed within a mathematics class), as well as during non-academic periods (e.g. steps to follow while ordering food in the cafeteria, playing a game at recess, or travelling around the school). Schedules also often involve a way to mark completion of each activity or step. For example, learners may remove the picture of a completed step, placing the picture in an "all done" compartment; learners may place a check mark in a box next to the picture of the step just competed.

In one example of visual schedules with learners with Down syndrome, Mechling and Gast (1997) examined the combined use of audio and visual prompting systems on independent task completion in four students with Down syndrome between 10 and 13 years of age. Photographs were affixed to a voice output device and, when selected, a recorded description of the step in the task sequence was played. For example, a photo of a bag of popcorn in a microwave oven was paired with the auditory message "Put bag in, like this" (p. 142). Verbal praise and access to a reinforcing activity were provided upon completion of the total task. The use of the self-prompting device resulted in an immediate increase in the number of correctly completed steps in the task for all four learners. Because both audio and visual prompts were used, it is not clear if either or a combination was responsible for changing the learners' performance. This warrants further investigation.

Another visually based strategy is *visual stories*, such as Carol Gray's Social Stories™ (Gray, 1994), which provide a description of a situation along with information about what will happen, what the learner should do and not do, and how the learner and others might behave. Visual stories can be represented in a variety of ways, including using written words, line drawings, and actual photographs. The learner may read the story him/herself or listen to an audio recording or as a caregiver reads. The learner reviews the story regularly and just prior to being in the situation about which the story is written. Several studies have empirically demonstrated the positive effects of using Social Stories™ with respect to making choices (Barry & Burlew, 2004), engaging in social interactions (Delano & Snell, 2006), and decreasing challenging behaviours (Crozier & Tincani, 2005); however, the participants were all learners with autism spectrum disorders. There are several aspects of visual stories that may lead to their effectiveness. Stories prime the learner with a preview of information or activities under low demand conditions (Wilde, Koegel, & Koegel, 1992) and often discuss contingencies for appropriate behaviour (Scattone, Tingstrom, & Wilczynski, 2006). Although the visual nature of these stories lends itself for use with learners with Down syndrome, empirical demonstrations are warranted.

Reinforcement can also be presented visually through the use of strategies such as token systems. Token systems involve the specification of a behaviour(s) to be addressed, tokens or points provided for engagement in the behaviours, and a "backup" reinforcer delivered to the learner in exchange for the tokens at the end of some period of time or accumulation of a number of tokens (Cooper *et al.*, 2007). Brooks *et al.* (2003) (discussed previously) implemented a token system with Hannah (a young girl with Down syndrome). Hannah's token system consisted of placing marks on a card that alerted her that she was closer to earning the opportunity to request attention from her teacher (the reinforcer). Blank spaces can be used to present visually how many tokens the learner must earn to receive reinforcement. The learner can see how close he/she is to receiving reinforcement. Dalton, Rubino, and Hislop (1973) demonstrated the use of a token system to decrease problem behaviour while at the same time enhancing performance in mathematics and language tasks in children with Down syndrome.

Social interest

The strengths in social development have long been noted for learners with Down syndrome. In addition to the interventions described previously that specifically incorporated social interaction to address pivotal skills (e.g. Feeley *et al.*, 2011), many tasks can be made social to increase learner engagement and success within the classroom and social interaction opportunities can be specifically planned as consequences for task performance. The grouping for instruction may also be one way to increase the social opportunities and, as a result, improve classroom performance. Taubman *et al.* (2001) examined the effectiveness of small group instruction with preschoolers, three of whom had Down syndrome. Within this small group, they provided three types of instruction: individual discrete trial instruction (the teaching opportunity was directed towards one member of the group), choral group instruction (the opportunity was presented concurrently for all participants in the group), and overlapping instruction (an opportunity was given to the group and then a highly individualized prompt was given to one child, with consequences delivered to all members concurrently). Tasks included pre-mathematics, language, and song activity tasks. A multiple baseline design across tasks indicated increases in performance across all three tasks. The authors reported anecdotally that children showed improvements in challenging behaviour. They suggested that escape-motivated behaviour may have decreased because the demands were distributed across the members of the group; attention-seeking behaviour may have decreased because of witnessing peers engaging in correct responding and receiving reinforcement (i.e. vicarious reinforcement). The group situation with opportunities to observe peers respond and receive reinforcement may be a particularly promising approach for learners with Down syndrome who show heightened social interest.

The application of strategies that address characteristic weaknesses and build upon the strengths of learners with Down syndrome can lead to successful classroom experiences for this population of learners from preschool through high school. These strategies can prevent challenging behaviour, facilitate the acquisition of skills across a range of developmental areas, and foster independence in learners with Down syndrome. There are at least a few studies suggesting that incorporating information about behavioural phenotype is effective. Continued demonstration of effectiveness is necessary, as well as direct comparison studies to determine whether greater effects emerge when interventions incorporate strengths than when they do not.

Intervention intensity: tailoring classroom instruction

One set of variables that may help optimize the effectiveness and efficiency of interventions for learners with Down syndrome discussed throughout this chapter is *intervention intensity*.

- With what intensity should a specific skill be taught for an individual learner with Down syndrome within a classroom setting?
- What intensity will maximize the likelihood of the learner acquiring specific skills so he/she can participate with his/her peers in classroom lessons?
- What intensity of intervention will ensure the learner acquires critical skills in a timely fashion to form a foundation of subsequent learning?

For example, for a six-year-old girl with Down syndrome, spelling instruction occurs during two classroom lessons each week, during which the learner has one opportunity to practise each of 10 new spelling words. Is this intense enough to result in acquisition of 10 new spelling words each week? If not, would spelling acquisition improve if intervention intensity increased to two spelling lessons each week with the class and two additional spelling lessons, one to one, with five opportunities to practise each new word? Although it is common for interventionists to assume that more is better, there has been almost no systematic study of intervention intensity, or how frequency, number, or length of intervention sessions (Warren, Fey, & Yoder, 2007) affects the performance of learners with Down syndrome.

Intervention intensity broadly refers to the quantity and quality of intervention (Warren *et al.*, 2007). Intensity may be directly related to whether learners acquire skills at all, how quickly they acquire those skills, and how well those skills generalize to other situations and maintain over time. These are all issues related to optimizing the efficiency and effectiveness of intervention.

Intervention intensity has often been approached by considering duration (i.e. minutes or hours per day, week, month, or year). Most notably, Lovaas' (1987) work with children with autism compared intensive behavioural intervention, provided at 40 hours per week, to the same intervention provided for only 10 hours per week. After approximately two years, Lovaas (1987) showed that almost 90 per cent of the children who received 40 or more hours of intervention demonstrated substantial improvements in intellectual functioning and transitioned to a "less restrictive" educational placement compared to those receiving less intense intervention. Subsequent research continues to show that intensity, as measured by duration, is an important factor to consider for individuals with autism (Eikeseth, Smith, Jaher, & Eldevik, 2002; McEachin, Smith, & Lovaas, 1993; Sallows & Graupner, 2005; Smith, Eikeseth, Klevstrand, & Lovaas, 1997).

Varied outcomes associated with different intervention intensities have been demonstrated in interventions for low birth weight, premature infants. Ramey *et al.* (1992) reported the intensity of intervention (as defined by the number of home visits, attendance at parent group meetings, and days attended at centres) had a strong positive relationship to the child's intellectual and social development at three years of age. Only a small proportion (1.9 per cent) of the children who fell in the highest participation group (the group with the top third frequency contact) had IQs below 70 at follow-up, but 13 per cent of the children within the lowest participation group (the group with the bottom third frequency contact) had IQ scores below 70 at follow-up.

Intervention intensity has also been attributed as the cause of poor outcomes of intervention. Warren *et al.* (2008) evaluated responsive education (an early communication intervention focused on responding to and reinforcing children's communicative attempts) and prelinguistic milieu teaching (intervention focused on establishing gaze, gesture, and vocalizations to comment and request) provided at low intensities (one hour per week over six months) to children with developmental delays. Following a lack of effects on communication and language development at six- and 12-month follow-up, they suggested that the intervention may be more effective at higher intensities of implementation.

While the duration approach to intensity is easily measured and understood, it neglects other important aspects of intensity that have the potential to alter outcomes. Warren *et al.* (2007) proposed a framework for examining intervention intensity. *Amount or quantity* of intervention includes several variables. *Dose* refers to the number of opportunities within an intervention session. For example, during a spelling lesson, there may be one opportunity to practise spelling a word, five opportunities for each word, or even more. *Dose frequency* refers to how often sessions or opportunities occur. For example, the spelling lesson (with the specified number of teaching opportunities) may occur once per week, three times per week, or every day. *Duration* refers to the length of time for which the intervention is delivered. For example, each spelling lesson may be 10, 20, or 30 minutes. These examples provide just a few values of intervention intensity. The range of values of each aspect of intervention intensity reflects a continuum from less to more intense.

Quality of intervention or *dose form* refers to *how* intervention occurs in terms of variables such as *who* conducts the intervention (professional vs. parent), the *setting* (school vs. home), and *student to interventionist ratio* (Jones & Feeley, 2011). Dose form has also been conceptualized on a continuum, with one end involving highly structured opportunities with repeated practice and the other end involving more naturally occurring instruction (Jones & Feeley, 2011). For example, spelling instruction targeting a month of the year (e.g. spelling the word February) may take place in a one-to-one format, with repeated opportunities presented in close temporal proximity by a teaching assistant who provides highly individualized reinforcers, or during a group lesson within a daily classroom routine (e.g. the student writing the heading on his journal entry) within the corresponding month (i.e. February) with one opportunity per lesson, in the absence of highly individualized consequences (e.g. verbal praise is provided to the group of students).

Only a few studies, all within speech and language intervention, have begun to approach intervention intensity using the model proposed by Warren *et al.* (2007). Two studies found non-significant effects of dose frequency (i.e. how often the intervention is implemented) on phonological awareness (Bellon-Harn, 2012) and semantic and morphologic performance (Ukrainetz, 2009), while others suggest greater dose frequency results in increased performance (Edeal & Gildersleeve-Neumann, 2011; Yoder, Fey, & Warren, 2012). Interestingly, after finding no main effect of dose frequency for milieu teaching, Yoder *et al.* (2012) examined covariates of outcomes and found children *without* Down syndrome benefited more from the more intense intervention than the less intense intervention. The authors suggest that aetiology represents an important moderator of intervention effect, and that children with Down syndrome required a different form of intervention, rather than just more of this same form of intervention.

It may be that skill areas that are part of the behavioural phenotype for a given disorder require a different intensity (quantity or quality) than other skill areas or those same skill areas for learners with a different disability. For example, Yoder and Warren (2002) and Fey *et al.* (2006) found conflicting results in their investigations of milieu teaching with responsive education for children with Down syndrome. Jones *et al.* (2010) suggested that these results may be due to the way skills were sequenced for intervention, especially for a skill such as requesting, which is characteristically impaired in learners with Down syndrome. Yoder and Warren (2002) began with more complex forms of requesting from the outset. Fey *et al.* (2006) began with a less complex form of requesting and then increased expectations in small steps as children progressed, which led to skill acquisition. This change in the form of intervention may explain the different findings.

For learners with Down syndrome, therefore, when addressing pivotal skills, more intensive intervention may be warranted, particularly if skill acquisition can be shown to happen faster with a more intensive intervention. For example, it may be that addressing verbal imitation warrants an intensive intervention, which, as we have demonstrated, is effective (Feeley *et al.*, 2011). Doing so may then enhance classroom performance as the learner will be able to perform following the teacher's model of words, phrases, etc. Presumably, once pivotal skills are acquired, more advanced skills can be acquired more quickly and perhaps the cascade of negative outcomes is also minimized more quickly and positive outcomes will be realized more quickly. With respect to enhancing the behaviour of learners with Down syndrome within classroom settings, if intensive intervention expediently addresses the skills needed for enhanced behaviour with corresponding decreases in challenging behaviour, then an intensive approach to intervention should be chosen to improve not only classroom performance, but overall quality of life.

Examining intervention intensity requires clearly defining dose, dose frequency, and dose form for particular interventions (Hoffman, 2009; Proctor-Williams, 2009). The first and second authors examined the effect of dose on skill acquisition in a young girl with Down syndrome named Sophia. The case example of Sophia illustrates one way in which investigators can begin to approach intervention intensity in interventions for children with Down syndrome.

Case example

Sophia was three years 11 months old at the start of the investigation. Sophia received early intervention services (including speech/language, occupational therapy, physical therapy, and special education services) in her home and at school. Despite receiving a number of services, Sophia's mother was dissatisfied with the gains Sophia was making relative to those attained by her twin brother, who was diagnosed with autism. Comparatively, Sophia's services were eclectic and delivered at a much lower intensity than the largely behaviour analytic interventions provided in one-to-one and small group settings received by her brother with autism. We hypothesized that varying the levels of intensity of the interventions provided to Sophia would result in measurable differences in her skill acquisition.

Sophia's performance on the Mullen Scales of Early Learning (Mullen, 1995) was too low to calculate an age-equivalent score, except for the Receptive Language subscale, on which she scored an age equivalent of 19 months, falling in the "very low" range (first percentile rank, T score = 20). Sophia used one or two-word utterances for requests (e.g. "I want"), greetings (e.g. "Hi"), and protests (e.g. "No"). She followed simple directions (e.g. "Knock"), but rarely interacted spontaneously, depending on teacher questions or prompts (e.g. "What do you want?").

Identifying and labelling objects were two skill areas identified for Sophia based on current areas of need as reported by her mother and interventionist observation. The skills addressed were selecting one of two objects (popcorn and juice) and labelling common objects (bowl and doll). Skills were paired by domain and difficulty, and randomly assigned to high-intensity intervention or low-intensity intervention. Therefore, two skills were targeted in high-intensity intervention and two targeted in low-intensity intervention.

Intervention involved multiple opportunities, prompting, and reinforcement as well as shaping procedures (i.e. reinforcing closer and closer approximations to the desired response), referred to as discrete trial instruction (Lovaas, 1987). High-intensity intervention consisted of 20 teaching opportunities during a 10-minute session; low-intensity intervention consisted of five teaching opportunities during a 10-minute session. This is an example of manipulation of dose (the number of opportunities within a session). We held dose frequency (i.e. the number of times the session was implemented per week) and dose form (i.e. the same interventionist implemented the same procedures with the same level of directiveness in the same environment) constant across both levels of intensity. Maintenance probes were conducted one week and three weeks after acquisition.

Sophia did not correctly identify any of the items, either expressively or receptively, prior to intervention. In the high-intensity condition, Sophia reached mastery criteria for both labelling and selecting one of two objects (seven sessions for "bowl" and one session for "juice") before meeting mastery criteria for either of the targets ("popcorn" and "doll") in the low-intensity intervention. She maintained both targets in high-intensity intervention at follow-up. After mastery of the targets in high-intensity intervention and 10 sessions of low-intensity intervention without mastery, we discontinued low-intensity intervention. Following intervention, Sophia's mother used these data to advocate for a change in services. Specifically, she advocated for five hours per week of high-intensity intervention (i.e. discrete trial instruction) in addition to Sophia's other services.

Sophia's results suggest that intervention intensity is a critical component in planning interventions for children with Down syndrome. The impact of intensity on classroom performance may be seen in whether a learner acquires skills, acquires those skills in a similar period of time as his/her peers, and whether the learner generalizes and maintains those skills over time. Intervention intensity may be one way to improve learner performance in the classroom. For example, regular classroom lessons may involve spelling practice three times each week with 1–2 opportunities to practise spelling each word during a 15-minute spelling practice session. This may be sufficient for most students to perform well, acquiring target spelling words each week. But, if a learner's performance indicates poor acquisition of target words, intensity might be the issue. Perhaps 4–5 opportunities to practise spelling each word with more spelling sessions each week would improve performance. The teacher's lessons could be supplemented with small group instruction and/or additional homework practice. Clearly the intensity should be dictated by learner performance; if increasing intensity to 4–5 opportunities per word with sessions every day leads to acquisition of target spelling words, then this intensity works for this learner for this skill area.

Sophia's case study illustrates how manipulating individual aspects of intervention intensity can produce measurable differences in intervention success. Although we held session duration constant (10 minutes) and varied the number of opportunities, we necessarily manipulated the intertrial interval, or the spacing of the opportunities (30-second intertrial interval in high-intensity intervention versus two-minute intertrial interval in low-intensity intervention). Thus, our results may reflect one or both manipulations of dose: the number of opportunities or the spacing of opportunities. Examining intervention intensity will require varying different aspects of the intervention in various combinations to determine which produces maximum effects on learning.

While dose, dose frequency, and duration may be relatively straightforward variables to manipulate, dose form may be the most important aspect of intervention intensity to consider. Comparatively, the definition of dose form is vague and largely represents how opportunities will be presented (i.e. the environment, the consequences). For example, Hoffman (2009) discussed how reading and interest level, genre, story structure, and cultural context are all components of the dose form of narrative language intervention. Part of the difficulty in defining dose form may also lie in distinguishing what is an aspect of intensity and what is inherent to the intervention. For example, do parent-directed, home-based interventions represent a different intensity level than therapist-directed, university-based interventions, or just different intervention philosophies? Many studies have attempted to approach the effects of dose form by comparing two interventions, but often fail to control for the other aspects of intervention intensity (e.g. Eikeseth *et al.*, 2002). Just as with other aspects of intensity, various manipulations of dose form while holding other aspects of intensity constant are required to make conclusions about intervention intensity.

There may also be interactions of intensity with other variables; individual characteristics (e.g. age), target skills (e.g. relative weaknesses), and urgency (e.g. severe challenging behaviour) may dictate the use of a given level of intervention intensity. For example, we hypothesize that addressing pivotal skills requires more intensive intervention because we can achieve skill acquisition more quickly than with lower intensity intervention. Addressing areas of relative strength (e.g. some social skills) may require less intensive intervention to achieve timely skill acquisition. That is, skill area interacts with intervention intensity; these hypotheses warrant direct comparison investigations. Our hypotheses reflect another example of how knowledge of behavioural phenotype can help guide improvements in interventions for learners with Down syndrome.

Summary and conclusion

Enhancing the performance of learners with Down syndrome in the classroom requires developing interventions that are at an optimal intensity using characteristic strengths to address challenging behaviour and pivotal skills. It is important to recognize the early pattern of challenging behaviour and early emerging impairments in pivotal skills that may negatively impact learning and classroom performance. We reviewed behaviour analytic interventions that have some evidence with learners with

Down syndrome and extensive evidence with learners with a range of disabilities, suggesting promise in considering a behaviour analytic approach to addressing the needs of learners with Down syndrome (Buckley, 2008). Building an evidence base of interventions for learners with Down syndrome requires the pursuit of empirical demonstrations specifically with learners with Down syndrome to begin to examine the needs presented by this population of learners. In addition, interventions must be carefully designed to incorporate information about the Down syndrome behavioural phenotype, both to address impairments and to build on strengths, to improve the effectiveness of intervention. With demonstrations of interventions that effectively address these areas, we can also begin to explore how the intensity of intervention impacts the efficiency of intervention to further maximize outcomes and opportunities for learners with Down syndrome.

References

Anderson, M. D., Sherman, J. A., Sheldon, J. B., & McAdam, D. (1997). Picture activity schedules and engagement of adults with mental retardation in a group home. *Research in Developmental Disabilities, 18*, 231–250.

Baer, D. M., & Sherman, J. A. (1964). Reinforcement control of generalized imitation in young children. *Journal of Experimental Child Psychology, 1*, 37–49.

Bakeman, R., & Adamson, L. B. (1984). Coordinating attention to people and objects in mother-infant and peer-infant interaction. *Child Development, 55*, 1278–1289.

Barry, L. M., & Burlew, S. B. (2004). Using social stories to teach choice and play skills to children with autism. *Focus on Autism and Other Developmental Disabilities, 19*, 45–51.

Bauer, S., Jones, E. A., & Feeley, K. M. (in press). Teaching responses to questions to young children with Down syndrome. *Behavioral Interventions.*

Belfiore, P. J., Lee, D. L., Scheeler, M. C., & Klein, D. (2002). Implications of behavioral momentum and academic achievement for students with behavior disorders: Theory, application, and practice. *Psychology in the Schools, 39*, 1–9.

Belfiore, P. J., Lee, D. L., Vargas, A. U., & Skinner, C. H. (1997). Effects of high-preference single-digit mathematics problem completion on multiple-digit mathematics problem performance. *Journal of Applied Behavior Analysis, 30*, 327–330.

Bellon-Harn, M. L. (2012). Dose frequency: Comparison of language outcomes in preschool children with language impairment. *Child Language Teaching and Therapy, 28*, 225–240. doi: 10.1177/0265659012445936.

Bono, M. A., Daley, T., & Sigman, M. (2004). Relations among joint attention, amount of intervention and language gain in autism. *Journal of Autism and Developmental Disorders,* 34, 495–505.

Brooks, A., Todd, A. W., Tofflemoyer, S., & Horner, R. H. (2003). Use of functional assessment and a self-management system to increase academic engagement and work completion. *Journal of Positive Behavior Interventions, 5*, 144–152.

Brown, F. (1991). Creative daily scheduling: A nonintrusive approach to challenging behavior in community residences. *Journal of the Association for Persons with Severe Handicaps, 16*, 75–84.

Buckley, S. (2008). The power of behavioural approaches: We need a revival. *Down Syndrome Research and Practice, 12*, 103–104.

Carr, E. G., Dunlap, G., Horner, R. H., Koegel, R. L., Turnbull, A. P., Sailor, W., . . . Fox, L. (2002). Positive behavior support: Evolution of an applied science. *Journal of Positive Behavior Interventions, 4*, 4–20.

Carr, E. G., & Durand, V. M. (1985). Reducing behavior problems through functional communication training. *Journal of Applied Behavior Analysis, 18*, 111–126.

Carr, E. G., Horner, R. H., Turnbull, A. P., Marquis, J. G., Magito McLaughlin, D., McAtee, M., … Doolabh, A. (1999). *Positive behavior support for people with developmental disabilities: A research synthesis* [Monograph]. Washington, DC: American Association on Mental Retardation.

Carr, E. G., Levin, L., McConnachie, G., Carlson, J. I., Kemp, D. C., & Smith, C. E. (1994). *Communication-based intervention for problem behavior: A user's guide for producing positive change.* Baltimore, MD: Paul H. Brookes.

Carr, E. G., & Owen-DeSchryver, J. S. (2007). Physical illness, pain, and challenging behavior in minimally verbal people with developmental disabilities. *Journal of Autism and Developmental Disorders, 37*, 413–424. doi: 10.1007/s10803-006-0176-0.

Carr, E. G., Smith, C. E., Giacin, T. A., Whelan, B. M., & Pancari, J. (1993). Menstrual discomfort as a biological setting event for severe challenging behavior: Assessment and intervention. *American Journal on Mental Retardation, 108*, 117–133.

Coe, D. A., Matson, J. L., Russell, D. W., Slifer, K. J., Capone, G. T., Baglio, C., & Stallings, S. (1999). Behavior problems of children with Down syndrome and life events. *Journal of Autism and Developmental Disorders*, 39, 149–156.

Cole, C. L., & Levinson, T. R. (2002). Effects of within-activity choices on the challenging behavior of children with severe developmental disabilities. *Journal of Positive Behavior Interventions, 4*, 29–37.

Cooper, J. O., Heron, T. E., & Heward, W. L. (2007). *Applied behavior analysis* (2nd ed.). Upper Saddle River, NJ: Merrill/Prentice Hall.

Cotton, S. M., & Richdale, A. L. (2010). Sleep patterns and behaviour in typically developing children and children with autism, Down syndrome, Prader-Willi syndrome and intellectual disability. *Research in Autism Spectrum Disorders, 4*, 490–500. doi: 10.1016/j.rasd.2009.11.006.

Crozier, S., & Tincani, M. J. (2005). Using a modified Social Story™ to decrease disruptive behavior of a child with autism. *Focus on Autism and Other Developmental Disabilities, 20*, 150–157.

Dalton, A. J., Rubino, C. A., & Hislop, M. W. (1973). Some effects of token rewards on school achievement of children with Down's syndrome. *Journal of Applied Behavior Analysis, 6*, 251–259.

Davis, C. A., Brady, M. P., Williams, R. E., & Hamilton, R. (1992). Effects of high-probability requests on the acquisition and generalization of responses to requests in young children with behavior disorders. *Journal of Applied Behavior Analysis,* 25, 905–916.

Delano, M., & Snell, M. E. (2006). The effects of social stories on the social engagement of children with autism. *Journal of Positive Behavior Interventions, 8*, 29–42.

Doss, L., & Reichle, J. (1991). Replacing excess behavior with an initial communicative repertoire. In J. Reichle, J. York, & J. Sigafoos (Eds), *Implementing augmentative and alternative communication: Strategies for learners with severe disabilities* (pp. 215–237). Baltimore, MD: Paul H. Brookes.

Drash, P. W., Raver, S. A., Murrin, M. R., & Tudor, R. M. (1989). Three procedures for increasing vocal response to therapist prompt in infants and children with Down syndrome. *American Journal on Mental Retardation, 94*, 64–73.

Dunlap, G., Kern-Dunlap, L., Clarke, S., & Robbins, F. R. (1991). Functional assessment, curricular revision, and severe behavior problems. *Journal of Applied Behavior Analysis, 24*, Special issue: Social validity: Multiple perspectives, 387–397.

Dykens, E. M. (2007). Psychiatric and behavioral disorders in persons with Down syndrome. *Mental Retardation and Developmental Disabilities Research Reviews, 13*, Special issue: Special issue on Down syndrome, 272–278.

Dykens, E. M., Shah, B., Sagun, J., Beck, T., & King, B. H. (2002). Maladaptive behaviour in children and adolescents with Down's syndrome. *Journal of Intellectual Disability Research, 46*, 484–492.

Edeal, D. M., & Gildersleeve-Neumann, C. E. (2011). The importance of production frequency in therapy for childhood apraxia of speech. *American Journal of Speech-Language Pathology, 20*, 95–110. doi: 10.1044/1058-0360(2011/09-0005).

Eikeseth, S., & Nesset, R. (2003). Behavioral treatment of children with phonological disorder: The efficacy of vocal imitation training and sufficient response-exemplar training. *Journal of Applied Behavior Analysis, 36*, 325–337.

Eikeseth, S., Smith, T., Jahr, E., & Eldevik, S. (2002). Intensive behavioral treatment at school for 4- to 7-year-old children with autism: A one-year comparison controlled study. *Behavior Modification, 26*, 49–68.

Ekstein, S., Glick, B., Weill, M., Kay, B., & Berger, I. (2011). Down syndrome and attention deficit/hyperactivity disorder. *Journal of Child Neurology, 26*, 1290–1295.

Feeley, K. M., & Jones, E. A. (2006). Addressing challenging behaviour in children with Down syndrome: The use of applied behavior analysis for assessment and intervention. *Down Syndrome Research and Practice, 11*, 64–77.

Feeley, K. M., & Jones, E. A. (2008). Strategies to address challenging behavior in young children with Down syndrome. *Down Syndrome Research and Practice, 12*, 153–163.

Feeley, K. M., Jones, E. A., Blackburn, C., & Bauer, S. M. (2011). Advancing imitation and requesting skills in toddlers with Down syndrome. *Research in Developmental Disabilities, 32*, 2415–2430.

Fey, M. E., Warren, S. F., Brady, N., Finestack, L. H., Bedin-Oja, S. L., Fairchild, M., & Yoder, P. J. (2006). Early effects of responsivity education/prelinguistic milieu teaching for children with developmental delays and their parents. *Journal of Speech, Language, and Hearing Research, 49*, 526–547.

Fidler, D. (2005). The emerging Down syndrome behavioral phenotype in early childhood: Implications for practice. *Infants and Young Children, 18*, 86–103.

Fidler, D. J., Most, D. E., & Philofsky, A. D. (2008). The Down syndrome behavioural phenotype: Taking a developmental approach. *Down Syndrome Research and Practice, Advance Online Publication*, www.down-syndrome.org/reviews/2069/. doi: 10.3104/reviews/2069.

Fidler, D. J., Philofsky, A., Hepburn, S., & Rogers, S. (2005). Nonverbal requesting and problem solving in toddlers with Down syndrome. *American Journal on Mental Retardation, 110*, 312–322.

Foster-Johnson, L., Ferro, J., & Dunlap, G. (1994). Preferred curricular activities and reduced problem behaviors in students with intellectual disabilities. *Journal of Applied Behavior Analysis, 27*, 493–504.

Garcia, E., Baer, D. M., & Firestone, I. (1971). The development of generalized imitation within topographically determined boundaries. *Journal of Applied Behavior Analysis, 4*, 101–112.

Gray, C. (1994). *Social stories.* Arlington, TX: Future Horizons.

Hall, A. M., Neuharth-Pritchett, S., & Belfiore, P. J. (1997). Reduction of aggressive behaviors with changes in activity: Linking descriptive and experimental analysis. *Education and Training in Mental Retardation and Developmental Disabilities, 32*, 331–339.

Hemmeter, M. L., Ault, M. J., Collins, B. C., & Meyer, S. (1996). The effects of teacher-implemented language instruction within free time activities. *Education and Training in Mental Retardation and Developmental Disabilities, 31*, 203–212.

Hetzroni, O. E., & Roth, T. (2003). Effects of a positive support approach to enhance communicative behaviors of children with mental retardation who have challenging behaviors. *Education and Training in Developmental Disabilities, 38*, 95–105.

Hodapp, R. M., Leckman, J. F., Dykens, E. M., Sparrow, S. S., Zelinsky, D. G., & Ort, S. I. (1992). K-ABC profiles in children with fragile X syndrome, Down syndrome, and non-specific mental retardation. *American Journal on Mental Retardation, 97*, 39–46.

Hoffman, L. M. (2009). Narrative language intervention intensity and dosage telling the whole story. *Topics in Language Disorders, 29*, 329–343.

Horner, R. H., Vaughn, B. J., Day, H. M., & Ard, W. R. (1996). The relationship between setting events and challenging behavior: Expanding our understanding of heavier support. In L. K. Koegel & G. Dunlap (Eds), *Positive behavioral support including people with difficult behavior in the community* (pp. 381–402). Baltimore, MD: Paul H. Brooks.

Hutchinson, J. M., & Belfiore, P. J. (1998). Adding a sequence of high preference mathematics problems to increase low-preference mathematics problems performance. *Proven Practice, 1*, 12–16.

Jones, E. A., & Feeley, K. M. (2011). Extending ABA intervention to developmental disabilities other than autism spectrum disorders: What are we waiting for? *The APBA Reporter, 27.* www.apbahome.net/newsletter.php?nid=27&aid=273.

Jones, E. A., Feeley, K. M., & Blackburn, C. (2010). A preliminary study of intervention addressing early developing requesting behaviours in young infants with Down syndrome. *Down Syndrome Research and Practice, 12*, 98–102. doi: 10.3104/reports.2059.

Kasari, C., & Freeman, S. F. N. (2001). Task-related social behavior in children with Down syndrome. *American Journal on Mental Retardation, 106*, 253–264.

Kazdin, A. E. (1973). The effect of vicarious reinforcement on attentive behavior in the classroom. *Journal of Applied Behavior Analysis, 6*, 71–78.

Kennedy, C. H., & Meyer, K. A. (1996). Sleep deprivation, allergy symptoms, and negatively reinforced challenging behavior. *Journal of Applied Behavior Analysis, 29*, 133–135.

Koegel, L. K., Koegel, R. L., Harrower, J. K., & Carter, C. M. (1999). Pivotal response intervention I: Overview of approach. *Research and Practice for Persons with Severe Disabilities, 24*, 174–185.

Krantz, P., & McClannahan, L. (1993). Social interaction skills for children with autism: A script fading procedure for beginning readers. *Journal of Applied Behavior Analysis, 31*, 191–202.

Kumin, L. (1994). Intelligibility of speech in children with Down syndrome in natural settings: Parents' perspective. *Perceptual and Motor Skills, 78*, 307–313.

Lalli, J. S., Browder, D. M., Mace, F. C., & Brown, D. K. (1993). Teacher use of descriptive analysis data to implement interventions to decrease students challenging behaviors. *Journal of Applied Behavior Analysis, 26*, 227–238.

Lee, D. L., Belfiore, P. J., Scheeler, M. C., Hua, Y., & Smith, R. (2004). Behavioral momentum in academics: Using embedded high-*p* sequences to increase academic productivity. *Psychology in the Schools, 41*, 789–801.

Lee, D. L., & Laspe, A. K. (2003). Using high-probability request sequences to increase journal writing. *Journal of Behavioral Education, 12*, 261–273.

Lovaas, O. I. (1987). Behavioral treatment and normal educational functioning in young autistic children. *Journal of Consulting and Clinical Psychology, 55*, 3–9.

Lovaas, O. I., Berberich, J. P., Perloff, B. F., & Schaeffer, B. (1966). Acquisition of imitative speech by schizophrenic children. *Focus on Autistic Behavior, 6*, 1–5.

Loveland, K., & Landry, S. (1986). Joint attention and language in autism and developmental language delay. *Journal of Autism and Developmental Disorders, 16*, 335–349.

Luiselli, J. K. (2008). Antecedent (preventative) interventions. In J. K. Luiselli, D. C. Russo, W. P. Christian, & S. M. Wilczynski (Eds), *Effective practices for children with autism: Educational and behavior support interventions that work* (pp. 393–412). Oxford: Oxford University Press.

Mace, F. C., & Belfiore, P. J. (1990). Behavioral momentum in the treatment of escape-motivated stereotypy. *Journal of Applied Behavior Analysis, 23*, 507–514.

Mace, F. C., Hock, M. L., Lalli, J. S., West, B. J., Belfiore, P., Pinter, E., & Brown, D. K. (1988). Behavioral momentum in the treatment of noncompliance. *Journal of Applied Behavior Analysis, 21*, 123–141.

Mahoney, G., Glover, A., & Finger, I. (1981). Relationship between language and sensorimotor development of Down syndrome and nonretarded children. *American Journal of Mental Deficiency, 86*, 21–27.

Marcus, B. A., & Vollmer, T. R. (1996). Combining noncontingent reinforcement and differ-

ential reinforcement schedules as treatment for aberrant behavior. *Journal of Applied Behavior Analysis, 29*, 43–51.
McComas, J. J., Thompson, A., & Johnson, L. (2003). The effects of presession attention on challenging behavior maintained by different reinforcers. *Journal of Applied Behavior Analysis, 36*, 297–307.
McEachin, J. J., Smith, T., & Lovaas, O. I. (1993). Long-term outcome for children with autism who received early intensive behavioral treatment. *American Journal on Mental Retardation, 97*, 359–372.
McGill, P. (1999). Establishing operations: Implications for the assessment, treatment and prevention of challenging behavior. *Journal of Applied Behavior Analysis, 32*, 393–418.
Mechling, L. C., & Gast, D. L. (1997). Combination audio/visual self-prompting system for teaching chained tasks to students with intellectual disabilities. *Education & Training in Mental Retardation & Developmental Disabilities, 32*, 138–153.
Mesibov, G. B., Browder, D. M., & Kirkland, C. (2002). Using individualized schedules as a component of positive behavior support for students with developmental disabilities. *Journal of Positive Behavior Interventions, 4*, 273–279.
Millichap, D., Oliver, C., McQuillan, S., Kasly, S., Lloyd, V., & Hall, S. (2003). Descriptive functional analysis of behavioral excesses shown by adults with Down syndrome and dementia. *International Journal of Geriatric Psychiatry, 18*, 844–854. doi: 10.1002/gps.930.
Mullen, E. (1995). *Infant Mullen scales of early learning*. Circle Pines, MN: American Guidance Service.
Mundy, P., & Crowson, M. (1997). Joint attention and early social communication: Implications for research on intervention with autism. *Journal of Autism and Developmental Disorders, 27*, 653–676.
Mundy, P., Sigman, M., Ungerer, J., & Sherman, T. (1986). Defining the social deficits of autism: The contribution of non-verbal communication measures. *Journal of Child Psychology and Psychiatry, 27*, 657–669.
Myers, B. A., & Pueschel, S. M. (1991). Psychiatric disorders in persons with Down syndrome. *Journal of Nervous and Mental Disease, 179*, 609–613.
National Autism Center. (2009). *National Standards Report*. Randolph, MA: National Autism Center. Retrieved from www.nationalautismcenter.org/nsp/.
Oliver, C., Hall, S., & Nixon, J. (1999). A molecular to molar analysis of communicative and challenging behaviors. *Research in Developmental Disabilities, 20*, 197–213.
O'Neill, R. E., Horner, R. H., Albin, R. W., Sprague, J. R., Storey, K., & Newton, J. S. (1997). *Functional assessment and program development for problem behavior: A practical handbook* (2nd edn). Pacific Grove, CA: Brooks/Cole.
O'Reilly, M. F. (1995). Functional analysis and treatment of escape-maintained aggression correlated with sleep deprivation. *Journal of Applied Behavior Analysis, 28*, 225–226.
Pierce, K. L., & Schriebman, L. (1994). Teaching daily living skills to children with autism in unsupervised settings through pictorial self management. *Journal of Applied Behavior Analysis, 27*, 471–481.
Pitcairn, T. K., & Wishart, J. G. (1994). Reaction of young children with Down's syndrome to an impossible task. *British Journal of Developmental Psychology, 12*, 485–489.
Proctor-Williams, K. (2009). Dosage and distribution in morphosyntax intervention current and future needs. *Topics in Language Disorders, 29*, 294–311.
Pueschel, S. M., Myers, B., & Sustrova, M. (1996). Psychiatric disorders and behavioural concerns in persons with Down's syndrome. In J. A. Rondal, J. Perera, L. Nadel, & A. Comblain (Eds). *Down's syndrome. Psychological, psychobiological, and socio-educational perspectives* (pp. 179–190). Philadelphia, PA: Whurr Publishers.
Ramey, C. T., Bryant, D. M., Wasik, B. H., Sparling, J. J., Fendt, K. H., & LaVange, L. M., (1992). Infant health and development program for low birth weight, premature, infants: Program elements, family participation, and child intelligence. *Pediatrics, 89*, 454–465.

Ramsey, M. L., DaShaunda, J., Patterson, P., & Kennedy, C. (2010). Using choice to increase time on-task, task-completion, and accuracy for students with emotional/behavior disorders in a residential facility. *Education and Treatment of Children, 33*, 1–21.

Rast, M., & Meltzoff, A. N. (1995). Memory and representation in young children with Down syndrome: Exploring deferred imitation and object permanence. *Development and Psychopathology, 7*, 393–407.

Repp, A. C., & Karsh, D. (1994). A hypothesis-based intervention for tantrum behavior of person with developmental disabilities in school settings. *Journal of Applied Behavior Analysis, 27*, 21–31.

Robinson, M. L. (2012). Behavioral phenotypes and medical conditions as plausible contextual factors for the display of challenging behavior in developmental disabilities: A heuristic model (Unpublished manuscript). SUNY Stony Brook, NY.

Robinson Joy, M. (2009). *Behavioral phenotypes as contextual factors for problem behavior in individuals with developmental disabilities* (Doctoral dissertation). Retrieved 12 March 2013 from http://dspace.sunyconnect.suny.edu/handle/1951/52235.

Roizen, N. J. (1996). Down syndrome and associated medical disorders. *Mental Retardation and Developmental Disability Research Reviews, 2*, 85–89.

Romaniuk, C., Miltenberger, R., Conyers, C., Jenner, N., Jurgens, M., & Ringenberg, C. (2002). The influence of activity choice on challenging behaviors maintained by escape versus attention. *Journal of Applied Behavior Analysis, 35*, 349–362.

Rondal, J. A. (1980). Verbal imitation by Down syndrome and nonretarded children. *American Journal of Mental Deficiency, 85*, 318–321.

Rondal, J. A., Lambert, J. L., & Sohier, C. (1981). Elicited verbal and nonverbal imitation in Down's syndrome and other mentally retarded children: A replication and extension of Berry. *Language and Speech, 24*, 245–254.

Ross, D. E., & Greer, D. (2003). Generalized imitation and the mand: Inducing first instances of speech in young children with autism. *Research in Developmental Disabilities, 24*, 58–74.

Sallows, G. O., & Graupner, T. D. (2005). Intensive behavioral treatment for children with autism: Four-year outcome and predictors. *American Journal on Mental Retardation, 110*, 417–438.

Sanchez-Fort, M. R., Brady, M. P., & Davis, C. A. (1995). Using high-probability requests to increase low-probability communication behavior in young children with severe disabilities. *Education and Training in Mental Retardation and Developmental Disabilities, 30*, 151–165.

Scattone, D., Tingstrom, D. H., & Wilczynski, S. M. (2006). Increasing appropriate social interactions of children with autism spectrum disorders using Social Stories. *Focus on Autism, 21*, 211–222.

Schroeder, G. L., & Baer, D. M. (1972). Effects of concurrent and serial training on generalized vocal imitation in retarded children. *Developmental Psychology, 6*, 293–301.

Sellinger, M. H., Hodapp, R. M., & Dykens, E. M. (2006). Leisure activities of individuals with Prader-Willi, Williams, and Down syndromes. *Journal of Developmental and Physical Disabilities, 18*, 59–71. doi: 10.1007/s10882-006-9006-8.

Shaw, R., & Simms, T. (2009). Reducing attention-maintained behavior through the use of positive punishment, differential reinforcement of low rates, and response marking. *Behavioral Interventions, 24*, 249–263. doi: 10.1002/bin.287.

Sherman, J. A. (1965). Use of reinforcement and imitation to reinstate verbal behavior in mute psychotics. *Journal of Abnormal Psychology, 70*, 155–164.

Smith, T., Eikeseth, S., Klevstrand, M., & Lovaas, O. I. (1997). Intensive behavioral treatment for preschoolers with severe mental retardation and pervasive developmental disorder. *American Journal on Mental Retardation, 102*, 238–249.

Smith, V., Mirenda, P., & Zaidman-Zait, A. (2007). Predictors of expressive vocabulary growth in children with autism. *Journal of Speech, Language, and Hearing Research, 50*, 149–160.

Taubman, M., Brierley, S., Wishner, J., Baker, D., McEachin, J., & Leaf, R. B. (2001). The effectiveness of a group discrete trial instructional approach for preschoolers with developmental disabilities. *Research in Developmental Disabilities, 22*, 205–219.

Thompson, R. H., Iwata, B. A., Conners, J., & Roscoe, E. M. (1999). Effects of reinforcement for alternative behavior during punishment of self-injury. *Journal of Applied Behavior Analysis, 32*, 317–328.

Turner, S., Alborz, A., & Gayle, V. (2008). Predictors of academic attainments of young people with Down's syndrome. *Journal of Intellectual Disability Research, 52*, 380–392.

Ukrainetz, T. A. (2009). Phonemic awareness: How much is enough within a changing picture of reading instruction. *Topics in Language Disorders, 29*, 344–359.

van Gameren-Oosterom, H. B. M., Fekkes, M., Buitendijk, S. E., Mohangoo, A. D., Bruil, J., & Van Wouwe, J. P. (2011). Development, problem behavior, and quality of life in a population based sample of eight-year-old children with Down syndrome. *PLoS ONE, 6*. Retrieved from www.plosone.org/article/info:doi/10.1371/journal.pone.0021879#.

Vollmer, T. R., Iwata, B. A., Zarcone, J. R., Smith, R. G., & Mazaleski, J. L. (1993). The role of attention in the treatment of attention-maintained self-injurious behavior: Noncontingent reinforcement and differential reinforcement of other behavior. *Journal of Applied Behavior Analysis, 26*, 9–21.

Warren, S. F., Fey, M. E., Finestack, L. H., Brady, N. C., Bedin-Oja, S. L., & Fleming, K. K. (2008). A randomized trial of longitudinal effects of low-intensity responsivity education/prelinguistic milieu teaching. *Journal of Speech, Language, and Hearing Research, 51*, 451–470. doi: 1092–4388/08/5102–0451.

Warren, S. F., Fey, M. E., & Yoder, P. J. (2007). Differential treatment intensity research: A missing link to creating optimally effective communication intervention. *Mental Retardation and Developmental Disabilities, 13*, 70–77.

Wilde, L., Koegel, L. K., & Koegel, R. L. (1992). *Increasing success in school through priming: A training manual.* Santa Barbara: University of California.

Wishart, J. (1993). Learning the hard way: Avoidance strategies in young children with Down's syndrome. *Down Syndrome Research and Practice, 1*, 47–55.

Wishart, J. G. (1998). Development in children with Down syndrome: Facts, findings, the future. *International Journal of Disability, Development and Education, 45*, 343–363.

Wishart, J. G. (2007). Socio-cognitive understanding: A strength or weakness in Down's syndrome? *Journal of Intellectual Disability Research, 51*, 996–1005.

Yoder, P., Fey, M. E., & Warren, S. (2012). Studying the impact of intensity is important but complicated. *International Journal of Speech-Language Pathology, 14*, 410–413. doi: 10.3109/1759507.2012.685890.

Yoder, P. J., & Warren, S. F. (2002). Effects of prelinguistic milieu teaching and parent responsivity education on dyads involving children with intellectual disabilities. *Journal of Speech, Language, and Hearing Research, 45*, 1158–1174.

Part II

Learning mathematics

Chapter 5

Mathematics profile of the learner with Down syndrome

Rhonda Faragher and Barbara Clarke

Abstract

Difficulty learning mathematics appears to be part of the effects of Down syndrome, and yet with quality teaching and the right support, learners with Down syndrome have demonstrated achievement in mathematics. In this chapter, we review the available literature on mathematics development of learners with Down syndrome and then discuss our research using task-based interviews to provide a description of how learners with Down syndrome develop mathematics concepts. We note limitations of our research and make suggestions for further work.

Introduction

The assumption that Down syndrome leads to intellectual disability is being challenged in the intellectual disability research community. In terms of mathematics education, there has been a similar revision of assumptions. Understanding of literacy development received early and intense research interest, which continues to this day. The chapters in this book on literacy indicate the scope of the work, progress made to date, and areas of current interest. By contrast, work in the field of mathematics development is far less advanced.

Teachers and parents have known for some time that learners with Down syndrome can and do learn mathematics; however, evidence in the research literature has been scant until recent years (Bird & Buckley, 2001). Even to this point, almost only aspects of number have been studied. Of these, most studies have focused on counting, using money, and using calculators (see, for example, Abdelhameed & Porter, 2006; Bochner, Outhred, Pieterse, & Bashash, 2002; Caycho, Gunn, & Siegal, 1991; Koller & Mulhern, 1977; Paterson, Girelli, Butterworth, & Karmiloff-Smith, 2006). From the research that has been undertaken, as well as the experiences of teachers and parents, it is understood that most learners with Down syndrome struggle with learning number and, for some, the difficulties can be considerable.

At this point, the cause of difficulties with learning number is not known. Some recent studies from the field of psychology (Camos, 2009; Paterson *et al.*, 2006) are beginning to identify areas of possible differences in cognitive development that may lead to impairments in the development of number. These tend to refer to language-based systems but the exact nature is yet to be understood.

It has been noted that students with Down syndrome struggle with the development of strategies, but if strategies are explicitly taught, students are able to make use of them and continue to do so in subsequent years (Irwin, 1991). Development of strategic thinking, including generalisation, is at the heart of mathematics and it may be that deficiency in these processes is at the heart of difficulties learning number. There is a clear need for research in the area of mathematical development of children with Down syndrome.

By contrast, there is considerable interest in the mathematical development of typically developing children[1] and, through a number of projects, a considerable amount of data has been obtained (Bobis *et al.*, 2005). Along with colleagues, we undertook a study, *Mapping the Mathematical Development of Children with Down Syndrome*, aimed at building on the research into typically developing young children, including the use of task-based cognitive interview tools (Faragher, Brady, Clarke, Clarke, & Gervasoni, 2008). Through this study, we aimed to map a developmental trajectory of children with Down syndrome in early mathematics concepts in the areas of number, geometry, measurement, and mathematical thinking.

This chapter summarises what is known to this point about the mathematics development of learners with Down syndrome from the published literature and results from our recent research.

An emerging field

Historically, research into the mathematical understanding of learners with Down syndrome has lagged behind other areas. Research from the field of psychology is beginning to provide interesting comparisons with typical development of the concepts of mathematics and that of learners with Down syndrome. Research from the fields of special education and mathematics education is much more limited, though beginning to emerge. Clearly, this is a fertile field for future research.

As the new millennium began, Bird and Buckley (2001) reviewed the literature available in the area of number development for learners with Down syndrome and noted only a few articles existed. More than a decade on, it is timely to reassess progress in the field. In this section, we review literature available and report findings under topic themes. We begin with studies of mathematics attainment. Following that, we review research according to mathematics content areas: numerosity, counting, money, and areas other than number (arithmetic). It is perhaps not surprising that the majority of articles that exist are to do with number and, within that field, counting. Finally, we review research on teaching approaches and use of calculating devices.

Attainment

Mathematics educators and researchers have grappled with the considerable challenges of assessing mathematics attainment of typically developing students. Many jurisdictions use large-scale testing of cohorts of students to compare performances of individuals, classes, schools, districts, and even countries. Researchers in the field of mathematics education have argued for assessments that provide richer information with greater reliability and validity than data collected on one day using methods which are easy to assess and grade.

Psychological tests of 'numerical ability' provide useful information but do not give the broad range of data on performance and attainment of concepts demanded by those who need to use the information for on-going teaching and learning. Unfortunately, little evidence of attainment other than that provided by psychological testing instruments exists for learners with Down syndrome. Often, too, this evidence arises from psychological testing undertaken while investigating research questions of a more general cognitive nature. Table 5.1 provides a list of such studies, including a brief summary of their findings.

It can be seen from the studies summarised in Table 5.1 that the majority of work has been in the area of understanding the cognitive basis of early number development.

Shepperdson (1994) did not test participants directly but asked professionals (e.g. teachers) 'to complete a list of 26 items on the young peoples' number abilities' (p. 98). These items were not specified (although they were briefly described) and it is unclear how they were generated. A similar approach was adopted by Turner and Alborz (2003) and de Graaf *et al.* (2013) in that researchers did not directly assess the children. Parents or tutors (not teachers) completed a checklist of skills. Both the Shepperdson and the Turner and Alborz studies compared cohort groups. By undertaking a study comparing two cohorts a decade apart in age, Shepperdson was able to identify effects of education development, reporting 'more of the seventies cohort possessed "academic" skills, compared with the sixties cohort at the same chronological age, but the skills of the seventies cohort were not of a substantially higher order' (p. 97). This would suggest developments in access to education or care had led to more children demonstrating academic attainment. The more recent study by de Graaf *et al.* (2013) extended the advantage of education to document the beneficial effect of education in inclusive settings rather than special school placements.

Numerosity

Paterson reported the numerosity discrimination of infants and children with Down syndrome (Paterson, 2001). Numerosity has been defined as the distinctive meaning given to the number of things in a set and is suggested as 'a cognitive counterpart to the term "cardinality" used by mathematicians and logicians' (Butterworth, 2005, p. 3). It is likely that numerosity is linked to numerical ability and number development but they are not synonymous terms. Paterson has provided interesting data on the performance of people with Down syndrome on standard numerosity tasks. Infants were studied to see if they were able to distinguish between two and three objects. It was astonishing that the children with Down syndrome did not appear to be able to distinguish between these quantities, considering that it is known that typically developing babies from birth and indeed many animals have been shown to demonstrate this ability (Devlin, 2005). Replication of the results of this study is needed before the findings are assumed to be a feature of Down syndrome. If corroborated by further research, implications for subsequent learning need to be established. It is also interesting as the task is overtly visual and this has been thought to be an area of relative strength for learners with Down syndrome.

Paterson then tested adults with a different test of numerosity—the ability to distinguish between various quantities of dots. It is not necessarily surprising that adults performed differently to infants in numerosity (assuming the failure on the infant task is not an aberration). As Dehaene (1999) argued, these aspects are substantially different and they are undertaken by different parts of the brain. The connection between

Table 5.1 Literature on numerical attainment of students with Down syndrome using psychometric testing

Author (Date)	*Participants*	*Testing instrument*	*Findings*
Shepperdson (1994)	Two cohorts 1 Born in the 1960s: n = *49* 2 Born in the 1970s: n = *26*	Professional asked to complete a list of 26 items on number abilities	• Some able to master simple skills in number • More in the 1970s cohort with numerical skills • Mean 1970s scores higher than 1960s cohort
Porter (1998)	Primary children in special schools Age 7–13 n = *58* total n = *15* DS	Two tasks: 1 count task (sets of sizes 3, 4, 5, 8, 9, 10) 2 'how many' 3 error correction task	• Considerable variation in performance • Just under a third able to count flawlessly (up to 10) • Just under a fifth could error detect
Paterson (2001)	Infants: n = *65* total n = 22 DS Adults: n = *17* total n = 9 DS	1 Numerosity[b]—infants: stimuli of test cards of objects 2 Numerosity[b]—adults: participants required to judge which of two numbers (as dots) was the larger	• Adults can discriminate between numerosities and demonstrate a distance effect as for typically developing controls (e.g. larger of 7 and 2 is easier than 7 and 8)
Turner & Alborz (2003)	n = *102* (in 1986) n = *101* (1991) n = *79* (2000)	Academic Attainments Index (completed by a parent or tutor)	• Higher scores were achieved by each successive age group up to age 20 • Some levelling off towards end of school • Some reached Key Stage 3 targets in number (p. 563)

Paterson, Girelli, Butterworth, & Karmiloff-Smith (2006)	Infants: *n* = *59* total *n* = *18* DS Older children and adults: *n* = *6* DS *n* = *8* Williams syndrome (WS)	1 Infant preferential looking paradigm[a] for numerosity[b] 2 Reaction times 3 Number battery measuring counting and simple arithmetic	Older children and adults: • All could count to 35 • Four could count backwards from 20 to 1 • Four knew 'next', 'before' within the counting sequence • All successful with putting numerals in order • Operations: variable success
Camos (2009)	Children: *n* = *12* DS Age: 4–7 years	Comparison dot displays to test for numerosity[b] discrimination	• Efficient core knowledge of numerosity[b] • Improvement in age with discrimination of large numerosities[b]
de Graaf, van Hove, & Haveman (2013)	Stratified random sample of 160 parents with children with Down syndrome, attending school (10 boys and 10 girls from each year) *n* = *121*	38 questions asked of parents covering 'basics', calculation, money, time	Data were reported as comparisons between school placements, rather than specific attainments

Notes

a Style of psych tests where babies look at cards with different numbers of dots on them. They look away after a while and only re-engage if the numbers change.

b Numerosity in these studies denotes the number of elements in a set—the cognitive counterpart to cardinality (Butterworth, 2005, p. 3).

the two and the further implications for general mathematics development are as yet unknown.

A further study of numerosity was undertaken by Camos (2009), whose participants were children with Down syndrome who were unable to count. The finding that the approximate numerical system is efficient in the children with Down syndrome led Camos to conclude that the findings 'pinpoint language as a major source of their difficulties in mathematics' (p. 445).

Counting

The development of counting by children with Down syndrome has received relatively large research attention. An early study by Caycho *et al.* (1991) applied the research methodology of Gelman and colleagues (Gelman & Cohen, 1988; Gelman & Gallistel, 1978; Gelman, Meck, & Merkin, 1986) used to investigate the counting development of typically developing children. They noted that counting competence on the tasks was related to receptive language and concluded that developmental level, rather than having Down syndrome, is associated with counting behaviour and that counting develops in a similar way to typically developing children. This finding was not supported by Porter's (1998) study in which she found that

> the children with Down syndrome had significantly higher scores for adhering to one-to-one correspondence than producing a stable conventional order of number words. This was the opposite pattern to the matched group and is in contrast to the pattern revealed by typically developing pre-schoolers.
>
> (p. 90)

As we observed in our study reported later in this chapter and explored in more detail in Chapter 6, learning the count word sequence appears to cause particular difficulties.

Nye, Fluck, and Buckley (2001) have extended the investigation of the comparison of the development of counting between learners with Down syndrome and those without. They too found children with Down syndrome experienced difficulties with production of the count sequence. Support from an adult was found to improve performance.

Other aspects of number

Research has been undertaken in the areas of computation, use of a calculator, and money. A recent study reported the performance of addition and subtraction calculations by students with Down syndrome (Noda Herrera, Bruno, Gonzalez, Moreno, & Sanabria, 2011) and in the process has added to our understanding of performance on broader aspects of number. The researchers conducted semi-structured interviews with 12 students with Down syndrome ranging in age from 12 to 31 years, in which participants were asked to solve number addition and subtraction problems. Noda Herrera *et al.* briefly reported findings on the participants' understandings of zero. It would appear this is the only study to do so. The students understood zero as the absence of objects but had difficulty using zero in algorithmic procedures. Other key findings were:

- Failure with verbal problems was attributed to comprehension rather than lack of the concept of addition or subtraction.
- One student used a derived fact for subtraction ('From 5 to 10 it's 5, so one less is 6'; p. 22).
- Students with Down syndrome progressed through the same stages and used the same strategies as other learners.
- Taught algorithms led to difficulties. These included mistakes caused by improperly learned procedures and encouragement to adhere to a process even when it was less efficient.

Many early calculator and money studies did not specify the type of intellectual impairment but, with Down syndrome being the largest cause of intellectual disability (Turner & Alborz, 2003), it can be assumed that many participants in the studies had Down syndrome. Research in the use of calculators emerged largely around the introduction of cheap, readily available calculators and ended as personal computers appeared. This matches the trend in the general education literature, in which it would seem that researchers of technology become interested in new trends. The value of the calculator as a tool (Horton, Lovitt, & White, 1992) and as a teaching device (Frederick-Dugan, Test, & Varn, 1991; Koller & Mulhern, 1977) has been documented.

Acquiring the concepts of financial literacy, including the use of money, would appear to be particularly difficult for learners with Down syndrome and a number of relevant studies exist (see, for example, Frederick-Dugan *et al.*, 1991; Stith & Fishbein, 1996; Wheeler, Ford, Nietupski, Loomis, & Brown, 1980). Bochner *et al.*'s (2002) study investigated the money management skills of young people with Down syndrome and found young people with Down syndrome could 'acquire basic competence in functional number and money management skills' (p. 103). These skills included identifying notes and coins, tendering money, identifying the cost of items, determining if change would be given, and finally calculating change. Further, they attribute success to 'opportunity to learn, expectations of success and ongoing meaningful practice' (p. 103). In a more recent study, a method for teaching the use of new technology such as automatic teller machines was investigated (Rowe & Test, 2012).

Areas other than number

The great majority of research in the field of mathematics development of learners with Down syndrome has been in the area of number development and counting. Lister and Lee (1992) undertook one of the first studies in other branches of mathematics when they investigated the conservation of number and length. They reported that the order of development of reasoning was similar to that of typically developing children. Importantly, they noted that the children with Down syndrome showed similar processes in problem solving (p. 11). Errorless learning is sometimes advocated for learners with Down syndrome (Buckley & Bird, 1993). However, Lister and Lee's study reported that participants with Down syndrome made progress as a result of cognitive conflict, which may suggest that learning is possible as a result of reconciling errors.

Increasingly, young people with Down syndrome are gaining access to inclusive secondary education. This has led to the emergence of case studies indicating progress in areas of more sophisticated mathematics. Italy has an inclusive education system and research has emerged of learners achieving success with algebra, linear functions, compound interest, and fractions. Some findings are particularly surprising, such as the student who came to understand the concept of the measurement of length through use of the distance formula from coordinate geometry (Monari Martinez & Benedetti, 2011).

In this section, we have presented a summary of literature on the mathematical learning of children with Down syndrome. In the following section, data are presented from a recent study on the mathematical development of children with Down syndrome we conducted in Australia.

Furthering our understanding of the mathematical development of children with Down syndrome

Through contact with parent support groups, 12 primary school-aged children were recruited to join our Australian study, ranging in age from six to 12 years. One child was home schooled, two were in a special school in a rural town, one in a special education unit attached to a primary school, and the rest attended regular primary school in inclusive classroom settings.

With a limited research base, methods to chart the mathematical learning of children with Down syndrome are yet to be developed. The choice of task-based interviews was appropriate, being a common technique used in a number of large-scale projects with mainstream children in Australia and New Zealand (Bobis *et al.*, 2005). We used the Early Numeracy Interview (Clarke *et al.*, 2002) and Extending Mathematical Understanding (EMU; Gervasoni, 2004) as the basis of an interview for use in this study. While these instruments were already demonstrably effective, modification, trial, and development was undertaken. The initial Early Numeracy Research Project (ENRP) included two special schools and teachers in those schools found the interview to be effective in providing a broad range of useful information about children with learning difficulties (though none with Down syndrome) (Clarke & Faragher, 2004), as illustrated by the following teacher quote.

> I have to admit I was really surprised when I did the testing on them, at how much two or three of them knew, they knew far more than I realised. A couple of them are being held back because they still can't do the counting, one, two, three, they go wrong. But when we go beyond that it's just amazing how much understanding they've got. I was just blown away by a couple of the results, I really was.
>
> (Special school teacher interview)

A pilot of the interview was conducted with a 10-year-old girl with Down syndrome. That interview was videotaped and analysed by four of the research team for difficulties that might affect the validity of the results. Amendments to the interview schedule included simplification of language, new tasks, and omission of some tasks.

We were aware of literature that indicated children interviewed in unfamiliar contexts by people they did not know reduced performance on literacy tasks (Brown & Semple, 1970). We therefore interviewed participants in their home or school, in the presence of their parents (or teacher), who watched from behind the child. The adults were invited to comment on the performance of the child, either by taking notes during the interview, or in a discussion following the interview. The interviews with children were videotaped. The lead researcher on the project undertook all interviews, with assistance from a colleague who operated the camera and assisted with motivating the child to continue involvement.

Each child in the main study was interviewed twice, once in the middle of the school year and the second interview towards the end of the year or early the following year to provide additional data points. There were a number of additional challenges involved in conducting the interviews, including the length of time and the engagement of the child. This is reported in more detail in Faragher *et al.* (2008) and mirrors much of what is written elsewhere in this book (particularly Chapter 4). While an interview schedule was developed, the interviewer was encouraged to modify as necessary to ensure more useful data—effectively a semi-structured interview. This allowed the interviewer to follow up on responses from the child, to double back to earlier tasks, to ask a similar task in a different way, and to add tasks, such as counting stickers. In order to do this, the interviewer needed to know the purpose behind the interview questions as well as to be able to make preliminary judgements about what was being observed in the interview while it was in progress.

This flexible approach to the interview was taken as a result of both the experiences from the special school within the ENRP and the research that suggested some syndrome-specific patterns of development. Typically, interview protocols on which this interview was based provide for an 'opt out' if the child is unsuccessful with a task. In this study, the interviewer used her judgement on when to continue or repeat a task.

Another major reason for the use of the flexible/semi-structured approach to the task-based interview was in response to the behaviour of the children. Avoidant behaviour has been extensively documented, even in very young children with Down syndrome (Wishart, 1996) and as discussed in Chapter 4. Therefore, we were not surprised (though we were certainly entertained!) by the many instances where children were using strategies to avoid attempting the tasks—e.g. changing the tasks, playing with the equipment, using behaviours to distract the interviewer (burping, being 'cute', changing the subject), and refusing to participate. It is important to note that children used avoidant strategies even when they were able to do the tasks. Our interview protocol and technique allowed us to work around these antics to gather data we could trust. Some studies on mathematics performance by children with Down syndrome give a more pessimistic view than the experiences of parents and teachers would suggest (Abdelhameed & Porter, 2006). The discrepancy may be due to research methods that are unable to take account of such behaviours.

One of the key features of the interview was the broad range of mathematical content that was included. As previously discussed, there has been a focus on early development of number in the previous research literature on children with Down syndrome.

The interview protocol

As for the Early Numeracy Interview and EMU, the interview involves asking children to perform tasks with objects. For example, we put a collection of plastic teddy bears on the table and ask the participant to put all the yellow teddies together and then to count them. In another task, we ask them to put one straw in each cup, having put five plastic cups on the table. The equipment was presented in a variety of interesting boxes and containers to encourage curiosity in the tasks. A number of the tasks would be recognised by those who know the literature well on early mathematical development. The focus was on eliciting thinking and on strategies used. The original Early Numeracy Interview has been characterised as a form of 'choose your own adventure'. The interviewer made a decision after each task, according to the script. Given success on a particular task, the interviewer continued with the next task in the domain as far as the child could go with success. Given difficulty with the task, the interviewer either abandoned that section of the interview and moved on to the next domain or moved into a 'detour', designed to elaborate more clearly the difficulty a child might be having with a particular content area.

A feature of the Early Numeracy Interview was the high ceiling that was achieved through inclusion of tasks designed to challenge all children. The script assumed a trajectory of learning based on previous work with typically developing children. We did not want to assume a trajectory for the purpose of this study and so the adaptation and flexibility was intended to help us to see what was possible rather than to provide comparison with typically developing children. We did ask the first question in a section using the same protocol to enable comparison but deviation was encouraged to enable the opportunity for children to 'show what they know'. This requires an intuitive approach to interviewing, balancing the needs of the research with the comfort and well-being of the child in the moment. As a parent or familiar teacher was always present, this provided the interviewer with an opportunity for eye contact or a quick question as needed. The interview contained the following main mathematical foci and more specific content.

Counting

Tasks in the first section involved counting small collections and the concepts of 'more', 'less', conservation of number, subitising, and one-to-one correspondence. Other tasks involve matching numerals to quantities; ordering numerals (0–9); and using ten-frames.[2] A number of the tasks were from a specific section of the Early Numeracy Interview—the First Year of School Mathematics Interview (FYSMI). Details of the FYSMI, including data from a large sample of mainstream children, were reported in Clarke, Clarke, and Cheeseman (2006).

Counting without objects

Tasks in this section included rote counting; counting forwards and backwards from different starting points; stating the number before and after a given number; counting on a hundreds chart; and counting by tens, fives, and twos. These tasks included a focus on the more abstract aspects of counting.

Place value

Place value tasks involved reading numerals up to four digits; writing numbers on a calculator; being able to read numbers using a calculator display; and ordering collections of two-, three-, or four-digit numbers. The calculator had been used in the original ENRP interview and overcame difficulties with writing and related skills, including reversing of numerals. These tasks were followed by tasks which required the children to use bundling sticks: one to make a given number, the other to write the number for a set of bundling sticks. Finally, the children were asked to identify a number covered on a 0 to 99 chart.

Addition and subtraction strategies

This section offered opportunities to demonstrate 'counting-on' and other basic and derived strategies. In recent years, there has been a shift in the teaching and learning of addition and subtraction from a focus on pen and paper algorithms and error diagnosis to building upon young children's intuitive knowledge and strategies (Clarke *et al.*, 2002). This shift has been described as moving from showing children *what to do* to showing them *how to think* (Sugarman, 1997). This was reflected in the tasks in this section of the interview. The tasks also included the use of a number line to add or subtract.

Multiplication and division strategies

The principle on which this section of the Early Years Interview was based is that a composite number is a collection or group of individual objects that must be viewed as a unit. For example, a child must view three objects as 'one lot of three' in order for the unit 'three' to be a countable unit. For a true understanding of multiplication and division, the child needs eventually to coordinate a number of equal-sized groups and recognise the overall pattern of composites, such as 'three sixes'. Steffe described this as a pre-multiplying scheme: 'For a situation to be established as multiplicative, it is necessary at least to co-ordinate two composite units in such a way that one of the composite units is distributed over elements of the other composite unit' (Steffe, 1994, p. 19). Initial tasks involved contexts for multiplicative thinking using plastic teddy bears.

Measurement (time)

At the start of the interview, the children are invited to simply 'draw a clock' on a piece of paper. This drawing is discussed at the start of this section of the interview to determine the child's understanding of the arrangement of the numbers, the purpose of the hands, and what a clock is used for. A real clock is then used to ask children to read times. Tasks in this section also include naming days and months, before and after questions for days and months, and being able to read and interpret a calendar.

Space/geometry

The final section of the interview included location tasks (including vocabulary such as 'beside', 'behind'); describing the location of a playground; shape-sorting tasks (looking for classification according to properties); being able to identify shapes in the environment, especially in different orientations; and recognition of similarity and difference for related shapes. This section was taken directly from the Early Numeracy Interview.

In the next section, we discuss some of the results of the study.

Results

In analysing the data, it was clear that a number of issues relating to the administration of the interview and the children's actions were important, along with the mathematical understanding that was evidenced.

Performance on the interview

Standard mathematics interview protocols such as the Early Numeracy Interview have a script to be followed by the interviewer. Prompting may be allowed, but only under specified circumstances and in a set manner. From the piloting of the interview for this Down syndrome study, it became clear that such an approach would yield little data we could trust. Some children would not answer questions even when later they revealed they were able to do so. Some children made up their own task, perhaps to avoid the one asked or because they were unsure what to do. Following a standard protocol would have meant that, in each of these instances, the child would have been recorded as unsuccessful and the interview would have moved to a different task, even though they may actually have been able to succeed at the task.

Some children adopted the strategy of latching on to keywords when they did not understand the task. These participants seemed to be resorting to words they knew, heard last, or enjoyed when the language of the interview was unclear to them. By carefully considering the response of the child and further probing, it was possible for the interviewer to detect when the task was not clear to the child. In these cases, modelling what was required or asking simpler questions as a scaffolding step were techniques adopted. Having the one researcher with considerable expertise interview all the children allowed greater scope for probing the children further. Some specific examples are found below within the discussion of the particular mathematics.

Modification to the interview became necessary for some participants when it appeared that the presentation of the tasks themselves was distracting. The standard interview protocol makes use of objects such as plastic teddy bears with the deliberate purpose of engaging participants. For some of our children, though, these objects seemed to be a distraction. Some children needed to arrange all the teddies to be facing the same way, but took so much time that they forgot what they needed to do for the task. Others engaged in the story of the teddies going to the beach and lying on beach towels (as a context for division), to the point of missing the mathematics. It could be that the children were glad of an alternative task to pursue or it could be that they were genuinely distracted from the mathematics. In either case, however, it became clear that small blocks could be used instead, making explicit the mathematics required.

Studying performance on the interview highlighted an important behaviour pattern exhibited by many of the children. Being aware of the work of Wishart (1996) and the discussion in Chapter 4, we expected some avoidant learning behaviour patterns to be exhibited. We did not expect the performance of Travis,[3] who deserved to win a prize in this category! Initially, he pretended not to be able to count at all. The interviewer tried many approaches, including offering to take turns and count smaller collections, to no avail. It did not seem likely that the boy was unable to count—he was successfully included in a regular upper primary school programme, and his mother was burying her head in her hands in dismay. The interviewer tried other approaches—counting with mistakes proved successful. Travis revealed in his face surprise at mistakes. The most successful, though, was the use of stickers. When he completed a task, he was given a sticker. He was told he could leave when he had 15. Astonishingly, he was then able to reveal not only that he could count to 15, but also that he could self-correct, work out how many more he needed, and confirm responses using a hundreds chart.

What could be the cause behind such behaviour? Many children with Down syndrome are labelled 'stubborn' or 'lazy'. We believe this is not the motivation in this case. We gave Travis a copy of his first interview on DVD and his mother told us that he watched the DVD over and over. He cheered himself on as he watched, saying, 'Come on Travis, you can do it!', only to sigh with disappointment when not successful. We believe this reveals a great deal. Travis wants to do well. Like other children, he wants to succeed. Unfortunately, in many situations, particularly tests, he may have experienced failure. It then is perhaps easy to understand why he would avoid answering a question than make an attempt with a good chance of failing. It may also explain why we notice children with Down syndrome being hesitant to experiment with new, more efficient strategies, such as counting on rather than counting all (Irwin, 1991). It might take more time, but if it works more often than not, it may be worth trusting the known strategy. There are typically developing children with the same reluctance to take risks with new mathematical strategies that are not consolidated, but improvement in mathematical learning, particularly in early number, is dependent on the increased use of more sophisticated strategies.

Mary was one of the older children interviewed and confidently worked on the first few tasks in the interview. She was then asked to take five blue teddies from a mixed collection, which she did successfully. Next the interviewer spread the teddies out and asked how many there were. Mary counted again, successfully. The intent was to see if she would identify the quantity without counting and arguably evidence conservation of number (see Clarke *et al.*, 2006, for discussion of the difficulties in interpreting this task). The interviewer again repeated the process and Mary again counted. While we would have expected that she could conserve number and understand that the count indicated the numerosity of the set, this task had not provided the necessary evidence. As the interviewer packed up the teddies, she had the blue teddies in a group under her hand. She then asked Mary how many there were and Mary quickly answered '5'. She was clearly demonstrating understanding of the cardinality of the set and conservation, though not in response to the question intended to elicit this knowledge but rather from an incidental question. This interaction again illustrates the challenges of more protocol-driven interviews with the behavioural practices of children with Down syndrome and the value of flexibility in the hands of a knowledgeable researcher in providing insights into mathematical understanding and thinking.

It is our view that interviewers of children with Down syndrome need to be flexible and highly skilled in understanding the mathematics underlying the interview questions in order to probe appropriately and provide valid data on individual understanding. This approach provided greater insight into the mathematical thinking and processing of the children we were studying.

Development of mathematics

One of the components of the research design was to interview each child twice with a gap of at least six months. We had intended that this would provide two data points for each child, effectively providing 24 points and enabling some quantitative and comparative analysis. However, the reality of the unreliability of the responses as well as limited progress by individual children made this problematic. What was originally thought to provide some general mapping of children with Down syndrome ended up providing data with limited reliability in relation to this purpose. The possibility of comparison with the extensive data set of typically developing children from the ENRP was therefore limited. However, we are able to make hypotheses and note progression with age.

Data analysis was undertaken by transcribing the videotapes and then documenting the responses of children. Interesting anecdotes or surprising responses were noted and written up in narrative form, including transcripts. These are the basis of the earlier discussions of Travis and Mary. We then used three categories for interpreting the children's responses across all questions—correct, partial, and incorrect. These data were entered on a spreadsheet and colour coded (illustrated in the tables in this chapter using dark, medium, and light shading, respectively), providing a visual and quantitative presentation of the results. This was a similar approach to Nye, Clibbens, and Bird (1995), except for 'partial' where they used 'can do with help'. In some circumstances, partial indicated that the child was assisted but also indicated partial completion. An example would be rote counting where the child did not reach the level of the original interview protocol but evidenced some counting (in which case, the highest count was also recorded).

Our presentation of data below focuses primarily on the individual narratives and some specific examples of collective data. In attempting to map the mathematical understanding of children with Down syndrome, we argue that such presentation is an existence proof or at least a starting point for further exploration of what is possible. The findings are discussed in each of the mathematical foci of the interview.

Counting

Through our analysis of the responses of emerging counters in our study, it would appear that they may be developing the concept of number in a different trajectory to typically developing children. This is the focus of Chapter 6 where more detailed analysis of the responses to the early number tasks is discussed.

Some of the traditional 'pre-number' concepts assessed were included in this section of the interview. An early task involves placing five plastic cups in front of the child and giving them nine plastic straws. They are then asked to place one straw in each cup to evidence one-to-one correspondence. Mary was progressing successfully with this task but once she had placed one in each cup she put a second one in each cup until all were used up. She then counted by twos to 10 while pointing to the cups. The interviewer repeated the instructions several times. She then decided to attempt the task again but this time specifically talked about her game and Mary's game. The interviewer said, 'You do my game first and then you can do your game', interpreting Mary's actions as playful rather than indicating a lack of understanding of the task and the concept of 'each' and related one-to-one correspondence. In response to this, Mary put a straw in each cup and then paused. When she was given permission to do her game, she added the extra straws. This appeared to vindicate the interviewer's interpretation of the previous interaction. It seemed that Mary knew what was being asked of her and could do it.

Table 5.2 presents the summative data from a series of questions which were part of the FYSMI and required sorting by colour, simple counting, and the conservation question discussed earlier. There are some missing data where the question was not asked or the children did not attempt the task. The proportion of missing data increased for tasks that were asked later in the interview. These will be evident in the following tables where cohort data are presented. The progression of children based on age is evident.

Counting without objects

Studying videotape excerpts indicated the extremely long response time exhibited by some participants when asked to oral count. One child took 90 seconds to give a correct response. Extended response times of learners with intellectual disabilities are well known to special educators (Mitchell, 2007). As an interviewer, it is possible to sit and wait. For a teacher, there are likely to be imperatives to jump in, to rephrase the question, or to teach the correct response (Rowe, 1986). As researchers, we are curious to know what Hun was thinking when he took 90 seconds to continue counting from 79 to 80. It is well known that counting across the decade is a difficulty for emerging counters as they learn the patterns inherent in our numeration system. However, this student was able to count confidently in tens. We do not know if the delay was about processing the task or retrieving information from memory. He did appear to be intently considering the task before continuing on successfully.

An additional task for supported counting with the 0–99 number chart was included on the basis of research into the challenges of the verbal count for children with Down syndrome. There is more discussion of the results in Chapter 6, but all children were able to 'rote count' at least as far with support of the symbols. It appears that the symbol supports the appropriate sequencing of the count words beyond what can be remembered.

When considering counting without objects, some of the children were highly proficient (see Table 5.3). The pattern is variable, though, and does not show a clear development with age. Some of the younger children were able to count to 32, while older children demonstrated only partial success. The support for counting given by the number chart is obvious from these data. All but one of the children counted further with the number chart than by rote counting alone. It can be seen that nine out of the 18 data points for this task (50 per cent) indicated some success at counting without objects. This jumped to around 88 per cent (15 out of 17) when supported by the number chart.

Mary seemed quite comfortable with the 0–99 chart. She named it when the interviewer produced it and went on to count confidently to 50, at which point she was asked to stop. She agreed to play a game where the interviewer covered a number with her finger while Mary had her eyes closed. The number 83 was covered. Mary answered 38 when asked what number was covered and did not give an explanation. Mary then wanted a turn and covered 100 for the interviewer. Mary then requested another turn and the interviewer covered 25. Mary correctly identified this number but again gave no explanation when asked. Both responses suggest some ability to see the pattern or the sequence of numbers. It is not clear what thinking or conceptualisation is evident but it seems to suggest some pattern-based thinking as the numerals were identified though the order for 83 was reversed. One of the major contrasts with

Table 5.2 Overall response to tasks focusing on colour and counting small collections

Activity	*Age at interview in years, months*									
	6, 2	*6, 4*	*6, 7*	*7, 0*	*7, 3*	*7, 9*	*8, 3*	*8, 8*	*9, 6*	*9, 11*
Put the yellow teddies together	no response	no response	correct	incorrect	no response	correct	no response	correct	correct	no response
How many are yellow?	incorrect	no response	correct	no response	no response	correct	partially correct	no response	correct	no response
Are there more green than yellow?	partially correct	no response	correct	no response	no response	correct	incorrect	correct	correct	correct
Get five blue teddies	incorrect	no response	incorrect	no response	partially correct	partially correct	incorrect	partially correct	correct	correct
Spaced out *How many now?*	correct	no response	incorrect	no response	correct	incorrect	partially correct	partially correct	correct	correct
Placed together *How many now?*	incorrect	no response	incorrect	no response	correct	partially correct	no response	no response	partially correct	correct

Activity	*10, 1*	*10, 1*	*10, 5*	*10, 6*	*10, 8*	*10, 10*	*11, 1*	*11, 2*	*11, 3*	*11, 8*	*11, 9*	*12, 3*
Put the yellow teddies together	incorrect	correct	correct	correct	correct	partially correct	no response	correct	correct	correct	correct	partially correct
How many are yellow?	correct	correct	correct	correct	correct	correct	correct	no response	correct	correct	correct	partially correct
Are there more green than yellow?	incorrect	incorrect	correct	incorrect	incorrect	correct	correct	correct	correct	correct	correct	partially correct
Get five blue teddies	incorrect	correct	partially correct	incorrect	correct	correct	correct	correct	correct	correct	correct	partially correct
Spaced out *How many now?*	incorrect	incorrect	correct	partially correct	partially correct	correct	correct	correct	partially correct	correct	correct	partially correct
Placed together *How many now?*	incorrect	incorrect	correct	partially correct	no response	correct	correct	correct	partially correct	partially correct	correct	partially correct

Notes
☐ = no response or subsequent question not asked
☐ = incorrect response
☐ = partially correct response
■ = correct response

Table 5.3 Overall results for rote counting including the use of the 0–99 chart for support

Activity	*Age at interview in years, months*																						
	6, 2	*6, 4*	*6, 7*	*7, 0*	*7, 3*	*7, 9*	*8, 3*	*8, 8*	*9, 6*	*9, 11*	*10, 1*	*10, 1*	*10, 5*	*10, 6*	*10, 8*	*10, 10*	*11, 1*	*11, 2*	*11, 2*	*11, 3*	*11, 8*	*11, 9*	*12, 3*
Counting without objects																							
1 to 32			14		14		4		>33			13	20				>33	25			36		40
From 53									59	59			54		54		59	59					
Count from 84									to 85	to 87							89	89			108		
Number chart																							
Count	20	7	14		12	14	10	12	>47	>43		20	>40				to 50					from 40	
Count backwards																							
From 10									missed 5														
From 24													23						24, 22, 21				

Notes
[white box] = no response or subsequent question not asked
[light box] = incorrect response
[grey box] = partially correct response
[dark box] = correct response

our previous experience of such interviews with typically developing children was the lack of explanation given by the children with Down syndrome. Most typically developing children and some children without Down syndrome in the two special school settings would attempt to explain their thinking. This component was very important in the ENRP and EMU interview. The strategies used were of particular interest as an indication of the sophistication of the mathematical thinking.

The ease with which most children could count backwards from 10 was striking and may reflect the experience many have with countdowns. Quite a few added 'blast off!' at the end. The competence they displayed with backwards from 10 was not matched with backwards from 24, which may match the challenge of counting forwards. It is largely a memory task.

Place value

Reading numeral cards was the first task in this section and further discussion is provided in Chapter 6. The responses to the task indicate a relative strength in reading numerals. One aspect of the interview was the use of the calculator for reading and writing numerals. The children were generally comfortable and familiar with the calculator.

One task required children to enter a number on a calculator that was orally presented to them—a writing number task. The display was cleared between numbers. The task was presented some time into the interview (up to 30 minutes from the start) and a small number of the younger children had disengaged. For those who engaged with the task, it can be seen in Table 5.4 that children from a young age were able to enter single digits. From nine years of age, this task would appear routine. It would appear that the writing of numerals is more difficult than the reading of numerals. Batman, for example, was highly accomplished at counting with and without objects. He also could read three-digit numbers fluently. However, his initial attempts to enter the number 15 were a source of frustration; he could not make the display show what he intended. Finally, after writing the number on paper and looking on a hundreds chart, he was able to enter the number correctly. Next, he entered 724 as the number is said: 700 20 4, said, 'seven hundred and twenty four'. It can be seen in the table that the same response was given by both children who reached this stage of the interview (Hun and Batman), and both were able to read these numbers. This difficulty with writing numbers is well established with pen and paper with typically developing children. The calculator was used with young children to avoid difficulties of interpreting their writing, including the possible reversal of digits. For older children with considerable school experience, it may be preferable to use physical writing for this task to ensure that the calculator is not confounding the difficulty. There is also a clear need to explicitly teach children to use calculators effectively, including the entry of numbers. It cannot be assumed that children know how to do this; however, with instruction, effective use can be expected (Koller & Mulhern, 1977).

The second set of calculator tasks involved the children entering digits and being asked to name the number without clearing the display between entries. All the children who were given this task were able to enter and name a single digit (10 out of 11, or 91 per cent), except for one boy who was successful on this task in his second interview five months later. Reading a two-digit number proved more challenging and children under 10 were not successful. Reading a three-digit number was only completed successfully by Batman, the oldest child in the study.

Table 5.4 Overall data on using a calculator to write numerals

Activity	*Age at interview in years, months*																						
	6, 2	*6, 4*	*6, 7*	*7, 0*	*7, 3*	*7, 9*	*8, 3*	*8, 8*	*9, 6*	*9, 11*	*10, 1*	*10, 1*	*10, 5*	*10, 6*	*10, 8*	*10, 10*	*11, 1*	*11, 2*	*11, 2*	*11, 3*	*11, 8*	*11, 9*	*12, 3*
Entering numbers																							
7																							
47															417								407
60															61								
15																					51		
724																			700, 24		700, 24	700, 24	700, 24
105																					1005		

Notes
□ = no response or subsequent question not asked
□ = incorrect response
■ = correct response

Addition and subtraction strategies

The first question with a focus on addition and subtraction was 'Show me six fingers' (part of the FYSMI). If successful, the child is asked to show it in a different way, with the intent of seeing if they are able to see six as three and three, or four and two, rather than just the number after five, thereby assessing part–part–whole aspects of number. Nelson (1999) claimed that 'there is no greater evidence that young children are developing true number sense than their emergent awareness that numbers are made up of other numbers' (p. 137). This is argued to be an important precursor to more sophisticated addition and subtraction strategies.

The tasks in this section of the interview were well beyond most of the children and in most cases they were not presented. The tasks often used larger numbers than these children were typically able to count and so evidence of their ability to use addition and subtraction strategies was limited. The first specific question involved the interviewer showing nine plastic teddies and covering these. A further collection of four is visible to the child, and the child is asked how many are there altogether. The task is to see if the child can count on in finding the total and follows a well-established protocol. In the future, it would be preferable to use smaller numbers to determine if the verbal count sequence was the difficulty rather than the knowledge of counting on.

During the interview with Hun (11 years old), he was presented with a subtraction task involving a context that required him to take 7 from 10. He chose to draw a number line and successfully answered the question. His recording is reproduced in Figure 5.1.

At the end of Hun's first interview, his mother shared an experience of a 'psych assessment' for school placement purposes. The psychologist had omitted the numeracy section but the report concluded that he would be unable to learn these concepts. His interview clearly showed this was not the case and his mother, while pleased with his achievements, was frustrated by some of the systemic issues that she believed were limiting his progress. Research of this nature is important to remove the misconception that children with Down syndrome automatically will be unable to learn mathematics.

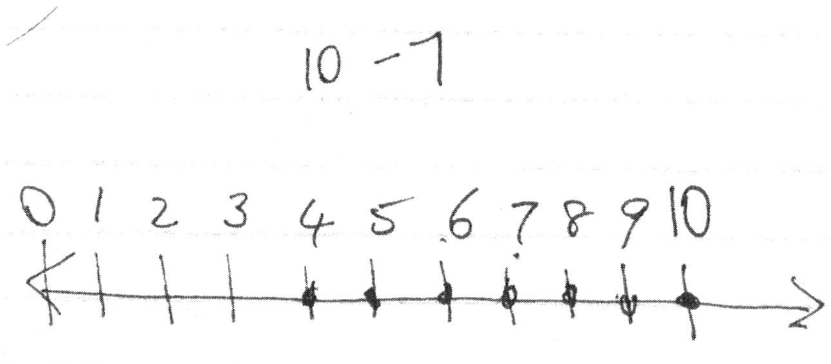

Figure 5.1 Number line drawn by Hun, 11 years old.

Multiplication and division strategies

Again most of the tasks in this section were not presented to the children. However, some children showed evidence of early multiplicative thinking during the teddy car task. In this task, children are asked to put two teddies in each of four cars (matchboxes). They are then asked how many teddies there are altogether. Mary was successful in understanding and completing the instructions and then counted by twos to give the answer of eight. She was also able to share 12 teddies equally between four "teddy mats"—evidencing early division understanding.

Hun could count by twos but did not use that strategy with the teddy cars. The context of the cars seemed to be a distraction as he physically drove the teddies into the matchboxes. This is an example of the issue raised earlier, where the context appears to distract some children from the mathematics of the task. However, it was engaging for Hun and perhaps kept him interested in the interview longer. Whether to keep the context is an open question. One of the features of the interview, particularly in the sections focusing on numerical operations, is the use of contexts. These are intended to both assess the conceptualisation of the mathematical operation (as in the case of eating strawberries as a context for subtraction) as well as engage the children.

Measurement (time)

In the ENRP interview, questions were asked relating to both length and mass measurement. As there were concerns about the time taken to interview children in the current study, it was decided not to include these sections. However, the tasks relating to time were included. As previously mentioned, the children were asked to draw a clock at the beginning of the interview. The intent of the clock task is to engage children in a discussion of time and the purpose of clocks. The quality of the drawing was not assessed, though inferences can clearly be drawn from the clocks created. Clarke (1998) suggested an increasing sophistication of children's drawings of clocks. Figure 5.2 shows a clock drawn by one of the children. This is from one of the higher performing children (Hun) and is relatively sophisticated, with numerals placed correctly in position. This would represent the stage where children recognise that partitioning

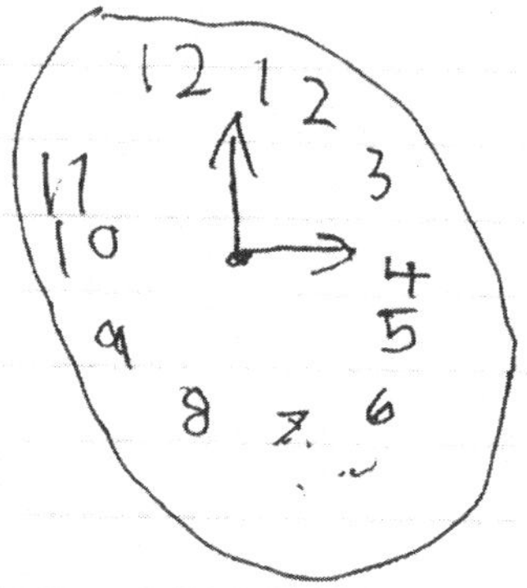

Figure 5.2 Clock drawn by Hun.

of the 12 numerals is important. Anecdotally this would be around seven or eight for typically developing children. As mentioned elsewhere in the book, visiospatial skills are a relative strength for children with Down syndrome and the geometric arrangement of the numbers on a clockface may indicate these forms of thinking or observing are more highly developed than other language-related aspects. More investigation is obviously needed to gain a clearer picture.

Clarke (1998) also talked of the importance of the concept of time, not just telling time. He advocated the use of this open-ended task of drawing a clock with primary-aged children. Such tasks also provide opportunity for children to demonstrate unexpected understandings or new ways of sharing their thinking. The intent was to have a conversation about time and the clock but this was not very effective in our study. Again there was limited explanation provided.

Eight out of 17 (47 per cent) were able to read 2 pm on an analogue clock, three correctly read the half hour (9:30) and one identified quarter past nine. In general, children found reading time on the analogue clock difficult. They also demonstrated little awareness of significant features of the clock, such as the arrangement of numbers and the purpose of the hands. Recent approaches to teaching the reading of analogue clocks (Van de Walle, 2004) emphasises teaching children to use the hour hand first. Research is needed to determine if a staged teaching approach with identifying the hands then telling time from the hour hand before moving to the minute hand would be an effective approach for children with Down syndrome.

Space/geometry

We had hypothesised that there might be a relative strength in this area of mathematics for children with Down syndrome. One of the major challenges was that this was the last part of the interview and the children were very tired and little useful data were collected.

A geometry-related question from early in the interview involved location language. The original task, part of the FYSMI, asked children to place a small plastic teddy in a specified position relative to another teddy. Margie was asked to place a green teddy behind a blue teddy that was in front of her on the table. She did not do this so the interviewer got out of her seat, moved over to the clear space with Margie and asked her to stand behind her. Margie did this successfully, showing some understanding of the concept 'behind' in this more physical context. This additional task became a feature of future interviews. More children were successful with this task as it required them to interpret position relative to themselves, rather than relative to another object.

This is an example of the need to understand the intent of the task and the likely processing of the child in order to successfully adapt 'on the run'. With typically developing children at the beginning of school this was not a necessary additional step. With children with Down syndrome (and possibly others with developmental delay), the additional task provided useful data.

Our study aimed to understand more of the development of mathematics by learners with Down syndrome. The interviews have proved rich sources of interesting data and provide some useful insights, but much more focused research is required.

Contribution of parents and teachers

As noted earlier, we made a deliberate effort to involve parents and teachers in this study. We found the comments of the adult observers to be insightful and helpful in understanding what we were seeing. It was also clear that particular emphases of adults affected the performance of the children. For example, one of our participants was taught at home by his mother and she had focused on counting. Her son was the most successful counter in our study, being able to count past 120, and count in twos, tens, and fives. As the interview proceeded, though, he was less successful in making use of numbers. His mother talked with the interviewer about this afterwards and decided she would move her focus to operations and understanding of number concepts.

Students who were attending regular schools were more used to standard 'mathematics classroom' objects. These include bundling sticks, which are rarely seen outside classrooms. Children were not always successful with these, but it was clear they knew what they were expected to do with them. One child proudly showed the interviewer the bundling sticks she used at home (stored in the book shelf near the dining table, along with her mathematics work books and other homework material).

Another child in a special school setting had been learning the days of the week and he loved demonstrating what he was able to do with his newly acquired understanding.

These examples indicate some of the many instances where we could detect responses to tasks had been influenced by explicit teaching in home or school contexts. This demonstrates the importance for parents and teachers of knowing what are the key ideas of mathematics. These important concepts can then be emphasised in teaching programmes and individual learning plans. Opportunities for learning and consolidation over time can then be provided. Children with Down syndrome take longer to learn many mathematics concepts and require considerable practice to ameliorate the effects of unstable learning. It is vital for teachers and parents to know the essential concepts to emphasise, consolidate, and practise over time.

We are clearly a long way from articulating even an indicative trajectory for mathematics learning for children with Down syndrome. We would argue that, while it has many similarities with typically developing children, there are some apparent differences that have implications for educators.

Implications and conclusions

In the analysis of our data on the mathematical development of learners with Down syndrome, we have noticed that none of the findings appear to be unique to individuals with Down syndrome. However, we are noticing clusters of similar phenomena, such as the relative strength in the use of symbols for the development of number concepts. We are exploring the idea now that we might be observing a syndrome effect. We are using the term 'syndrome' in the sense that it refers to a combination of related phenomena. This may lead us to propose a profile of strengths and weaknesses in mathematical development that can assist teachers to overcome some of the detrimental effects of Down syndrome for learners. We advocate further research in this area and particularly studies which move beyond the investigation of early number into other areas of mathematics learning. Through this, additional strengths may be found that may compensate for areas of weakness.

A clear requirement for educators is to support students with Down syndrome to be risk takers in their learning. It is important to appreciate that avoidant behaviours are not due to stubbornness or laziness but may be an inherent learning style for children with Down syndrome, perhaps developed to protect against failure. We can help children by explicitly teaching and encouraging more efficient strategies for tasks and providing consistent opportunities for practice to ensure these strategies become part of the competent repertoire of the child. The apparent lack of ability or at least experience in providing explanations of their mathematical thinking needs to be further explored.

Highly structured protocols provide reliable comparisons for researchers but limit the opportunities for some children to evidence the richness of their mathematical understanding. Structured interview protocols (such as the Early Numeracy Interview) that are designed to elicit different strategies, encourage conversations, and highlight children's thinking provide greater insights about the learning of individual children than is possible with other testing. A more flexible approach in the form of semi-structured interviews has provided richer and more valid data for children with Down syndrome. A knowledgeable interviewer is required for this method to be effective. It requires sophisticated knowledge of the mathematical development of young children as well as the skills to engage the children, to intervene or stay silent, to persist, and to know when to move on.

In assessment, providing opportunities and tools for the child to demonstrate what they know and can do as part of the regular learning process, and not just in formal testing procedures, would be important. Assessment using one-to-one task-based interviews in a flexible way could be considered by teachers as well as researchers. These do not need to be administered formally but can be incidental during teaching sessions.

Our research leads us to believe that there is unlikely to be a simple solution for helping students with Down syndrome to learn mathematics more effectively. Over the years, many kits and programmes have been developed, such as number dots, *Numicon*, and money skill resources. All of these are likely to assist at least some children with number learning; however, approaches to assist learners develop concepts across the broader discipline of mathematics are likely to be multi-faceted.

The richness and breadth of mathematical-related experiences and knowledge are important for enhancing the opportunities for all. More research is clearly needed but well-established, good mathematical learning practices along with informed and sensitive teaching and on-going assessment can provide important opportunities for children with Down syndrome. We were delighted to have the opportunity to interview these children and to share their mathematical stories and understandings.

Acknowledgement

The authors wish to acknowledge the contribution of the children with Down syndrome and their parents and teachers, as well as the insights reflected in this paper of colleagues in the research team: Jo Brady, Ann Gervasoni, and Jan Kruger.

The research was jointly funded by the Mathematics Teaching and Learning Research Centre of the Australian Catholic University, as well as SiMERR (ACT)—the Centre for Science, ICT and Mathematics Education in Rural and Regional Australia.

Notes

1 Of course, human diversity ensures there is no such thing as a 'typically developing' child. We use this term as shorthand for children without intellectual disabilities, and specifically in this context, without Down syndrome.

2 Ten-frames are visual representations of numbers up to 10 shown by dots on a card. For example, 7 would be represented as:

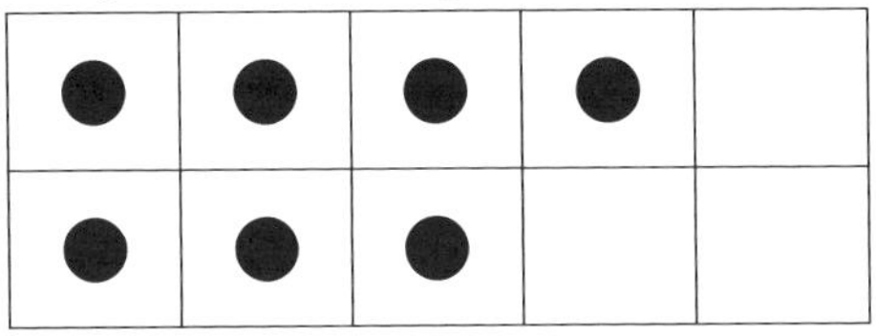

3 The names are pseudonyms created by the children themselves.

References

Abdelhameed, H., & Porter, J. (2006). Counting in Egyptian children with Down syndrome. *International Journal of Special Education, 21*, 176–187.

Bird, G., & Buckley, S. (2001). *Number skills for individuals with Down syndrome. An overview.* Hampshire, UK: The Down Syndrome Educational Trust.

Bobis, J., Clarke, B. A., Clarke, D., Thomas, G., Wright, R., Young-Loveridge, J., & Gould, P. (2005). Supporting teachers in the development of young children's mathematical thinking: Three large scale cases. *Mathematics Education Research Journal, 16*, 27–57.

Bochner, S., Outhred, L., Pieterse, M., & Bashash, L. (2002). Numeracy and money management skills in young adults with Down syndrome. In M. Cuskelly, A. Jobling, & S. Buckley (Eds), *Down syndrome across the lifespan* (pp. 93–106). London: Whurr Publishers.

Brown, R. I., & Semple, L. (1970). Effects of unfamiliarity on the overt verbalisation and perceptual motor behaviour of nursery school children. *British Journal of Educational Psychology, 40*, 291–298.

Buckley, S. J., & Bird, G. (1993). Teaching children with Down syndrome to read. *Down Syndrome Research and Practice, 1*, 34–39. doi: 10.3104/perspectives.9.

Butterworth, B. (2005). The development of arithmetical abilities. *Journal of Child Psychology and Psychiatry, 46*, 3–18.

Camos, V. (2009). Numerosity discrimination in children with Down syndrome. *Developmental Neuropsychology, 34*, 435–447.

Caycho, L., Gunn, P., & Siegal, M. (1991). Counting by children with Down syndrome. *American Journal on Mental Retardation, 95*, 575–583.

Clarke, B. A., Clarke, D. M., & Cheeseman, J. (2006). The mathematical knowledge and understanding young children bring to school. *Mathematics Education Research Journal, 18*, 78–102.

Clarke, B. A., & Faragher, R. M. (2004). Possibilities not limitations: Teaching special needs children. In B. Clarke, D. M. Clarke, G. Emanuelsson, B. Johansson, D. V. Lambdin, F. K. Lester, … K. Wallby (Eds), *International perspectives on learning and teaching mathematics* (pp. 379–394). Goteborg, Sweden: National Center for Mathematics Education.

Clarke, D. (1998). Children's understanding of the clock in the digital age. *Primary Educator, 4*, 9–12.

Clarke, D. M., Cheeseman, J., Gervasoni, A., Gronn, D., Horne, M., McDonough, A., … Rowley, G. (2002). *Early numeracy research project final report.* Melbourne, Australia: Mathematics Teaching and Learning Centre, Australian Catholic University.

de Graaf, G., van Hove, G., & Haveman, M. (2013). More academics in regular schools? The effect of regular versus special school placement on academic skills in Dutch primary school students with Down syndrome. *Journal of Intellectual Disability Research, 57*, 21–38. doi: 10.1111/j.1365-2788.2011.01512.x.

Dehaene, S. (1999). *The number sense. How the mind creates mathematics.* London: Penguin.

Devlin, K. (2005). *The math instinct. Why you're a mathematical genius (along with lobsters, birds, cats, and dogs)*. New York: Avalon.

Faragher, R., Brady, J., Clarke, B. A., Clarke, D. M., & Gervasoni, A. (2008). Narrowing the gap: Empowering teachers and parents through understanding how children with Down syndrome develop mathematically. In L. Graham (Ed.), *Proceedings of the 'Narrowing the Gap: Addressing Educational Disadvantage' Conference* (pp. 56–62). University of New England, Armidale, NSW: SiMERR.

Frederick-Dugan, A., Test, D. W., & Varn, L. (1991). Acquisition and generalization of purchasing skills using a calculator by students who are mentally retarded. *Education and Training in Mental Retardation. 26*, 381–387.

Gelman, R., & Cohen, M. (1988). Qualitative difference in the way Down's syndrome and normal children solve a novel counting problem. In L. Nadel (Ed.), *The psychobiology of Down's syndrome* (pp. 51–99). Cambridge: MIT/Bradford Press.

Gelman, R., & Gallistel, C. R. (1978). *The child's understanding of number.* Cambridge: Harvard University Press.

Gelman, R., Meck, E., & Merkin, S. (1986). Young children's numerical competence. *Cognitive Development, 1*, 1–29.

Gervasoni, A. (2004). *Exploring an intervention strategy for six and seven year old children who are vulnerable in learning school mathematics.* Unpublished doctoral thesis, La Trobe University, Bundoora.

Horton, S. V., Lovitt, T. C., & White, O. R. (1992). Teaching mathematics to adolescents classified as Educable Mentally Handicapped using calculators to remove the computational onus. *Remedial and Special Education, 13*, 36–60.

Irwin, K. C. (1991). Teaching children with Down syndrome to add by counting-on. *Education and Treatment of Children, 14*, 128–141.

Koller, E. Z., & Mulhern, T. J. (1977). Use of a pocket calculator to train arithmetic skills with trainable adolescents. *Education and Training of the Mentally Retarded, 12*, 332–335.

Lister, C., & Lee, S. (1992). Processes of development in understanding of length in individuals with Down syndrome. *Early Child Development and Care, 81*, 1–13.

Mitchell, D. (2007). *What really works in special and inclusive education: Using evidence-based teaching strategies*. New York: Taylor and Francis.

Monari Martinez, E., & Benedetti, N. (2011). Learning mathematics in mainstream secondary schools: Experiences of students with Down's syndrome. *European Journal of Special Needs Education, 26*, 531–540. doi: 10.1080/08856257.2011.597179.

Nelson, G. D. (1999). Within easy reach: Using a shelf-based curriculum to increase the range of mathematical concepts accessible to young children. In J. V. Copley (Ed.), *Mathematics in the early years* (pp. 135–145). Reston, VA: National Council of Teachers of Mathematics.

Noda Herrera, A., Bruno, A., Gonzalez, C., Moreno, L., & Sanabria, H. (2011). Addition and subtraction by students with Down syndrome. *International Journal of Mathematical Education in Science and Technology, 42*, 13–35. doi: 10.1080/0020739X.2010.500698.

Nye, J., Clibbens, J., & Bird, G. (1995). Numerical ability, general ability and language in children with Down's syndrome. *Down Syndrome Research and Practice, 3*, 92–102.

Nye, J., Fluck, M., & Buckley, S. (2001). Counting and cardinal understanding in children with Down syndrome and typically developing children. *Down Syndrome Research and Practice, 7*, 68–78.

Paterson, S. J. (2001). Language and number in Down syndrome: The complex developmental trajectory from infancy to adulthood. *Down Syndrome Research and Practice, 7*, 79–86.

Paterson, S. J., Girelli, L., Butterworth, B., & Karmiloff-Smith, A. (2006). Are numerical impairments syndrome specific? Evidence from Williams syndrome and Down's syndrome. *Journal of Child Psychology and Psychiatry, 47*, 190–204.

Porter, J. (1998). The understanding of counting in children with severe learning difficulties and nursery children. *British Journal of Educational Psychology, 68*, 331–345.

Rowe, D. A., & Test, D. W. (2012). Effects of simulation to teach students with disabilities basic finance skills. *Remedial and Special Education* (online). doi: 10.1177/0741932512448218.

Rowe, M. B. (1986). Wait time: Slowing down may be a way of speeding up! *Journal of Teacher Education, 37*, 43–50. doi: 10.1177/002248718603700110.

Shepperdson, B. (1994). Attainments in reading and number of teenagers and adults with Down's syndrome. *Down Syndrome Research and Practice, 2*, 97–101.

Steffe, L. P. (1994). Children's multiplying schemes. In G. Harel & J. Confrey (Eds), *The development of multiplicative reasoning in the learning of mathematics* (pp. 3–41). Albany, NY: State University of New York Press.

Stith, L. E., & Fishbein, H. D. (1996). Basic money-counting skills of children with mental retardation. *Research in Developmental Disabilities, 17*, 185–201.

Sugarman, I. (1997). Teaching for strategies. Teaching and learning early number. In I. Thompson (Ed.), *Teaching and learning early number* (pp. 142–153). Buckingham, UK: Open University.

Turner, S., & Alborz, A. (2003). Academic attainments of children with Down's syndrome: A longitudinal study. *British Journal of Educational Psychology, 73*, 563–583.

Van de Walle, J. A. (2004). *Elementary and middle school mathematics: Teaching developmentally* (5th edn). Boston, MA: Pearson.

Wheeler, J., Ford, A., Nietupski, J., Loomis, R., & Brown, L. (1980). Teaching moderately and severely handicapped adolescents to shop in supermarkets using pocket calculators. *Education and Training of the Mentally Retarded,* 15, 105–112.

Wishart, J. G. (1996). Avoidant learning styles and cognitive development in young children. In B. Stratford & P. Gunn (Eds), *New approaches to Down syndrome* (pp. 173–205). London: Cassell.

Chapter 6

Developing early number concepts for children with Down syndrome

Barbara Clarke and Rhonda Faragher

Abstract

This chapter reviews the literature on aspects of early number learning for children with Down syndrome. It reports on data relating to early number from a larger study undertaken to map the mathematical development of children with Down syndrome. The study used semi-structured, task-based, one-to-one interviews. From the analysis of video data, it would appear that the children in our study are developing counting in different ways from typically developing children. It seems that the development of number understanding by these children is enhanced by the use of symbols, but more research is needed. Suggested teaching approaches are proposed, as are further areas for research.

Introduction

As discussed in Chapter 5, the cause and nature of difficulties with learning number for children with Down syndrome is not known, but there are some promising developments. Some recent studies from the field of psychology (Camos, 2009; Paterson, Girelli, Butterworth, & Karmiloff-Smith, 2006) are beginning to identify areas of possible differences in cognitive development that may impair the development of number. These tend to refer to language-based systems but the exact nature is yet to be understood.

A recent study (Paterson *et al.*, 2006), where the mathematical development of children and adults with Williams syndrome was used as a contrast, provided clear evidence for syndrome-specific number development for children and adults with Williams syndrome but concluded that the development of aspects of number in children with Down syndrome paralleled typically developing children, though with significant delay. However, some of their more specific findings suggest variations that could be explained by different patterns of development of number for children with Down syndrome. Of course, as with typically developing children, there is considerable variation between children with Down syndrome in relation to numerical ability (Gelman & Cohen, 1988).

There has generally been a paucity of research into the mathematical development of children with specific learning difficulties (Rousselle & Noel, 2007), particularly compared to the research into reading and language development. However, there is increased interest, particularly in light of research with brain imaging (Dehaene, 1997). There is growing evidence that genetic factors play a role in mathematical achievement and development (Paterson *et al.*, 2006; Rousselle & Noel, 2007) and it is timely to investigate the role of the educator in supporting the mathematical development of diverse students, particularly for children with Down syndrome.

By contrast, there has been considerable interest in the mathematical development of typically developing young children, particularly in Australia. Through a number of school-based, system-wide projects, a considerable amount of data on the number development of young children in school settings has been gathered (Bobis *et al.*, 2005). Within this context, there has been some research on interventions for children 'at risk' (Gervasoni, 2004; Wright, Martland, & Stafford, 2000). However, these tend to be based on assumptions of similar patterns of mathematics learning to typically developing children, which may not be valid for the development of children with specific learning difficulties or syndrome-specific issues. These do however provide support for the complexities of the development of number for children with difficulties learning mathematics.

Much of this practice-based literature builds on research on early childhood mathematical learning, including the work of Gelman and Gallistel (1978). They generated five principles that they argued were key to learning to count:

- one–one principle
- stable-order principle
- cardinal principle
- abstraction principle
- order irrelevance principle.

In understanding the cardinal principle, the child would know that the count indicates the number in the set. The abstraction principle is often left out of early counting lists for practitioners (e.g. Reys, Lindqwuist, Lambdin, & Smith, 2009) as it refers to the understanding that counting does not require actual objects but can be abstracted as evidenced when children *count-on*.

A study that built on the research into typically developing young children including the use of task-based cognitive interview tools to map the mathematical development of children with Down syndrome (Faragher, Brady, Clarke, Clarke, & Gervasoni, 2008) is reported in detail in Chapter 5. In this chapter, we will report some of our findings related to the early number development of the children within that study who were emergent counters. We use the term 'emergent counters' for those children who were still struggling with counting a small collection of objects. Wright *et al.* (2000) used the term *emergent counting* to refer to the lowest level of a learning framework for counting. At this level, students were unable to consistently count a given number of objects. They argue that this is due either to their lack of knowledge of the counting sequence or to difficulties with one-to-one correspondence—the first two of the counting principles.

Background literature

Learning to count

One area with a relatively strong research literature is 'counting for children with Down syndrome'. In early research, Cornwell (1974) concluded that, while children with Down syndrome were able to count using rote procedures, they had relative difficulty with development of concepts such as cardinal understanding. Gelman and Cohen (1988), when focusing on the use of the counting principles by children with Down syndrome, also concluded that these children learn to count by rote only. Two components of learning to count seem relevant here: the production and sequencing of counting words and the evidence of counting skills through object counting. It is well established that children with Down syndrome have impaired verbal short-term memory and that this may be a contributing factor for their smaller counting word vocabulary and shorter verbal counting sequences (Bird & Buckley, 2001).

Children first learn to say a range of counting words, and then an order develops with a gradual increase in the length of the correctly sequenced string representing the number that a child can successfully reach through rote counting. The successful counting of a collection of the same count or enumeration is more difficult. For typically developing children starting school in the Early Numeracy Research Project (ENRP) study, 57 per cent could successfully rote count to 20 and beyond, while 39 per cent could count a collection of 20 objects (Clarke, Clarke, & Cheeseman, 2006). Of course once an understanding of the extended number system develops, then the string can theoretically become infinite and is only limited by knowledge of place value terminology.

The total counting word vocabulary for typically developing children is larger than what they can produce correctly sequenced (Fuson, 1988). This is also the case for children with Down syndrome (Porter, 1999). Young children with Down syndrome have a significantly reduced range of count words compared to typically developing children.

In a study of counting skills where children with Down syndrome were matched with children with severe learning difficulties based on their count score, Porter (1999) found differences between the two groups. She argued that children with Down syndrome have particular difficulties learning the number string or counting sequence when compared with both typically developing children and children with severe learning difficulties. In addition, she found that children with Down syndrome were relatively higher in one-to-one correspondence than production of the stable-order number string.

Caycho, Gunn, and Siegal (1991) found that children with Down syndrome were just as able as typically developing children at object counting when matched according to receptive vocabulary. This was supported by Nye (2003), whose study also found no difference in the understanding of cardinality (in this case, as assessed by the 'how many?' question after the count, a 'give x' task, and a novel counting task) for groups matched for non-verbal mental age. These results are in contrast to earlier results and provide support that children with Down syndrome can develop conceptually based understandings of counting and cardinality.

It is common in studies of this type that children are matched in some cognitive aspect with typically developing children in order to make a valid comparison. The matching can be across a range of measures and these are chosen by the researchers. A common comparison is through mental age as identified by standard measures such as the Stanford-Binet (Thorndike, Hagen, & Sattler, 1986). This approach was used by Gelman and Cohen (1988). However, other cognitive components are used when there is a clear argument for them. For example, Caycho *et al.* (1991) matched for receptive vocabulary, arguing that it was relevant given the verbal aspect of counting.

This may explain some of the differences in results. While these differing results suggest more research is needed to produce more trustworthy findings, it is encouraging that evidence is indicating conceptual understanding of counting for children with Down syndrome.

Subitising

The ability to subitise (quickly determine the quantity of a set) is quite robust in typically developing preschool children. For example, there is evidence of very young children being able to distinguish numerosities of two and three (Starkey & Cooper, 1995). Early research (Gelman & Gallistel, 1978) hypothesised that children were using a count to determine the quantity in subitising situations. More recently it has been argued that serial counting is not required and that it is a separate cognitive process (Dehaene, 1997). Benoit, LeHalle, and Jouen (2004) argue for subitising as the developmental pathway for acquiring the meaning of the first few number words.

Paterson, Brown, Gsödl, Johnson, and Karmiloff-Smith (1999) found that children with Down syndrome were unable to distinguish between set sizes of two and three items when compared with a matched cohort of typically developing children and a cohort of children with Williams syndrome. Nye, Clibbens, and Bird (1995) used standard dice patterns to assess the subitising of 16 children with Down syndrome aged 7–12.5 years. Of these, five were able to subitise the six dots but nine were not successful with any of the patterns presented, further indicating limitations in the skill for children with Down syndrome. Subitising is a visual process (Dehaene, 1997) and, given the relative strength of children with Down syndrome in visual skills, these results seem surprising.

Ordering and relative size of numbers

There is increasing acknowledgement of the importance of the perception of the size of numbers in the development of key number understanding. It is well recognised that there are two aspects that affect the difficulty of number comparison tasks—a distance effect and a magnitude effect. The distance effect is where the greater the difference between numbers, the easier the task of distinguishing between them, so determining which is the larger of 80 and 100 is easier than for 81 and 82. The magnitude effect is that the larger the numbers, the harder it is to distinguish them, even if the difference in the set is the same. For example, distinguishing the larger of 72 and 74 is harder than distinguishing between 2 and 4. There is some evidence of a link between magnitude comparison skills and cardinality understanding for typically developing children (Rouselle, Palmers, & Noelk, 2004). Some researchers argue for the existence of an analogue magnitude system (Wagner & Johnson, 2011) which supports number development through a form of internal number line. This system is important in the development of more advanced numerical concepts.

Paterson *et al.* (2006) found that infants with Down syndrome were unable to detect a change in small numerosities (contrasting with robust findings for typically developing infants). However, after an initial delay in the development of numerosity comparison, once they were able to represent small numbers, this developed to match the typically developing children in the study. This work is yet to be replicated but suggests a relative strength in the analogue magnitude system.

Ordering numerals or quantities is an extension of simple comparison and a key component of place value understanding (Clarke *et al.*, 2002). Comparison based on quantity, where the numbers are fully represented, is different from comparison involving symbols (Rouselle & Noel, 2007). Moving to more advanced comparison or ordering requires understanding of place value. This is beyond the scope of this chapter but there is some discussion of place value in Chapter 5.

How all these aspects are linked in the development of mathematics for typically developing young children is still unclear and for children with Down syndrome even less is known.

As detailed in Chapter 5, semi-structured mathematical assessment interviews were conducted with 12 children twice each during 2007 and 2008 as part of a project that aimed to map the mathematical development of primary-aged children with Down syndrome. These interviews were videotaped, viewed, and analysed.

The interviews were based on the instrument developed and used in the ENRP (Clarke *et al.*, 2002) and still used extensively in schools in Victoria, Australia. The interview is used by teachers to provide comprehensive data on the mathematical thinking of children aged 5–8 as well as for comparison between children and cohorts.

The interview was implemented in this project in a more flexible form than the original design to ensure maximum opportunities for individual children to show what they knew rather than as a protocol-driven instrument. Tasks were first asked in the same form of wording as the original instrument but follow-up questioning, instructions, or guidance were provided at the discretion of the interviewer. An initial pilot with a 10-year-old with Down syndrome provided useful insights and supplementary tasks. One of the authors (Faragher) conducted the interviews using both her significant knowledge of the mathematical intent of the tasks and her expertise interacting with children with Down syndrome.

Results for early counting and numerosity

It appeared quite early in the analysis that some unexpected responses were emerging from the data. There seemed to be greater success in the recognition of numerals when compared with our expectations based on experience with traditionally developing children. We will present detailed data from one of the children, Gina,[1] in order to share some insights into the detail provided through the video and the form of the questions and interactions. Relevant and related responses from three other children who were early or emergent counters will be presented subsequently.

Gina

Gina (aged eight) attended her local primary school and her parents supplemented her education with private tutoring in mathematics and English as well as music lessons. The first interview was undertaken in her home and the second at an office at the university. In the first interview, she was greatly distracted but was much more focused in the second. A feature of the interview structure is the number of opportunities to return to concepts. During the initial pilot of the interview, it was found that the child was able (or willing) to evidence particular understandings in one task but not on another, even though they were closely related.

Gina was not successful in counting a handful of plastic teddy bears. Her handful was eight teddies and, after dropping one on the floor, the interviewer asked her how many teddies there were. After about a minute, during which time Gina rearranged them, the interviewer again asked, 'So how many are there? Can you count them for me?' After a short time, the interviewer moved one teddy at a time and said, 'One, two,… you do it'. Gina then slowly put the teddies in a line. She had six in a line and as she moved the seventh she quietly said, 'Six'. This was the first oral response in about two minutes. At no point during this time did Gina say or sequence aloud any other counting words.

There were a number of other occasions during Gina's interview where she was given an opportunity to count a small collection, or rote count. Early in the interview, there is a sequence of questions based on the First Year of School Interview from the ENRP (Clarke *et al.*, 2006) that focus on a collection of teddies, sorting them by colour, and making a group of four. Gina successfully selected the four yellow teddies but was not able to count them. There was limited evidence during this sequence of reciting the count. This was despite the interviewer starting the count and pointing several times. When asked to get five blue teddies, Gina selected all of the eight blue teddies that were in the collection. Gina was asked if there were five but she continued to rearrange the blue teddies with no oral response. The interviewer then removed the additional three and asked again, 'How many are there?' Table 6.1 provides a brief transcript with actions as Gina was asked questions focused on counting the five blue teddies, and a related conservation-of-number question which investigates if the child understands that the number of teddies remains the same in any arrangement.

Despite the multiple opportunities to count during the entire interview, only in the interaction in Table 6.1 did Gina recite independently the counting words or use them to support the counting of a small collection. In this case, the collection was five but she attributed a value of six to the count.

There was evidence that Gina could recognise numerals. For example, when working with a 0–99 chart, Gina successfully named the numerals 3–9. The interviewer (hiding the zero) pointed to the chart and said 'one, two', then Gina spontaneously and quickly took the interviewer's finger and pointed and recited the numerals up to nine, in order. She also independently recognised 3 in 33. We believe that symbolic support enabled her to recite the sequence of counting words to nine. In what ways is this knowledge supporting her number development or in what ways can it be used to build her understanding? The only other task that involved the use of numerals was a dot-matching task that included all numerals and dot collections of 0, 1, 2, 3, 4, 5, and 9. Here Gina identified the numerals 1, 2, 3, 4, and 5 and independently matched the dot representation of 1 and 3.

The answer is one

Sometimes, children with Down syndrome exhibit behaviours that hinder the assessment of their mathematical understanding. In Gina's case, giving an answer 'one' seemed to be 'avoidance' behaviour. This is a learned (albeit potentially unhelpful) behaviour, and not in any sense misbehaviour. There were seven occasions during the interview when Gina gave an answer 'one'. On only one occasion was this an appropriate response. It appeared from the analysis of the video that it was her 'default' response. It would seem to be an attempt to disengage with the question, perhaps to

Table 6.1 A summary of the words and actions of the interviewer and Gina

Interviewer's actions and words	*Gina's actions and words*
Five blue teddies are placed in a row. *Now we have some teddies. Let's count them. You count them with me.* *Here we go. Ready?*	
	Takes another teddy.
Removes the extra teddy. *Here we go.* Points and counts. *One, two, three, four, five*	
Five.	*Five.*
Spreads out the teddies as she talks. *They're going for a march right out there. Spread them out. We will make them now stand apart.* *How many teddies are there now?*	
	Pointing and counting independently. *One, two, three, four, five.* Then said, *Six.*
Let's try again. One . . . Pointing to the first two teddies in order.	
	One, two, one, three. Pointing appropriately as she recites the number words.
Starts pointing again in order. *One, two, three, four.*	
	Four, five. Pointing to the appropriate teddies.
We've got five. Pushes them up in a closer line. *Let's push them up close together. How many have I got now?*	
	One, two, [cough] *one, two, one, two.* Pointing, but not appearing to use one-to-one correspondence.
Start from there. Pointing to the first teddy in the line.	
	One, two, one, two.
Three.	
	Three.
Yep, three.	
	One, two. Pointing to the fourth and fifth.
Are we back to two? I think we've had enough of this.	She then moves the teddies into a group.

effectively avoid thinking about the question, or maybe to provide a response when knowing what to do is unclear. A particular example is quite enlightening:

> Gina was presented with some dot cards and numeral cards and asked to find the number to match the dots. She did not show evidence of matching but pointed to the numeral 3 and said 'three'. The interviewer used this as a cue to ask if she knew any other numbers. During this sequence, the interviewer picked up the numeral 4 and asked Gina what number it was. Gina responded quickly by saying 'one' and then said 'four' quietly. It was as if 'one' was her standard answer and then she realised that she actually could read the numeral.

Gina was an engaging child but struggled with much of the interview. She was one of the youngest of the children whom we interviewed. However, a picture was beginning to emerge from our work of a preference for the visual presentation of numerals over oral in supporting early number development.

Cameron

Cameron also provides a fascinating insight into emergent counters with Down syndrome. He was 10 at the time of his interviews and attended special school in a rural centre. In the first interview, Cameron had struggled to count small sets of objects, or to say the count sequence to five. His mother took this as a focus for intervention between the two interviews and, by the second session, Cameron was consistently counting five objects. The involvement of parents in the support and teaching of their children was a feature of the parents who were involved in our study and their role is worthy of further study.

Cameron's second interview was conducted in the school staff room, which was not a very convenient place for the placement of the video camera. As a result, some of his responses were not able to be identified. He was cooperative but displayed a range of avoidance behaviours that were typical of those we were seeing in other children. For example, he appeared when he was counting some of the objects to be having some sort of role play conversation using the teddies. People coming in and out of the room as well as noises from outside were distracting to him, with the result that he was not very focused on what he was doing for most of the interview.

Cameron could count to five and count a collection of five objects. He showed evidence of the first three counting principles in this process, including the cardinality principle. On one occasion during the interview Cameron recited the counting sequence up to six, but he was only able to rote and object count to five consistently. When required to count beyond five, he was more likely to say eight. He was showing no evidence of what Fuson (1988) calls the *chant* stage, where the rote count is larger than the object count.

Arguably, he is no longer an emergent counter but that would assume that the skills he has developed in being able to count to five would be transferable to larger sets. For typically developing children, the rote count is considerably higher than the actual count but that is not the case here. He also clearly reverts to the practices of emergent counters beyond five.

Cameron appeared to rely on counting to determine the numerosity of a set. Even in the subitising and matching tasks he did not provide evidence of recognising a set of two or three from dot cards. As previously discussed, subitising not only seems to be delayed in children with Down syndrome but also raises the question as to whether our teaching practices, with their focus on the count to determine numerosity, limit opportunities for the development of this important magnitude-related activity. Cameron, in another part of the interview, was able to indicate, without counting, which had more—a set of three or a set of four teddies.

Cameron's interview appears to highlight the challenges of memorising the counting sequence for children with Down syndrome. Since he has evidenced successful use of the counting principles showing sophisticated knowledge of counting, the difficulties he was having moving beyond five in his oral count seemed surprising. Are there better ways to develop early number understandings than our initial reliance on oral counting?

Similarly, one of the other children was more successful on some of the counting tasks and beyond emergent counting but was inconsistent with the oral count after 10, only being successful to 13 on one occasion. Even so, he was very confident with numeral recognition and successful at reciting the count to 19 using the 0–99 number chart with some pointing by the interviewer. He was 10 years old and could confidently show 10 fingers.

In terms of numeral recognition, Cameron was able to recognise the numerals 3 and 8 when shown them on cards and also showed evidence of recognising 5 and 2 during the matching tasks. He appeared distracted during the matching task and more interested in handling the cards than focusing on what was being asked.

While Cameron was able to say the count words up to five, he was still learning about zero. For the subitising task, the children are briefly shown a dot card at a time and asked how many dots there are. One of the cards is intentionally blank. This card was the source of great consternation to Cameron.

INTERVIEWER: I'm going to show you the cards really quite quickly
CAMERON: Ohh
INTERVIEWER: ...and you have to tell me how many dots you see. Okay. Are you ready?
CAMERON: I'm ready.
INTERVIEWER: They're going to come fast.
[Cameron is shown a card with two dots—he counts, 'one, two'. He is then shown a card with four dots. He continues to try to count them after the card is withdrawn]
INTERVIEWER: That was fast, wasn't it!... What about this one?
CAMERON: Oh! No dots!
INTERVIEWER: No dots! Do you have a word for that?
CAMERON: You tricked me!

In the next task, Cameron was asked to match numeral cards to the dot cards. He was unable to reconcile the blank card. He asked for it to be taken away. When it was left with the group, he asked for a pen to draw a cross on it. At no time did he give a name for zero, nor did he appear to recognise that a blank card could have meaning or connection with numbers. There was a corresponding numeral card showing the numeral 0.

Therefore, it was surprising when later in the interview, while reading the numerals on the 0–99 chart, Cameron said 'zero'. It would appear that he has a label for the symbol but, at this stage, he does not have the concept of zero and so cannot think of matching. In other words, he may have the symbol only as a label but does not connect this to its numerosity.

A similar pattern was observed with the number seven. As noted earlier, Cameron was confidently able to count up to five objects. He knew the word 'seven' but used this along with other number words in seemingly random order when attempting rote or object counting. He was not able to name the symbol when completing the ordering tasks. This was in contrast to the calculator task where he was asked to enter the number seven. Without hesitation, he entered 7 on the calculator. In this instance, Cameron could clearly recognise the symbol 7 on the calculator key. The calculator may represent a more familiar context than number cards. He may be more used to numbers on keypads, such as phones.

Margie

Margie was six years of age at the time of her second interview. In this interview, she was quite enthusiastic and engaged and she seemed to exhibit less of the avoidance behaviours evidenced by other children. These did increase later in the interview as she appeared to tire.

As previously mentioned, these interviews are characterised by multiple opportunities for children to show what they know—for example, children are given the opportunity to count a small number of objects many times during the interview. The first task in the interview asks the child to take a handful of teddies, to estimate how many, and then they are asked how many there are. In Margie's case, she took five for her handful. She was not successful in either of her two attempts to count these. However, when asked again how many there were, she said 'five' and then counted backwards to one, pointing appropriately. This was novel to us and we concluded that she was more confident with her backward count than her forward counting sequence. There was further evidence in the rote counting section of the interview where she was able to successfully count backwards from 10. This is not the case for typically developing children (Clarke *et al.*, 2006).

With one exception, Margie was only successful forward counting a collection of five objects when supported by the interviewer pointing. The exception was when she was presented with five dots on a card and she successfully counted those independently. There was no evidence of subitising and when asked how many dots there were on a card, including cards showing two or three dots, counting was her strategy of choice. However, when asked to show six fingers, this was done quickly and correctly. She was six years old and we speculate that she was familiar with representing her age. The interviewer went on to ask her to check by counting. While Margie had been confident in her representation of six, this question could be viewed as reinforcing the value being placed on counting to the determinant of the numerosity or magnitude of the set. Margie was not able to accurately count her fingers. While the intent was to provide a further opportunity to count, asking at this stage may have been counterproductive to her development of an understanding of magnitude or quantity.

Margie showed evidence of being familiar with a range of numbers as she referred to many during her verbal counting, including her rote counting. However, when asked to rote count, she was successful only to 10 without prompting. When using the 0–99 chart as a support, she read the numerals in order successfully to 12.

Margie's interview suggests a greater strength in the use of symbols relative to the oral count as she showed evidence of recognising each digit. When completing a later task in the interview, where numerals are presented to read, she recognised 3 and 8 but said 'eight' and 'three' when presented with 83. When shown 18, she said 'one' then 'eight'. When asked by the interviewer, 'What is it when we say it together'?', she said 'eighteen'. This was a surprising response as typically developing children rote count to higher numerals than they can read (Clarke *et al.*, 2006)

Shrek[2]

Shrek was one of the more challenging interviews as it was conducted in a small office on the floor (his preference). He did not respond to a number of questions. He was able to independently count four yellow teddies and to indicate correctly that there were more yellow teddies (count of four) than green teddies (count of three), suggesting some understanding of magnitude. He was inconsistent with his use of the counting sequence beyond two, both when attempting to count a collection as well as rote counting. He successfully pointed and counted five objects on three occasions when they were in a line, with the interviewer indicating the first. He did not show evidence of knowing the count—cardinality. He showed numeral recognition of 1, 2, 3, 4, 5, and 6 during the matching and ordering tasks. One of the surprises in his interview was when he recognised 4 on the dot card and matched the numeral without appearing to count.

There was one interesting interaction where he was reading the numeral cards. He was presented with a 9 card and, when asked what it was, said 'six'. The interviewer corrected him saying it was nine and Shrek tilted his head, appearing to realise that it was an upside down 6. It is difficult to interpret the thinking or knowledge that is evident here but it did support our growing contention that the children are more comfortable with the symbols or numerals than the oral count word. It was in this section of the interview that Shrek was the most engaged.

For the task of ordering the numeral cards, the interviewer put the numeral 1 down in front of Shrek and asked him, 'What comes next?'. He said 'two' and found the correct numeral card, placing it next to the 1. When asked what would be next, he said 'three' but selected the card with 5. The interviewer corrected this by supporting him to identify the 3 card. He successfully selected the 4 card and placed it next to the 3 and then did the same with the 5 card. When asked what comes next he said 'six'—the first time he had evidenced going beyond five in rote or object counting. Typically when learning to count, the ability to break the count and to know what comes after a number without the support of the complete sequence is a later skill than rote and object counting. Wright *et al.* (2000) would consider such a skill to indicate perceptual counting. Ordering numerals appears to require some level of understanding of the abstraction principle and might suggest that, with the support of the numeral cards, a higher level of numeric understanding is evidenced.

During the subitising task, where cards with dots are shown briefly, Shrek successfully identified the five dot card quickly. It was not in the standard dice formation but a 2×2 array and the additional dot on the side. It was the only pattern that he identified during the sequence of subitising tasks. As previously mentioned, he also successfully identified the numerosity of four when matching, with no evidence of counting—effectively subitising during an earlier part of the interview.

Discussion

There seems to be some evidence from our study that children with Down syndrome are more comfortable with the numerical symbol than the verbal number. Another child in our study, Annie, in her second interview was asked to show six fingers. This task, mentioned above in relation to Margie's interview, is designed to evidence part–part–whole understandings (Clarke *et al.*, 2006), the understanding that a number can be composed of smaller numbers. Children are then asked to show six in a different way to see if they are able to break the number into three and three, or four and two, rather than the less sophisticated understanding of six as the number after five, or a number in the counting system. In Annie's case, she used her fingers to make the symbol or shape of 6. As authors, we have conducted the interview over 100 times and never encountered this response. She appears to be seeing the symbol as an object and not automatically connecting the number name to numerosity/cardinality. Annie was one of our more accomplished counters and she was quite able to count sets of six objects. It is therefore surprising that she gave a physical representation of the numeral 6 rather than showing six fingers.

In our analysis of the responses of emerging counters in our study and illustrated through discussion in this chapter, it would appear that our participants with Down syndrome are developing their understanding of number in a different way to traditionally developing children. Margie, Cameron, and Gina, who were unable to say the oral count word sequence successfully, were able to count to 10 using symbolic support of the 0–99 chart. This would be different to traditionally developing children who would develop the oral count words first, and at a younger age, with symbols and sense of quantity emerging later.

The observation from our research would match that suggested by studies in neuropsychology (Camos, 2009). There is growing evidence that there are two quite distinct core knowledge systems for acquiring number concepts (Dehaene, 1997; Spelke, 2000; Xu, 2003). The exact nature of these systems is still under debate (Butterworth, 2005); however, Lipton and Spelke (2005) claimed that 'converging behavioral and neuroimaging results provide evidence for two systems: a language-independent, approximate system and a language-dependent system that stores learned facts' (Lipton & Spelke, 2005, p. 979). Camos' (2009) study investigated the discrimination of large numerosities in children with Down syndrome to assess the approximate numerosity system, concluding 'the approximate numerosity system … is efficient in children with DS. These findings point at language-based systems as the source of their difficulties' (Camos, 2009, p. 435).

We can think about the development of the concept of number as having three distinct components: word labels, symbols, and understandings of quantity (Lipton & Spelke, 2005, who refer to the understandings of quantity as 'non-symbolic numerosities'). This relationship is displayed visually in Figure 6.1.

The ways typically developing children gain robust understandings of number have received some attention. The connection between symbol and quantity has been investigated (Dehaene, 1997). Some studies (Siegler & Booth, 2004) look at the link between words or symbols and their location on a number line. The research by Lipton and Spelke explicitly investigated the link between number labels and quantity. They conclude, 'children's success at mapping number words to non-symbolic numerosities depends specifically on their success at counting to those words' (Lipton

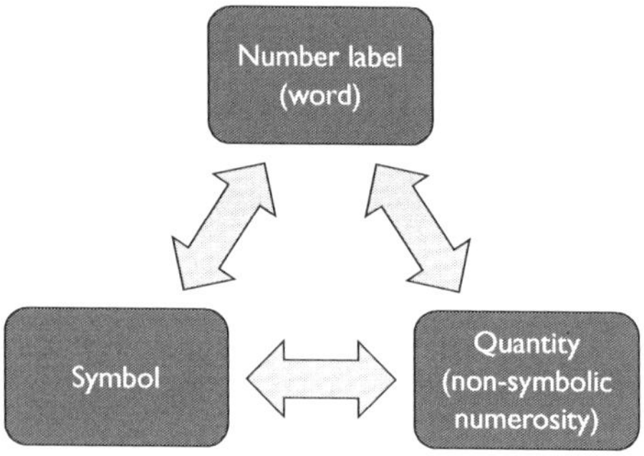

Figure 6.1 Three components in the concept of number (Lipton & Selke, 2005).

& Selke, 2005, p. 987). It may be that children with Down syndrome do not form these mappings in the same way as typically developing children. Research would suggest that some aspect of the language-dependent exact system is the source of difficulties for children with Down syndrome (Camos, 2009) and would match our observation of children in our study using the symbols before understanding the connection with cardinality. It may be that, if teachers were to focus on the link between symbol and quantity while introducing the number label, progress may be enhanced.

Paterson *et al.* (2006) discuss results from patients who have had brain surgery and are unable to perform number tasks such as calculations and subitising, but have no difficulty with spoken number language. They ask if such findings are applicable to genetic-based syndromes where different development occurs. While each connection within Figure 6.1 may be necessary to ensure robust understanding of number, is the order of development a given?

Fidler and Nadel (2007) encourage instruction that is presented with visual support due to the relative weakness in verbal processing for children with Down syndrome. This would be consistent with an instructional or educative approach that focuses on the link between symbol and quantity.

Are children with Down syndrome being disadvantaged through our reliance on verbal counting as the way into an understanding of number or numeration? The use of verbal language for number and counting dominates in most interactions with young children. Educators generally recommend delaying the introduction of symbols to young children. For example,

> Language is crucial to the learning of mathematics because it is through discussion that learners can come to terms with mathematical ideas, develop ways of expressing concepts and processes and take on the ways of thinking as their own. In due course, this verbal description and explanation of what is happening needs to give way to symbolic expressions that are often seem to characterise mathematics.
>
> (Booker, Bond, Sparrow, & Swan, 2010, p. 25)

It is known that many children with Down syndrome experience difficulties with language due to deficits in the phonological loop structure of memory and due to hearing loss. Learning to read through the initial use of sight words is often undertaken before children are able to speak (Buckley, 1995) and speech becomes a 'second language' after print. We believe we can use this relative strength in the use of symbols to enhance the learning of early number concepts (Faragher, Brady, Clarke, & Gervasoni, 2008).

Numerosity, defined as the cognitive counterpart of cardinality, denotes the number of things in a set (Butterworth, 2005). Typically, the use of the oral counting sequence is associated with and assumed in the ability to determine the numerosity of the set. Is it the only way or can other strategies be enabled to support this?

Strategies and implications

There has been an increasing emphasis in the literature (Buckley, 1995; Porter, 1999) on the potential value of the use of symbols to support children with Down syndrome to learn to count. While knowing the count words and the order is important in later development, is it dependent on the verbal count sequence? What other aspects are important and what might instruction look like if the initial focus is on the symbol and the quantity rather than the word?

Porter (1999) found in the qualitative analysis of student responses to counting tasks that the results were consistent with the children not having formed appropriate connections between adjacent numbers. Might this be encouraged through the visual ordering of the numerals rather than our general reliance on the oral sequencing? In our study, Shrek was able to order numerals but not produce the equivalent oral counting sequence.

The supported counting using the 0–99 chart in the interview was not part of the original ENRP instrument but was included in these interviews to provide alternative opportunities to count. The chart had been used to identify place value understanding later in the interview through the covering of a number and asking children to identify it and justify their answer. With the support of the chart, three of the emergent counters could recite the counting sequence beyond the level of their rote counting. One of the features of the chart is the order of the numerals as well as the obvious pattern of counting that leads to place value-related concepts.

We recommend a de-emphasis on the verbal count as a necessary prerequisite to other key aspects of early number learning. We think there may be an argument for focusing on counting to five for children with Down syndrome to support the development of counting principles and understanding. What value is there in oral counting beyond 10 when this was clearly very difficult for the children in the study? For typically developing children, counting supports place value development as well as multiplicative thinking. Is it more productive to focus on other models that support the development of these and other important mathematical skills and that will lead to more productive learning for children with Down syndrome? As we observed with Margie and Cameron, it seems that counting dominates our interactions and may be counterproductive.

Ordering of the numerals is inherent in the count and is a key aspect of the learning of number. It is relevant across both the exact and the approximate systems. 'Walking the count' using a counting line has the potential to internalise the sequence but also to support the order. Tools such as a counting or number roll are recommended for use in mathematical intervention and have much potential. Much of this work has a place in the preschool and early intervention settings.

Numicon, a commercial resource where the quantity is linked to the symbol, has had some successful use with children with Down syndrome in the United Kingdom (Numicon, n.d.). The mathematical features of these are similar to ten-frames (e.g. Gervasoni, 1997) and support both the magnitude understanding as well as early computational strategies. In particular, they support early place value understanding, with their focus on 5 and 10. We would argue for such tools to be used but also for more focused research on their use with learners with Down syndrome, identifying the underlying mathematical processes being developed rather than the material itself.

Teachers and teaching

Supporting Porter (1999), we would argue for the need to enhance educators' knowledge of the counting principles as tools to see the development of children with Down syndrome in relation to counting. The importance of understanding the mathematical thinking of children to support development is well established in the mathematics education literature (Sowder, 2007). Learning the count words in sequence is often seen as the most important component of early number learning. However, there is a range of other necessary aspects to number learning and we may be over-emphasising the use of the oral count. For children with Down syndrome, it may be better if oral counting is not given primacy.

Differentiated instruction is advocated within the early years classroom in many countries. Effective differentiation in the context of a classroom inclusive of children with special needs requires robust knowledge of children's mathematical understanding. The importance of effective assessment to determine these, as well as the ability to interpret the resulting data, is essential.

Acknowledgement

We acknowledge, with gratitude, the contribution of the children and their parents to this research. We acknowledge, too, the contribution of our colleagues Ann Gervasoni, Doug Clarke, and Jo Brady in the initial development of the project. This chapter reports some findings from a larger study undertaken by researchers at the Australian Catholic University and Monash University. The research was jointly funded by the Mathematics and Literacy Education Research Flagship of ACU, as well as SiMERR (ACT)—the Centre for Science, ICT and Mathematics Education in Rural and Regional Australia.

Notes

1 Names of the children are pseudonyms, chosen by the children themselves. We have their permission, and their parents' permission, to report their contributions to this research.
2 'Shrek' was the name selected by the child to identify himself within the project.

References

Benoit, L., LeHalle, H., & Jouen, F. (2004). Do young children acquire number words through subitizing or counting? *Cognitive Development, 19*, 291–307.

Bird, G., & Buckley, S. (2001). *Number skills for individuals with Down syndrome. An overview.* Hampshire: The Down Syndrome Educational Trust.

Bobis, J., Clarke, B. A., Clarke, D., Thomas, G., Wright, R., Young-Loveridge, J., & Gould, P. (2005). Supporting teachers in the development of young children's mathematical thinking: Three large scale cases. *Mathematics Education Research Journal, 16*, 27–57.

Booker, G., Bond, D., Sparrow, L., & Swan, P. (2010). *Teaching primary mathematics.* (4th edn). Frenchs Forest, NSW: Pearson.

Buckley, S. (1995). Teaching children with Down syndrome to read and write. In L. Nadel & D. Rosenthal (Eds), *Down Syndrome: Living and learning in the community* (pp. 158–169). New York: Wiley-Liss.

Butterworth, B. (2005). The development of arithmetical abilities. *Journal of Child Psychology and Psychiatry, 46*, 3–18.

Camos, V. (2009). Numerosity discrimination in children with Down syndrome. *Developmental Neuropsychology, 34*, 435–447.

Caycho, L., Gunn, P., & Siegal, M. (1991). Counting by children with Down syndrome. *American Journal on Mental Retardation, 95*, 575–583.

Clarke, B. A., Clarke, D. M., & Cheeseman, J. (2006). The mathematical knowledge and understanding young children bring to school. *Mathematics Education Research Journal, 18*, 78–102.

Clarke, D. M., Cheeseman, J., Gervasoni, A., Gronn, D., Horne, M., McDonough, A., & Rowley, G. (2002). *Early numeracy research project final report*. Melbourne, Australia: Mathematics Teaching and Learning Centre, Australian Catholic University.

Cornwell, A. C. (1974). Development of language, abstraction, and numerical concept formation in Down's syndrome children. *American Journal of Mental Deficiency, 79*, 179–90.

Dehaene, S. (1997). *The number sense: How the mind creates mathematics*. London: Penguin.

Faragher, R., Brady, J., Clarke, B. A., Clarke, D. M., & Gervasoni, A. (2008). Narrowing the gap: Empowering teachers and parents through understanding how children with Down syndrome develop mathematically. In L. Graham (Ed.), *Proceedings of the 'Narrowing the Gap: Addressing Educational Disadvantage' Conference* (pp. 56–62). University of New England, Armidale, NSW: SiMERR.

Faragher, R., Brady, J., Clarke, B. A., & Gervasoni, A. (2008). Children with Down syndrome learning mathematics: Can they do it? Yes they can! *Australian Primary Mathematics Classroom, 13*, 10–15.

Fidler, D. J., & Nadel, L. (2007). Educating children with Down syndrome: Neuroscience, development, and intervention. *Mental Retardation and Developmental Disabilities Research Reviews, 13*, 262–271.

Fuson, K. E. (1988). *Children's counting and concepts of number*. New York: Springer Verlag.

Gelman, R., & Cohen, M. (1988). Qualitative differences in the way Down syndrome and normal children solve a novel counting problem. In L. Nadel (Ed.), *The psychobiology of Down syndrome* (pp. 51–99). Cambridge, MA: MIT Press/Bradford books.

Gelman, R., & Gallistel, C. (1978). *The child's understanding of number*. Cambridge, MA: Harvard University Press.

Gervasoni, A. (1997). Classroom challenge: Helping students develop powerful visual images of number. *Prime Number, 12*, 28–31.

Gervasoni, A. (2004). Exploring an intervention strategy for six and seven year old children who are vulnerable in learning school mathematics. Unpublished PhD thesis, Latrobe University, Bundoora, Australia.

Lipton, J. S., & Spelke, E. S. (2005). Preschool children's mapping of number words to nonsymbolic numerosities. *Child Development, 76*, 978–988.

Numicon (n.d.). Oxford University Press. Accessed on 24 May 2012 from www.numicon.com/Index.aspx.

Nye, J. (2003). Numerical development in children with Down syndrome: The role of parent–child interaction. Unpublished PhD thesis, University of Portsmouth.

Nye, J., Clibbens, J., & Bird, G. (1995). Numerical ability, general ability and language in children with Down syndrome. *Down Syndrome Research and Practice, 3*, 92–102.

Paterson, S. J., Brown, J. H., Gsödle, M. K., Johnson, M. H., & Karmiloff-Smith, A. (1999). Cognitive modularity and genetic disorders. *Science, 286*, 2355–2358.

Paterson, S. J., Girelli, L., Butterworth, B., & Karmiloff-Smith, A. (2006). Are numerical impairments syndrome specific? Evidence from Williams syndrome and Down's syndrome. *Journal of Child Psychology and Psychiatry, 47*, 190–204.

Porter, J. (1999). Learning to count: A difficult task. *Down Syndrome Research and Practice, 6*, 85–94.

Reys, R., Lindquist, M., Lambdin, D., & Smith, N. (2009). *Helping children learn mathematics* (9th edn). New York: John Wiley & Sons.

Rousselle, L., & Noel, M.-P. (2007). Basic numerical skills in children with mathematics learning disabilities: A comparison of symbolic vs non-symbolic number magnitude processes. *Cognition, 102*, 361–395.

Rouselle, L., Palmers, E., & Noel, M.-P. (2004). Magnitude comparison in pre-schoolers: What counts. Influence of perceptual variables. *Journal of Experimental Child Psychology, 87*, 57–84.

Siegler, R., & Booth, J. L. (2004). Development of numerical estimation in young children. *Child Development, 75*, 428–444.

Sowder, J. (2007). The mathematics education and development of teachers. In F. K. Lester (Ed.), *Second handbook of research on mathematics teaching and learning* (pp. 157–223). Charlotte, NC: Information Age Publishing and National Council of Teachers of Mathematics.

Spelke, E. S. (2000). Core knowledge. *American Psychologist, 55*, 1233–1243.

Starkey, P., & Cooper, R. (1995). The development of subitizing in young children. *British Journal of Developmental Psychology*, 13, 399–420.

Thorndike, R. L., Hagen, E. P., & Sattler, J. M. (1986). *Technical manual, Stanford-Binet Intelligence Scale: Fourth edition*. Chicago: Riverside Publishing Company.

Wagner, J. B., & Johnson, J. C. (2011). An association between understanding cardinality and analogue magnitude representations in preschoolers. *Cognition, 119*, 10–22.

Wright, B., Martland, J., & Stafford, A. (2000). *Early numeracy: Assessment for teaching and intervention*. London: Paul Chapman Publishing.

Xu, F. (2003). Numerosity discrimination in infants: Evidence for two systems of representations. *Cognition, 89*, B15–B25.

Chapter 7

Research on number knowledge of students with Down syndrome

An experience from Indonesia

Rumiati and Robert J. Wright

Abstract

This chapter presents the results of a small-scale research study on the number knowledge of students with Down syndrome in Indonesia. Five students with Down syndrome and ages ranging from seven to 19 years, from a special education school in Yogyakarta city, were interviewed to document their abilities in identifying numerals, solving number problems involving the use of unscreened and screened collections of counters, and solving one-digit and two-digit number problems in horizontal format. The approach and the schedule of assessment tasks in the interview were adapted from that used in Mathematics Recovery (Wright, 2008). The interviews were conducted individually and videotaped in order to capture subtle clues related to students' abilities. The number knowledge of the five students with Down syndrome is described, compared, and discussed.

Background to the study

Number is an important part of everyday life. In this modern era, life could be difficult for people who do not understand number since the use of number is ubiquitous. It is important to teach number to students with Down syndrome. Understanding how children with Down syndrome develop their number knowledge has been a particular interest of relatively few educational practitioners and researchers (Abdelhameed, 2007, 2009; Brigstocke, Hulme, & Nye, 2008; Faragher, Brady, Clarke, & Gervasoni, 2008). Yet, there is an urgent need for more research focusing in this area, especially on how to help students with Down syndrome enhance their number knowledge and reach their highest potential. This chapter discusses the number knowledge of students with Down syndrome in a special education school in Indonesia, based on a small-scale research project conducted by the first author.

Children with Down syndrome have difficulty in learning number word strings (Porter, 2000). Compared to typically developing children, children with Down syndrome produced significantly fewer number words altogether and shorter standard number word sequences, and could not count larger sets than those their counterparts could count (Nye, Fluck, & Buckley, 2001). A study by Brigstocke *et al.* (2008) also suggests that number as well as arithmetic is a particular area of difficulty for children with Down syndrome. Despite this evidence, individual differences among children with Down syndrome should be studied to better understand their learning. Recent research shows that, even though children with Down syndrome have a deficit in counting (Abdelhameed, 2007), appropriate teaching approaches during intervention benefited them (Abdelhameed, 2009; Buckley, 2007). Children with Down syndrome can do and learn mathematics (Faragher *et al.*, 2008). This suggests that determining and documenting what a child with Down syndrome is able to achieve is an important key to advancing their number skills and to determining the most appropriate teaching approach for them (Buckley, 2007).

The Mathematics Recovery (MR) programme has a distinctive approach to assessing young children's numerical knowledge (Wright, Martland, & Stafford, 2006) using a one-to-one, videotaped interview. There are a number of parallels with the Early Numeracy Interview discussed in Chapters 5 and 6. The interview involves presenting numerical tasks carefully in order to determine the extent of the child's number knowledge. In some cases, the presentation of tasks involves the use of counters and a screen. Videotaping the assessment interview is advocated in order to eliminate the need to take notes and to enable the interviewer to give full attention to the interviewee. The approach used in the MR programme enables detailed documentation of children's current number knowledge (Williams, 2008). The schedule of assessment tasks provided by the MR programme was used and adapted for this study to document the number knowledge of children with Down syndrome.

Research questions

The research questions chosen for the study are:

1 What abilities do students with Down syndrome have related to identifying numerals?
2 What abilities do students with Down syndrome have related to solving number problems involving screened and unscreened collections of counters?
3 What abilities do students with Down syndrome have related to solving one- and two-digit number problems in horizontal format?

Methodology

The study was conducted in a special education school in the inner city of Yogyakarta. The school is a co-educational school catering to 126 students from kindergarten to high school, with ages from five to 19 years. These children were assigned to a class or level according to their chronological age. There are 49 teachers in this school and the ratio between teachers and students is 1:2.6, which is considered ideal for a special education school in Indonesia. Among the 126 students, 12 (five boys and seven girls) students were diagnosed as individuals with Down syndrome based on physical observation and a dermatogliphy test carried out by a medical specialist. The vice-principal helped the interviewer to identify these students. Table 7.1 shows the sex, level, grade, and age of students with Down syndrome in the school. All names have been changed in order to preserve the students' anonymity. The data collection involved observation and interviews.

Table 7.1 Sex, level, grade, age, and duration of interview of students with Down syndrome

Code	*Sex*	*Name*	*Level*	*Grade*	*Age*	*Duration of interview*
1	G	No name	Kindergarten		5 years 0 months	N/A
2	G	Tera	Kindergarten		7 years 8 months	19 m 51 s
3	B	No name	Elementary school	1	8 years 0 months	N/A
4	G	No name	Elementary school	4	11 years 0 months	N/A
5	B	Asto	Elementary school	3	11 years 5 months	5 m 6 s
6	G	Dona	Elementary school	4	12 years 3 months	3 m 12 s
7	B	No name	Elementary school	5	13 years 9 months	N/A
8	B	No name	Elementary school	4	14 years 8 months	N/A
9	G	No name	Elementary school	6	14 years 11 months	N/A
10	G	Kaila	Junior high school	8	15 years 2 months	31 m 8 s
11	B	No name	Junior high school	8	18 years 10 months	N/A
12	G	Pinta	Senior high school	11	19 years 8 months	67 m 50 s

Notes
m = minutes, s= seconds.

Observations

The observation took place before the interview. During the period of observation, the interviewer introduced herself to the teachers and students. Conversations with teachers were carried out whenever necessary. The observations took place twice. The purpose of the observations was to familiarize the students with the interviewer.

Interviews

The interviews were conducted in the middle of February 2011. The students' consent was sought directly prior to each interview. Five students agreed to be interviewed. The other students refused to be interviewed. This chapter discussed only the five children who were interviewed. Three students (two from elementary and one from senior high school) were interviewed in their classrooms in the presence of their teachers. The youngest student (seven years two months) was interviewed in the presence of her mother. The other students agreed to be interviewed in the library without their teacher or parents being present.

The approach to assessment in the MR programme and the MR assessment schedule were designed to be used by teachers with typically developing children. Modifications were considered necessary for the research approach. The interviewer decided to take a flexible approach based on similar arguments to those of Faragher *et al.* (2008). The interviews consisted of three parts: Part 1 had the purpose of assessing the child's ability to identify numerals. Numerals are the written and read symbols for numbers—for example, the numeral '3' is read as 'three'. This part was designed for all students in the kindergarten, elementary, and secondary schools. In this part, the interviewer showed the children several numerals written on a card, one by one, and asked the child, 'What number is this?' In some cases, the interviewer asked the child to show a number of fingers corresponding to the displayed numeral. The numerals which are identified by the child are noted.

Part 2 was designed for the junior and senior high school students. In this part, the interviewer placed out several counters and asked the student, 'How many counters are there?' (see Figure 7.1). Initially, the number of counters was less than 10. If the student was able to count at least to 10, the number of counters was increased. If the student was able to count correctly, the interviewer would put out three counters and then add four more, and screen all of the counters and ask the child, 'How many counters are there altogether behind this screen?' The task was repeated several times in order to provide opportunities for the child to solve the task. If the student was able to solve the first problem, the number of counters was increased, but no more than 20 counters were used.

For junior and senior high school students who were successful in Part 2, the interviews were continued in Part 3. This part was designed to assess children's ability to solve one- or two-digit number problems in horizontal format. The interviewer showed a card with a number problem written on it and asked, 'Please solve this problem?' When the student gave a correct answer, the interviewer asked the student how she or he found the answer. After the interview, the interviewer wrote reflective notes about her impressions of the student's ability and the strategies used by the student.

Data analysis

The data consisted of video recordings of the interviews, along with reflective and observation notes. In attempting to draw valid meaning from the data, the first author followed the methods proposed by Miles and Huberman (1994). The reflective notes for each student were re-read and the video recordings were re-viewed in order to identify events where the children were solving number problems. Significant events on the video recordings were described and then interpreted and discussed, and contrasted with the reflective and observation notes, as well as results from previous studies on number knowledge of children with Down syndrome (Abdelhameed, 2007,

Figure 7.1 A kindergarten student with Down syndrome tries to count several counters.

2009; Brigstocke *et al.*, 2008; Buckley, 2007; Faragher, 2004; Faragher & Brown, 2005; Faragher *et al.*, 2008; Germain, 2001, 2002; Haslam, 2007; Horner, 2007; McConnochie & Sneath, 2007; Nye *et al.*, 2001; Nye & Clibbens, 1995; Paterson, 2001; Porter, 2000; Rietveld, 2005; Wing & Tacon, 2007).

Results

The following are descriptions of each student's number knowledge based on the interviews.

Tera (7 years 8 months)

Tera was interviewed by her mother. She was able to count objects up to four. When her mother showed her 10 strips, she counted one, two, three, and four. Her mother asked her to repeat the counting and she tried to continue several times but she always made mistakes for numbers beyond four. When her mother showed her several counters, she was also able to count up to four, but made mistakes for numbers beyond four.

When her mother showed her the numerals 1 to 10 on a card one at a time, she was also able to identify numerals up to 4. For numerals beyond 4, she made mistakes. The following is an excerpt from her interview

MOTHER: (shows the numeral 1). What number is this?
TERA: One.
MOTHER: (shows the numeral 2). What number is this? Like a duck?
TERA: Two.
MOTHER: (shows the numeral 3). What number is this?
TERA: (draws the numeral 3 with her left hand in the air). Three.
MOTHER: Good. (shows number 4). What number is this?
TERA: (silent for around three seconds, then draws the numeral 4 with her left hand in the air).
MOTHER: What is after 3?
TERA: Like chair?
MOTHER: Yes, what is that?
TERA: Mmmm ... fo ... ur ...
MOTHER: Good. (shows the numeral 5). What number is this?
TERA: Two.
MOTHER: No ... Two is like duck. What is this?
TERA: Five.
MOTHER: (shows number 6). What number is this?
TERA: One.
MOTHER: No ... One is like this (shows card with number 1). How about this?
TERA: Mmmm ... six.
MOTHER: (shows 7). What number is this?
TERA: Five.
MOTHER: No, 5 is this one (shows card with the numeral 5). This is not 5. What is after 6? Se...
TERA: Ven.

Asto (11 years 5 months)

Asto was interviewed by the first author. When the interviewer raised her finger symbolizing one, and asked, 'What is this?', he said 'one' while mimicking her gesture. Then, when the interviewer raised two fingers, he said 'two', while also mimicking this gesture. When one more finger was raised, Asto again mimicked the gesture, and said that that was 'six'. Then he added one more finger. There were now four in all, but he again said that it was 'six'.

Asto was shown the numeral 1, which was written on a card, and was asked, 'What number is that?' He said 'one'. Then, he was able to correctly identify the numerals 2 and 3. However, when the task was repeated, he seemed confused. Thus he could not identify numerals robustly.

Dona (12 years 3 months)

Dona was interviewed by the first author. Dona was shown numerals one at a time. Each numeral was written on a card and the numerals were presented in the following order: 3, 5, 7, 9, 8, 4, 2, 6. She was able to identify all of the numerals. For the numeral 1, she said that it was seven. When told that was incorrect, she said that it was one. When shown 0, she said that it was 10. She identified the numerals 11, 12, and 13 on her first attempt. She had difficulty in identifying other numerals, but for number 20, she said that it was 'two ten'. Dona was not given any of Part 2 since she was reluctant to continue the interview.

Kaila (15 years 2 months)

Part 1: Kaila was shown one-digit then two-digit numerals one at a time, not in numerical order, and she was able to identify all of them. The numerals in the order in which they were presented are: one-digit numerals—7, 4, 5, 1, 0, 9, 8, 3, 6, 10 and two-digit numerals—59, 12, 48, 15, 21, 23, 19, 11, 13, 83, 77, 56, 77, 56, 25, 20, 86. However, when she was shown three-digit numerals, she made mistakes. It seemed likely that she had never been taught to identify three-digit numerals. For 234, she said 'twenty three thirty four'; for 710, she said 'seven ten', and for 999 she said 'nine nine nine'.

Part 2: Four yellow counters were presented to Kaila and she was asked to count them. Kaila counted these counters by pointing at them one by one. Furthermore, three black counters were presented, and she was able to state the number of counters immediately and apparently without counting by ones. After that, the interviewer asked, 'How many counters are there altogether?' Without counting, Kaila answered 'four'. When the interviewer repeated the question, Kaila counted all seven counters one by one and answered correctly: 'seven'. Furthermore, when five yellow counters and eight black counters were presented, Kaila was also able to count the number of counters correctly.

Since Kaila was able to solve number problems involving unscreened collections of counters, the interviewer then presented problems involving screened collections. The following is an excerpt from the interview:

INTERVIEWER: There are three yellow counters (puts down three yellow counters). There are two black counters (puts down two black counters, then screens the counters). How many counters are there altogether?

KAILA: How many? (She puts her hand on her head, and after 10 seconds, opens five fingers on the left hand and closes those fingers one by one while counting one, two, three, and after a short pause, continues four, five.) The answer is five.
INTERVIEWER: Very good.

Similar problems were presented to Kaila, in which the number of counters used was increased. She was not able to solve the following tasks presented with two screened collections: 5 + 8, 9 + 9, and 8 + 7. In attempting to solve these tasks, she always counted from one and she always stopped at the wrong number.

Part 3: Kaila was presented with the following number task written on a card in horizontal format: 16 + 10. She used a counting-on strategy, in which she opened her 10 fingers and closed these fingers one by one while saying '17, 18, 19, 20, 21, 22, 23, 24, 25, 26'. She used the same strategy for 5 + 6, 9 + 4, and 16 + 9. For 29 + 18, she also used the same strategy; however, when attempting to keep track of 18 counts, she stopped when she ran out of her 10 fingers and so answered '39'.

Pinta (19 years 8 months)

Part 1: When the interviewer placed a pile of numeral cards in front of Pinta, she played with the cards. When the interviewer asked her, 'Do you know what these are?', she said she did not know. Her teacher, who was also present, told her that these are numbers. While she continued to play with the cards, the interviewer asked her to name numerals one at a time and not in numerical order. She was able to identify 1 to 9. This task was repeated to make sure that her ability to identify these numbers was reasonably robust and she was able to identify these numerals again correctly. Pinta was also able to identify several two-digit numerals such as 11, 12, 13, 15, 19, and 20. However, she made mistakes for other larger numbers. For 23, she said 'two and three', and on some occasions, she said 'twenty-one' for 12 and 'twenty' for 50.

Part 2: When the interviewer presented four black counters she was able to count them and similarly with three yellow counters. When asked 'How many counters are there altogether?', she said without counting, 'There are five people'. When asked to count, she counted the collections separately. For the black counters she counted '1, 2, 3, 4', and for the yellow counters she counted '1, 2, 3'. When the interviewer said, 'I want to know how many there are altogether', instead of counting, she wrote number 12 on a piece of paper.

When six counters were presented, and the interviewer asked, 'How many counters are there?', Pinta counted them correctly. She also counted nine green counters. When asked to count all the counters (six yellow counters and nine green counters), she said that she did not know. When a collection of 25 counters was presented and she was asked to count, Pinta counted '1, 2, 3, 4, 5, 6, 7, 8, 9, 20' and said 'Too many counters'. When asked to re-count, she did the same. She said that she did not know what was after nine. When 15 counters were put in a row, Pinta counted all these counters and said the number of the counters was 17. Again, seven black counters were presented, followed by six yellow counters. Pinta was able to count each collection separately. The interviewer mixed the two collections and asked, 'How many are there altogether?' Instead of counting all of the counters, Pinta separated the yellow counters and counted them correctly, and then counted the black counters correctly.

When the interviewer told her again, 'I asked you how many are there altogether?', she said, 'Ah. I don't know'.

During the interview, Pinta wanted to write these numerals. She was able to write 1 to 10 correctly. When asked to continue, she wrote 15, and then she said that she did not want to continue. Instead she wrote 1 to 10 again.

Discussion

Interviewing typically developing students requires skill and knowledge. Interviewing students with Down syndrome was challenging. Innovative and individual approaches were necessary. The amount of time for each interview as shown in Table 7.1 includes the time needed to establish rapport with the student. The actual time taken to pose tasks related to number knowledge differs among students. Dona was interviewed for only 3 minutes 12 seconds in her class, and then she did not want to continue, while Pinta was interviewed for 67 minutes and 50 seconds because, between tasks, she seemed to enjoy playing with the interview materials, such as cards, counters, and strips. The number knowledge of each student as indicated in the interviews is summarized in Table 7.2.

The results of this study support previous research findings that counting is one of the areas of difficulty of students with Down syndrome. However, this is not necessarily the case for all students. Some students with Down syndrome are able to use counting to solve number problems. The following are answers to the research

Table 7.2 Summary of the number knowledge of each student based on interviews

No.	*Name, Age*	*Level*	*Part 1*	*Part 2*	*Part 3*
1	Tera 7.8*	Kindergarten	Able to identify numerals 1–4	Not asked	Not asked
2	Asto 11.5	Elementary school	Not able to identify numerals	Not asked	Not asked
3	Dona 12.3	Elementary school	Able to identify numerals 2–9, 11, 12, and 15. Makes mistakes with other numerals	Not asked	Not asked
4	Kaila 15.2	Junior high school	Able to identify one-and two-digit numerals	Able to count from one to find the number of items in two screened collections	Able to solve number problems in horizontal format, with the second addend in the range 1–9 using a counting-on strategy
5	Pinta 19.8	Senior high school	Able to identify one-digit numerals and some two-digit numerals	Able to count small numbers of visible items	Not asked

Note
7.8 = 7 years and 8 months (etc.).

questions based on the data from the study. These serve to summarize the findings of the study:

1 *What abilities do students with Down syndrome have related to identifying numerals?* Only one of the five students was able to identify two-digit numerals. The other students showed various abilities, ranging from being unable to identify any numerals to being able to identify one-digit numerals only.
2 *What abilities do students with Down syndrome have related to solving number problems involving unscreened and screened collections of counters?* The secondary school students, Kaila and Pinta, were at different stages of counting. While Kaila was able to solve number problems involving screened collections of counters, Pinta could not, notwithstanding that Pinta is older than Kaila and has been in school longer than Kaila. This suggests that, at least for these older students, age and the duration of schooling were not the only variables in determining the number knowledge of students with Down syndrome.
3 *What abilities do students with Down syndrome have related to solving one- and two-digit number problems in horizontal format?* Kaila, a junior high school student, was the only student who was able to solve addition problems in horizontal format. She also was able to solve number problems involving screened collections of counters. In doing so, she counted from one and used her fingers to keep track of three counts and then two more counts. Furthermore, she was able to count on to solve number problems in horizontal format, involving one-digit addends and two-digit addends. Overall, she was the most advanced in terms of number knowledge. As well, she communicated better than the other students. During a class observation prior to the interview, she seemed more advanced in number knowledge than three other students who did not have Down syndrome. Kaila is able to recall her home phone number; she is also able to handle questions about dates and days more fluently than the other students. According to her and her teacher, Kaila started to learn number at an early age. Her parents, who were quite wealthy, sent her to a private course on writing, reading, and numeracy. Among wealthy parents in the city, the course is regarded as being of good quality and it is not specifically for children with special needs or Down syndrome.

There was an interesting event during the interview with Tera. According to her mother, Tera (seven years eight months) had been attending a regular kindergarten for two years. However, she was assessed by her teacher as not appropriate for the regular school and was transferred to a special education school. At the time of her interview, she had been attending the special education school for seven months. When asked to identify the numerals 1 and 2, Tera was able to do so quickly. However, for numerals 3 and 7, she drew the numeral in the air before saying the number word. Her responses to these numeral identification tasks show that, even though she is not able to say immediately the number words, she has a means of communicating particular numerals. Children with Down syndrome are known to have significant difficulty with speech. Nevertheless, we do not advocate that children with Down syndrome should learn to speak prior to learning about numbers and numerals. These activities can occur concurrently. Thus we believe that, as indicated in Kaila's case, early education and early intervention related to both speech and number will yield positive results.

Conclusion

This chapter suggests, through the case studies, that even though children with Down syndrome show limited number knowledge, early identification and intervention are likely to make a difference. Kaila, who has enjoyed appropriate education and early intervention, has higher ability levels related to number knowledge than the other students with Down syndrome.

References

Abdelhameed, H. (2007). Do children with Down syndrome have difficulty in counting and why? *International Journal of Special Education, 22*, 1–11.

Abdelhameed, H. (2009). Use of the behavioural approach in teaching counting for children with Down syndrome. *International Journal of Special Education, 24*, 1–10.

Brigstocke, S., Hulme, C., & Nye, J. (2008). Number and arithmetic skills in children with Down Syndrome. *Down Syndrome Research and Practice* (online), 74–77. Retrieved from www.down-syndrome.org/reviews/2070/reviews-2070.pdf. doi: 10.3104/reviews.2070.

Buckley, S. (2007). Teaching numeracy. *Down Syndrome Research and Practice, 12*, 11–14.

Faragher, R. (2004). I can do math too: Count me in. *Australian Primary Mathematics Classroom, 9*, 23–27.

Faragher, R., Brady, J., Clarke, B., & Gervasoni, A. (2008). Children with Down Syndrome learning mathematics: Can they do it? Yes they can! *Australian Primary Mathematics Teacher, 13*, 10–15.

Faragher, R., & Brown, R. I. (2005). Numeracy for adults with Down syndrome: It's a matter of quality of life. *Journal of Intellectual Disability research, 49*, 761–765.

Germain, R. (2001). Access to numeracy: A case study. *British Journal of Special Education, 28*, 182–186.

Germain, R. (2002). A 'positive' approach to supporting a pupil with Down syndrome during 'dedicated numeracy time'? *Down Syndrome Research and Practice, 8*, 53–58.

Haslam, L. (2007). Sam's progress with learning mathematics. *Down Syndrome Research and Practice, 12*, 32–33.

Horner, V. (2007). Teaching number skills and concepts with Stern structural arithmetic materials. *Down Syndrome Research and Practice, 12*, 27–31.

Miles, B. M., & Huberman, A. M. (1994). *Qualitative data analysis: An expanded sourcebook*. Thousand Oaks, CA: Sage.

McConnochie, J., & Sneath, G. (2007). Katrina's progress with learning mathematics. *Down Syndrome Research and Practice, 12*, 34–37.

Nye, J., & Clibbens, J. (1995). Numerical ability, general ability and language in children with Down's syndrome. *Down Syndrome Research and Practice, 3*, 92–102.

Nye, J., Fluck, M., & Buckley, S. (2001). Counting and cardinal understanding in children with Down syndrome and typically developing children. *Down Syndrome Research and Practice, 7*, 68–78.

Paterson, S. (2001). Language and number in Down syndrome: The complex development trajectory from infancy to adulthood. *Down Syndrome Research and Practice, 7*, 79–86.

Porter, J. (2000). Learning to count: A difficult task. *Down Syndrome Research and Practice, 6*, 85–94.

Rietveld, C. M. (2005). Classroom learning experiences of mathematics by new entrant children with Down syndrome. *Journal of Intellectual & Developmental Disability, 30*, 127–138.

Williams, P. (2008). *Intervention in mathematics in primary schools*. London: Department for Children, Schools and Families.

Wing, T., & Tacon, R. (2007). Teaching number skills and concepts with Numicon materials. *Down Syndrome Research and Practice, 12*, 22–26.

Wright, R. J. (2008). Mathematics recovery: An early number program focusing on intensive intervention. In A. Dowker (Ed.), *Mathematics difficulties: Psychology and intervention* (pp. 203–223). San Diego, CA: Elsevier.
Wright, R. J., Martland, J., & Stafford, A. K. (2006). *Early numeracy: Assessment for teaching and intervention*. London: Paul Chapman Publishing/Sage.

Chapter 8

Learning mathematics in the secondary school

Possibilities for students with Down syndrome

Rhonda Faragher

Abstract

Many learners with Down syndrome find arithmetic difficult. The source of the difficulty is still unknown. However, arithmetic is only a small part of mathematics and it is not necessarily the case that learners who struggle with arithmetic will find other areas of mathematics difficult. Access to study of mathematics across the breadth of the discipline is crucial for learners as this underpins numeracy: defined here in the Australian sense as the ability to use mathematics in the context of daily life. Numeracy in turn has a direct effect on a person's quality of life.

This chapter explores the possibilities of learners with intellectual impairments studying mathematics at the secondary school level and discusses the move towards learning year level-appropriate curriculum, a concept defined in the chapter. Two case studies are presented of students with Down syndrome in the early years of secondary school undertaking year level-appropriate mathematics teaching with focused support. These cases produced astonishing results and are used to explore implications for teachers and researchers in the inclusion of learners with Down syndrome in secondary mathematics programmes. The chapter concludes with a consideration of the implications of teaching year level-appropriate curriculum for secondary school students with Down syndrome.

Introduction

The expectation that learners with Down syndrome will have difficulties with mathematics is almost universal and research would support the contention, at least for number skills (Bird & Buckley, 2001). What is less clear is the performance of learners with Down syndrome on other aspects of mathematics. A few documented or anecdotal cases suggest higher mathematics may not be out of the reach of learners with Down syndrome with good teaching and the right support. Some literature (Monari Martinez, 1998; Monari Martinez & Pellegrini, 2010) has reported students with Down syndrome successfully learning algebra. In a fascinating paper, Monari Martinez and Benedetti (2011) report students learning coordinate geometry, including the distance formula, and financial mathematics, including solving exponential and logarithmic equations. Further, a student in Melbourne, Australia, passed the state-wide external examination in General Mathematics at the completion of secondary school (I. Cook, Education Officer, Down Syndrome Association of Victoria, personal communication, 30 March 2011) and a student in New Zealand passed a similar examination (parent, personal email communication, 19 March 2010).

Accomplishments by individuals give a sense of what might be possible if all learners were given access to a secondary mathematics curriculum. As Shepperdson notes:

> We do not know what proportion of people with Down's syndrome would learn academic skills, or what level they would achieve if they were all exposed to regular teaching. Nor do we know how far abilities would remain more stable, or how far people would continue to make gains, if they continued to be taught from their teens into adulthood.
>
> (Shepperdson, 1994, p. 101)

Students with intellectual impairments who have been educated in inclusive primary classrooms are increasingly seeking inclusive secondary schooling (Forlin, 2005). Inclusive schooling is more than enrolling the student in the school: access to the secondary curriculum is necessary as well. This requires designing an appropriate programme for students with intellectual impairments and yet the planning can be a challenging process. This chapter considers some of the issues involved in planning for learning mathematics at the secondary school level for learners with Down syndrome.

Background

Numeracy and its connection to mathematics

If students with Down syndrome are to be taught a secondary mathematics curriculum, we should first question whether this is desirable, before we consider what and how mathematics would be taught. At the heart is the difference between mathematics and numeracy.

Mathematics is a rich discipline of human thought and very hard to encapsulate in a short definition. Mathematics has been regarded as the science of pattern but pattern here means more than pattern in the common language usage. It involves underlying structure and deciding what stays the same as we change features of a problem. Many people are surprised to learn that new mathematics is being generated all the time. For example, new mathematics was required for the movie *Tangled*. In order to draw human hair and animate it, thousands of complex equations were required (Toney, 2010).

Mathematics is far more than textbook exercises. The skills taught may be important as they give us the 'tools of the trade'— the techniques for doing mathematics—but mathematics is much more than that. Learners need to have opportunities to engage in the richness of mathematics through a broad study of the discipline and opportunities to solve problems. It might be argued that this is of little value for some learners. However, the study of mathematics underpins numeracy and, as I will argue, this has direct ramifications on a person's quality of life.

In Australia, numeracy has been defined as 'the effective use of mathematics to meet the general demands of life at school and at home, in paid work, and for participation in community and civic life' (Ministerial Council on Education Employment Training and Youth Affairs [MYCEETYA], 1997, p. 130). The sense of numeracy being the *use* of mathematics is consistent with definitions from some other countries, such as the Netherlands. Some countries use the term 'mathematical literacy' in a similar sense to numeracy. For a detailed discussion of the definition of numeracy and its connection to mathematics, a full account is available in the National Numeracy Review (Council of Australian Governments Human Capital Working Group, 2008).

The concept of numeracy has evolved over the last 50 years and is still developing. To this point, we know the following. Numeracy is about *using* mathematics. This implies you must know mathematics before you can use it. The use must also be *effective*. Numeracy encompasses more than number work. It includes all the branches of mathematics, such as geometry, measurement, statistics, and algebra. Indeed, the more mathematics you know and are able to call on in whatever situation, the more numerate you will be. Finally, numeracy requirements *vary*, depending on time, culture, and context.

Numeracy requirements change over time. The mathematics demands of contexts have changed as new technologies have emerged. It is no longer necessary to calculate using written methods rapidly and without error, as electronic calculators are available in various forms, including electronic cash registers. By contrast, sophisticated analysis of data and interpretation of quantitative representations are increasing in importance (Steen, 2001).

Numeracy is also dependent on culture. Canadians must be familiar with the imperial and metric systems of measurement. Australians need only the metric system. Indigenous Australians living in remote and seemingly featureless environments have a need for a sophisticated system of location, an aspect of geometry not required by those living in urban settings (Harris, 1980).

Numeracy depends on the context. Each context brings its own mathematical demands and a person may be more or less numerate in different situations; for example, builders measure to the nearest millimetre to ensure gaps are not present in walls. A road crew could paint road markings without needing to be so precise. To be numerate, a person has to understand the mathematical requirements of the context in which they are operating. Just knowing the mathematics is not sufficient—the application to the context is needed as well.

The influence of the context of mathematics has been studied by Lave, and the field is now known as 'Situated Cognition'. Her seminal work documented everyday arithmetic practices in different settings (Lave, 1988). People undertake mathematics in different ways depending on the context they are in. School procedures are taught to ensure correct results by following the same procedure, regardless of the numbers involved. Adults in life contexts are more likely to use ad hoc methods that are chosen for ease based on the numbers involved and the level of precision required.

Numeracy is most often developed in context. That is, we learn how to apply the mathematics in the situations where it is needed. We learn 'tricks of the trade', the level of precision required, how to judge the reasonableness of results, and so on. Mathematics may be learned in school or other contexts but the application is made in the situation, so numeracy has to be developed in situ, or simulated environments (Rowe & Test, 2012).

Is mathematics important for learners with Down syndrome?

For many adults, mathematics is seen as a difficult subject and many would argue they have used little mathematics since completing their school studies. It is possible to remove a great deal of mathematics from our lives—we can use calculators, others can shop for us, arrange our transport, and so on. However, this comes at a loss of independence. When we become fluent to the point of automaticity with mathematics techniques, it is easy to forget mathematics is being used. The more contexts a person engages with in their lives, the more opportunities for doing mathematics and the more the requirements for mathematics there are. If opportunities to learn mathematics are curtailed, numeracy development will also be reduced. The more mathematics a person can undertake, the more they are able to engage in the contexts of their lives in an informed way.

Being numerate contributes significantly to a person's quality of life (Faragher & Brown, 2005). There is a surprising resonance between the two concepts: numeracy and quality of life. The core ideas of quality of life all have direct counterparts with numeracy. As Roy Brown points out in Chapter 1 in this book, the principles of quality of life include choices, self-image, perception, lifespan, holism, empowerment, and variability. Numeracy demands change as the contexts of a person change. In the field of quality of life, this reflects the principles of holism and lifespan. Another example of the synergy between the two concepts would be the effect of self-image and perceptions. For example, in the report of an investigation of the mathematical needs of adults in the United Kingdom, Cockroft (1982) identified adults who avoided mathematics due to their lack of confidence. How we feel about ourselves as learners (perceptions) and what we believe others think of us as learners (self-image) deeply affect our willingness and ability to undertake the mathematical demands of our lives and therefore both our numeracy and quality of life.

Depriving people with intellectual disabilities of the opportunities to learn mathematics directly contributes to undermining their future quality of life. For some learners, the opportunity to learn mathematics can have an immediate impact on quality of life, as in the case examples to follow where learners gained a great deal of satisfaction from their accomplishment with mathematics. In the longer term, learners may have access to a greater variety of employment; mathematics can be the gatekeeper to many occupations.

Learning rich mathematics from across the discipline is necessary for numeracy attainment. This in turn has an impact on a person's quality of life. Therefore, opportunities for learning mathematics are essential; but is learning more advanced mathematics possible for students with Down syndrome? This will be explored in the following section.

Mathematics at secondary level for learners with Down syndrome

Although the research literature in this area is virtually non-existent, some case examples are emerging of accomplishments of secondary school-aged learners with Down syndrome in mathematics. In the following section, two different cases from Australia are described and implications drawn.

Case 1: Martin[1]

Martin was 15 years old at the time of the study and enrolled in his local secondary school. Each week, he had five mathematics lessons: three were spent in the class with his age-peers while the remaining two were in the special education unit where he worked one-on-one with the special education teacher.[2] His time in the unit focused on life skills, such as the use of coins. In the regular classroom, he would have worksheets to complete on his own. These worksheets were unrelated to the content being studied by the other students and were chosen to keep him occupied without requiring assistance from the teacher, such as dot-to-dot puzzles. Martin's special education teacher contacted me for assistance, as she was unhappy with Martin's programme. She felt he was not making progress in his functional skills. Also, his parents were keen for Martin to be included more in the regular school programme. Most importantly, for the teacher, Martin was unhappy. He was misbehaving and clearly indicating he thought the worksheets were too simple for him. He also felt any work in the special education unit involving manipulative materials (such as counters and blocks) was infantile and he was very reluctant to participate.

A visit to the school was arranged for me to meet with the student and his teachers and consider options for his programme. They agreed to trial a Numeracy Development Plan (NDP) and document the planning process. There are five stages to the NDP, explained more fully in Faragher (2010) and described briefly as follows:

1 *Undertake a context audit.* List the contexts of the life of the person, including potential contexts. For example, a student may wish to find a part-time job.
2 *Establish what will be taught.* Note the numeracy demands of each context, and determine which need to be taught explicitly, separating these from mathematics skills the person is already using competently.
3 *Invite the person to prioritise the list.* Prioritising the list allows the person to choose to study areas of personal importance. Sometimes these can be areas causing particular difficulty and embarrassment, such as inability to use cash to make purchases.
4 *Establish who will do the teaching.* In a school setting, who will do the teaching is usually a straight-forward matter. However, decisions about the role of the allocated mathematics teacher, the special education teacher, and parents are required.
5 *Establish where the teaching will occur.* In school settings, the classroom is the main context for learning. Determining what will be taught in the mathematics classroom, what in the special education classroom, and what will be taught in other subjects and contexts is required.

There were three main sessions in the planning process, involving me as the researcher and three learning support teachers: Robyn, who had teaching responsibilities for Martin, and Ann and Sue, who assisted in the unit.

Session one: The student worked with his teachers to list the contexts of his life. While the conversation was observed, the session was not audio-taped but notes were taken. The student's parents had agreed to his talking with the teachers and the researcher about his goals but not to be involved further in the research project.

Session two: The three teachers and the researcher worked together, using the stages above to develop a NDP. This was audio-taped.

Session three: The researcher conducted an audio-taped interview with the main teacher about the planning process.

Secondary school as context

Early on, it became clear that the mathematics classroom, itself, was a legitimate context for a Year 9 schoolboy. During the first session of the planning process, Martin talked with the teachers, speaking of his interest in ten-pin bowling and other activities he pursued. Naturally, a large part of the life of a secondary student involves attendance at school, including classes and break times, and so school was added to his list of contexts.

The second session began with a discussion of scoring in ten-pin bowling to work on order of numbers and the use of the number line on display in the classroom. The discussion led to a shift in the teachers' thinking. Rather than considering a completely alternative programme, the teachers began to investigate including material from the regular class programme—both content (negative numbers) and resources (number line). I raised the possibility of the mathematics classroom as a context—studying mathematics from the regular programme rather than from the perspective of what is needed in adulthood. Initially, this was greeted with scepticism.

ANN: We do that with another student but we find with [Martin] that he is so far behind. For example, at the moment they are doing cos, sine and tan. Now the only thing he can get out of that is, 'This is a triangle'. And um you know we would be hard pushed to justify with [Martin] how we could even use the triangle later on, let alone the trigonometry. You know. There's not a lot that ... I mean it could end up looking the same if you gave him a page of triangles but apart from that.

The teacher's dissatisfaction with achieving only superficial content similarity was evident. Merely 'looking like the others' was not enough to justify the student's inclusion in a mathematics programme. At this point in the planning process, we began to tackle the essence of the problem.

RESEARCHER: ...It's more about whether that's the best use of his time, I think, is the issue you are grappling with. Is that right?

ANN: Yes. I think what we're trying to do is give him the maths that he will then be able to use. That is why we have concentrated so hard on the money and that kind of thing. Whereas with the other child who is in the class with the intellectual impairment that is not quite as great, I can actually go into each class once a week and see what they're doing and I can think, 'He will never use this' but I can simplify it so he is with the class doing something quite similar. But I would never consider doing that for [Martin] because I have never thought that he would ever use it.

In most countries, teachers of students in regular classroom programmes do not have the choice to decide whether the mathematics programme is worth teaching or not. Except for students working on Individual Education Plans (IEPs), teachers must follow the mandated syllabus programmes. However, in preparing IEPs for students with intellectual and developmental disabilities, there is a considerable dilemma to be faced about whether to include the study of mathematics for its own sake or concentrate on life skills. This quandary arose in the work of Elisabetta Monari Martinez (1998) in a study reporting the experience of students with Down syndrome and their teachers as they worked through a unit on algebra. She argued that it was inappropriate to deny potential enjoyment and accomplishment to students just because they had Down syndrome.

Monari Martinez's work was raised in discussion with the teachers and became a turning point for considering what might be possible for Martin. The development of Ann's thinking can be seen below.

RESEARCHER: One of the things, even with the [other] kids, you have to go over again which is the hypotenuse and which is the adjacent and some of that sort of work.

ANN: Maybe he could learn that. Maybe it's the sort of thing that's not necessarily going to be able to be used later but something that he will be able to feel he is achieving now.

The comment of the teacher acknowledges the present value of learning, not just for future use. Brown and Brown (2003, p. 90) describe the contribution to quality of life of 'cherishing everyday pleasures'. Feelings of achievement and accomplishment add to enjoyment of everyday activities. In addition, accomplishment contributes to a person's self-image and, therefore, quality of life, as Roy Brown writes in Chapter 1 of this book (and see also Schalock *et al.*, 2002). Ann considered another aspect of self-image in Martin's work in the regular classroom. 'I have noticed with his English, he often wants to do what the kids in class are doing.' On more than one occasion, the teachers demonstrated their concerns for Martin's self-image, noting efforts they were making to offer content that was appropriate to his age. It could be argued, for a teenager, self-image has particular prominence, perhaps compounding effects on quality of life. Numeracy involves the use of mathematics in life contexts. Being a numerate Year 9 secondary student in an inclusive programme requires being able to engage in the mathematics of the classroom. The classroom is a life context and so being engaged in this mathematics has the potential to have a positive impact on quality of life.

Robyn, Martin's support teacher, returned to the need to include life skills, commenting, 'I still think … I'm still really keen to stick with the money thing'. Martin was known to have difficulties with the use of money and had once brought a $50 note to school. He was found buying ice-creams for most of the other students in his grade—with few having any compunction about accepting his largess! Lunch breaks at school represented another context and one in which he had a clear need to understand the use of money. In order to meet the needs of other contexts of his life, Robyn decided to continue work on life-skills aspects when Martin was working with her in the special education unit, supplementing the regular classroom mathematics programme.

The modified programme

The final stages of the NDP process involve deciding who will do the teaching, where it will take place, and when it will be done. Initially the teachers felt they were not able to provide a good programme because there were not enough lessons in the special education unit. Sue commented, 'He really has to do it himself [when working in the mathematics classroom], we don't have enough hours'. However, as the planning meeting progressed, the teachers began to formulate an alternative strategy. Other students are not required to teach themselves in the classroom and this certainly should not be the expectation of a student with intellectual impairment. The teachers came to the view that others could be available to assist. Peer tutoring was considered, as was the possibility of involving the class teacher more. (The mathematics class teacher would normally have been involved in the planning process; however, at the time he was struggling with general duties. He resigned from his position soon after.)

As a result of the planning discussions, it was decided Martin would be taught a modified programme based on the content of the standard Year 9 class programme during the three lessons he was in the regular classroom. Robyn undertook the modification of the programme. She developed support materials to be used in the regular mathematics classroom to supplement the standard curriculum materials. In addition, his lessons in the special education unit would be devoted to learning additional functional topics, including financial literacy, carrying out simple number calculations with the aid of a ruler or calculator, and time management. These are skills required for adulthood (Carnellor, 2004), as well as some current contexts.

In the months following, Robyn regularly corresponded with me by email. She sent work samples as well as classroom observation records. We also shared ideas for solutions to problems that arose (see, Faragher, 2007, for more explanation).

The work samples showed evidence of Martin's remarkable progress with trigonometry. He used task cards (containing the steps needed to complete an exercise) to assist him. One sample showed the steps Martin took to find an unknown angle in a right-angled triangle using the sine ratio. With the assistance of his calculator, he followed the steps on the task card to find the answer to questions on his test paper. The task cards are described in greater detail later in this chapter.

Robyn's anecdotal records indicated that other students in the class could assist Martin because he was working on similar tasks to theirs. They, too, were solving trigonometry problems. For Martin, the exercises followed the exact steps on his task card. Other students in the class did not have this level of support and moved beyond exercises that were straightforward to include problems with multiple steps or which required interpretation. According to Robyn, Martin was much happier in the classroom because he was now doing work that was similar to the other students in the class. This had a surprising side effect: Martin was also much more willing to participate in the lessons in the special education unit. Robyn and Sue hypothesised that Martin had changed his view of himself as a learner and how he believed his teachers viewed him. An alternative hypothesis is that he was more receptive to work in the special education unit as it was more focused on particular skills he needed, and he had asked to be taught. For example, the focus on coins was changed to a focus on notes—much more necessary for a teenager.

Through the NDP process, the listing of contexts of Martin's life led to an understanding of the richness of the mathematics requirements for teenagers with Down syndrome. Aside from the initial, obvious contexts, such as sport, the various contexts of school life needed to be included. Lunchtime, with opportunities to purchase food from the school shop, class lessons with a need for telling time, reading timetables, and organisation, as well as the mathematics class lessons themselves indicated a diverse range of requirements across the discipline of mathematics.

Being able to do similar (though less complex) mathematics problems as other students in the class leads to feelings of satisfaction and accomplishment. There is also a feeling of belonging—of being included. Students have the chance to share in classroom conversations. As a result of the modified mathematics programme developed using the NDP process, Martin's enjoyment of lessons improved, as evidenced by his behaviour. Robyn reported he enjoyed working on the same topics as his classmates. He was seen to ask other students for assistance and to work with them. Also, results on his tests demonstrated the effectiveness of his learning.

Case 2: Rachel

A 14-year-old girl with Down syndrome was studying Year 8 mathematics at a mainstream secondary girls' school. This was the first time a student with Down syndrome had attended the school and the teaching staff were anxious to develop an appropriate mathematics programme. They became particularly concerned when Rachel's teacher asked her to add 10 and 10 and was given the answer 25! I was invited in to the school to provide advice and support for the teacher.

As for the previous case, there were three main aspects to this research.

Stage one: The researcher met with the classroom mathematics teacher. Notes were taken.
Stage two: The classroom teacher developed the teaching materials
Stage three: The researcher observed Rachel at work on two occasions. The sessions were videotaped and work samples collected.

The first stage involved a planning meeting that was held with the classroom mathematics teacher, Linda, and myself. The teacher discussed her concerns about finding an appropriate programme for the student, who was clearly many years behind the mathematics achievement of the other students in the Year 8 class.

Linda's first suggestion was to go back to Year 2 worksheets to follow a common recommendation to start teaching where the learner is up to. Unfortunately, this can lead to a cycle of revisiting work without progression. There was also the very real challenge for a secondary teacher to teach concepts from the early primary school years alongside the standard secondary programme.

This initiated a discussion about learners with Down syndrome and their difficulties with number. Although we are beginning to have some insight into the source of the difficulties, the research community is far from understanding the problem, much less being able to offer approaches to overcome learners' difficulties. If Linda were to revert to teaching Year 2 concepts, it is not certain that the student, Rachel, would be any more successful. The discussion moved to consideration of the experience gained from research described in Case 1. The teacher was intrigued. My suggestion was to begin with the standard programme for Year 8 and modify as necessary.

Engaging with year level-appropriate content

Following the initial planning meeting, Linda, the teacher, developed a unit on percentage for use with the class. She implemented the programme in the classroom three weeks later and gave direction to a learning support assistant, who did not prepare materials but assisted Rachel in the classroom to understand the mathematics taught by Linda.

The teacher was astonished by the progress made by Rachel. Her work was documented with a video recording in which Rachel can be seen completing the calculation 23 per cent of 189. Rachel uses her calculator to enter fractions (using a fraction key), perform the calculation, and then convert the answer from fractional to decimal form. Figure 8.1 shows Rachel's workbook (taken just three weeks after the initial planning meeting with Linda).

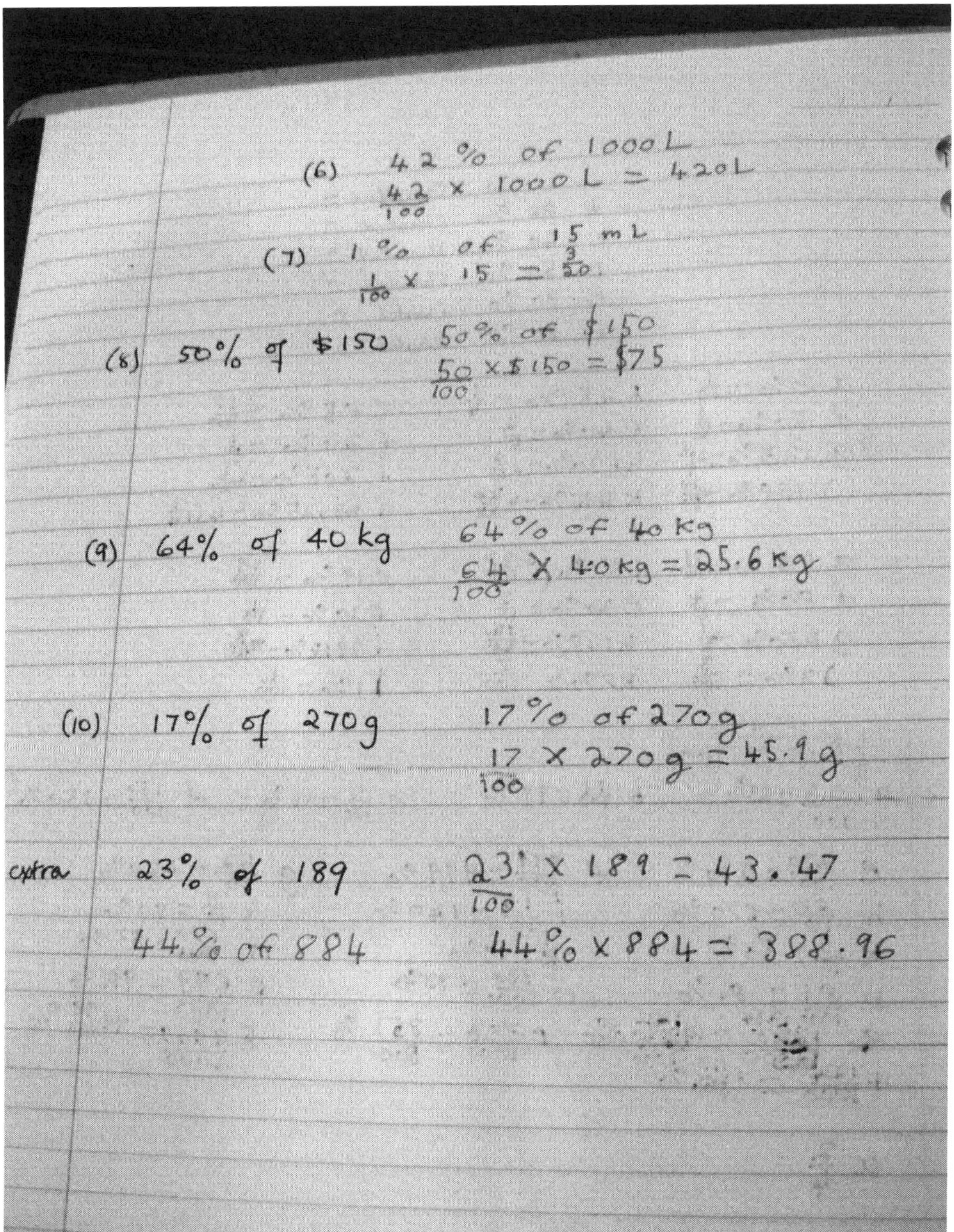

Figure 8.1 Sample of Rachel's workbook.

According to Linda, Rachel has been very proud of her achievements and enjoys being in the mathematics class. She was delighted with the student's success, particularly as percentage is regarded as a difficult topic at Year 8 level for many learners without intellectual disabilities. The teacher went on to plan units on introductory algebra.

Observing Rachel complete the percentage exercise raised the question: Does she understand what she is doing? Is she working on the 'like this, do that' model of teaching and learning? A second example of following a procedure was seen in an observation lesson on the calculation of area of rectangles. Following the rule of multiplying the two numbers together, Rachel was working away on a procedure and correctly using her calculator to record the answer to the area of rectangles. She became stuck, though, when the shape drawn was a square. One side length was marked but the other was marked with a small line, indicating the lengths were the same. Rachel asked me for assistance. Initially I thought her problem was caused because she did not understand the notation for congruent sides of the square. However, even when that was explained, she still did not know what to do. She was looking for the second number to enter into her calculator. It became clear that she had not been making any connection to area at all. She had been following a process that involved manipulating numbers. Although the worksheet had diagrams drawn, not one of them was actually the size or shape indicated by the numbers. It would, therefore, have been more surprising if Rachel had made a connection between the diagrams and an actual area!

Skemp (1976) wrote of the difference between instrumental and relational understanding. Instrumental understanding is where learners can follow a procedure correctly. Relational understanding is deeper; the learner understands why the procedure works. It may well be likely that Rachel had acquired instrumental understanding and not relational understanding. However, it is unlikely other students in the class had developed relational understanding either. Many classrooms practices, and the textbook materials they rely on, focus on instrumental understanding (Stein, Grover, & Henningsen, 1996). Further research is needed to ascertain whether learners with Down syndrome can achieve relational understanding of mathematical procedures but there is no indication at this stage that they cannot.

In an age where calculators are readily available, the value of written procedures for computation has been questioned in the curriculum for all learners (Usiskin, 1998). For learners with Down syndrome, the conversation appears not to have been as advanced. Students are still spending a great deal of time learning number work, including written computation procedures, even though this is often an area of mathematics of relative weakness for learners with Down syndrome. It is also an area of diminishing importance. As noted at the beginning of this chapter, numeracy requirements change with time. Written procedures for computation no longer have the critical importance they had last century. In the case of Rachel, computation is an area of difficulty but she adopted the use of a calculator as a prosthetic device (Wheeler, Ford, Nietupski, Loomis, & Brown, 1980) and has demonstrated adept usage. This enabled her to access other aspects of the mathematics curriculum alongside her age peers while avoiding wasting school time trying to learn procedures of little value and with a low probability of success.

Discussion of cases

What to teach

When students reach secondary school, decisions about what to teach can be challenging. Fundamental mathematics concepts are introduced in the primary years and are the focus of the general curriculum, including for children with Down syndrome. Once a child reaches secondary school, the pressure to prepare for post-school options leads to challenging decisions often characterised as a choice between further study of mathematics or moving more to life skills and numeracy. One of Martin's teachers raised this when she commented, 'Mind you, he's 16 soon and I guess I feel very much the push of time and also where he will happily go and be able to have a fulfilling life'.

Tension exists between functional, utilitarian numeracy and mathematics. As both Janet Carr and Roy Brown have advocated earlier in this book, we need to take a life-span view to the education of learners with Down syndrome. With advances in life expectancy, young children can look forward to a long adulthood, for many into their seventies. While making realistic provision for adulthood, school mathematics programmes need to ensure possibilities are not limited. This can be achieved by carefully exploring the contexts of a student and possible contexts in the future. In the early years of secondary education, in order to ensure options are retained, learners need access to the learning objectives of the general mathematics curriculum as well as application of mathematics into other areas of the curriculum (numeracy), such as financial literacy and management of time. In Martin's case, these aspects of numeracy were undertaken in the special education unit, effectively requiring him to learn the general mathematics course in just three out of five classes—two lessons fewer than other students. If aspects of mathematics were genuinely required for numeracy, it would imply there would be opportunities throughout the school day to learn these areas of mathematics. Numeracy, as a cross-curriculum priority, should be included on a student's individual education plan and addressed in all classes.

As a sensitising notion (Taylor, 1994), quality of life helps us to look at disability in a new light. This is important in guiding the teaching of mathematics to people with intellectual disabilities, tailoring teaching to specific individual requirements. Quality of life involves the interplay of a number of core ideas, identified in the consensus statement (Schalock *et al.*, 2002). It may seem a waste of precious school time to be working in a classroom on mathematics content that is likely to have little use in adulthood. However, if we consider perceptions, values, choices and personal control, and self-image, we can appreciate the importance to quality of life for the student in being included in the general mathematics class. Mathematics is a rich and beautiful subject worthy of study in its own right and everyone should be entitled to access its study. Many people enjoy mathematics and it was noted that both the students whose cases are reported in this chapter enjoyed the feeling of success when able to respond correctly to exercises like other students. There is also the under-explored possibility that learners may acquire concepts that have been considered prerequisite while learning more advanced concepts. Both Martin and Rachel had not accomplished basic arithmetic but were studying higher-level mathematics. Through this work, they may acquire greater understanding of arithmetic, though this was not investigated in the case studies. Monari Martinez and Benedetti did, however, in their 2011 study, where they report: 'Incredibly, applying the two points distance formula and verifying the result, Martina learned to measure the distance of two points with a ruler and to understand the concept of "millimetres"' (Monari Martinez & Benedetti, 2011, p. 536). This is a remarkable finding, indeed: a student who has not understood measurement develops the concept through the study of coordinate geometry.

Learning year level-appropriate curriculum

Learning the curriculum as specified for the year level of the student and augmented by functional skills does not mean every learner in the class is taught the same material. Incorrect inclusive practice has at times assumed that students with disability included in regular classrooms need to manage with the same instruction as the other students. This is not the case. It is inequitable to treat everyone the same. Meeting the educational needs of learners means making accommodations to assist them to achieve the learning goals. In the case studies previously discussed, the instructional materials were modified by the teachers, to enable achievement of learning outcomes in the content area.

'Year level appropriate' refers to the match between curriculum or other content and the schooling age of students. Earlier research in this area (Spooner & Browder, 2006) has used the term 'age-appropriate curriculum'. This would be an appropriate term where the student with intellectual disability is in the same year level as students of the same age. This is not always the case. Many children repeat school years or commence school at an older age.

Modifying a standard mathematics programme to include a student with Down syndrome is a complex undertaking. Some suggested approaches are available in the literature (see, for example, Browder & Spooner, 2006). For Martin, the special education teacher undertook the modification. For Rachel, it was the mathematics class teacher. Monari Martinez (1998) suggests that mathematics teachers provide a student with a written sequence of steps. Implementation of this strategy for Martin required planning modifications to current topics. Simplified instructional worksheets on current classroom topics were prepared and given to the student once the classroom teacher had completed the introductory lessons. These worksheets developed a sequence of steps to be followed in solving basic problems, and the simple, repeatable steps were reiterated on a purpose-designed card (see Figure 8.2). Martin, like many secondary students with Down syndrome, was a confident reader. The use of cards made it possible for him to use the formula, *Sine ratio = Opposite side ÷ hypotenuse side*, for example, in a predictable process to solve problems. Modelling by the teacher, followed by adequate practice with immediate corrective feedback, effectively gave the student confidence in his skills. Similar laminated cards were provided to him for other topics that he covered at the same time as his peers, but at a modified level (an approach described by Browder, Ahlgrim-Delzell, Pugalee, & Jimenez, 2006). The cards were stored on a split ring that the student was able to carry in his pencil case.

A similar approach was undertaken for Rachel. The exercise of calculating a percentage of a number was broken down into steps. Rachel was shown how to change the question into a set format (changing the number as percentage into a fraction with 100 as the denominator). She was then shown the button to use on her calculator. Task cards were not used for teaching Rachel, who was able to remember the steps involved, along with the use of her calculator. As Clarke and Faragher advocate in Chapter 5, students with Down syndrome need to be taught explicitly how to use a

Sine ratio

Write down the rule:

Sine θ = Opposite side ÷ hypotenuse side

Write in the numbers:

Sine θ = (____ ÷ ____)

Use your calculator to work out the answer for Sine θ :

Use your calculator to find θ :

ANS Shift $\sin^{-1}$

Figure 8.2 An example of a task card used by Martin.

calculator. With regular practice, most can become accomplished in their use. Other studies (see, for example, Koller & Mulhern, 1977; Wheeler *et al.*, 1980) provide detailed approaches to teaching the use of a calculator.

Neither Martin nor Rachel is remarkable for their mathematical aptitude. It would be too easy to dismiss their achievements by assuming they must in some way be unique or extraordinary compared with other learners with Down syndrome. What was remarkable was the willingness of their teachers to take a considerable risk. They were dealing with students who appeared not to have prerequisite knowledge for the work being planned. It seemed unlikely that the students would be successful and there were few examples from research or practice to draw on. The success of the students is testament to what can be achieved with inspired teaching.

Although year level curriculum was the focus of the two case studies, the teachers also raised the issue of continuing to teach mathematics for practical applications, including time and money. The issue of teaching functional mathematics is addressed in the following section.

Teaching functional mathematics

Emphasising mathematics skills that might be needed for the future warrants caution. As part of a larger study of the numeracy requirements of adults with Down syndrome, Faragher (2007) presented findings from a survey of parents and carers. In this study, respondents indicated they felt able to teach the mathematics needed in the context of adult life. Many reported instances (such as using a telephone and budgeting) where learning had been much more efficient when in the context where the skills were needed or the learner had a clear self-directed purpose for learning. What parents did not feel confident to do was to teach other areas of mathematics. They regretted schools devoting too much time to life skills and not enough to teaching academic work where teachers had the expertise. Few opportunities exist for learners to continue learning mathematics after leaving school. Even so, some focus on clearly functional mathematics was considered necessary by the carers, with the concepts of *time* and *use of money* being raised as particularly troublesome, yet important.

Time is an extraordinarily difficult attribute to measure, as it is not a physical quantity. It also has more than one aspect: sequencing of events, duration of time, and telling time by reading clocks and watches. Many education programmes place most emphasis on reading the time, and yet, it is arguably the easiest of the three aspects. It is one with a tangible object and a set process that can be taught. Understanding that time is actually something that can be measured is a complex, abstract concept and difficulties manifest themselves in sequencing events and understanding duration. The following vignette illustrates one person's challenging experience with time.

Rhonda and Sarah

A few years ago I was part of a friendship group for young adults with intellectual disabilities. One of our members, Sarah, lived in supported accommodation with two other friends. A support worker visited the home on a daily basis but the three lived largely independently. One evening I was driving Sarah back to her home when she asked me to take her to a pharmacy as she had diarrhoea. As I had no knowledge of her medical history, I asked her to speak with the pharmacist. He asked her how long she had been experiencing the problem. Her reply was 'six months'. The pharmacist was taken aback and suggested she seek advice from a doctor.

Subsequent discussion with my friend's mother revealed that the condition was more like six hours in duration.

The anecdote above raises the importance of developing an understanding of the duration of time and the language involved. It also highlights the considerable difficulties that may arise when those with a casual connection to a person, particularly health professionals, are making decisions based on responses when these may not be accurate. Care must also be taken when a person with Down syndrome is asked to recount events. Recounts involve understanding duration and sequencing of events as well as the use of language to convey the understanding.

The second area of difficulty raised by families is financial literacy. This topic is receiving greater attention in the general mathematics curriculum in many countries, and particularly in Australia. Aside from the arithmetic, there are deep concepts involved in the use of money. Money, while intensely practical, is an abstraction of the underlying numerical concepts and money is not a representation that supports the development of these concepts.

The equivalence of coins is another issue that is also quite complex. Not all the difficulties are with numeracy. Coins can be difficult to handle. The size does not routinely correspond with the amount. Some coins, such as the US 'dime', do not have the value marked on them. Other aspects are to do with the underlying mathematics. For example, counting coins involves counting the value (such as counting in 10s for coins of 10c value), rather than counting objects (how many coins do I have?). The patterns involved vary from country to country. In the United States, patterns are based around 25s—the quarter dollar. In Singapore, patterns are based around 10s and 50s. Travellers often are starkly aware of adjustments that need to be made to automatic routines for tending coins.

As noted earlier, numeracy demands change with time. This is particularly evident in the area of financial literacy. In countries where electronic finance is dominant, there is a need to focus less on coins and more on the use of electronic transactions. The following anecdote shows an accommodation made to compensate for difficulties with the use of coins.

Ruth and coins

My daughter, Ruth, struggles with calculation. She finds inordinate difficulty with understanding the value of coins, such as counting coins as objects rather than multiples of the value of the coin. Determining if change will be received remains a challenge, let alone determining the amount of the change. This is not for want of experience and opportunities for practice over many years.

In recent times, she has opened a day-to-day account that is linked to her savings account. The day-to-day account is accessed by the use of a debit card and she has learnt to operate an automatic teller machine (ATM) as well as point-of-sale devices. Typically, she withdraws cash from ATMs, usually $20 or $50. She prefers to use notes for transactions and, while she can name coins, using them in transactions remains a difficulty and requires modelling and questioning for each transaction.

This limitation of coin usage might be regarded as a debilitating deficit of functional skills with potential for considerable limitations of numeracy in adult contexts. However, a friend observed a remarkable accommodation. She took my daughter on a shopping trip. My daughter was aware she only had $3 in her account but a bulging wallet of coins. At Ruth's request, my friend took her to a bank where my daughter walked straight up to a coin counting machine, emptied her wallet, and collected the receipt, which she then took to a teller for depositing into her account. My friend was astonished—she had not even been aware such machines existed.

Ruth had been shown how to use a coin machine once, some months ago. One teaching experience had been sufficient for her to use this as a strategy to overcome her inability to use coins, which has been the subject of countless teaching experiences. Further, she has adopted this strategy without direction from an adult.

Conclusion

Mathematics is the underpinning of numeracy, which in turn affects a person's quality of life. Young people with Down syndrome can look forward to a long adulthood full of possibilities for new contexts and opportunities for learning.

Engaging with secondary school mathematics content is an important way to continue the development of mathematical understanding across the discipline. It also allows learners to engage in the conversations and experiences of other learners in an inclusive classroom setting. The remarkable conclusion from the two case studies presented here and other similar anecdotal accounts would suggest that it is indeed possible to engage meaningfully with year level-appropriate curriculum while not having mastered earlier concepts.

Continuing work in areas of mathematics such as financial literacy may be helpful. However, the financial world is changing. Few of us manually calculate change for shopping transactions any more, if we ever did outside school exercises. Being numerate in modern financial contexts needs further investigation but would include being able to operate electronic devices, such as the use of debit cards and automatic teller machines.

So little is known about the possibilities of teaching secondary level mathematics to learners with Down syndrome. Teachers have little research evidence to guide their practice. Practice-based evidence is being accumulated, which is giving us some encouragement that year level-appropriate curriculum is possible and, indeed, desirable.

When all students with Down syndrome are taught secondary mathematics content in a sustained way, with adequate time allocation and opportunities for learning that continue into adulthood, we will be in a position to fill the research gap identified by Shepperdson (1994, p. 101) and raised at the beginning of this chapter: we will know what can be achieved by people with Down syndrome with respect to mathematical attainment.

Notes

1 Both Martin and, later, Rachel are pseudonyms.
2 The author wishes to acknowledge this and other teachers who assisted with the development of the ideas in this chapter.

References

Bird, G., & Buckley, S. (2001). Number skills for individuals with Down syndrome—An overview. Hampshire, UK: The Down Syndrome Educational Trust.

Browder, D. M., Ahlgrim-Delzell, L., Pugalee, D. K., & Jimenez, B. A. (2006). Enhancing numeracy. In D. M. Browder & F. Spooner (Eds), *Teaching language arts, math, & science to students with significant cognitive disabilities* (pp. 171–195). Baltimore, MD: Brookes.

Browder, D. M., & Spooner, F. (Eds). (2006). *Teaching language arts, math, & science to students with significant cognitive disabilities.* Baltimore, MD: Brookes.

Brown, I., & Brown, R. (2003). *Quality of life and disability. An approach for community practitioners.* London: Jessica Kingsley Publishers.

Carnellor, Y. (2004). Encouraging mathematical success for children with learning difficulties. Southbank, Victoria: Social Science Press.

Cockroft, W. H. C. (1982). Mathematics counts: Report of the committee of inquiry into the teaching of mathematics in schools. London: HMSO.

Council of Australian Governments Human Capital Working Group. (2008). *National numeracy review report*. Canberra, ACT: COAG.

Faragher, R. M. (2007). *Numeracy in the context of adulthood and Down syndrome.* Doctoral thesis, Flinders University of South Australia, Adelaide.

Faragher, R. M. (2010). Developing numeracy to enhance quality of life. In R. Kober (Ed.), *Enhancing the quality of life of people with intellectual disabilities. From theory to practice* (pp. 401–411). London: Springer.

Faragher, R. M., & Brown, R. I. (2005). Numeracy for adults with Down syndrome: It's a matter of quality of life. *Journal of Intellectual Disability Research, 49*, 761–765.

Forlin, C. (2005). Guest editorial. Moving onwards and upwards: Inclusive education in secondary schools. *The Australasian Journal of Special Education, 29*, 87–91.

Harris, P. (1980). *Measurement in tribal aboriginal communities*. Darwin, NT: Northern Territory Department of Education.

Koller, E. Z., & Mulhern, T. J. (1977). Use of a pocket calculator to train arithmetic skills with trainable adolescents. *Education and Training of the Mentally Retarded,* December, 332–335.

Lave, J. (1988). *Cognition in practice: Mind, mathematics and culture in everyday life.* Cambridge: Cambridge University Press.

Ministerial Council on Education Employment Training and Youth Affairs (MYCEETYA). (1997). *National report on schooling in Australia 1997*. Melbourne: MYCEETYA.

Monari Martinez, E. (1998). Teenagers with Down syndrome study algebra in high school. *Down Syndrome Research and Practice, 5*, 34–38.

Monari Martinez, E., & Benedetti, N. (2011). Learning mathematics in mainstream secondary schools: Experiences of students with Down's syndrome. *European Journal of Special Needs Education, 26*, 531–540. doi: 10.1080/08856257.2011.597179.

Monari Martinez, E., & Pellegrini, K. (2010). Algebra and problem-solving in Down syndrome: A study with 15 teenagers. *European Journal of Special Needs Education, 25*, 13–29. doi: 10.1080/08856250903450814.

Rowe, D. A., & Test, D. W. (2012). Effects of simulation to teach students with disabilities basic finance skills. *Remedial and Special Education* (online). doi: 10.1177/0741932512 448218.

Schalock, R., Brown, I., Brown, R. I., Cummins, R. A., Felce, D., Matikka, L., & Parmenter, T. (2002). Conceptualization, measurement, and application of quality of life for persons with intellectual disabilities: Report of an international panel of experts. *Mental Retardation, 40*, 457–470.

Shepperdson, B. (1994). Attainments in reading and number of teenagers and young adults with Down's syndrome. *Down Syndrome Research and Practice, 2*, 97–101.

Skemp, R. R. (1976). Instrumental understanding and relational understanding. *Mathematics Teaching, 77*, 20–26.

Spooner, F., & Browder, D. M. (2006). Why teach the general curriculum? In D. M. Browder & F. Spooner (Eds), *Teaching language arts, math, and science to students with significant cognitive disabilities* (pp. 1–13). Baltimore, MD: Brookes.

Steen, L. A. (Ed.). (2001). *Mathematics and democracy. The case for quantitative literacy.* Princeton, NJ: National Council on Education and the Disciplines.

Stein, M. K., Grover, B. W., & Henningsen, M. (1996). Building student capacity for mathematical thinking and reasoning: An analysis of mathematical tasks used in reform classrooms. *American Educational Research Journal, 33*, 455–488.

Taylor, S. J. (1994). In support of research of quality of life, but against QoL. In D. Goode (Ed.), *Quality of life for persons with disabilities: International perspectives and issues* (pp. 260–265). Cambridge, MA: Brookline Books.

Toney, J. (2010). *Disney's 'Tangled' and beautiful mathematics.* Retrieved 11 February 2013 from http://scienceblogs.com/deanscorner/2010/12/29/disneys-tangled-and-beautiful/.

Usiskin, Z. (1998). Paper-and-pencil algorithms in a calculator and computer age. In L. J. Morrow & M. J. Kenney (Eds), *The teaching and learning of algorithms in school mathematics (Yearbook of the National Council of Teachers of Mathematics)* (pp. 7–20). Reston, VA: NCTM.

Wheeler, J., Ford, A., Nietupski, J., Loomis, R., & Brown, L. (1980). Teaching moderately and severely handicapped adolescents to shop in supermarkets using pocket calculators. *Education and Training of the Mentally Retarded*, April, 105–112.

Part III

Literacy development

Chapter 9

Developing the reading skills of children with Down syndrome

Kelly Burgoyne, Becky Baxter, and Sue Buckley

Abstract

Children with Down syndrome have a distinct profile of language and memory delays and difficulties which have implications for the development and teaching of literacy in this group. In this chapter, we review what is known about reading skills and the teaching of reading in children with Down syndrome. We discuss how language, speech, and phonology are related to reading and the possibility that reading instruction and reading progress may have benefits for aspects of language and memory. Writing abilities are also reviewed. Finally, we identify the implications of current knowledge for instruction.

Introduction

The ability to read is crucial for children's participation in many academic and social activities at home and at school. Beyond school age, literacy skills remain key to successful inclusion in the labour market and the social community as well as essential for success in society today. In addition to these benefits, reading can be a rewarding and enjoyable activity in itself: parental reports demonstrate that many children with Down syndrome are interested in learning to read and frequently choose to spend time reading and looking at books for pleasure in their free time (Al Otaiba, Lewis, Whalon, Dyrlund, & McKenzie, 2009; Ricci, 2011; Ricci & Osipova, 2012; Trenholm & Mirenda, 2006; van Bysterveldt, Gillon, & Foster-Cohen, 2010a). Reading is a priority goal for many parents of children with Down syndrome (Ricci & Osipova, 2012; Trenholm & Mirenda, 2006; van Bysterveldt *et al.*, 2010a), many of whom spend time teaching their child to read and engaging in reading activities with them (van Bysterveldt *et al.*, 2010a), often starting when children are at an early age (Al Otaiba *et al.*, 2009; van Bysterveldt *et al.*, 2010a). Estimates of the number of books children have access to at home suggest parents provide print-rich home literacy environments (Al Otaiba *et al.*, 2009; van Bysterveldt *et al.*, 2010a) in which reading and engaging with print is a valued and commonly occurring activity. Learning to read is therefore a valuable and important goal for all children and one that many children with Down syndrome can achieve.

In this chapter, we review what is known about reading skills and the teaching of reading in children with Down syndrome. We discuss how language, speech, and phonology are related to reading and the possibility that reading instruction and reading progress may have benefits for aspects of language and memory. Writing abilities are also reviewed. Finally, we identify the implications of current knowledge for instruction.

It is important to note that much of the research on which the following chapter is based stems from work with Western, English-speaking cultures and may not therefore transfer directly to other cultures/languages. It should also be noted that not all children with Down syndrome in the West have access to good literacy teaching; our understanding of what this group may achieve is still developing.

Before reviewing the research, it is important to consider a number of issues pertaining to assessment and reporting of reading attainments; this chapter therefore begins with a brief discussion of some of these issues.

Assessing and reporting reading attainments

There are a number of issues related to assessment and reporting which should be noted, as these have a bearing on the conclusions we can reach from the research evidence. One of the biggest complications when evaluating the research literature is a lack of consistency of measures across studies. Reading ages and standard scores (though problematic in some respects) can be useful indicators of the level of reading and allow comparison with other studies in a way which cannot be done with raw scores when different measures are used; in many studies, however, raw scores are the only data provided. In addition, whilst group studies often only report average scores, the large variability seen in this population supports consideration of the range of scores as well as the average. Similarly, studies typically differ in reporting background information, such as school placement, type and frequency of literacy instruction received, access to and participation in external services, and hearing and visual impairments—all of which may impact on literacy attainment and should be considered.

Most published studies report word reading attainments but when considering reading skills it is important to know how far children have progressed in alphabetic reading skills and how well they understand what they read. Few studies report on phonics attainment and even fewer report on comprehension.

A fundamental issue is the lack of appropriate assessment tools for use with individuals with Down syndrome. Many measures rely on verbal instructions and a verbal response; clearly, difficulties with speech and language will affect performance on verbally mediated tasks such that these may underestimate the level of ability individuals can achieve. Similarly, standardised measures of speech, language, and literacy are often taken to measure the progress children make and to evaluate the impact of intervention. Given the significant delays in speech and language skills experienced by many children with Down syndrome, difficulties with generalisation, and the populations that typical standardised assessments are designed to measure, such measures may lack sensitivity to discrete gains that may have been made. Future research should aim to develop more fine-grained assessment tools that are more appropriate for this group of learners.

There are also issues associated with formally assessing individuals with Down syndrome which are likely to impact on performance. Speech delays and/or disorders may cause difficulties for interpreting verbal responses; having someone who is familiar with the child sit in on assessments if the assessor does not know the child can be useful. Similarly, building a relationship with a child and learning about what interests and motivates them, and their ability to sustain attention, as well as becoming accustomed to their speech, can aid with conducting and interpreting assessments.

Learning to read: word recognition and comprehension

Effective reading is to read with meaning. This involves the development of two separate, though interacting, components: word recognition and language comprehension. The majority of work with children with Down syndrome to date has explored the word recognition component of reading; much less is currently known about reading comprehension ability and how to support the development of comprehension skills for this group of children. Accordingly, this chapter first reviews the research in relation to the development of word recognition skills in children with Down syndrome, and teaching programmes which aim to support word recognition, before considering comprehension skills. Though this structure reflects the relative attention each component has received from research, this does not imply that comprehension is less important; ensuring that children link the process of reading to meaning and understand what they read is important from the outset.

Word recognition

Most individuals with Down syndrome are able to acquire some measurable level of word reading ability (Burgoyne *et al.*, 2012; Byrne, MacDonald, & Buckley, 2002; Fidler, Most, & Guiberson, 2005; Laws & Gunn, 2002). Studies which include students across a wide age range (e.g. Fidler *et al.*, 2005; Laws & Gunn, 2002) and individuals attending schools for students with special educational needs (e.g. Laws & Gunn, 2002) are difficult to interpret as the frequency and type of literacy instruction individuals have previously had or currently have access to is unclear. Recent research with children in mainstream schools who have access to regular literacy instruction may provide a clearer picture of the number of children with Down syndrome who can learn to read. Such evidence suggests that around 90 per cent of children with Down syndrome in mainstream schools learn to read, though levels of reading attainment and rates of progress vary widely (e.g. Burgoyne *et al.*, 2012; Cardoso-Martins, Peterson, Olson, & Pennington, 2009; Goetz *et al.*, 2008; Hulme *et al.*, 2012; Laws, 2010). For example, Laws (2010) reports data from an unpublished study which found an average reading age of 5:10 (years:months) for 28 children with Down syndrome aged between five and 11 years (average chronological age = 7:09). Twenty-seven months later, reading ages were between 5:00 and 10:03 (average reading age = 6:7); gains in reading ages between the two time points were between two months and two years. Similarly, a longitudinal study of 49 children with Down syndrome, average age of 10:04, in mainstream schools reported a wide range of ability at the start of the study with standard scores ranging between 55 and 115 (Hulme *et al.*, 2012). The group of children with Down syndrome made progress in reading over two years in school, albeit at a slower rate than that made by a group of typically developing children matched for word reading at the start of the study (average age 6:05). Whilst many individuals are able to develop some level of reading ability, some children with Down syndrome are able to acquire reading skills at a level that is in line with their chronological age (e.g. Groen, Laws, Nation, & Bishop, 2006), with group studies suggesting that this is the case for approximately 10 per cent of individuals with Down syndrome (Burgoyne *et al.*, 2012: 9 per cent; Cardoso-Martins *et al.*, 2009: 10.5 per cent; Hulme *et al.*, 2012: 8 per cent; Laws, 2010: 11 per cent; Nash & Heath, 2011: 8 per cent).

Word reading strengths and weaknesses

For most children with Down syndrome (though not all—see Fowler, Doherty, & Boynton, 1995; Groen *et al.*, 2006), word recognition is in advance of decoding ability, as measured by nonword reading tasks (Fowler *et al.*, 1995; Hulme *et al.*, 2012; Kay-Raining Bird, Cleave, & McConnell, 2000; Kennedy & Flynn, 2003; Næss, Melby-Lervåg, Hulme, & Lyster, 2012; Nash & Heath, 2011; Roch, Florit, & Levorato, 2011; Roch & Jarrold, 2008; Verucci, Menghini, & Vicari, 2006). Decoding skills are reliant on a phonological approach to reading, and difficulties with decoding are a predicted consequence of poor phonological awareness, as typically seen in Down syndrome (see the evidence reviewed below). Better real-word reading could indicate a preference for a visual or logographic approach to reading. Frith (1985) described three stages of development in typical literacy: The initial logographic phase is characterised by whole word recognition, an inability to decode, and spelling restricted to familiar words; children who have progressed to the alphabetic phase begin to apply letter sound rules to decode and blend and can spell semi-phonetically; at the final stage (orthographic), the child acquires conventions, starts to recognise larger chunks, such as suffixes and prefixes, and is able to read words through analogy. There is some evidence for logographic reading in Down syndrome—for example, they have particular difficulties reading nonwords that are visually dissimilar to real words (Gombert, 2002) and show strengths in irregular word reading (Roch & Jarrold, 2008). There is also some evidence that word identification correlates with visual perception in this group (Fidler *et al.*, 2005). However, this could reflect a lack of instruction in phonological decoding strategies rather than a dependence on visual cues. Furthermore, there is a significant relationship between word and nonword reading in Down syndrome (Fowler *et al.*, 1995; Kay-Raining Bird *et al.*, 2000).

What factors influence reading development?

A number of factors have been related to reading ability in individuals with Down syndrome, including cognition (Laws, Buckley, Bird, MacDonald, & Broadley, 1995; Sloper, Cunningham, Turner, & Knussen, 1990), speech accuracy (Laws, 2010), phonological representations (Dodd & Thompson, 2001), phonological awareness (Laws, 2010; Lemons & Fuchs, 2010b), and language skills (Burgoyne *et al.*, 2012; Hulme *et al.*, 2012). Hearing loss has also been reported as a factor (Laws, 2010; Laws & Gunn, 2002); however, the research on the relationship between hearing and reading is inconclusive as not all studies report a relationship (e.g. Kennedy & Flynn, 2003; Groen *et al.*, 2006).

These factors are not separate and discrete but rather all interact as a set of skills that the child brings with them to the task of reading. This section discusses the relationship between these factors in terms of their role in supporting reading development. It is important to note, however, that this relationship is not one way but rather is reciprocal in nature and these aspects may in turn further develop as a result of reading experience (Hulme *et al.*, 2012; Simpson, 2011).

Several areas of development which predict reading in the typically developing population are delayed in children with Down syndrome compared to measures of non-verbal mental age, including speech, language, and verbal short-term memory (Roberts, Price, & Malkin, 2007). We can therefore predict that children with Down syndrome will experience difficulty with both spoken and written language acquisition.

During the first year of life, children are exposed to the sounds of their language and are developing the foundations for speech and language learning. Around two thirds of children with Down syndrome are reported to have some form of hearing loss (Roberts *et al.*, 2007). Therefore, from the very beginning, many children with Down syndrome have more difficulty accessing the sounds around them, which may impact on the quality of their developing phonological representations.

Accurate phonological representations are important for reading and spelling; inaccurate representations create difficulties when mapping sounds to words, regardless of how skilled the child is at blending or segmenting and translating to letters (Snowling & Stackhouse, 2006). The development of fully specified phonological representations is also related to verbal short-term memory, where sounds and words are rehearsed and stored. Verbal short-term memory is related to reading in typically developing children (Gathercole & Baddeley, 1993) and in individuals with Down syndrome (Laws, 2010) and plays an important role in reading-related measures such as phonological awareness tasks, which require both storage and manipulation of phonemes. Children with Down syndrome score poorly on tests of verbal short-term memory; however, the extent to which this is due to a selective deficit in verbal short-term memory or rather reflects additional factors, such as speech difficulties (Jarrold, Nadel, & Vicari, 2008), is unclear. Thus, difficulties with hearing and verbal short-term memory skills will impact on the development of fully specified phonological representations, which in turn will affect the mapping of these stored representations for literacy.

The accuracy of speech output/production will also impact the development of a child's speech sound system and literacy skills. If a child is unable to articulate the speech sounds of the language being learned, they will develop a phonology that is different from the adult model (Hua & Dodd, 2006). Problems with muscle strength or with coordination are often reported in children with Down syndrome (see Abbeduto, Warren, & Conners, 2007); these may then affect the development of the speech sound system. Children with speech sound disorders demonstrate impairments in quality and access to phonological representations, and word reading (Anthony *et al.*, 2011). Given the speech difficulties found in children with Down syndrome (Dodd, McCormack, & Woodyatt, 1994; Ni Cholmain, 1994), it is not surprising speech accuracy has also been found to correlate with final word reading scores after taking chronological age into consideration (Laws, 2010). The skills required for successful phonological awareness and literacy development are thought to arise from an intact speech processing system (Snowling & Stackhouse, 2006) with a measure of children's phoneme awareness knowledge in preschool being described as the best single predictor of reading performance in the early years for typically developing children (Gillon & Dodd, 2005). Speech sound disorders have been found to be associated with phonological awareness impairments (Anthony *et al.*, 2011; Peterson,

Pennington, Shriberg, & Boada, 2009). It is believed that the disruption of the speech sound system will have a knock-on effect for skills such as phonological awareness and the severity of the speech problem, when measured by speech intelligibility, has been suggested to be a significant predictor on phonological awareness tasks (Stackhouse & Wells, 1997). This puts children with Down syndrome within the highest risk group for literacy difficulties given the specific difficulty in speech development.

For typically developing children, phonological awareness is a strong predictor of reading (Muter, Hulme, Snowling, & Stevenson, 2004) and essential to the development of alphabetic reading skills. Phonological awareness is the ability to reflect on and manipulate the sounds in spoken language. This can be measured in different ways: by the ability to separate words into syllables, to identify and produce rhyme, to match words that begin with the same sound, and to manipulate individual sounds (or 'phonemes') in words—for example, by blending, segmenting, and deleting them. A recent review of 20 studies (Lemons & Fuchs, 2010b) indicates that, though phonological awareness skills are typically delayed in children with Down syndrome relative to typically developing groups and to word reading skills, they nonetheless play a role in the reading development of this group. It is not yet clear the extent to which phonological awareness skills are an essential precursor to reading in Down syndrome; recent studies suggest that, as for typically developing children, phoneme awareness may develop in children with Down syndrome as they learn to read (e.g. Hulme *et al.*, 2012).

A recent longitudinal study (Hulme *et al.*, 2012) reported differential relationships between phonological awareness and reading for children with Down syndrome and typically developing children. In this study, phoneme awareness was a concurrent and longitudinal predictor of reading for typically developing children. This relationship did not hold for children with Down syndrome: for this group, initial reading level was predicted by vocabulary; however, neither phoneme awareness nor vocabulary predicted later reading skills. It should be noted, however, that there was a high degree of longitudinal stability in reading for the group with Down syndrome, making identification of significant predictors difficult. Relationships between reading and phoneme awareness were stronger for those children with the highest levels of phoneme awareness, suggesting that a certain level of phonological awareness is needed to benefit from it.

Language skills beyond phonology have been found to predict reading progress in children with Down syndrome in other research. Burgoyne *et al.* (2012) also found language (a composite measure of vocabulary and grammar), rather than phoneme awareness, to significantly predict reading progress in an intervention study conducted over 40 weeks with 57 primary-aged children with Down syndrome. Taken together, this work highlights an important role for vocabulary and wider language skills for the reading development of children with Down syndrome, which is supported elsewhere in the literature (Laws, 2010; Lorenz, Sloper, & Cunningham, 1985).

Chronological age is also related to reading progress in children with Down syndrome (Burgoyne *et al.*, 2012; Hulme *et al.*, 2012) in that older children tend to make less progress than younger children. This is likely to at least partly reflect the change in priority afforded to reading instruction throughout the school years and suggests that, for this group of children, it is important that time and attention is allocated to the teaching of reading beyond the initial stages of school.

Interventions to support word reading

Increasing understanding of the foundations of reading development has shaped the design of interventions which aim to help children learn to read. Following research with typically developing children who have reading difficulties, work with children with Down syndrome has progressed through different approaches to reading instruction, including those which follow a whole-word approach, phonological awareness training, and recently more comprehensive teaching approaches which combine multiple targets for instruction. These approaches are discussed below.

Whole-word reading

The relatively good visual skills (Fidler *et al.*, 2005) of children with Down syndrome support the potential for a sight word or 'look and say' approach to the teaching of reading (i.e. teaching whole words with no emphasis on letter–sound relationships) for this group. This approach aims to teach children a bank of words they can recognise by sight. It has been suggested that instruction should start with this approach and ensure children can read and understand simple sentences before targeting alphabetic strategies (Buckley, Bird, & Byrne, 1996). Recent evidence may offer some support for this suggestion: children with more sight words made more progress in other reading skills (i.e. decoding) during reading intervention than children with fewer sight words (Lemons & Fuchs, 2010a). However, more work is needed to support this.

Evidence from case studies, parent reports, and a small group study suggest that children with Down syndrome can begin to learn to read through sight word learning activities from an early age (2–3 years; e.g. Appleton, Buckley, & MacDonald, 2002; Dickinson, 2002; Groen *et al.*, 2006; Kotlinski & Kotlinski, 2002). In a small group study (Appleton *et al.*, 2002), 18 children with Down syndrome, aged 2–4 years, received parent-delivered instruction in sight word learning. After six months, the children could recognise an average of 17 words, though the range was large (0–67 words), with some children unable to read any of the words.

Historically, reading instruction for children with Down syndrome has tended to favour whole-word teaching and there are a number of manual and electronic programmes available which follow this approach. It should be noted, however, that many of these programmes lack scientific rigorous evaluation, which is necessary to support their efficacy. Furthermore, there are limitations to this approach to reading instruction: sight word reading is limited to words which have been trained and does not therefore support independent reading; instruction must include a wider range of components if children are to become effective readers (Buckley *et al.*, 1996).

Phonological awareness training

The relationship between phonological awareness and reading has prompted evaluations of this type of instruction for children with Down syndrome. Evidence from this work suggests that children with Down syndrome can make gains in specific phonological awareness skills following relatively short periods of teaching (e.g. Burgoyne, Duff, Snowling, Buckley, & Hulme, 2013; Kennedy & Flynn, 2003; Lorenz *et al.*, 1985; van Bysterveldt, Gillon, & Moran, 2006; van Bysterveldt, Gillon, & Foster-Cohen, 2010b). Effects appear to be largely restricted to those skills that are explicitly targeted with little evidence of generalisation; for example, a small-scale study (Kennedy & Flynn, 2003) reports gains in targeted phonological awareness skills (alliteration detection, initial phoneme isolation) and spelling for three children with Down syndrome aged 6:11–8:10 years following eight hours of one-on-one instruction but no evidence of generalisation to untrained tasks (i.e. segmentation). This type of instruction can also be effective for young children: van Bysterveldt, Gillon, & Moran (2006) found a small group (N = 7) of 4–5 year-old children with Down syndrome made significant progress in letter–sound knowledge, print concepts, and phoneme awareness after just four hours of parent-delivered intervention. Furthermore, explicitly linking goals to stimulate areas of phonological development that are critical for reading success with goals to stimulate correct phonological production can lead to gains in speech production accuracy (van Bysterveldt *et al.*, 2010b).

Though phonological awareness skills are an important foundation for reading, interventions which target phonological awareness may not necessarily impact on reading ability (e.g. Cleave, Kay-Raining Bird, & Bourassa, 2011). Evidence from typically developing children suggests that the teaching of phonology is most effective when it is combined with reading instruction and when the links between sounds and letters are made clear (phonological linkage hypothesis; Hatcher, Hulme, & Ellis, 1994); thus, combining reading with phonology instruction may be more likely to impact on reading skills. Consistent with this approach, Burgoyne *et al.* (2013) report significant gains in both targeted phonic skills (phoneme blending) and in word reading following instruction which combined specific activities to support phoneme blending with wider reading instruction, evaluated with 10 children with Down syndrome over six weeks of teaching. It is worth noting, however, that no significant effects were found on nonword reading skills; it therefore remains possible that gains in real-word reading were not due to the gains made in phoneme blending but were achieved using alternative strategies. Furthermore, the children had all been receiving language and reading instruction as part of a larger study (Burgoyne *et al.*, 2012, discussed below) and no long-term follow-up was carried out to assess maintenance of skills.

A combined reading and phonology approach was also evaluated by Cologon, Cupples, and Wyver (2011), combining activities targeting blending at the onset-rime and phoneme level with word and sentence reading. Seven children with Down syndrome, aged 2:11 to 10:08, received 10 hours of intervention over 10 weeks. Significant gains were found on measures of phonological awareness (word blending, nonword blending, and segmentation), word and nonword reading, letter–sound knowledge, and word and short-passage comprehension. Furthermore, gains were maintained over six months following intervention. Taken together, this evidence suggests that more comprehensive programmes which integrate multiple components are more effective than phonological awareness training in isolation.

Comprehensive reading programmes

A growing body of evidence demonstrates that phonics-based reading instruction which combines the teaching of phonics with wider reading instruction such as sight word teaching and real book reading can be effective for many children with Down syndrome (e.g. Baylis & Snowling, 2011; Goetz *et al.*, 2008; Lemons & Fuchs, 2010a; Lemons, Mrachko, Kostewicz, & Paterra, 2012). These studies report significant gains in reading and foundational skills following periods of regular, targeted intervention, which appear to be maintained once intervention ends (Baylis & Snowling, 2011; Goetz *et al.*, 2008). Limitations of much of this work include small sample sizes, short-term training periods, inclusion criteria (e.g. a baseline level of language or reading ability), and a lack of control groups and randomised controlled trials (RCTs).

More recently, research has demonstrated that combining language intervention with phonics-based reading instruction can be more effective for children who have language as well as reading difficulties (Duff *et al.*, 2008). Recent work has evaluated this combined approach in the first RCT of a reading and language intervention for children with Down syndrome (Burgoyne *et al.*, 2012). The intervention consisted of two components: a reading strand and a language strand (see Table 9.1 for breakdown of activities). The reading strand included work on book reading, letters, sounds and phonology, and sight word learning, whilst the language strand targeted new vocabulary learning and using new vocabulary in spoken and written sentences following the multiple context approach (Beck, McKeown, & Kucan, 2004).

The teaching programme was evaluated with 54 primary school-aged children with Down syndrome (aged 5:02 to 10:00 at the start of the study). All children were in mainstream primary schools; no exclusion criteria beyond school placement was adopted and the group represented a wide range of abilities, including children with little or no existing reading skills and children with low levels of language. Children were randomly allocated to intervention and waiting control groups; the intervention group received intervention over 40 weeks in school, whilst the waiting control group continued with their typical literacy instruction (following the National Curriculum and supported by a teaching assistant) for the first 20 weeks, after which they then received the reading and language intervention over the next 20 weeks in school. Teaching assistants working with the children in mainstream schools were trained to deliver the intervention to individual children in daily 40-minute sessions.

The effects of the programme were evaluated using a large battery of standardised and bespoke tests. Children were assessed at the beginning of the project (prior to intervention), at the end of the first 20 weeks (where the intervention group had completed 20 weeks of intervention, and the waiting control group had received 20 weeks of teaching as usual), and after 40 weeks (at which point the intervention group had completed 40 weeks of intervention and the waiting control group 20 weeks). There were no differences between the two groups of children at the start of the project, as expected given randomisation to groups. The authors next compared the two groups of children at the 20-week phase. At this time point, the children in the intervention group had made more progress on many of the measures and were significantly ahead

Table 9.1 Reading and language teaching programme (Burgoyne *et al.*, 2012)

Reading strand (20 mins)	
Reading easy level book	2–3 mins
Reading new instructional level book	5 mins
Sight word vocabulary	2–3 mins
Letters, sounds, phonology	5 mins
Introduce new instructional level book	5 mins
Language strand (20 mins)	
Vocabulary: Introduce new words	5 mins
Vocabulary: Reinforce meaning of new words	5 mins
Expressive language: Use new words in written language	5 mins

of those in the waiting control group on measures of single word reading, letter–sound knowledge, phoneme blending (a test of phonological awareness), and expressive vocabulary taught as part of the intervention. These measures were those that were most closely aligned with the intervention content; there were no significant group differences on wider measures of language and literacy, such as grammar, nonword reading, and spelling. Both groups made progress over the second 20-week phase; though the intervention group remained numerically ahead of the control group on many of the outcome measures, there were no significant group differences at the end of the trial.

Consistent with previous studies of reading intervention, there was wide variation in the amount of progress children made in reading over the course of the intervention; some children made no or only very small gains on the standardised test of single word reading while other children made large gains. The authors found three significant predictors of reading growth in response to intervention: the first was age, in that children who were younger made more progress in reading; language was also a significant predictor, as children who had higher initial levels of receptive language (a composite measure of vocabulary and grammar) also made more progress; and lastly, intervention attendance predicted reading growth: children who received more intervention sessions made greater progress in reading.

This study is the largest evaluation of a reading programme for children with Down syndrome to date, and the first RCT to evaluate a combined reading and language programme for this group of learners. Consistent with previous work, Burgoyne *et al.* (2012) found many children with Down syndrome can benefit from regular, targeted instruction to support their reading and language skills following a comprehensive programme of teaching which included phonics-based reading instruction and work on vocabulary and sentence skills. Also consistent with earlier work, progress in reading and language skills varied widely within the group and language skills were identified as an important predictor of reading growth.

Summary of word reading section

Many individuals with Down syndrome acquire useful levels of reading, though there is wide variability in attainment. Many factors affect reading development in children with Down syndrome, as with all children, and we are learning more about the complex interrelationships between these skills and how they affect reading. This evidence has been used to develop intervention programmes, the efficacy of which should be evaluated through rigorous scientific approaches. Evidence from such research increasingly supports a comprehensive and multicomponent approach to the teaching of reading for individuals with Down syndrome.

The research reviewed above has dealt with the word recognition component of reading; as discussed earlier, effective reading demands that text is read with meaning. This chapter will now turn to look at the reading comprehension skills of children with Down syndrome.

Reading comprehension

Reading comprehension is a complex skill that involves multiple components, including language (grammar, semantics, and pragmatics), working memory, background knowledge, and processes including inferential processing, and comprehension monitoring (Cain & Oakhill, 2006). Language (Chapman & Kay-Raining Bird, 2011) and memory (Jarrold, Purser, & Brock, 2006) are known to be affected in individuals with Down syndrome; it is reasonable therefore to expect difficulties with comprehension. The available evidence suggests that this is the case with word recognition typically in advance of reading comprehension for this group (e.g. Byrne *et al.*, 2002; Groen *et al.*, 2006; Nash & Heath, 2011; Roch & Levorato, 2009; Verucci *et al.*, 2006). Though children make gains in comprehension over time, progress is slower than in word reading such that the discrepancy between word reading and reading comprehension increases with age (Boudreau, 2002; Byrne *et al.*, 2002; Laws & Gunn, 2002; Roch & Levorato, 2009). Reading comprehension is typically stronger than listening comprehension, which shows slower progress over time (Roch *et al.*, 2011).

The discrepancy between accuracy and comprehension is comparable to that seen in 'poor comprehenders', leading to comparisons with this group: Poor comprehenders have difficulties with comprehension despite age-appropriate reading accuracy and exhibit oral language difficulties, such as poor vocabulary knowledge (Catts, Adlof, & Weismer, 2006; Nation, Clarke, Marshall, & Durand, 2004), similar to those found in children with Down syndrome. Work which identifies effective intervention approaches with poor comprehenders may therefore suggest potential avenues for supporting comprehension skills in individuals with Down syndrome; these are discussed further below. There are, however, some important differences between these groups (for example, cognitive impairment) and evidence for learning strengths in Down syndrome (e.g. visual) which must be considered when modifying existing intervention approaches. It is also important that such interventions be subjected to rigorous scientific evaluation; to date, there are no such evaluations available for review, with few published studies addressing reading comprehension intervention for this group and those that are available being limited to single case studies.

The reading comprehension difficulties seen in individuals with Down syndrome are related to language weaknesses and verbal memory (Levorato, Roch, & Beltrame, 2009; Levorato, Roch, & Florit, 2011; Nash & Heath, 2011; Roch *et al.*, 2011; Roch & Levorato, 2009). After controlling for word reading, Nash and Heath (2011) found significant relationships between vocabulary and comprehension for 13 individuals with Down syndrome, and a strong (though non-significant) relationship between verbal memory and comprehension. This suggests a potential causal role for underlying language skills in the comprehension difficulties of individuals with Down syndrome, consistent with research with poor comprehenders (Clarke, Snowling, Truelove, & Hulme, 2010). The implication here is that intervention which targets language skills may be effective in supporting comprehension. This is supported by evidence from a recent meta-analysis which highlights the benefits of vocabulary instruction to passage-level comprehension (Elleman, Lindo, Morphy, & Compton, 2009) and a large-scale RCT with poor comprehenders showing sustained and increasing gains in comprehension following a programme of oral language instruction (Clarke *et al.*, 2010). A similar approach, modified to make use of the strengths of children with Down syndrome (e.g. visual strengths), may hold promise as an effective method of supporting reading comprehension for this group of learners.

Inferential comprehension may be of particular difficulty for children with Down syndrome. Inference questions require the reader to go beyond what is explicitly stated in the text to establish meaning by integrating different parts of the text, using previous world knowledge, and using the surrounding context. Individuals with Down syndrome appear to find these questions more difficult than questions which tap literal understanding (Groen *et al.*, 2006; Nash & Heath, 2011). Though more evidence is needed to confirm this, it is perhaps unsurprising given the language delays seen in this population; indeed, there is a strong relationship between inferencing and vocabulary in Down syndrome (Nash & Heath, 2011). Inferencing skills can be targeted through intervention: McGee and Johnson (2003) report 20-month gains in comprehension for 6–10-year-old typically developing poor comprehenders following just three weeks of training. This type of intervention may also be effective for children with Down syndrome; however, research which clarifies the nature of their comprehension difficulties and the underlying causes of those difficulties is necessary to warrant such specific intervention targets.

Training children how to use effective strategies for comprehension—for example, accessing prior knowledge and experiences, predicting from text, and retelling stories—can also support comprehension. Strategic processing facilitates comprehension by enabling the reader to actively process text and develop a more detailed and coherent representation during reading that is supported by personal experience and background knowledge. Individuals with Down syndrome may use and benefit from world knowledge to support their comprehension: Levorato *et al.* (2009) found listening comprehension significantly improved when sentences were presented within a brief context than when presented alone, with 14 of 16 individuals showing improved comprehension when provided with contextual support. Though replication of this work is necessary, other research (e.g. Morgan, Moni, & Jobling, 2004; see Chapter 10) supports the potential for instruction which fosters the use of comprehension strategies for this population.

Impaired verbal memory is common in individuals with Down syndrome (Jarrold & Baddeley, 1997) and is related to the comprehension difficulties of this group (Nash & Heath, 2011; Levorato *et al.*, 2011). In contrast to verbal memory, visual memory skills are relatively strong. Weaknesses in verbal memory may be supported by strategies which utilise visual memory; by visually representing verbal information, memory can be improved. Visual imagery training can be effective for supporting comprehension, as shown in research with poor comprehenders (Oakhill & Patel, 1991) and children with specific language impairment (Joffe, Cain, & Maric, 2007). Visualisation strategies may also be effective for individuals with Down syndrome: A study of 52 individuals with Down syndrome aged 7–57 years (de la Iglesia, Buceta, & Campos, 2005) and a case study of a 17-year-old with Down syndrome (Lecas, Mazaud, Reibel, & Rey, 2011) report significantly better recall of story information following mental imagery training. Further research is needed to evaluate whether training in visualisation supports comprehension in addition to recall. Furthermore, the ages of participants included in this research makes extrapolation of findings difficult given the high-level nature of the training; evaluations with school-aged children are therefore important.

Summary of reading comprehension section

For many individuals with Down syndrome, text comprehension is an area of significant difficulty. Text comprehension problems are related to impairments in language and verbal memory. We have much to learn about how best to support comprehension difficulties in this group and research in this area is badly needed. Though there are important differences between poor comprehenders and individuals with Down syndrome which must be considered when modifying existing interventions, evidence from poor comprehenders suggests several possible approaches to intervention for comprehension difficulties in individuals with Down syndrome.

Does reading have other benefits?

Learning to read is a rewarding and enjoyable experience in itself. Furthermore, access to the world of books and reading is likely to have benefits for the language development of children with Down syndrome in the same way as it does for all children. In typical development, there is a reciprocal relationship between reading progress and development in other areas, including working memory, phonological awareness (Ellis & Large, 1988; Gathercole & Baddeley, 1993), and vocabulary (Gathercole & Baddeley, 1989, 1993). There is also some evidence of this reciprocity in studies of children with Down syndrome in that individuals who read tend to have better language abilities than those who are non-readers (Cardoso-Martins *et al.*, 2009; Laws *et al.*, 1995; Laws & Gunn, 2002). It is important to note, however, that much of the research is correlational, which does not allow for causal relationships to be inferred. However, a recent longitudinal study (Hulme *et al.*, 2012) found reading skills to be a significant longitudinal predictor of later phoneme skills for children with Down syndrome, as for typically developing children. This suggests that learning to read contributes to the development of phoneme awareness for both groups of children.

Print can be used to support practice with spoken language and articulation, both of single words and of sentences. Research such as Locke (1994, 1997) suggests that, as a child begins to express inflectional morphology, a more sophisticated control is promoted in phonology. Buckley and Johnson-Glenberg (2008) go on to suggest the benefits of using the visual learning and whole-word reading strength of children with Down syndrome to map on to and support production practice; using reading activities to practice production of sentence grammar not yet fully used in spontaneous talk in an attempt to support the development of phonology. Whilst there is anecdotal evidence to support the benefits of reading for developing speech and language skills, there are few studies which address this question and the available evidence is inconclusive.

A longitudinal study of reading development in a group of 14 children with Down syndrome followed progress over a four-year period (Laws *et al.*, 1995). The sample was split into two groups—'readers' and 'non-readers'— in Year 4 and found no significant difference in age, non-verbal ability, vocabulary, understanding of grammar, or short-term memory between the groups at the start of the study. At the end of the four-year study, the readers scored significantly higher on tests of vocabulary, grammar, and memory than non-readers. The authors therefore suggest that reading may lead to gains in these related skills. They also note, however, that the two groups were predominantly in different school environments, with the non-readers in special schools and the readers in mainstream schools. Therefore, these gains may be at least partly due to school environment.

A separate five-year follow up study (Laws & Gunn, 2002) found that readers significantly outperformed non-readers on non-verbal ability, language comprehension and production, phonological memory, and phonological awareness at the beginning of the study (Time 1). However, the readers had not made significantly more progress on the measures at the end of the five-year period (Time 2) than the non-readers, which might have been expected if reading has benefits for speech and language skills. One caution when interpreting these results, however, is that there were several more 'new readers' at Time 2 (readers at Time 2 who had been non-readers at Time 1) and their scores on all measures were included in Time 1 readers' results (despite the fact that they were not readers at Time 1). No information was recorded about the length of time these 'new readers' had been reading or the amount, type, or quality of reading instruction any of the children had received. Without this information, it is difficult to interpret the findings of this research.

A further study by Laws (2010) investigated whether learning to read has benefits for receptive vocabulary, verbal short-term memory, and speech production in a group of 28 children with Down syndrome, aged 5–11 years at the start of a two-year study (unpublished data cited in Laws, 2010). In this study, early letter knowledge, phonological awareness, expressive and receptive vocabulary, and speech accuracy were reported to correlate with final word reading scores. The children were divided into two groups based on their initial reading skills: a 'low' group, who had reading ages of up to five years 10 months, and a 'high' group, whose reading ages were six years four months and higher. As in Laws and Gunn (2002), a relationship between reading and the various language measures was investigated. The 'high' readers made 'considerably' more reading progress on measures of word recognition ability (significance not reported). However, while the readers did have significantly better receptive vocabulary scores, this was true at all time points; there was no evidence they had made more progress on this measure than the 'low' reader group over time. Laws and Gunn suggest that there is little clear evidence to support the view that reading leads to gains in oral language, verbal short-term memory, and speech development. Reasons for the outcomes suggested by the authors include the possibility that the sample ages may have been too high: to investigate the relationship between these factors, a sample of children at the early stages of reading and speech and language development would be helpful, particularly given the wide variability in scores on the variety of assessments (for example, some 'low' readers scored amongst the highest on the receptive vocabulary measures). In addition, data are not presented for expressive vocabulary or wider language measures, which have also been suggested to be linked with literacy development. Furthermore, some of the measures used may not have been sensitive enough to detect small differences over time (e.g. a measure of percentage of consonants correct to capture changes in speech accuracy).

There are advantages to print over spoken language in that print is tangible, visible, and permanent so that it can be processed at the speed of the reader and revisited in ways that spoken language cannot. Text may therefore support learning, comprehension, and memory of spoken vocabulary and language. For children with Down syndrome, reading comprehension is stronger than listening comprehension (Roch *et al.*, 2011), which supports an advantage for text for this group. Recent research further demonstrates the benefits of print: Mengoni, Nash, and Hulme (2013) demonstrated that children with Down syndrome are better able to remember spoken words when they are presented alongside flashcards of the written word. In this study, 17 children with Down syndrome (aged 7–16 years) showed improved memory for nonwords which had been presented with a flashcard of the nonword spelling than for nonwords which had been accompanied by Greek or Cyrillic letters. The advantage of orthography was the same for this group as it was for a group of typically developing children matched for word reading ability. The authors suggest that orthography provides a means of confirming the phonology of the new word, and another representation of the word in memory, which aids retrieval. It may also enable easier and more accurate access to the phonology of the word. This research suggests that seeing a word in print can support children with Down syndrome to learn new spoken words as it does for typically developing children. It is important to note, however, that all the children with Down syndrome were good readers (the average reading age for the group was seven years) and it is not clear whether the benefits of print are the same for children whose reading skills are less well developed or whether the same benefits would be seen above the single-word level. In addition, memory for new words was tested immediately after learning; as the authors did not test long-term learning of the new words, it cannot be assumed that these benefits hold beyond immediate testing. Indeed, the group with Down syndrome scored lower on tests of expressive vocabulary, which suggests difficulties with long-term retention of word learning.

In summary, whilst there is reason to suggest that reading may have benefits for the development of speech, language, and memory, the research to date is inconclusive; further studies are needed to clarify this.

Writing abilities

The majority of studies report only the reading abilities of the individuals with Down syndrome; only one experimental research study reports on their ability to express themselves in written form (Kay-Raining Bird, Cleave, White, Pike, & Helmkay, 2008). In this study, 21 students with Down syndrome aged from 8:6 to 19:10 years were matched on word reading ability with 17 typically developing children. The children were asked to tell or write a story based on picture sequences. There were two writing conditions—handwriting and word processing. Both groups of children produced oral narratives that had more different words and sentence structures and described more episodes than either of their written narratives, though there were individual differences, with one child from each group producing written language that was more complex than their oral narratives. Handwritten narratives contained more episodes and punctuation than word-processed narratives so that the predicted benefits of word processing in reducing the motoric demands of handwriting for the children with Down syndrome were not confirmed, though the authors comment that the children had less experience of word processing than handwriting at this time. Children with Down syndrome produced written narratives that were as linguistically complex as those of the typically developing children matched for word reading. There were also no differences in spelling accuracy, although children with Down syndrome tended to use shorter words. The only significant difference was handwriting legibility, which was poorer in the group with Down syndrome.

In exploring individual differences, it is interesting to note that receptive vocabulary predicted written narrative performance for the children with Down syndrome but surprisingly a measure of phonological awareness did not predict spelling ability. Interpreting these findings is complex as the children with Down syndrome are older than the typically developing group so have had more time to develop their skills, but the typically developing group were significantly more advanced on measures of mental age and vocabulary comprehension, which suggests that the children with

Down syndrome had reading and writing skills that were ahead of what might be expected given their language and cognitive skills at this time. However, while age predicted narrative skills for the typically developing children, age was not a predictor for the children with Down syndrome.

Spelling abilities were also reported as close to word reading abilities in another study (Byrne *et al.*, 2002) and in both these studies the children with Down syndrome were being educated in mainstream classrooms. A further longitudinal study, using a teacher report checklist, also reports comparable reading and writing skills for a group of children with Down syndrome (Sloper *et al.*, 1990; Turner & Alborz, 2003). This group varied in educational placement, with most being educated in special education settings.

Writing abilities were considered in a survey exploring the literacy experiences of individuals with Down syndrome conducted with Canadian families (Trenholm & Mirenda, 2006). Information was provided by parents/guardians for 224 children and adults with Down syndrome ranging from infancy to 41 years. They report that over 70 per cent of respondents for all age groups except the under-fives were very or somewhat interested in learning to write. Writing abilities were reported to increase with age. In the 5–9 year age group, 46.4 per cent were reported to be able to write or copy their name or other familiar words and 25 per cent were writing in work books. Children in the 9–13 year age range were reported to have a wider range of writing abilities, with 69.6 per cent able to write or copy their names or familiar words and 52.5 per cent writing in workbooks. In the 13–19 age range, 59.5 per cent were able to write their names or familiar words, 62.2 per cent were writing in workbooks, and 51.4 per cent were writing simple answers to questions. This survey indicates that more than half of the teenagers had developed useful writing abilities.

Further information on the writing abilities of children or adults comes from case studies (for example, see Bird, Beadman, & Buckley, 2001; Bird & Buckley, 2001, 2002; Buckley, 2001). Here again, wide variability is seen, with some children with Down syndrome writing and composing stories at age-appropriate levels but most progressing more slowly.

Given the delays in developing the necessary motor control for handwriting, the use of software to support writing may be considered. Prest and Mirenda (2010) report the findings of an exploratory study of the use of symbol-supported software and suggest that it has a positive role to play in helping students develop and increase their writing if appropriate staff support is available.

There is clearly a need for further research into the development of writing abilities. There is a need to separately investigate the motor elements of writing skill development from the ability to begin to put words, answers, and thoughts on paper or even on a computer screen. Children with Down syndrome take longer to develop the fine motor ability to form legible letters and words in handwriting; however, they may be able to use assistive technology to record their words and thoughts.

Future directions

As discussed at the beginning of this chapter, one of the most challenging issues for research with individuals with Down syndrome is the lack of assessment tools which are appropriate for this group of learners. Measures which are sufficiently fine-grained to capture small gains in learning are imperative to demonstrate progress. Tools which do not place restrictive demands on areas in which individuals with Down syndrome have particular difficulties (e.g. verbal skills, memory, and fine motor skills) would enable a more accurate assessment of ability.

Interventions which have been shown to be effective for other populations with reading difficulties offer a useful starting point for addressing the reading difficulties of children with Down syndrome. Such interventions, adapted to suit the profile of individuals with Down syndrome, require rigorous scientific evaluations to be recommended for practice. These are in particular need in the area of comprehension. It is important that intervention efficacy is replicated across a number of well-designed and controlled studies. There are benefits to both case study/small group and large-scale studies in evaluating intervention approaches. Interventions should also be assessed in realistic contexts.

Though we know more about teaching approaches that are effective for this group of children, research consistently shows that (as in research with typically developing groups) some individuals only make limited or no gains in response to intervention. It is therefore important to evaluate individual differences in response to intervention: research should aim to identify which children benefit from a particular intervention and which may not, and explore the reasons behind this differential treatment response and possible alternative approaches which may be more successful.

Given that children can be taught to recognise words from an early age and that this may support the development of other skills, there is a need for more research which considers the literacy skills of young children with Down syndrome. Longitudinal studies which clearly identify the instruction that children receive from an early age, the duration and frequency of such instruction, and the impact of this on development are needed.

New technologies open up new possibilities for literacy development and a wide range of instructional resources are now available on the internet. These types of resources are often very motivating for children and offer a useful addition to traditional teaching. Such resources may offer particular potential for the development of writing skills. Future research should evaluate these methods.

Practical implications

The research reviewed above suggests a number of practical implications for professionals and parents teaching reading to children with Down syndrome.

- Parents and professionals can start teaching reading and foundational skills known to be important for speech, language, and literacy development from an early age (preschool). These skills include listening discrimination and sound work, understanding of print, letter–sound knowledge, and early phonological awareness.
    - Early book reading with your child, developing enjoyment and interest in books and reading, will be important. It will support language development as well as demonstrating some early reading principals—for example, cover/title, words, reading from left to right, understanding print has meaning, emphasising sounds in words, and highlighting letters.
    - Listening games such as sorting items by initial sounds, I-spy, sound lotto, syllable marking, etc. are suitable for preschool children and will target some of the early listening and speech skills related to literacy development.

- Supported reading should be encouraged from a very early age, where the child is supported to read key phrases/sentences at an appropriate language level with adequate support. This may mean reading in imitation or reading some key words independently. From the beginning, the speech and language delays of the individual child must be taken into consideration. Children with Down syndrome will not bring the same level of vocabulary knowledge, language, or speech skills to the task of reading; this needs to be taken into consideration throughout word reading, phonological awareness, and reading comprehension tasks, and adaptations will need to be made.
    - Ensure understanding of instruction words used in teaching activities (e.g. first, next, last, blend, segment, letter, sound, phoneme, grapheme). Early phonic programmes commonly use high-frequency function words, which may include unknown vocabulary for those with language delays (e.g. pit, pin, tin, at, is, and it are commonly included in the early words used to target blending). Target vocabulary may need to be explicitly taught or more suitable familiar, concrete vocabulary may need to be chosen.
- Given the relative speech, language, and verbal short-term memory difficulties in children with Down syndrome and the visual learning strength, visual supports such as letters, words, sentences, pictures, and objects should be used to support learning new skills, particularly those which rely on these weaker areas of the learning profile.
    - Visually showing children how to 'blend' and 'segment' by breaking up the letters of a word and putting letters together will support understanding of these terms and learning new skills. Provide visual supports such as pictures and words to support activities. Use flashcards of words to support spoken language learning.
- From the very beginning, ensure children are reading for meaning. When children are first introduced to words, books, and stories, the fact that we read to 'get the message' should be emphasised. Reading comprehension should continue to be an area of focus throughout reading, starting with understanding single words through to complex language and sentence structures.
    - Early readers should match words and phrases to the corresponding pictures to demonstrate reading comprehension. Later readers should work on answering questions on text they have read as well as retelling and summarising parts of a story/text; visual choices and supports for intelligibility may also be needed for the child to demonstrate their understanding.
- Reading should be functional and enjoyable from the beginning. Children enjoy reading about themselves and the things they are interested in and have knowledge about. This will further support their understanding of what they are reading.
    - Personal books can be made to depict the child's family, familiar activities, and interests. Activities should be incorporated into fun games and should be varied to maintain focus and interest. Fun and motivating ways of presentation, such as the use of computers/iPads®, should be included.

- Multi-sensory activities can be a way of encouraging practice and increasing a child's interest through everyday activities.
  - Magnetic letters, which can be manipulated, are useful in supporting children to recognise letters by touch and sight, and in sounding out and manipulating letters to form different words.
  - Placing words and letters in the sand tray or water for children to find, writing with different materials including chalk and paint, and making letter shapes from Play-Doh™ are all effective multisensory teaching activities.
- Ensure time for adequate repetition and practice. At the early stages of literacy development, children will need daily practice to learn new skills. As these skills develop, time for repeated reading of new material and concepts will be required as well as reviewing past skills.
  - Lessons often move quickly and children will need extra time to consolidate and build on new skills with lots of experience for generalisation to a variety of situations. Recently acquired skills will need revision and need to be built into everyday experiences in order to be retained and strengthened.
- Much of the research has demonstrated that parents and support staff in schools can effectively deliver literacy teaching given adequate training and knowledge. In addition, it is important for parents and professionals to work collaboratively to support repetition, consistency, and generalisation across environments.
  - Regular review meetings should be organised to discuss individual targets and strategies. Developing a home–school link book to inform all individuals concerned of current activities, targets, and progress is also useful.
- Text and words should be chosen to meet the current reading and language levels of the child. Children with Down syndrome often have better word reading than reading comprehension skills. It is important to provide appropriate reading materials depending on the teaching target, word reading ability, or reading comprehension. They should not be given text to read if they are not able to read it for meaning.
  - Input from the child's speech and language therapist may be needed for guidance around appropriate language levels for reading material. Individual SLT (speech and language therapy) and curriculum targets can be incorporated into reading and lesson plans.
- Some children with Down syndrome 'take off' with reading while for others it can be a slow road to success. Perseverance will be needed to ensure continued progress and it should be remembered that, while reading progress may be going more slowly, being engaged in reading activities may be fostering other skills.
  - Make reading activities fun and encourage enjoyment. For older children, make sure reading materials are age appropriate and motivating. Whilst there are some reading schemes available, these are limited. Making books on the child's interests and reading texts such as magazines, annuals, website materials, etc. will help to support enjoyment.

- Ensure children are able to manage the 'jump' from one reading level to the next; finely graded books will be needed to support progress and success.
- Ensure the opportunity for the child to choose books from school/library to share and read alongside parents. These books are more likely to be age/interest appropriate and support motivation.

- Learning and activities will need to be individualised. While it is important to know the learning profile associated with Down syndrome, it will also be crucial to know about the individual's strengths, difficulties, and interests and to regularly adapt activities and assessments to meet the child's needs.
    - As the child progresses, teaching will need to include regular reviews, recognising that previous teaching targets have been met and setting new ones to ensure continued progress.
- Children with Down syndrome can be sensitive to failure and it will be important to build confidence and enjoyment in literacy activities. They will also need new activities modelled to support verbal instructions and lots of practice and experience with support before support is reduced.
    - The use of errorless learning will support the child's learning and confidence with new skills; provide enough support to ensure the child succeeds and gradually withdraw support over time.
- Clear assessment and/or measurement strategies should be put into place to ensure that small steps in progress that may be made by the individual child are not overlooked by general classroom measures and comparison with typically developing peers. On-going assessment of recent targets should be in place for the individual child.
    - For example, word reading lists can be made into posters that are reviewed regularly to show progress.
    - An on-going record of handwriting progress should be kept so that improvements are documented (e.g. through keeping dated examples, videos, and photographs of more practical multisensory activities).
- Do not allow delayed literacy skills to limit the child's access to lesson objectives and inclusion in classroom activities. Be clear on the learning objective for the child and reduce all other literacy demands.
    - Word cards, scribes, letters, computers, etc. can be used to differentiate class activities and support recording.
- Ensure adequate time to work on literacy skills throughout school or until the child has become a proficient reader. As the child moves through school, explicit teaching of reading, spelling, and handwriting in the classroom becomes much less of a focus as typically developing children become proficient. Structured teaching will need to continue and this is likely to need more consideration and planning.
    - Keep an updated 'All about me' book with recent targets and examples of strategies and motivating rewards for new staff and for consistency.

- Reading together and sharing books should be encouraged at all ages, including for those children who are not independent readers. Books can be made to record examples of work and topics covered, as well as developed to share personal experiences and events. This will encourage repetition and allow the child to revisit previous experiences and be included in the literate world.
    - In school, examples of work supported by additional pictures, photos, and sentences should be developed across the curriculum. They can be used as a measure of progress as well as allowing the child to look back on previous work to consolidate learning
    - Encourage and support the child to keep a 'conversation diary' with pictures, leaflets, photographs, etc. of places they have been and experiences they have had. These should be accompanied with sentences at an appropriate language level for the child that they can use to support their conversation with others.

Conclusion

As discussed within this chapter, reading is an important life skill for all children and opportunities should be provided across settings for children with Down syndrome to access appropriate reading instruction. Whilst more research is needed, and several areas of further research have been highlighted, the authors have presented some practical guidance based on current evidence. As demonstrated, reading and writing are achievable goals for many children with Down syndrome and practitioners should bear in mind the research findings on literacy for this population while differentiating teaching strategies and materials to meet the individual needs of the child.

References

Abbeduto, L., Warren, S. F., & Conners, F. A. (2007). Language development in Down syndrome: From the prelinguistic period to the acquisition of literacy. *Mental Retardation and Developmental Disabilities, 13*, 247–261.

Al Otaiba, S., Lewis, S., Whalon, K., Dyrlund, A., & McKenzie, A. (2009). Home literacy environments of young children with Down syndrome: Findings from a web-based survey. *Remedial and Special Education, 30*(2), 96–107.

Anthony, J. L., Greenblatt-Aghara, R., Dunkelberger, M. J., Anthony, T. I., Williams, J. M., & Zhang, Z. (2011). What factors place children with speech sound disorders at risk for reading problems? *American Journal of Speech-Language Pathology, 20*, 146–160.

Appleton, M., Buckley, S., & MacDonald, J. (2002). The early reading skills of preschoolers with Down syndrome and their typically developing peers: Findings from recent research. *Down Syndrome News and Update, 2*, 9–10.

Baylis, P., & Snowling, M. J. (2012). Evaluation of a phonological reading programme for children with Down syndrome. *Child Language Teaching and Therapy, 28*, 39–56.

Beck, I. L., McKeown, M. G., & Kucan, L. (2002). *Bringing words to life: Robust vocabulary instruction*. New York: The Guildford Press.

Bird, G., Beadman, J., & Buckley, S. (2001). *Reading and writing for children with Down syndrome (5–11 years)*. Portsmouth, UK: Down Syndrome Education International.

Bird, G., & Buckley, S. (2001). *Reading and writing for infants with Down syndrome (0–5 years)*. Portsmouth, UK: Down Syndrome Education International.

Bird, G., & Buckley, S. (2002). *Reading and writing development for teenagers with Down syndrome (11–16 years)*. Portsmouth, UK: Down Syndrome Education International.

Boudreau, D. (2002). Literacy skills in children and adolescents with Down syndrome. *Reading and Writing: An Interdisciplinary Journal, 15*, 497–525.

Buckley, S. (2001). *Reading and writing for individuals with Down syndrome: An overview*. Portsmouth, UK: Down Syndrome Education International.

Buckley, S. J., Bird, G., & Byrne, A. (1996). Reading acquisition by young children with Down syndrome. In B. Stratford & P. Gunn (Eds), *New approaches to Down syndrome* (pp. 268–279). London: Cassell.

Buckley, S., & Johnson-Glenberg, M. C. (2008). Increasing literacy learning for individuals with Down syndrome and Fragile X syndrome. In J. E. Roberts, R. S. Chapman, & S. F. Warren (Eds), *Speech & language development and intervention in Down syndrome & Fragile X syndrome* (pp. 233–254). Baltimore, MD: Paul H. Brookes Publishing Co.

Burgoyne, K., Duff, F., Clarke, P., Buckley, S. J., Snowling, M., & Hulme, C. (2012). Efficacy of a reading and language intervention for children with Down syndrome: A randomised controlled trial. *Journal of Child Psychology and Psychiatry, 53*, 1044–1053.

Burgoyne, K., Duff, F., Snowling, M., Buckley, S., & Hulme, C. (2013). Training phoneme blending skills in children with Down syndrome. *Child Language Teaching and Therapy* (online). doi: 10.1177/0265659012474674.

Byrne, A., MacDonald, J., & Buckley, S. (2002). Reading, language and memory skills: A comparative longitudinal study of children with Down syndrome and their mainstream peers. *British Journal of Educational Psychology, 72*, 513–529.

Cain, K., & Oakhill, J. (2006). Profiles of children with specific reading comprehension difficulties. *British Journal of Educational Psychology, 76*, 683–696.

Cardoso-Martins, C., Peterson, R., Olson, R., & Pennington, B. (2009). Component reading skills in Down syndrome. *Reading and Writing, 22*, 277–292.

Catts, H. W., Adlof, S. M., & Weismer, S. E. (2006). Language deficits in poor comprehenders: A case for the simple view of reading. *Journal of Speech, Language, and Hearing Research, 49*, 278–293.

Chapman, R. S., & Kay-Raining Bird, E. (2011). Language development in childhood, adolescence and young adulthood in persons with Down syndrome. In J. Burack, R. Hodapp, G. Iarocci, & E. Zigler (Eds), *The Oxford handbook of intellectual disability and development* (2nd edn) (pp. 167–183). Toronto, Canada: OUP.

Clarke, P. J., Snowling, M. J., Truelove, E., & Hulme, C. (2010). Ameliorating children's reading comprehension difficulties: A randomized controlled trial. *Psychological Science, 21*, 1106–1116.

Cleave, P., Kay-Raining Bird, E., & Bourassa, D. (2011). An evaluation of a treatment programme for teaching phonological awareness skills to children with Down syndrome. *Canadian Journal of Speech-Language Pathology and Audiology, 35*, 332–343.

Cologon, K., Cupples, L., & Wyver, S. (2011). Effects of targeted reading instruction on phonological awareness and phonic decoding in children with Down syndrome. *American Journal of Intellectual and Developmental Disabilities, 116*, 111–129.

de la Iglesia, J. C. F., Buceta, M. J., & Campos, A. (2005). Prose learning in children and adults with Down syndrome: The use of visual and mental image strategies to improve recall. *Journal of Intellectual and Developmental Disability, 30*, 199–206.

Dickinson, L. (2002). The use of a reading program and signing to develop language and communication skills in a toddler with Down syndrome. *Down Syndrome News and Update, 2*(1), 2–4.

Dodd, B., McCormack, P., & Woodyatt, G. (1994). Evaluation of an intervention programme: Relationships between children's phonology and parents' communicative behaviour. *American Journal on Mental Retardation, 98*, 632–645.

Dodd, B., & Thompson, L. (2001). Speech disorder in children with Down syndrome. *Journal of Intellectual Disability Research, 45*, 308–316.

Duff, F. J., Fieldsend, E., Bowyer-Crane, C., Hulme, C., Smith, G., Gibbs, S., & Snowling,

M. J. (2008). Reading with vocabulary intervention: Evaluation of an instruction for children with poor response to reading intervention. *Journal of Research in Reading, 31*, 319–336.

Elleman, A. M., Lindo, E. J., Morphy, P., & Compton, D. L. (2009). The impact of vocabulary instruction on passage-level comprehension of school-age children: A meta-analysis. *Journal of Research on Educational Effectiveness, 2*, 1–44.

Ellis, N., & Large, B. (1988). The early stages of reading: A longitudinal study. *Applied Cognitive Psychology, 2*, 47–76.

Fidler, D. J., Most, D. E., & Guiberson, M. M. (2005). Neuropsychological correlates of word identification in Down syndrome. *Research in Developmental Disabilities, 26*, 487–501.

Fowler, A., Doherty, B., & Boynton, L. (1995). The basis of reading skill in young adults with Down syndrome. In L. Nadel & D. Rosenthal (Eds), *Down syndrome: Living and learning* (pp. 182–196). New York: Wiley-Liss.

Frith, U. (1985). Beneath the surface of developmental dyslexia. In K. E. Patterson, J. C. Marshall, & M. Coltheart (Eds), *Surface dyslexia* (pp. 361–397). London: Routledge and Kegan Paul.

Gathercole, S., & Baddeley, A. (1989). Evaluation of the role of phonological STM in the development of vocabulary in children: A longitudinal study. *Journal of Memory and Language, 28*, 200–213.

Gathercole, S., & Baddeley, A. (1993). *Working memory*. Hove, UK: LEA.

Gillon, G., & Dodd, B. (2005). Understanding the relationship between speech and language impairment and literacy difficulties: The central role of phonology. In B. Dodd (ed.), *Differential diagnosis and treatment of children with speech disorder* (2nd edn) (pp. 289–304). London: Whurr Publishers Ltd.

Goetz, K., Hulme, C., Brigstocke, S., Carroll, J. M., Nasir, L., & Snowling, M. (2008). Training reading and phoneme awareness skills in children with Down syndrome. *Reading and Writing, 21*, 395–412.

Gombert, J. E. (2002). Children with Down syndrome use phonological knowledge in reading. *Reading and Writing: An Interdisciplinary Journal, 15*, 455–409.

Groen, M. A., Laws, G., Nation, K., & Bishop, D. V. M. (2006). A case of exceptional reading accuracy in a child with Down syndrome: Underlying skills and the relation to reading comprehension. *Cognitive Neuropsychology, 23*, 1190–1214.

Hatcher, P. J., Hulme, C., & Ellis, A. W. (1994). Ameliorating early reading failure by integrating the teaching of reading and phonological skills: The phonological linkage hypothesis. *Child Development, 65*, 41–57.

Hua, Z., & Dodd, B. (2006). *Phonological development and disorders in children: A multilingual perspective*. Clevedon, UK: Multilingual Matters Ltd.

Hulme, C., Goetz, K., Brigstocke, S., Nash, H., Lervag, A., & Snowling, M. (2012). The growth of reading skills in children with Down syndrome. *Developmental Science, 15*, 320–329.

Jarrold, C., & Baddeley, A. D. (1997). Short-term memory for verbal and visuo-spatial information in Down syndrome. *Cognitive Neuropsychiatry, 2*, 101–122.

Jarrold, C., Nadel, L., & Vicari, S. (2008). Memory and neuropsychology in Down syndrome. *Down Syndrome Research and Practice*. Accessed on 19 March 2013 from www.down-syndrome.org/reviews/2068/. doi: 10.3104/reviews/2068.

Jarrold, C., Purser, H., & Brock, J. (2006). Short-term memory in Down syndrome. In T. P. Alloway & S. E. Gathercole (Eds), *Working memory and neurodevelopmental disorders* (pp. 239–266). New York: Psychology Press.

Joffe, V. L., Cain, K., & Maric, N. (2007). Comprehension problems in children with specific language impairment: Does mental imagery training help? *International Journal of Language and Communication Disorders, 42*, 648–664.

Kay-Raining Bird, E., Cleave, P. L., & McConnell, L. (2000). Reading and phonological awareness in children with Down syndrome: A longitudinal study. *American Journal of Speech-Language Pathology, 9*, 319–330.

Kay-Raining Bird, E., Cleave, P. L., White, D., Pike, H., & Helmkay, A. (2008). Written and oral narratives of children and adolescents with Down syndrome. *Journal of Speech, Language and Hearing Research, 51*, 436–450.

Kennedy, E. J., & Flynn, M. C. (2003). Training phonological awareness skills in children with Down syndrome. *Research in Developmental Disabilities, 24*, 44–57.

Kotlinski, J., & Kotlinski, S. (2002). Teaching reading to develop language. *Down Syndrome News and Update, 2*, 5–6.

Laws, G. (2010). Reading as an intervention for vocabulary, short-term memory and speech development of school-aged children with Down syndrome: A review of the evidence. In J. Holmes (Ed.), *Advances in child development and behaviour, Vol. 39* (pp. 131–162). Burlington, MA: Academic Press.

Laws, G., Buckley, S. J., Bird, G., MacDonald, J., & Broadley, I. (1995). The influence of reading instruction on language and memory development in children with Down's syndrome. *Down's Syndrome: Research and Practice, 3*, 59–64.

Laws, G., & Gunn, D. (2002). Relationships between reading, phonological skills and language development in individuals with Down syndrome: A five year follow-up study. *Reading and Writing: An Interdisciplinary Journal, 15*, 527–548.

Lecas, J.-F., Mazaud, A. M., Reibel, E., & Rey, A. (2011). Using visual strategies to support verbal comprehension in an adolescent with Down syndrome. *Child Language Teaching and Therapy, 27*, 84–96.

Lemons, C. J., & Fuchs, D. (2010a). Phonological awareness of children with Down syndrome: Its role in learning to read and the effectiveness of related interventions. *Research in Developmental Disabilities, 31*, 316–330.

Lemons, C. J., & Fuchs, D. (2010b). Modelling response to reading intervention in children with Down syndrome: An examination of predictors of differential growth. *Reading Research Quarterly, 45*, 134–168.

Lemons, C. J., Mrachko, A. A., Kostewicz, D. E. & Paterra, M. F. (2012). Effectiveness of decoding and phonological awareness interventions for children with Down syndrome. *Exceptional Children, 79*, 67–90.

Levorato, C. M., Roch, M., & Beltrame, R. (2009). Text comprehension in Down syndrome: The role of lower and higher level abilities. *Clinical Linguistics & Phonetics, 23*, 285–300.

Levorato, C. M., Roch, M., & Florit, E., (2011). Role of verbal memory in reading text comprehension of individuals with Down syndrome. *American Journal on Intellectual and Developmental Disabilities, 116*, 99–110.

Locke, J. L. (1994). Gradual emergence of developmental language disorders. *Journal of Speech and Hearing Research, 37*, 608–616.

Locke, J. L. (1997). Theory of neurolinguistic development. *Brain and Language, 58*, 265–326.

Lorenz, S., Sloper, T., & Cunningham, C. (1985). Research supplement: Reading and Down syndrome. *British Journal of Special Education, 12*, 65–67.

McGee, A., & Johnson, H. (2003). The effect of inference training on skilled and less skilled comprehenders. *Educational Psychology, 23*, 49–59.

Mengoni, S. E., Nash, H., & Hulme, C. (2013). The benefit of orthographic support for oral vocabulary learning in children with Down syndrome. *Journal of Child Language, 40*, 221–243.

Morgan, M., Moni, K., & Jobling, A. (2004). What's it all about? Investigating reading comprehension strategies in young adults with Down syndrome. *Down Syndrome Research and Practice, 9*, 37–44.

Muter, V., Hulme, C., Snowling, M. J., & Stevenson, J. (2004). Phonemes, rimes, vocabulary, and grammatical skills as foundations of early reading development: Evidence from a longitudinal study. *Developmental Psychology, 40*, 663–681.

Næss, K.-A. B., Melby-Lervåg, M., Hulme, C., & Lyster, S.-A. H. (2012). Reading skills in children with Down syndrome: A meta-analytic review. *Research in Developmental Disabilities, 33*, 737–747.

Nash, H., & Heath, J. (2011). The role of vocabulary, working memory, and inference making ability in reading comprehension in Down syndrome. *Research in Developmental Disabilities, 32*, 1782–1791.

Nation, K., Clarke, P., Marshall, C. M., & Durand, M. (2004). Hidden language impairments in children: Parallels between poor reading comprehension and specific language impairment? *Journal of Speech, Language, and Hearing Research, 47*, 199–211.

Ni Cholmain, C. (1994). Working on phonology with young children with Down syndrome: A pilot study. *Journal of Clinical Speech and Language Studies, 1*, 15–35.

Oakhill, J., & Patel, S. (1991). Can imagery training help children who have comprehension problems? *Journal of Research in Reading, 14*, 106–115.

Peterson, R. L., Pennington, B. F., Shriberg, L. D., & Boada, R. (2009). What influences literacy outcome in children with speech sound disorder? *Journal of Speech, Language and Hearing Research, 52*, 1175–1188.

Prest, J., & Mirenda, P. (2010). Using symbol supported writing software with students with Down syndrome: An exploratory study. *Journal of Special Education Technology, 25*, 1–12.

Ricci, L. (2011). Home literacy environments, interest in reading and emergent literacy skills of children with Down syndrome versus typical children. *Journal of Intellectual Disability Research, 55*, 596–609.

Ricci, L., & Osipova, A. (2012). Visions for literacy: Parents' aspirations for reading in children with Down syndrome. *British Journal of Special Education, 39*, 123–129.

Roberts, J., Price, J., & Malkin, C. (2007). Language and communication development in Down syndrome. *Mental Retardation and Developmental Disabilities, 13*, 26–35.

Roch, M., Florit, E., & Levorato, C. (2011). Follow-up study on reading comprehension in Down's syndrome: The role of reading skills and listening comprehension. *International Journal of Language and Communication Disorders, 46*, 231–242.

Roch, M., & Jarrold, C. (2008). A comparison between word and nonword reading in Down syndrome: The role of phonological awareness. *Journal of Communication Disorders, 41*, 305–318.

Roch, M., & Levorato, M. C. (2009). Simple view of reading in Down syndrome: The role of listening comprehension and reading skills. *International Journal of Language and Communication Disorders, 44*, 206–223.

Simpson, S. (2011). Working with children with written language difficulties. In M. Kersner & J. Wright (Eds), *Speech and language therapy: The decision-making process when working with children* (pp. 201–214). London: David Fulton Publishers Ltd.

Sloper, P., Cunningham, C., Turner, S., & Knussen, C. (1990). Factors relating to the academic attainments of children with Down's syndrome. *British Journal of Educational Psychology, 60*, 284–298.

Snowling, M. J., & Stackhouse, J. (2006). *Dyslexia speech and language* (2nd edn). London: Whurr Publishers Limited.

Stackhouse, J., & Wells, B. (1997). *Children's speech and literacy difficulties*. London: Whurr Publishers Limited.

Trenholm, B., & Mirenda, P. (2006). Home and community literacy experiences of individuals with Down syndrome. *Down Syndrome Research & Practice, 10*, 30–40.

Turner, S., & Alborz, A. (2003). Academic attainments of children with Down's syndrome: A longitudinal study. *British Journal of Educational Psychology, 73*, 563–583.

van Bysterveldt, A. K., Gillon, G. T., & Foster-Cohen, S. (2010a). Literacy environments for children with Down syndrome: What's happening at home? *Down Syndrome Research & Practice*. Accessed on 19 March 2013 from www.down-syndrome.org/reports/2111/reports-2111.pdf.

van Bysterveldt, A. K., Gillon, G., & Foster-Cohen, S. (2010b). Integrated speech and phonological awareness intervention for preschool children with Down syndrome. *International Journal of Language and Communication Disorders, 45*, 320–335.

van Bysterveldt, A. K., Gillon, G. T., & Moran, C. (2006). Enhancing phonological awareness and letter knowledge in preschool children with Down syndrome. *International Journal of Disability, Development and Education, 53*, 301–329.
Verucci, L., Menghini, D., & Vicari, S. (2006). Reading skills and phonological awareness acquisition in Down syndrome. *Journal of Intellectual Disability Research, 50*, 477–491.

Chapter 10

Challenging literate invisibility

Continuing literacy education for young adults and adults with Down syndrome

Karen B. Moni and Anne Jobling

Abstract

Literacy plays a crucial role throughout the lives of all individuals and increasingly so for individuals with intellectual disabilities. Literacy adds significantly to the quality of life of individuals with intellectual disabilities, both academically and emotionally (Erickson, 2005; Moni & Jobling, 2000, 2001). With a focus on living independently, literacy can contribute to the development of skills in problem solving, choice making, and communication, which are required for daily life in the community (Ashman & Suttie, 1995; Erickson, 2005; van den Bos, Nakken, Nicolay, & van Houten, 2007). Despite the obvious importance and advocacy for developing literacy skills for successful and rewarding participation in the community across the lifespan, limited research has been undertaken to investigate the literacy education of young adults and adults with intellectual disabilities.

This chapter discusses the notion of "literate invisibility" (Kliewer, Biklen, & Kasa-Hendrickson, 2006). The first part of the chapter explores why, until recently, the literacy skills of young adults and adults with Down syndrome have appeared to be invisible to educators, the community, and researchers, suggesting some of the contexts and causes that have contributed to the neglect of the needs and aspirations of young adults and adults around literacy education. The second part of the chapter discusses recent research evidence for the continuing literacy development of young adults and adults with Down syndrome, focusing initially on research in teaching reading. In this section, the roles of oral language, digital literacies, and popular culture in literacy and literacy learning are discussed. The third part argues for the need for research that draws on socio-cultural theories of learning that embrace a broader understanding of literacy development and education to encompass wider educational and research contexts, build effective teaching strategies, and focus on the individual's purposes for literacy. The fourth part presents a case for a lifelong learning perspective that provides support and on-going literacy education for young adults with intellectual disabilities, including Down syndrome. This leads into a final section that considers implications for practice.

Introduction

The development of literate citizens is crucial to the sustainability of a democratic society (Ehren, Lenz, & Deshler, 2004). Thus, there have been many government initiatives and policies to advance the literacy learning of a range of groups within society (see MCEETYA, 2008; Erickson, 2005), recognising that all citizens have the motivation and capability to continue learning and developing literacy throughout life (Kearns, 2005). Internationally, UNESCO in a 2001 resolution designated the years 2003–2012 as the Decade of Literacy, stating that:

> Literacy for all is at the heart of basic education for all [and] creating literate environments and societies is essential for achieving the goals or eradicating poverty, reducing child mortality, curbing population growth, achieving gender equality and ensuring sustainable development, peace and democracy.
>
> (UNESCO, 2006, p. 19)

The role of literacy in the lives of young people with intellectual disabilities within this broader social policy context has been neglected. While there is a range of policies and general provisions for individuals with disabilities which have recognised the rights of individuals with physical and sensory disabilities to have opportunities to continue their education, the provision of, and access to, educational opportunities for those with intellectual disabilities have been largely ignored. Nowhere is this more evident than in the lack of opportunities for young adults and adults to continue to develop literacy skills in post-compulsory education.

For the past few years, it has been recognised that literacy plays an increasingly crucial role throughout the lives of individuals with intellectual disabilities, including Down syndrome, with research showing that literacy skills add significantly to the quality of life academically, emotionally, and in terms of physical well-being (Moni & Jobling, 2000, 2001; Erickson, 2005). For adults, where there is a focus on participation in all aspects of society and independent living, the on-going development of literacy builds the capacities of individuals to read, write, speak, and engage in a range of print, multimedia, and oral texts, and also contributes to the development of skills in problem solving, choice making, communication, and in sustaining effective social networks which are required to negotiate daily life in the community (Ashman & Suttie, 1995; van den Bos *et al.*, 2007).

Despite the obvious importance of and advocacy for developing literacy skills for successful and rewarding participation in the community, the recognition that there is both a place and a need for on-going literacy education in post-school contexts has been slow to develop, leaving young adults underprepared to meet the demands of post-secondary learning and work environments (Gregg, 2012; Hart, Grigal, & Weir, 2010). This is partly due to deep-seated historical, community, and educational misconceptions about Down syndrome, and partly due to the limited research that has been undertaken to investigate the literacy education of young adults and adults with Down syndrome (Carr, 2000). The next section of the chapter considers some of the contexts for this and also suggests why there needs to be increasing attention on the literacy needs and skills of young adults and adults with Down syndrome in research.

Challenging literate invisibility

Kliewer, Biklen, and Kasa-Hendrickson coined the term "literate invisibility" in their 2006 article about the denial of both literacy education and literate citizenship for individuals with intellectual disabilities. They argued that understanding and developing literacy for individuals with intellectual disabilities remains at the margins because of entrenched views about the nature of disability as static and biological, and therefore immutable. In other words, there is a perpetuating belief that individuals with intellectual disabilities are unable to learn literacy. The major outcome of this belief is an absence of suitable educational programmes in the community that focus on literacy development—denying individuals the right to an education that is supposedly for all (Kliewer *et al.*, 2006). A second aspect of this invisibility is the denial of any literacy competence of individuals with intellectual disabilities. This means that these learners are often constructed as having deficits in literacy that must be remediated, rather than having strengths that should be developed in an on-going way.

A third area of invisibility, beyond those discussed by Kliewer and his colleagues, is invisibility in research. There is very limited research in the area of literacy development beyond childhood that focuses *specifically* on the needs of young adults with Down syndrome. Research into literacy development in older children and young adults with intellectual disabilities includes participants with a broad spectrum of intellectual disability, including Down syndrome, and the results are rarely reported in terms of differentiating among the disabilities. This means that we often have to extrapolate implications for on-going literacy education for individuals with Down syndrome from this broader research context.

While research has begun to make the literacy and academic skills of individuals with Down syndrome more visible (e.g. Boudreau, 2002; Turner & Alborz, 2003), there is still some way to go before there is widespread commitment from educators and, in the case of adults, community-based service organisations providing education that both meets the needs of these particular learners and focuses on developing literacy skills across the lifespan. The challenge for professionals, families, and individuals is to try and create research, educational, and social contexts where young adults with Down syndrome become more visible and educational barriers can be broken down. This chapter is a response to this challenge.

In the next section, some of the contexts that have created, or which are outcomes of, literate invisibility for individuals with intellectual disabilities are discussed further.

Narrow definitions of literacy

Literacy instruction for individuals with disabilities has focused mainly on reading and, in particular, on decoding and lower-order reading of simple signs or directions (Katims, 2001; Lundberg & Reichenberg, 2013). Much of the research has been conducted in clinical settings and with testing materials that are not based on authentic texts. While this research has provided a lot of useful information about developing reading in the early years of school and in interventions, it has been less useful in terms of understanding and supporting the literacy development of adolescents and young adults in educational programmes. One reason for this is that this narrow view of literacy does not account for aspects of literacy that are prevalent in contemporary understandings of literacy in the broader education community, such as speaking and listening, and viewing or engagement with multimedia. Nor does it consider the ever-widening social uses for literacy in the lives of young adults as they take advantage of increasing opportunities to participate in society, or the enabling affordances and advances in technology. Continued focus on traditional skills-based models of reading and writing in research and in teaching helps to perpetuate literate invisibility as this focus promotes a deficit model that does not account for strengths and competences in verbal and visual domains, and keeps pedagogy focused on skill-and-drill activities rather than engagement with a broad range of age-appropriate text and multimedia that motivate adolescents and young adults to learn.

Community attitudes

Early research into broader community attitudes towards individuals with intellectual disabilities revealed negative perceptions and attitudes, but more recently community perceptions are broadening and becoming more positive, particularly around social aspirations, relationships, and participation in the community (Gilmore, 2006).

However, attitudes towards individuals with Down syndrome and their place in educational settings continue to be more negative than positive, in both the general community and peer groups, and in professional contexts by teachers and community service organisations, charged with providing programmes for individuals with intellectual disabilities. For example, Pace, Shin, and Rasmussen (2010) in their study of community attitudes towards individuals with Down syndrome found that many adults continue to hold negative attitudes. They reported that a quarter of their respondents felt that children with Down syndrome should go to special schools, 30 per cent felt that these students were distracting in the regular classrooms, and 18 per cent believed that employing people with Down syndrome in the workplace would lead to more accidents. Young people were similarly negative about working and socialising with people with Down syndrome.

Limited opportunities for academic learning in secondary contexts

In the contexts of secondary schools, the curriculum area where students learn most explicitly about literacy and develop their literacy skills is English. The focus in English is on developing students' abilities to compose, comprehend, and critically evaluate texts in a wide range of genres for personal, social, and cultural purposes, and the subject is characterised by the breadth of language experience offered to students. Historically, however, students with intellectual disabilities who need extra academic support have been perceived as needing "literacy" rather than "English" skills and, in many high schools, these students have often been withdrawn from English to attend remedial literacy classes in small, cramped classrooms, where literacy has been something done to them rather than with them, and where the curriculum may bear little resemblance to what happens in the regular classroom (Illesca, 2005). Tuition in these withdrawal sessions has for the most part focused on functional aspects of literacy and basic skills and has tended to focus on completion of skill-and-drill worksheets (van Kraayenoord, Moni, Jobling, & Ziebarth, 2003). Such practices have the potential to further marginalise and render these students invisible by restricting their access to activities in which they have both literate competence and expertise—for example, in popular culture (Moni & Jobling, 2008).

Teacher attitudes and pedagogical knowledge

There is a large body of literature investigating teacher attitudes and practices in which it has been reported that both pre-service and trained teachers feel stressed and insecure about catering for students with special needs in the regular classroom

(Avramidis, Bayliss, & Burden, 2000; Forlin, Jobling, & Carroll, 2001; Jobling & Moni, 2004). The teachers discussed in these and other studies developed negative attitudes towards inclusion and had doubts about their abilities to teach students with disabilities as well as continuing to express their concerns about a general lack of preparation and confidence in providing for students who have disabilities and difficulties (Jobling & Moni, 2004).

Limited post-school options

Post-school options in education for young adults are provided either by short-term courses in vocational (Technical and Further Education: TAFE) settings or by service organisations. Many young adults who participate in mainstream literacy courses operating through the TAFE systems find that, while the instructors and teachers may adapt their pace of instruction and allow students to take longer to complete units of work compared to adults without a disability, many VET (vocational education and training) and TAFE courses do not always accommodate the specific needs of individuals with a disability (Moni & Hay, 2012).

Among providers of adult programmes for individuals with intellectual disabilities, there is a perpetuating belief that, as schools have tried to teach them to read and write and mostly failed, further instruction would be of little benefit to them in their adult life-skills programmes (Farrell & Elkins, 1994). Programmes therefore have developed a narrow literacy focus on functional skills, such as sight words for cooking or numbers for bus transport access (van Kraayenoord, 1992; Hendrick, Katims, & Carr, 1999; Young, Moni, Jobling, & van Kraayenoord, 2004). However, the effectiveness of such programmes has been hampered by the limited knowledge and training of disability support staff in literacy and in strategies for developing the capabilities of individuals with intellectual disability more effectively (Moni, Jobling, & van Kraayenoord, 2007). These issues, when combined with a lack of on-going documentation of effective teaching and learning strategies, as well as limited age-appropriate resources and evaluation of the programme goals and specific objectives, have meant that there have been few opportunities for community programmes to expand the literacy potential of adults in their services (Moni, Jobling, Morgan, & Lloyd, 2011).

Research evidence for the continuing literacy development of young adults and adults with Down syndrome

In recent years, people with Down syndrome have achieved levels of literacy that were once regarded by the community as unattainable (Cardoso-Martins, Peterson, Olson, & Pennington, 2009). Such achievements have been possible because of an increased recognition of the need to maintain literacy as part of lifelong learning. A small, but growing body of research supports the view that, when children and young adults with Down syndrome are provided with opportunities to broaden their literacy education through appropriate teaching and learning strategies, they continue to develop and improve their language and literacy skills into adolescence and beyond (Martin, Klusek, Estigarribia, & Roberts, 2009; Morgan, Moni, & Jobling, 2004, 2009; Reichenberg, 2013), although there is a considerable variation in both the range and the levels of achievement (Goetz *et al.*, 2008; Martin *et al.*, 2009; Snowling, Nash, & Henderson, 2008).

The next section discusses recent research evidence for the continuing literacy development of young adults and adults with Down syndrome and focuses initially on reading. The roles of oral language, digital literacies, and popular culture in literacy and literacy learning are discussed and the implications for education are highlighted.

Reading comprehension

Reading is the "gold standard" literacy skill for all learners in our society. It is the foundation for all other literacy skills and for every aspect of learning. It is also relatively easy to measure different aspects of reading skills using a range of standardised tests, and therefore easy to compare the achievements of different groups of students. So it is not surprising that much of the research into literacy development has focused on developing reading skills. Much of this research has been with young children, focusing on the efficacy of early intervention and short programmes based on phonics and/or word recognition. In brief, this research has found that children with Down syndrome can benefit from structured phonics-based interventions and explicit training in phonological awareness (see Roch & Jarrold, 2008; van Bysterveldt, Gillon, & Moran, 2006, for a programme that was taught by parents).

Buckley and Johnson-Glenberg (2008) provide some evidence of children being able to read in primary and secondary settings, although they also comment that this research has focused on word recognition rather than comprehension and there needs to be more work in this area. Nash and Heath (2011) also note that earlier work was done on single word recognition or comprehension at the phrase or sentence level rather than passages of connected texts, such as genuine stories, which may therefore not be able to reflect reading performance in real-life settings and for genuine purposes. Recently, studies have moved beyond developing word recognition and phonological awareness to focus on reading comprehension of more natural texts and in classroom settings. In this research, there is a consensus among researchers that comprehension is consistently the significant area of difficulty for many individuals with Down syndrome (Buckley & Johnson-Glenberg, 2008; Lundberg & Reichenberg, 2013; Moni & Jobling, 2001; Nash & Heath, 2011). However, research about how well young adults and adults with Down syndrome can read and comprehend written information is more limited and, in some instances, has to be inferred from broader research into intellectual disabilities (Jones, Long, & Finlay, 2006).

Small-scale case studies undertaken with young adults with Down syndrome in the last decade point to the continued development of literacy skills through tailored and explicit instruction (Bochner, Outhred, & Pieterse, 2001; Gallaher, Jobling, Moni, & van Kraayenoord, 2002; Pershey & Gilbert, 2002). Morgan, Moni, and Jobling (2004, 2009) undertook action research to investigate the use of specific reading comprehension strategies with six young adults with Down syndrome. This study found that a structured programme of focusing on specific reading comprehension strategies led to improvements in reading comprehension, rate and accuracy. The study also revealed a uniform deficit among the participants in understanding question words, which had negative implications for enhancing reading comprehension. For example, it affected their responses to strategic questioning; maintenance of coherent, responsive dialogue; recall of prior knowledge, past experiences, and texts; construction of meaning; and their ability to retell. These findings suggest that the meanings of question words should be explicitly taught prior to using questioning as a teaching strategy, and in reading comprehension activities.

More recently, van den Bos *et al.* (2007) conducted a direct intervention programme with a group of 38 adults with mild intellectual disabilities. This programme aimed to improve the reading comprehension of the participants. They reported that the use of expository texts with explicit teaching of strategies for prediction and clarifying was most effective.

Three studies have found that reciprocal teaching is effective in enhancing reading comprehension of young adults with intellectual disabilities (Alfassi, Weiss, & Lifshitz, 2009; Lundberg & Reichenberg, 2013; Reichenberg, 2013). In these studies (which included young adults with Down syndrome), reciprocal teaching was used to actively engage students, individually and in small groups, in talking about texts. In all three studies, the authors found that there were improvements in levels of comprehension, and that the social settings both scaffolded and challenged the participants to think more deeply about the texts. The authors concluded that their findings support the use of socio-cultural approaches to teaching literacy for this population.

There is strong evidence from a 14-year research and teaching project that has challenged the literate invisibility of young adults with intellectual disabilities through the development, implementation, and evaluation of a literacy programme designed to meet the needs of young adults with an intellectual disability, the majority of whom have Down syndrome. Data related to receptive language, vocabulary, and reading comprehension were collected from participants enrolled in the programme in each two-year cycle since 1998, using a range of standardised instruments. The findings showed significant differences in receptive language, vocabulary, and reading accuracy and comprehension across three data collection points (Moni & Jobling, 2001, 2013).

The findings of these studies reveal that, when young adults with intellectual disabilities are provided with long-term opportunities to develop literacy through appropriate explicit pedagogies and learning strategies, they continue to improve their receptive language, vocabulary, and reading skills.

Broadening our understanding about literacy in the lives of young people with Down syndrome

This part argues for the need for research that draws on socio-cultural theories of learning that embrace a broader understanding of literacy development and education to encompass wider educational, social and research contexts, build effective teaching strategies, and focus on the individual's needs and purposes for literacy.

Traditional perspectives about literacy have focused on reading and writing. In recent years, however, it has been recognised that literacy encompasses a wider set of skills and strategies. Contemporary understandings focus on multi-literacies, recognising that in order to understand the world learners need to engage with texts in print, oral, and multimedia domains, in a wide range of contexts. This is exemplified in the following statement by UNESCO:

> There is no single notion of literacy as a skill which people possess or not, but multiple literacies. We all engage in both oral and written practices and in learning new literacies at different stages of our lives, for example, the literacy demands of

> digital technologies. The concept of "situated literacies" draws attention to how the social, cultural and political context shapes the ways in which people acquire and use literacy.
>
> (UNESCO, 2008, p. 10)

Historically, this broader, more social understanding of literacy and concomitant broader approaches to teaching literacy to individuals with Down syndrome have not been widely evident in approaches to both research and teaching. However, there is now increasing recognition that literacy education for individuals with Down syndrome, similar to that advocated for other learners, needs to adopt a more socio-cultural approach to literacy to enable learners to develop skills, habits, and strategies that are wider than the traditional skills of reading and writing and encompass age-appropriate resources, multimedia, and content within a balanced literacy programme (Alfassi *et al.*, 2009; Coyne, Pisha, Dalton, Zeph, & Smith, 2012). In the following section, we focus on some of these broader literate practices. The first aspect that is receiving increasing attention is the development of oral language.

Oral language

Research into the development of oral language has been a strong focus for individuals with Down syndrome, and there is no clear evidence that there is a critical language learning time, or a ceiling for language acquisition (Hesketh & Chapman, 1998; Rondal, 1995). Much of the work on oral language development has been conducted with young children. In reviewing this research, Martin *et al.* (2009) and Roberts, Price, and Malkin (2007) provide detailed overviews of the language and communication characteristics of individuals with Down syndrome, discussing many of the features of a consistent, although variable, profile. As part of their work, they made several points that have implications for continuing literacy education. In brief, educators need to consider the strengths that they can build on, which include being able to use a variety of communicative strategies, to stay on topic, and to recount using visual/concrete prompts. As social skills, and an understanding of social context, play an important role in developing language, these should be taught in conjunction with language skills. The development and production of expressive language and more complex syntax remain challenges. This means that learners need to be constantly exposed to and engaged in a range of language events and need explicit teaching in how to negotiate these.

While it is widely agreed that there is a need for early intervention to support communication, a continued focus on promoting language development is also important throughout school and adolescent years. Chapman and others argue that the relative strengths in vocabulary, vocabulary comprehension, and verb diversity of adolescents and young adults may be a result of the greater diversity and increased opportunities in educational and vocational experiences available to many young adults (Chapman, 1999). If this is so, then we need further research undertaken in educational and vocational settings to investigate the kinds of strategies available to teachers for enhancing oral language across the lifespan (Rondal, 2007).

There is now a growing body of evidence that young adults with Down syndrome can communicate and that communication can be improved (Abbeduto *et al.*, 2003; Fowler, Doherty, & Boynton, 1995; Moni, 2006). Research has reported that receptive language and vocabulary comprehension are relative strengths (Addebuto *et al.*, 2003; Miller *et al.*, 1999). Vocabulary production has also been noted as a relative strength of adolescents, more than in younger children. However, overall, there is a consensus that comprehension of syntax and language production remains a challenge for older as well as younger learners (Chapman, 1999; Laws & Bishop, 2003; Nash & Heath, 2011). There is some research to suggest that this gap between comprehension and production increases through childhood and adolescence (Laws & Bishop, 2003) and thus teachers need to build on comprehension strengths and provide opportunities to develop language production during this period and beyond.

One aspect of oral language that has been studied in individuals with Down syndrome is oral narrative skills. These are important in literacy instruction in general and in reading instruction in particular. Several studies have shown that, while individuals with Down syndrome can be supported in eliciting narratives, typically these narratives have fewer words, more limited semantic diversity, and less cohesion than those of typically developing peers (Cleave, Raining-Bird, Czutrin, & Smith, 2012). Recent research focusing on specific skills in narratives with young adults with Down syndrome found that, in terms of macro skills, there are relative strengths in understanding elements of story grammar, such as introductions, character development, and conclusions (Finestack, Palmer, & Addebuto, 2012). Cleave and her colleagues (2012) took a developmental approach to understanding how narrative skills change across time for children and adolescents and found that narrative skills developed over a one-year period in vocabulary, but not in length or syntactic complexity, suggesting that semantic skills are a relative strength for individuals with Down syndrome. In this study, when visual supports were provided to scaffold the narratives, more story information was elicited (Cleave *et al.*, 2012). The findings of both of these studies have important implications for developing literacy programmes as they point to the need to focus on both core language skills and narrative structure when developing narrative skills. They also highlight the usefulness of providing visual supports using technology.

Digital literacies

Technology is integrated into our homes, communities, social networks, and workplaces as well as being an essential part of education. Devices such as iPods®, iPads®, tablets, and mobile smart phones are relatively inexpensive and have been readily adopted by young adults and their families to support both social and educational purposes (Light & McNaughton, 2012). There is strong evidence that children and young adults with Down syndrome access technology in general and computers in particular. For example, a recent survey conducted in the US of children and young adults with Down syndrome (aged 4–21) found that 80 per cent of their respondents (n = 561) started computer use by the age of six, with 85 per cent using computers for entertainment, and 80 per cent for learning. The most commonly reported applications are the internet, including email, educational software, and games (Feng, Lazar, Kumin, & Ozok, 2010; Moni, Jobling, & Lloyd, 2012). In thinking about technology and literacy, we need to distinguish between technology use for literacy purposes and using technology to support literacy learning, the manipulation of technology (e.g. through different input systems such as keyboards, speech recognition, and word prediction), and the use of assistive technologies for broader communication purposes.

In this regard, the research literature is replete with anecdotal and advocacy accounts of the motivational and technical aspects of using these technologies for individuals with intellectual disabilities; however, rigorous studies and those that focus specifically on young adults with Down syndrome are harder to find (Hu, Feng, Lazar, & Kumin, 2011; Kaghora *et al.*, 2013), with most studies focusing on usability issues (Kumin, Lazar, Feng, Wentz, & Ekedebe, 2012).

In brief, the literature on usability and individuals with Down syndrome has found that children and young adults can use computers independently, and while they often have difficulty with the fine motor skills needed to type, they can manipulate a mouse effectively and be taught to use multi-touch screens (e.g. iPads®) to high levels of competency (Kumin *et al.*, 2012). It is interesting to note that many of the usability studies use explicit teaching, modelling, opportunities for repeated practice, genuine tasks (e.g. accessing Facebook), and concrete materials to support skills training, and that these are teaching strategies advocated in the broader research community as being effective for learners with Down syndrome. A recent systematic review of research into iPod® and iPad® use within the broader field of intellectual disability supports this view, concluding that these tools can be used to enhance academic, leisure, employment, and transitioning skills (Kaghora *et al.*, 2013). The implications for teaching young adults with Down syndrome to access technologies initially are clear. However, as these and other authors note, users need letter recognition, reading, and visual literacy skills to undertake tasks effectively—for example, password use remains a perennial issue—and it is in these literacy aspects where there needs to be more research and educational focus.

In terms of using technology for literacy and social purposes, Kaghora (2011) worked with three teenagers with severe intellectual disabilities to teach them how to use an iPod® independently to access and watch age-appropriate videos for entertainment. She found that functional use of the iPod® could be taught quickly through task analysis and video modelling, and skills were retained after follow-up. Similarly, Lloyd, Moni, and Jobling (2005) used task analysis, explicit teaching, and modelling in a classroom study of 10 young adults with Down syndrome in which these young adults learned to create, open, and save a word document to a folder using texts on a topic of interest that they had written themselves. In both of these studies, being able to use the technology for their own leisure and educational purposes was a key motivator, which highlights the importance of having a genuine purpose for technology use that drives persistence and mastery of relevant skills.

There is no doubt that one of the benefits of technology is access to wider opportunities for individuals with Down syndrome to engage in literate practices that allow them to apply their skills and knowledge in genuine literacy events, using a broad range of texts, and for purposes that are age appropriate and align with their interests. One of the key areas where young adults can use technology to develop their literacy is through accessing and studying popular culture.

Popular culture has long been an important inclusion in literacy classrooms because it integrates new forms of media-mediated texts and plays an important role in the lives of young adults outside of school (Duncan-Andrade, 2004; Evans, 2005). Young adults with Down syndrome are immersed in and engage with popular culture independently and frequently in similar ways to their peers without intellectual disabilities (Moni & Jobling, 2008). They watch a lot of TV and enjoy similar kinds of programmes as typically developing 15–24 year olds, including reality TV, soaps, sport, and comedies. Inclusion of popular culture in literacy education goes beyond the potential for motivation and engagement, however, because knowing about music, TV, movies, etc. is important social capital that can be drawn on to make their expertise visible in the classrooms and build literacy using their strengths (Moni & Jobling, 2008). The kinds of activities that have been included in one post-school literacy programme include developing plotlines of key events and developing character portraits, writing reviews and newspaper articles using graphic novels or comic versions of texts (e.g. Shakespeare), scripting scenes for recreating TV shows and interviewing stars or characters, and developing PowerPoints™ of biographies of movie stars or singers using selected short documentaries and YouTube clips as a starting point (Moni & Jobling, 2008).

Future directions: a lifespan perspective

Just as life opportunities have increased for individuals with Down syndrome, research and community interest has also grown regarding what happens to individuals with Down syndrome after they leave school. A key example of this is that families are increasingly demanding opportunities for their children that are available to young adults and adults without disabilities (Martinez, Conroy, & Cerreto, 2012; Ricci & Osipova, 2012). Continuing education and literacy education, in particular, feature highly in the goals and aspirations parents and caregivers have for their adults with Down syndrome (Moni *et al.*, 2012; Trenholm & Mirenda, 2006).

In response to increasing expectations that people with intellectual disabilities should be able to participate in tertiary education, there has been a move to develop post-school educational programmes and inclusive college education programmes in several countries that enable young adults to continue their education (see, for example, Grigal, Hart, & Weir, 2012; Mock & Love, 2012; O'Connor, Kubiak, Espiner, & O'Brien, 2012). While these programmes provide students with the social experience of college and are important in terms of changing attitudes of peers without a disability, there needs to be more research about the academic outcomes of these programmes for students with Down syndrome.

The literacy skills of older adults with intellectual disabilities are becoming more visible. For example, one study of adults with intellectual disabilities attending a community programme found that clients had a range of emergent literacy skills in sight vocabulary, reading, and writing, and had definite ideas about what they wanted to achieve in the area of literacy. The majority preferred to read leisure rather than functional literacy material, with books and magazine materials predominating. Self-selected reading material was usually a book about a topic that interested them (Young *et al.*, 2004). Consequently, community-based service organisations are becoming more interested in developing literacy activities and programmes for their older clients and are partnering with researchers to develop accredited literacy programmes (Bachmann & Moni, 2011; Moni *et al.*, 2011).

These aspirations and initiatives means that there is an increasing need to undertake research into literacy development in young adults in a range of contexts in order to develop evidence-based programmes that support these individuals, not only in their formative years of schooling but also as they move into adulthood and beyond.

Considerations for practice

Addressing literate invisibility for young adults and adults with Down syndrome involves the development of continuing literacy education programmes that recognise both the needs and the strengths of these learners and how these impact on learning. In this chapter, we draw together some of the key ideas from research that may provide useful considerations for practice.

- Make literate competence more visible by adopting a broad definition of literacy so literacy activities and development focuses on areas of relative strength, including oral language, visual literacy, and popular culture.
- Focus planning on providing opportunities for repetition of tasks but with varying contexts and content, rather than repetition for skill and drill. Repetition and practice can be planned using hands-on activities, concrete materials, and visual stimuli—modelling, think-alouds, and strategic questioning are key strategies
- Use evidence-based strategies that have been shown to be effective in teaching young adult learners with disabilities generally and with young adults with Down syndrome in particular. These include: explicit teaching, reciprocal teaching, guided reading and writing, providing visual support for learning, and developing macro and micro skills.
- Young adults need to engage with texts that align with their interests, prior knowledge, and abilities. Age appropriateness should be an important consideration in text selection and in activity design—for example, digital and popular media texts are more appealing than low-level reading texts designed for a much younger audience.
- Explicitly teach the meaning of question words.
- Concrete materials provide an anchor that enables learners to link an imagined experience to a real one in their lives. They assist vocabulary development about a topic in that, rather than asking learners to describe something abstract, the object can be brought into the classroom and discussed by the whole class so that a broader range of ideas/words is generated. For example, learners can be asked to use all of their senses to describe an object, such as a piece of rich fabric or some driftwood, which may then be included in a writing activity.
- Use visual images and ICT supports for reading and writing. Photos are a great resource for getting learners with Down syndrome to talk, write, and read (Moni & Jobling, 2010). Learners can use photos to recount experiences or to sequence events—for example, about a holiday, or for a set of wedding or birthday photos. Writing activities include writing captions/bubbles for photos, writing about photos, naming the people and places in the photos, and creating a photo journal. Reading activities can include reading back the story, reading the captions, and recognising names.
- Use a range of scaffolding techniques to support writing, including writing together.
- Explicitly teach the structure of typical communicative events, such as telling anecdotes, beginning and maintaining a conversation, asking for help, and elaborating answers, and recast and re-phrase questions and responses to questions so learners have an opportunity to hear a model of an elaborated response.

- Begin literacy activities with talking. This builds vocabulary, focuses on prior experience, and enables learners to rehearse and predict ideas in texts they are going to read or create.
- Model oral language skills such as turn taking, initiating conversations, and showing interest when others are speaking.
- Recognise the range of uses of technology and distinguish between technology use for learning, for developing literacy, and for leisure. Understanding these different roles will make the evaluation of the myriad apps available much easier, especially if age appropriateness is also kept in mind.

Conclusion

In this chapter, we have drawn from the general field of research into literacy education and intellectual disabilities, and the small, but growing body of research with young adults and adults with Down syndrome, to argue for the need to adopt a lifespan approach to literacy education for young adults and adults with Down syndrome that is underpinned by socio-cultural approaches to teaching and learning, and a broad definition of literacy, that is developmental and based on the needs of learners, and that considers age appropriateness and the educational context.

However, literate invisibility for young adults with Down syndrome remains an issue in terms of programme development, community expectations, recognition of competency, and research focus. In this chapter, we have unpacked some of the historical reasons for this, acknowledging that this is a growing area of research that is producing important information for professionals and families involved in teaching and supporting literacy for young adults and adults with Down syndrome. However, we also argue that there is a lot more research needed about the role literacy plays in the lives of these individuals and how to support literacy effectively across the lifespan if we are to meet aspirations of "literacy for all" for this population.

References

Addebuto, L., Murphy, M. M., Cawthon, S. W., Richmond, E. K., Weissman, M. D., Karadottir, S., & O'Brien, A. (2003). Receptive language skills of adolescents and young adults with Down or Fragile X syndrome. *American Journal on Mental Retardation, 3*, 149–160.

Alfassi, M., Weiss, I., & Lifshitz, H. (2009). The efficacy of reciprocal teaching in fostering the reading literacy of students with intellectual disabilities. *European Journal of Special Needs Education, 24*, 291–305.

Ashman, A., & Suttie, J. (1995). Changing existing services for older people with an intellectual disability. *Australian and New Zealand Journal of Developmental Disabilities, 20*, 189–204.

Avramidis, E., Bayliss, P., & Burden, R. (2000). A survey of mainstream teachers' attitudes towards the inclusion of children with special educational needs in the ordinary school in one local education authority. *Educational Psychology, 20*, 193–213.

Bachmann, V., & Moni, K. B. (November, 2011). *Accredited qualifications for tertiary students with an intellectual disability*. Paper presented at ASSID, Adelaide.

Bochner, S., Outhred, L., & Pieterse, M. (2001). A study of functional literacy skills in young adults with Down syndrome. *International Journal of Disability, Development and Education, 48*, 67–90.

Boudreau, D. (2002). Literacy skills in children and adolescents with Down syndrome. *Reading and Writing: an Interdisciplinary Journal, 15*, 497–525.

Buckley, S., & Johnson-Glenberg, M. C. (2008). Increasing literacy learning for individuals with Down syndrome and Fragile X syndrome. In J. E. Roberts, R. S. Chapman, & S. Warren (Eds), *Speech and language development and intervention in Down syndrome and Fragile X syndrome* (pp. 233–254). Baltimore, MD: Brookes.

Cardoso-Martins, C., Peterson, R., Olson, R., & Pennington, B. (2009). Component reading skills in Down syndrome. *Reading and Writing, 22*, 277–292.

Carr, J. (2000). Intellectual and daily living skills of 30-year-olds with Down syndrome: Continuation of a longitudinal study. *Journal of Applied Research in Intellectual Disabilities, 13*, 1–16.

Chapman, R. S. (1999). Language development in children and adolescents with Down syndrome. In J. F. Miller, M. Leddy, & L. A. Leavitt (Eds), *Improving the communication of people with Down syndrome* (pp. 41–60). Baltimore, MD: Paul H. Brookes.

Cleave, P., Raining-Bird, E., Czutrin, R., & Smith, L. (2012). A longitudinal study of narrative development in children and adolescents with Down syndrome. *Intellectual and Developmental Disabilities, 50*, 332–342.

Coyne, P., Pisha, B., Dalton, B., Zeph, L. A., & Smith, N. C. (2012). Literacy by design: A universal design for learning approach for students with significant intellectual disabilities. *Remedial and Special Education, 33*, 162–172.

Duncan-Andrade, J. M. R. (2004). Your best friend or your worst enemy: Youth popular culture, pedagogy, and curriculum in urban classrooms. *The Review of Education, Pedagogy and Curriculum Studies, 26*, 313–327.

Ehren, B. J., Lenz, B. K., & Deshler, D. D. (2004). Enhancing literacy proficiency with adolescents and young adults. In C. A. Stone, E. R. Silliman, B. J. Ehren, & K. Apel (Eds), *Handbook of language and literacy: Development and disorders* (pp. 681–701). New York: Guilford.

Erickson, K. (2005). *Literacy and persons with developmental disabilities: Why and how*. Paper commissioned for the EFA Global Monitoring Report 2006, Literacy for Life, UNESCO.

Evans, J. (2005). Introduction: The changing nature of literacy in the twenty-first century. In J. Evans (Ed.), *Literacy moves on: Popular culture, new technologies and critical literacies in the elementary classroom* (pp. 1–12). Portsmouth, NH: Heinemann.

Farrell, M., & Elkins, J. (1994). Literacy for all? The case of Down syndrome. *Journal of Reading, 38*, 270–280.

Feng, J., Lazar, J., Kumin, L., & Ozok, A. (2010). Computer usage by children with Down syndrome: Challenges and future research. *ACM Transactions on Accessible Computing, 2*(3), Article 13 (March). doi: 10.1145/1714458.1714460.

Finestack, L. H., Palmer, M., & Addebuto, L. (2012). Macrostructural narrative language of adolescents and young adults with Down syndrome or Fragile X syndrome. *American Journal of Speech-Language Pathology, 21*, 29–46.

Forlin, C., Jobling, A., & Carroll, A. (2001). Pre-service teachers' discomfort levels towards people with disabilities. *The Journal of International Special Needs Education, 4*, 32–38.

Fowler, A., Doherty, B., & Boynton, L. (1995). The basis of reading skill in young adults with Down syndrome. In L. Nadel & D. Rosenthal (Eds), *Down syndrome: Living and learning* (pp. 182–196). New York: Wiley-Liss.

Gallaher, K., Jobling, A., Moni, K. B., & van Kraayenoord, C. E. (2002). Reading with Abby: A case study of the impact of a series of literacy tutoring sessions on a young adult with Down syndrome. *Down Syndrome Research and Practice, 8*, 59–67.

Gilmore, L. (2006). Perceptions of Down syndrome in the Australian community. *Journal of Developmental Disabilities, 12*, 1–13.

Goetz, K., Hulme, C., Brigstocke, S. Carroll, J. M., Nasir, L., & Snowling, M. (2008). Training reading and phoneme awareness skills in children with Down syndrome. *Reading and Writing, 21*, 395–412.

Gregg, N. (2012). Increasing access to learning for the adult basic education learner with learning disabilities: Evidence-based accommodation research. *Journal of Learning Disabilities, 45*, 47–63.

Grigal, M., Hart, D., & Weir, C. (2012). A survey of postsecondary education programs for students with intellectual disabilities in the United States. *Journal of Policy and Practice in Intellectual Disabilities, 9*(4), 223–233.

Hart, D., Grigal, M., & Weir, C. (2010). Expanding the paradigm: Postsecondary education options for individuals with autism spectrum disorder and intellectual disabilities. *Focus on Autism and Other Developmental Disabilities, 20*, 1–17.

Hendrick, W. B., Katims, D. S., & Carr, N. J. (1999). Implementing a multimethod, multilevel literacy program for students with mental retardation. *Focus On Autism and Other Developmental Disabilities, 14*, 231–239.

Hesketh, L. J., & Chapman, R. S. (1998). Verb use by individuals with Down syndrome. *American Journal of Mental Retardation, 103*(3), 288–304.

Hu, R., Feng, J., Lazar, J., & Kumin, L. (2011). Investigating input technologies for children and young adults with Down syndrome. *Universal Access in the Information Society, 12*, 89–104. doi: 10.1007/s10209-011-0267-3.

Illesca, B. (2005). Temporary validation: The challenges of "remedial literacy" programs. In B. Doecke & G. Parr (Eds), *Writing = Learning* (pp. 166–181). Kent Town: Wakefield Press.

Jobling, A., & Moni, K. B. (2004). "I never thought I'd have to teach these people." *Asia Pacific Journal of Teacher Education, 32*, 5–22.

Jones, F. W., Long, K., & Finlay, W. M. L. (2006). Assessing the reading comprehension of adults with learning disabilities. *Journal of Intellectual Disability Research, 50*, 410–418.

Kaghora, D. M. (2011). Three students with developmental disabilities learn to operate an iPod® to access age-appropriate entertainment videos. *Journal of Behavioral Education, 20*, 33–43.

Kaghora, D. M., van der Meer, L., Ramdoss, S., O'Reilly, M. F., Lancioni, G. E., Davis, T. N., & Sigafoos, J. (2013). Using iPods® and iPads® in teaching programs for individuals with developmental disabilities: A systematic review. *Research in Developmental Disabilities, 43*, 147–156.

Katims, D. S. (2001). Literacy assessment of students with mental retardation: An exploratory investigation. *Education and Training in Mental Retardation and Developmental Disabilities, 36*, 362–372.

Kearns, P. (2005). *Achieving Australia as an inclusive learning society: A report on future directions for lifelong learning in Australia*. Canberra: Adult Learning Australia.

Kliewer, C., Biklen, D., & Kasa-Hendrickson, C. (2006). Who may be literate? Disability and resistance to the cultural denial of competence. *American Educational Research Journal, 43*, 163–192.

Kumin, L., Lazar, J., Feng, R., Wentz, B., & Ekedebe, N. (2012). A usability evaluation of workplace-related tasks on a multi-touch tablet computer by adults with Down syndrome. *Journal of Usability Studies, 7*, 118–142.

Laws, G., & Bishop, D. V. M. (2003). A comparison of language abilities in adolescents with Down syndrome and children with specific language impairment. *Journal of Speech, Language and Hearing Research, 46*, 1324–1340.

Light, J., & McNaughton, D. (2012). Supporting the communication, language and literacy development of children with complex communication needs: State of science and future priorities. *Assistive Technology, 24*, 334–344.

Lloyd, J., Moni, K. B., & Jobling, A. (2005). Breaking the hype cycle: Using the computer effectively with learners with intellectual disabilities. *Down Syndrome Research and Practice, 9*, 68–74.

Lundberg, I., & Reichenberg, M. (2013). Developing reading comprehension among students with mild intellectual disabilities: An intervention study. *Scandinavian Journal of Educational Research, 75*, 89–106.

Martin, G. E., Klusek, J. Estigarribia, B., & Roberts, J. E. (2009). Language characteristics of individuals with Down syndrome. *Topics in Language Disorders, 29*, 112–132.

Martinez, D. C., Conroy, J. W., & Cerreto, M. C. (2012). Parent involvement in the transition process of children with intellectual disabilities: The influence of inclusion on parent desires and expectations for postsecondary education. *Journal of Policy and Practice in Intellectual Disabilities, 9*, 279–288.

Miller, J. F., Leddy, M., & Leavitt, L. A. (Eds). (1999). *Improving the communication of people with Down syndrome*. Baltimore, MD: Paul H. Brookes.

Ministerial Council on Education, Employment and Training Youth Affairs (MCEETYA). (2008). *The Melbourne declaration on educational goals for young Australians.* Retrieved from www.curriculum.edu.au/verve/_resources/National_Declaration_on_the_Educational_Goals_for_Young_Australians.pdf.

Mock, M., & Love, K. (2012). One state's initiative to increase access to higher education for people with intellectual disabilities. *Journal of Policy and Practice in Intellectual Disabilities, 9*, 289–297.

Moni, K. B. (August, 2006). *Literacy and lifelong learning: Developing oral language with young adults*. Paper presented at the Ninth World Congress on Down Syndrome, Vancouver.

Moni, K. B., & Hay, I. (2012). Secondary school and transitions. In A. Ashman & J. Elkins (Eds), *Education for inclusion and diversity* (4th edn) (pp. 325–358). French's Forest: Pearson Education.

Moni, K. B., & Jobling, A. (2000). LATCH–ON: A literacy course for young adults with Down syndrome. *Journal of Adolescent and Adult Literacy, 44*, 40–49.

Moni, K. B., & Jobling, A. (2001). Reading-related literacy learning of young adults with Down syndrome: Findings from a three year teaching and research program. *International Journal of Disability, Development and Education, 48*, 337–394.

Moni, K. B., & Jobling, A. (2008). A case for including popular culture in literacy education for young adults with Down syndrome. *Australian Journal of Language and Literacy, 31*, 260–278.

Moni, K. B., & Jobling, A. (2010). Using photographs to scaffold literacy activities with young adults with intellectual disabilities. *Down Syndrome Research and Practice, 12*, 98–102.

Moni, K. B., & Jobling, A. (August, 2013). *Outcomes from a longitudinal literacy research program for adults with intellectual disability.* Paper presented at Asia-Pacific Third Regional Conference, Tokyo.

Moni, K. B., Jobling, A., & Lloyd, J. (July, 2012). *Understanding young adults' and family goals for post school literacy education*. Paper presented at IASSID World Congress, Halifax, Nova Scotia.

Moni, K. B., Jobling, A., Morgan, M., & Lloyd, J. (2011). Promoting literacy for adults with intellectual disabilities in a community-based service organization. *Australian Journal of Adult Learning, 51*, 456–478.

Moni, K. B., Jobling, A., & van Kraayenoord C. E. (2007). "They're a lot cleverer than I thought": Challenging perceptions of support staff in community-based disability services. *International Journal of Adult Learning, 26*, 439–460.

Morgan, M. F., Moni, K. B., & Jobling, A. (2004). What's it all about? Investigating reading comprehension strategies in young adults with Down syndrome. *Down Syndrome Research and Practice, 9*, 37–44.

Morgan, M., Moni, K. B., & Jobling, A. (2009). Who? Where? What? When? Why? How? Question words: What do they mean? *British Journal of Learning Disabilities, 29*, 178–185.

Nash, H., & Heath, J. (2011). The role of vocabulary, working memory and inference making ability in reading comprehension in Down syndrome. *Research in Developmental Disabilities, 32*, 1782–1791.

O'Connor, B., Kubiak, J., Espiner, D., & O'Brien, P. (2012). Lecturer responses to the inclusion of students with intellectual disabilities auditing undergraduate classes. *Journal of Policy and Practice in Intellectual Disabilities, 9*, 247–256.

Pace, J. E., Shin, M., & Rasmussen, S. A., (2010). Understanding attitudes toward people with Down syndrome. *American Journal of Medical Genetics Part A,* 152A, 2185–2192.

Pershey, M. G., & Gilbert, T. W. (2002). Christine: A case study of literacy acquisition by an adult with developmental disabilities. *Mental Retardation, 40*, 219–234.

Reichenberg, M. (2013). "I liked the text about the little bird." Five intellectually disabled persons talk about texts. *Scandinavian Journal of Educational Research, 15*(2), 108–124. doi: 10.1080/15017419.2012.676565.
Ricci, L., & Osipova, A. (2012). Visions for literacy: Parents' aspirations for reading in children with Down syndrome. *British Journal of Special Education, 39*, 123–129.
Roberts, J. E., Price, J., & Malkin, C. (2007). Language and communication development in Down syndrome. *Mental Retardation and Developmental Disabilities Research Reviews, 13*, 26–35.
Roch, M., & Jarrold, C. (2008). A comparison between word and nonword reading in Down syndrome: The role of phonological awareness. *Journal of Communication Disorders, 41*, 305–318.
Rondal, J. A. (1995). *Exceptional language development in Down syndrome: Implications for the cognition–language relationship*. Cambridge: Cambridge University Press.
Rondal, J. (2007). Language rehabilitation. In J. Rondal & A. Rasore-Quartino (Eds), *Therapies and rehabilitation in Down syndrome* (pp. 63–87). Chichester, UK: John Wiley and Sons.
Snowling, M. J., Nash, H. M., & Henderson, L. M. (2008). The development of literacy skills in children with Down syndrome: Implications for intervention. *Down Syndrome Research and Practice* (online), 62–66. doi: 10.3104/reviews/2066.
Trenholm, B., & Mirenda, P. (2006). Home and community literacy experiences of individuals with Down syndrome. *Down Syndrome Research and Practice, 10*, 30–40.
Turner, S., & Alborz, A. (2003). Academic attainments of children with Down syndrome: A longitudinal study. *British Journal of Educational Psychology, 73*, 563–583.
UNESCO (2006). *EFA Global Monitoring Report: Literacy*. Paris: United Nations Educational Scientific and Cultural Organization.
UNESCO (2008). *The global literacy challenge: A profile of youth and adult literacy at the mid-point of the United Nations Literacy Decade, 2003–2012.* Paris: United Nations Educational Scientific and Cultural Organization.
van Bysterveldt, A. K., Gillon, G. T., & Moran, C. (2006). Enhancing phonological awareness and letter knowledge in preschool children with Down syndrome. *Journal of Disability, Development and Education, 53*, 301–329.
van den Bos, K. P., Nakken, H., Nicolay, P. G., & van Houten, E. J. (2007). Adults with mild intellectual disabilities: Can their reading comprehension ability be improved? *Journal of Intellectual Disability Research, 51*, 835–849.
van Kraayenoord, C. E. (Ed.). (1992). *A survey of adult literacy provision for people with intellectual disabilities*. Brisbane: The University of Queensland, Fred and Eleanor Schonell Special Education Research Centre.
van Kraayenoord, C. E., Moni, K. B., Jobling, A., & Ziebarth, K. (2003). Broadening approaches to literacy education for young adults with Down syndrome. In M. Cuskelly, S. Buckley, & A. Jobling (Eds). *Down syndrome across the lifespan* (pp. 93–106). Whurr: London.
Young, L., Moni, K. B., Jobling, A., & van Kraayenoord, C. E. (2004). Literacy skills of adults with intellectual disabilities in two community-based day services. *International Journal of Disability, Development and Education, 51*, 83–98.

Chapter 11

Down syndrome

A story from a developing country

Rumiati

Abstract

The purpose of this chapter is to describe experiences and viewpoints about educating children with Down syndrome in a developing country. The chapter includes affordances and challenges currently facing Indonesia, and priorities to be addressed for improving the quality of education for children with Down syndrome, and thereby raise their quality of life. Although the title of this chapter states Down syndrome specifically, it also contains ideas which apply to educating children with any disability and special needs in general.

Introduction

I am a researcher at the Centre for the Development and Empowerment of Mathematics Teachers and Educational Personnel (PPPPTK Matematika or Pusat Pengembangandan Pemberdayaan Pendidik dan Tenaga Kependidikan Matematika) in Indonesia. This is a government institution under the Ministry of National Education. The institution conducts in-service training, workshops, and seminars focusing on mathematics in order to improve the competency and capacity of mathematics teachers. I was awarded an Australian Partnership Scholarship from Ausaid to study a Master's degree in Australia from 2008 to 2010. The title of my thesis was an investigation of the number knowledge of first and second grade children in an Indonesian school.

My interest in education for children with Down syndrome arose in 2010, a year before I wrote this chapter. For that reason, the ideas I present in this chapter are likely to be premature and tentative. I am in transition from a person with no or very little knowledge of children with Down syndrome and disabilities, to someone who wants to work and contribute to new knowledge in the area. The inspiration was triggered by Rhonda Faragher. I met her in 2010 at the 33rd Mathematics Education Research Group of Australia (MERGA) conference at Fremantle (Western Australia). She and Barbara Clarke presented a paper entitled 'Developing early number skills: Some interesting results from children with Down syndrome'. The reason I went to her presentation was because I have a brother with Down syndrome and I was intrigued by the title of her paper, which suggested that a child with Down syndrome can learn and do mathematics.

Attending Rhonda's presentation about Down syndrome has opened my eyes to a new world and a range of possibilities. Even though I have a sibling with Down syndrome, my interactions with him are quite brief. He lives with my parents, rice farmers, in a village four hours by bus from the city in which I work and live. He was born in 1996 as the fourth and youngest child, and the only son of my then 44-year-old mother. I left my parents' house in 1993 to undertake a bachelor's degree at another city. When he was born, neither my parents nor I knew that he was a baby with Down syndrome. While he was growing up, they gradually became aware that he was different and slower in development than other children—for example, at two years of age, he was unable to walk or talk.

In many cases in developing countries, it is a shock and also a shame to have a family member with a disability. People, including one's extended family, tend to perceive this as a curse or punishment because of the parents' sins or bad deeds. Having a family member with a disability could be a burden (Hodes, 2007; Juang Sunanto, 2011). My parents' first reaction was to deny his disability, by saying that he was no different from other children. They needed a lot of time to accept that he was different from typically developing children.

Due to my parents' denial, at the age of seven, my brother was sent to a regular public school in our neighborhood. The teachers at the school advised us that he was different from his peers and should be educated in a special education school. My parents wanted to send him to a special education school, but it was difficult for them because the school was some distance from our home. They did not have a means of transportation. In addition, they found out that the classes in the special education school were very crowded; there was only one teacher for eight children while, according to the headmaster, ideally, there is one teacher for a maximum of six children. Since my brother was regarded as the most difficult student, he was the most likely to be excluded on the grounds that he needed individual teaching. At this time, my parents took the view that he could not be educated in school. They did not know what course of action to take and they felt helpless and isolated. They wanted to send him to a school to receive education, but neither my parents nor I had the means to do that. As rice farmers with no land ownership, my family was regarded as a less wealthy family according to Indonesian socio-economic culture.

As the first daughter in my family, I consider myself lucky because I received a good education at public schools. My parents did not finish primary education and were hardly able to read and write. Also, I received a scholarship to do a bachelor's degree, which I completed in 1999. In 2002, after serving as a mathematics teacher in a senior high school for four years, I started working as a government employee at the Ministry of National Education. With shame and sorrow, due to my limited knowledge and ignorance, I have to confess that I paid very little attention to my brother's education.

My initial interaction with Rhonda changed my attitude towards my brother. Before I met her, I thought it was a shame to talk about my brother, especially in public. I embrace him the way he is, but my role is a passive one. I think he is unable to do anything. Since meeting Rhonda, I have read many articles and other publications about Down syndrome. I compared pictures of my brother with pictures of children with Down syndrome from other countries and I can see that they have similarities. After making these comparisons, I have no doubt that my brother is a child with Down syndrome (see Figure 11.1 for a montage of photographs). I began to wonder, if I had known and accepted him as a child with Down syndrome earlier, would my attitude have been different? Ideally, there should be no regrets; I love my brother, but I do feel sorry that I gave him very little attention. This chapter is written

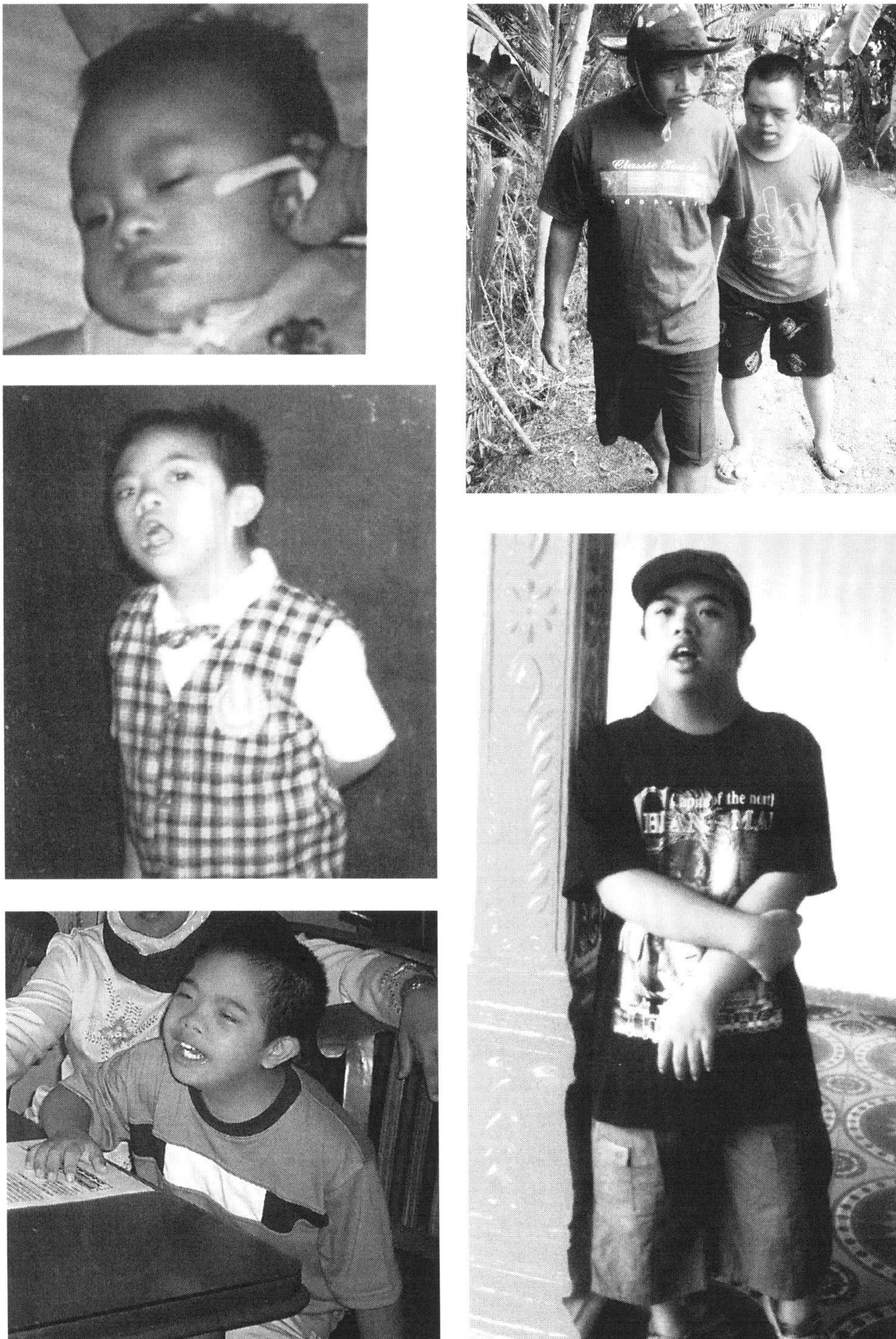

Figure 11.1 My brother as a child, and as a teenager with our father. I wish I had acknowledged him as a child with DS.

from the perspective of my blooming interest in the education of children and young people with Down syndrome and my wish to do something to improve the lives of my brother and other children with similar disabilities.

Current situation: affordances and challenges

How many people with Down syndrome are there in Indonesia? For two reasons, the number is difficult to calculate. First, diagnosis depends on the parents' or family members' knowledge of Down syndrome. They may not be aware that a child or family member has Down syndrome. Second, once they learn that one of their family members has Down syndrome, they may prefer to conceal the child's disability instead of talking openly or seeking help. In developing countries, it is not uncommon for Down syndrome to go unrecognized in babies and for parents to adopt an attitude of hiding away babies who potentially have a disability (McConkey, 2002).

According to a recent survey, there are around 300,000 children with Down syndrome in Indonesia (Kompas, 2010b). Furthermore, according to data from the Directorate of Special Education and Special Service Education of the Ministry of National Education, in 2007, there were 72,325 children attending special education schools (public and non-public schools). Among these children, 42,866, or 59 per cent, are children with an intellectual disability. However, the Directorate does not state the number of children with Down syndrome attending these special schools. Thus, the number of children with Down syndrome remains unknown.

These numbers suggest that a large proportion is missing out on schooling. This is one of the problems in our country. In the following, I discuss affordance, challenges, and priorities to be addressed, in order to improve the quality and also accessibility of education for children with special needs, including those with Down syndrome.

Affordances

National policy advocating people with disability

McConkey (2002) reviews three critical strategies that are transforming the future of people with Down syndrome from one of despair and hopelessness to a valued and positive lifestyle in their family and the community. One of the strategies is through a national policy which advocates for people with a disability. In Indonesia, the groundwork has been laid (Amendment of the Indonesian Constitution, 1945). Verse 1 states that every citizen has a right to receive education. Furthermore, Verse 2 states that every citizen has a duty to participate in basic education and the government shall pay for that basic education. This Constitution has resulted in several laws. First, the National Education System Law, Number 20, Year 2003, Verse 5 (1) states that every citizen has an equal right to receive a high quality of education, and Verse 5 (2) states that citizens with physical, intellectual, mental, and social disability have the right to receive special education. Second, the Child Protection Law, Number 23, Year 2002, and Verse 1 (15) states those children with disability have the right to be protected, and Verse 51 states that children with a physical or mental disability shall have equal opportunity and accessibility to receive education in a regular or special school. Third, Disability Law, Number 4, Year 1997, Verse 5 states that citizens with a disability have equal rights and opportunity to improve their quality of life, while Verse 6 states that they have a right to receive education. Furthermore, Indonesia is a signatory to The United Nations Convention on the Rights of Persons with Disabilities, the convention which was adopted on 13 December 2006 and opened for signature on 30 March 2007.

As mentioned above, there is a choice of schools for children with a disability—special school or inclusive school. A special school is expected to serve children with special needs, including gifted children. The students are grouped into classes or groups according to their type of impairment or special need. There are 10 types: Type A—visual impairment; Type B—hearing/speechless impairment; Type C—intellectual disability; Type D—physical disability; Type E—social disability or disruptive children, HIV or AIDS and drug victim children; Type F—autism; Type G—multiple disability; Type H—learning disability such as dyslexia, dyscalculia, dysgraphia, dysphasia, and dyspraxia, slow learner (IQ 70–90); Type I—gifted children with IQ of more than 125, talented children; and Indigo—that is, children who are claimed to possess special, unusual, and/or supernatural traits or abilities. A unit of a special education school usually serves only one to five types of special needs. Children with Down syndrome usually are included in Type C, children with intellectual disability.

Since 2000, the Indonesian government has tried to develop inclusive education. This was not totally new because in the 1980s there was a movement called 'integrated education', which was quite similar to inclusive education. However, following a world trend towards inclusive education, the government chose to use that term. *The Salamanca Statement on Inclusive Education* (1994) and *The Dakar Commitment on Education for All* (2000) (PLB, 2007) have influenced the stake holders to take a positive view on inclusive education. The Bandung Declaration during a national seminar held by the Indonesian government in Bandung, West Java on 8–14 August 2004 shows a commitment: 'Indonesia goes to Inclusive Education'. The National Seminar was continued with an international conference held in Bukittinggi, West Sumatra on 26–29 September 2005, resulting in a statement that inclusive education shall be considered as the approach to improving the quality of schooling and guaranteeing' education for all'. As well, the Indonesian government, through its Ministry of Education, supports inclusive education through regulation Number 70, Year 2009. The regulation states that students with physical, intellectual, mental, and social disability have the right to enter inclusive education depending on their needs (Verse 3). According to this regulation, an inclusive school can be a regular school which also admits children with special needs, or a special school which also admits typically developing children. As well, every district shall have at least one inclusive school for each level, and every class shall have at least one child with a disability. Finally, the government shall provide to each inclusive school at least one teacher with expertise in special needs (Figure 11.2 shows students working in a special education class).

Parents' associations

Family involvement is also among the three strategies suggested by McConkey (2002) to improve the quality of life of people with Down syndrome. The Indonesian Association for Down syndrome or 'Ikatan syndrome down Indonesia' (ISDI) was established on 21 April 1999 in Jakarta (the Indonesian capital). This non-profit organization plays an important role providing support for parents or families, even though the members also consist of medical practitioners, special education practitioners, teachers and

Figure 11.2 Teaching and learning in a special education class.

volunteers. The purpose of this organization is to inform the community about children with Down syndrome through newspapers and activities such as dancing, playing music, sport, or other social activities. They have regular meetings to share information and experiences on how to educate children with Down syndrome.

Challenges

In the effort to improve the quality of life and the quality of education of children with Down syndrome in Indonesia, there are at least two significant challenges to be addressed: 1) the negative attitude towards disabilities, 2) policy versus implementation.

Negative attitude towards disabilities

Negative attitudes towards disabilities may stem from parents, family members, or the community. There has been a change in the attitudes to and beliefs about children with a disability in many parts of Indonesia. However, when a baby with Down syndrome is born into a family, there are at least three factors which affect the quality of their education: acceptance, wealth, and knowledge of the parents, carers, or family members (Figure 11.3). If these factors work together in a positive way, children with a disability may receive a high quality of education.

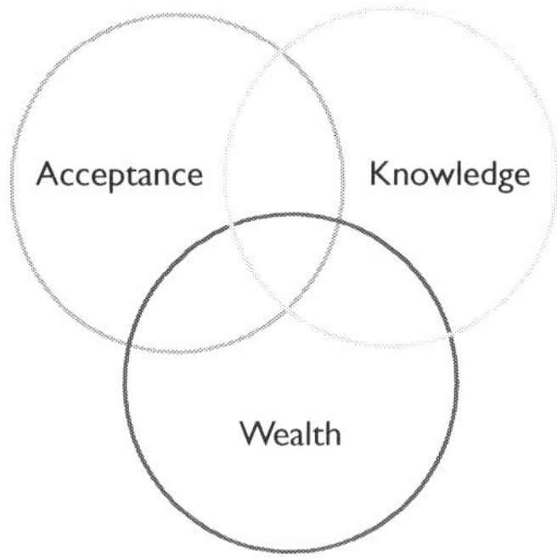

Figure 11.3 Factors which influence attitudes towards disability.

Acceptance. Similar to what occurs in Vietnam (Hodes, 2007), only very rarely do parents or family feel proud to have a child with a disability. The level of acceptance of families differs. If the disability is noticed at birth, the child is very susceptible to rejection. In the case of Down syndrome, early identification is rare. Pre-natal screening is limited to parents who are wealthy and educated. Understanding that a child has a mental disability will develop over time, when parents see that their child's development is slower than that of 'normal' babies. The parents and family may react by ignoring or concealing the child's disability. They may allow the child to grow up without responding in any specific way. Acceptance from the parents, however, is important for the survival of a child with Down syndrome.

*Wealth.*When a child is born into a wealthy family, the family is able to pay for medical services, treatment, and education. However, if the same child is born into a less wealthy family, these services are unaffordable. A disabled child born into a poor family is the most unfortunate child. While other family members are struggling to fulfill their daily needs, the child is very susceptible to neglect.

Knowledge. While the two factors of acceptance and wealth are important, there is also the important factor of knowledge. In order to improve the quality of life of children with Down syndrome, parents as well as family should have knowledge about how to educate and care for them. Although it is unlikely that a family member will have prior experience in educating a child with Down syndrome, knowledge on how to raise and educate children with Down syndrome can be obtained from books as well as from other parents who have a child with this disability. Once the child is accepted, we move to the next issue. There should be access to information so parents and family members will not feel alone. Forming a parental support group is a necessity. In the end, the parents' support groups may work together to change negative attitudes of the community towards people with Down syndrome.

According to Juang Sunanto (2011), there are three stages of community attitudes towards people with a disability: (1) neglect them, (2) protect them, (3) train and educate them. From time to time, communities will change from one stage to another. However, since the community consists of individuals, the community attitude is affected by how individual members react to the disability. In order to change the community attitude, people and families who do not have children with a disability must be included. It is necessary to develop a friendly environment. People tend to be afraid of something they do not know or they do not understand. Due to their misunderstanding, people may reject a disabled person. There were several cases in Indonesia where pregnant women were afraid to meet a person with a disability due to their superstitions that they will give her bad luck, and her baby will be born with a similar disability. This superstition should be removed by spreading correct information that a disability and Down syndrome do not occur in that way.

Policy versus implementation

Even though there has been good will from government to raise the quality of education of children with a disability as well as their quality of life, implementation of the policy is still facing many difficulties. Lack of resources as well as lack of expertise is not uncommon in developing countries like Indonesia. While many of the citizens are still struggling to fulfill their basic needs, people with a disability in these countries, including people with Down syndrome, who have limited or no ability to contribute to the family, are most vulnerable to neglect. Job opportunities are available to the more able compared with those with a disability. One way to narrow the gap is to educate and train these children to have skills that enable participation in paid work. However, the number of special schools is limited and many regular schools are not yet ready to accept children with special needs. It is not surprising that many children with a disability are still excluded from school. This is much less of a problem in the affluent world, which is rich with professional expertise (McConkey, 2002).

Furthermore, in special education schools, there are limited numbers of books which provide guidance to teachers who teach children with Down syndrome. Teachers will use teaching methods based on their experience, and they call it 'teacher method'. The limited information about how children with Down syndrome learn makes it difficult for new teachers to gain insight into the teaching of children with Down syndrome. There is an important need for information about how children with Down syndrome learn a range of subject matters, such as science, mathematics, and technology. (See Chapters 5–8 of this book.)

Considering these affordances and challenges, I propose four priorities to be addressed in order to improve the quality of education for children with a disability, including children with Down syndrome.

Priorities to be addressed

Changing negative attitude towards people with disability

There are at least two means to promote a positive attitude towards people with a disability. The first is through a formal path, such as health practitioner and teacher education, and the second is through an informal path, such as using mass media. It is not common for a student teacher who is preparing to teach subjects such as mathematics and science to take a course on disability. Thus the Ministry of National Education should appeal to teacher education institutions to require students to take one course on disability. In Indonesia, the informal paths to promote positive attitudes towards Down syndrome have been started by ISDI. This should be continued and further developed. Relevant published articles include: 'Teori Baru Penyebab Down syndrome' (New theory on the cause of Down syndrome) (Kompas, 2010b),

'Anak Down syndrome harus bias mandiri' (Children with Down syndrome should be educated to be independent) (Kompas, 2010a), and 'Down syndrome harus diberi peluang' (Down syndrome should be given a chance) (Kompas, 2008).

Changing negative attitudes also can be done by modifying infrastructure to be more disability friendly. Having more accessible buildings means that we are more likely to see and experience people of disabilities and that would lead to changes in attitudes. Buildings and public facilities, including public transport, should cater for people with a disability. Radical change, such as replacing buildings, is impossible. However, in the case of new buildings, architects should be encouraged to consider this issue. Modifications of and improvements to the environment are needed for Down syndrome people because their body characteristics differ from those of normal people. Some people with Down syndrome may be afraid to walk along a narrow path or on steps. They need buildings with features such as wider paths.

A new paradigm for catering for disability has commenced but it has not yet spread widely. It has been suggested that the term 'children with a disability' be changed to 'children with special needs' or 'children with special needs in education' (Juang Sunanto, 2011). The later term promotes a more positive view and can include gifted children.

Enforcing the implementation of inclusive education

Early identification is very important. Many parents with a child with Down syndrome want to send their child to school. However, the location of the school is often too far from their home. This problem could be solved by forcing a regular school to be an inclusive school. However, this would require the headmaster and teachers to have a positive attitude to disability and the knowledge to know what help and support is needed. Therefore, this is suggested as the second priority to be addressed.

Forming parental support groups in wider areas

As mentioned above, one of the affordances in educating people with Down syndrome in Indonesia is the existence of parents' associations. Currently however, the parents association is present only in the national capital. In other parts of Indonesia, there are still many Down syndrome children and their families who are unreached, living in isolation from support. Supporting the formation of parental support groups in wider areas is important. As regular schools become inclusive schools, the networks among these schools may encourage the formation of parent support groups. Therefore, this is suggested as the third priority.

Increasing the availability and numbers of professionals and experts in the area of disability

The last (but not least) priority to be addressed is the need to increase the numbers of professionals and experts in the area of disability. As McConkey (2002) stated, the affluent world is rich in professional expertise, training opportunities, and career structures that are accompanied by a growing number of specialists, but this is not the case for poorer nations. There should be good will for the government to provide training opportunities and career structures, as well as scholarships for people who want to work and study in areas of disability.

Conclusion

This chapter described the current situation on educating children with Down syndrome in Indonesia. Nevertheless, what is described in this chapter does not apply to every part of Indonesia. The situation in different parts of Indonesia can vary considerably. While typically developing children in remote areas may have very limited access to education, children with a disability in these areas will have none. As well, the situation described here does not apply to all developing countries; however, several features, such as negative attitude towards disabilities and inconsistency between policy versus implementation, are likely to be relevant.

Education does make a difference. The key to successful education is to focus on what children can do and build from there, instead of taking a pessimistic view on what they cannot do. The reasons for educating children with Down syndrome should be the same as those for educating every typically developing child: every child has the right to be educated in order to reach their highest potential and to have a higher quality of life.

Furthermore, I would like to quote McConkey (2002):

> Down syndrome is not a disaster for either the person or the family but rather a road less travelled. It is a journey that increasingly is becoming better signposted with improved facilities en route and one that brings rich rewards to those who venture forth in hope and with determination.
>
> (McConkey, 2002, p. 208)

We are in a developing country and we have just woken up from a long sleep. We need to reflect on our own experiences and also to learn from developed countries that there is hope for children with Down syndrome. We are aware that the road is still long and hard. Nevertheless, with belief and determination, our dreams can eventuate. 'A high quality of education' is possible for every child, including those with Down syndrome, or other disability and special needs. We choose to travel on the road less travelled and it will make a difference.

Acknowledgement

The author wishes to thank IASSID Asia-Pacific Scholarship Programme-*SINGA scholarship* for providing travel funds to attend a writing conference in Portsmouth in the process of developing this chapter. Thanks to my parents who let me include their pictures in this chapter. Finally, to my brother, I want to say thank you and forgive me for not being there while you grew up. I hope I will be able to do more for you in the future.

References

Hodes, M. (2007). Early intervention in Vietnam. *Down Syndrome Research and Practice, 12*, 38–41.

Juang Sunanto. (2011). Pendidikan Luar Biasadi Indonesia. Retrieved on 10 August 2011 from http://file.upi.edu/Direktori/FIP/JUR._PEND._LUAR_BIASA/196105151987031-JUANG_SUNANTO/PLB.diInodesia.pdf.

Kompas. (27 November 2008). Down syndrome harus diberi peluang. Retrieved on 10 August 2011 from http://kesehatan.kompas.com/read/2008/11/27/15413189/.Down.Syndrome.Harus.Diberi.Peluang.

Kompas. (24 January 2010a). Anak Down syndrome harus bias mandiri. Retrieved on 10 August 2011 from http://kesehatan.kompas.com/read/2010/01/24/15030726/Anak.Down.Syndrome.Harus.Bisa.Mandiri.

Kompas. (29 March 2010b).Teori Baru Penyebab Down syndrome. Retrieved on 10 August 2011 from http://kesehatan.kompas.com/read/2010/03/29/11191896/Teori.Baru.Penyebab.Down.Syndrome.

McConkey, R. (2002). Creating positive lifestyles for people with Down syndrome in developing countries. In M. Cuskelly, A. Jobling, & S. Buckley (Eds), *Down syndrome across the life span* (pp. 195–201). Philadelphia: Whurr.

PLB. (2007). *Pedoman umum penyelenggaraan inklusif.* Jakarta: Direktorat Pembinaan Sekolah Luar Biasa.

Chapter 12

Where we are, where we would like to be, and (perhaps) how we get there

Rhonda Faragher and Barbara Clarke

This book emerged from a desire to collect in one place what we know about educating learners with Down syndrome that has been gleaned from research and decades of learning from practice by parents, teachers, and other professionals. And what an exciting time this is to be undertaking such a task. In most countries, babies born with Down syndrome can expect to live long, healthy, and fulfilling lives with opportunities for inclusion in education, community life, and employment. Education is the mechanism by which much of the preparation for high quality of life in adulthood is achieved.

This book was developed by a group of researchers from the International Association for the Scientific Study of Intellectual and Developmental Disability, Down Syndrome Special Interest Research Group. It was considered timely to collate research findings, identify promising practices, and recommend strategies for educating students with Down syndrome. The chapters provide rich insights into what is currently known about learners with Down syndrome across a range of areas. They offer advice for practitioners and give future directions for researchers. In this final chapter, we will bring together some key issues arising from current practice, highlight areas of continued research need, and focus on future implications.

Throughout this book, the joys and challenges of educating people with Down syndrome are evident. We, along with the authors of chapters, take the view that Down syndrome is not a problem to be fixed. There are similarities and differences when learners are compared with those without Down syndrome and some of the differences can be challenging at times. It is important to acknowledge the complexities that are involved in any educational endeavour and these may be multiplied when students with intellectual disabilities are involved. A number of authors have cautioned about simple solutions or claims of interventions that provide an "answer" to the education of learners with Down syndrome. It will be challenging for the teacher, the parent, and others involved, but for many, it can be some of the best teaching experiences they have.

It is also acknowledged by many authors that, as with more typically developing children, each learner with Down syndrome is distinctive. There is considerable variation in ability, interest, and context. The people with Down syndrome who introduced this book and who have the final word in the epilogue are testament to this variation. We hope you have the opportunity to meet many other people with Down syndrome. We acknowledge the value of highlighting relative strengths and weaknesses related to the syndrome for the purposes of enhancing education but warn against this providing a specific "recipe" for the educator to use. In extending the metaphor, we would argue that there is a range of ingredients necessary but the skilled practitioner can use these to create the best outcome for the learner.

Where we are

In many middle-to-high income countries, education of learners with Down syndrome has radically changed over the last 50 years. This is partly due to the increase in life expectancy well into adulthood. But it is also due to changes in attitudes, led in part by parents responding to and driving the human rights agenda. From limited education by parents or charitable organizations, to education in special schools, to inclusive education in mainstream schools, the last few decades have brought remarkable transformations for learners. Teachers, other professionals, and parents have also experienced this transformation. It has led to dramatic changes in our understanding of what might be possible for learners and also the challenges of providing the best education and support for all learners in the classroom, including those with Down syndrome.

Quality of life

Quality of life forms a way of framing the broad approach both to the study of intellectual disability and to the consideration of policy and systemic decisions (see Chapter 1). We would also argue that it has strong implications for schooling and the decisions made by educators. For example, providing choice enhances feelings of control and children are more likely to engage and persist with a task that they have chosen. Quality of life concerns where we are now but also takes a lifespan view that leads us to consider the future. In this chapter, we return later to issues of quality of life as we discuss where we would like to be for educating learners with Down syndrome.

Cognitive aspects

Research understanding of cognitive profiles related to Down syndrome is still developing. Variations in measurement, comparison groups, and individual variation between those with Down syndrome makes this a complex task and it is important that this complexity is understood to prevent generalizations and premature conclusions. Indicated areas of strength and weakness are discussed in detail in Chapter 2 but there are on-going challenges to identify appropriate teaching methods and specific interventions. Some explicit practices, particularly in relation to language development, are contributing to significant improvement in cognitive progress. Young children with Down syndrome, though following a delayed or different developmental trajectory, can learn to read with resulting benefits for speech and language development as well as making progress possible through much of the traditional primary school curriculum.

There are many areas related to cognitive abilities and learning in need of investigation. Some assumptions have never been tested and, for certain strategies, evidence is needed to substantiate the approaches and to extend across different contexts and time.

Supporting language and mathematical development for learners with Down syndrome

Research into language development provides helpful insights and Chapters 9 and 10 suggest some promising practices. The research on mathematical development is more limited, with some tentative but helpful findings documented in Chapters 5–8.

Some common strategies are emerging across both areas. Ensuring time for adequate repetition and practice were key messages in the discussion of both literacy and mathematics. At the early stages of literacy and number development, children will need daily practice to learn new skills. Early intervention is required to support future learning. Given the relative speech, language, and verbal short-term memory difficulties in children with Down syndrome and the relative strength of visual learning, visual supports such as letters, words, and symbols should be used to support learning new skills, particularly those which rely on these areas of the learning profile, such as reading and early number.

Behaviour and motivations

Behaviour patterns can be major challenges for the educator of children with Down syndrome. This was evident in many of the chapters. In our research reported in Chapter 5, we noticed challenging behaviour patterns and had to find ways around them in order to gather our data. Teachers, learning support assistants, and parents also need to find ways to overcome these behaviours in order to support and enable learning. The barriers can be great but the opportunities provided by the strengths in social situations have potential. The importance of the social is a feature of the behaviour of children with Down syndrome. This was discussed extensively and a model for supporting teachers and care-givers was highlighted by Jones, Neil, and Feeley in Chapter 4. They reviewed behaviour analytic interventions that have some evidence with learners with Down syndrome and extensive evidence with learners with a range of disabilities, suggesting promise in considering a behaviour analytic approach to addressing the needs of learners with Down syndrome.

It is important to recognize the early pattern of challenging behaviour and early emerging impairments in pivotal skills that may negatively impact learning and classroom performance. Behaviours such as playfulness can be interpreted by educators as a negative but examples are provided of constructive interpretations of these and how they can be used to reinforce productive behaviours for learning.

It has been hypothesized that social and cognitive motivations are competing and that in children with Down syndrome the motivation to engage socially is more pressing than the motivation to engage with challenging cognitive tasks. To date this hypothesis has not been tested explicitly, but it clearly has important implications for classroom practice and would thus be a useful focus for future research.

Where we would like to be

We now return to the themes raised in the introductory chapter as we consider where we see the future for learners with Down syndrome and discuss what authors of this book consider to be major implications and challenges for future research.

Inclusive practices

In most middle- and high-income countries, the inclusion of students with Down syndrome in the regular classroom is established practice. This has been transformative for students with Down syndrome but can also be for other learners in these classrooms (Boyle, Scriven, Durning, & Downes, 2011). An understanding by the educators involved in teaching and supporting the learner in an inclusive setting of the specific strengths and weaknesses (both cognitive and behavioural) is clearly important. For example, the strengths of learners with Down syndrome in imitation and social interest suggest the need to carefully consider how to ensure successful learning in an inclusive environment. When we set up programmes, it is always with an eye towards maximizing learning within inclusive environments as well as within other environments as necessary to ensure the child with Down syndrome is learning important skills.

In addition, consideration of pedagogical strategies is needed. Some suggested approaches have arisen from research and/or practice and have been raised in this book. We summarize some here.

Year level-appropriate curriculum was raised as a possible approach in Chapter 8 where learners may not have acquired knowledge and skills in mathematics that have in the past been presumed to be prerequisite for the content being taught to other learners in the class. This had led to some learners demonstrating accomplishment with seemingly more advanced concepts of mathematics while still being unable to perform basic arithmetic. A similar strategy has been proposed for literacy where it is advocated that delayed literacy skills should not limit the child's access to lesson objectives and inclusion in classroom activities. Instead, use of word cards, scribes, and letters can be used to overcome this barrier—a similar role to that of the calculator in mathematics used to perform the arithmetic. Appropriate supportive tools within the classroom are relevant for other areas as well.

Learning for enjoyment and purpose reflects the underlying value of education. An argument can be made that sometimes, some things just have to be done for benefit later. However, if learning is restricted to drill for possible future use, challenging behaviours are likely to result. Instead, we advocate all formal learning be designed from the view that learning can and should be enjoyable. For example, reading should serve a purpose and be enjoyable from the beginning. Children enjoy reading about themselves and the things they are interested in and have knowledge about. This can be used to advantage when designing reading materials and lessons.

Research in literacy is relatively strong in the field of Down syndrome. Mathematics research is rarer. Research in other curriculum areas, such as history, drama, visual art, and science, is yet to establish a substantial body of literature. There are many examples of people with Down syndrome engaging in these disciplines, particularly in the performing arts, and education research would be welcome to support our understanding of how learners engage with these areas. Perhaps it is time to move beyond the idea of education for functional skills, of which clearly literacy and numeracy have a major part, and into the area of learning for enjoyment and purpose. Here, studies of language and literacy as well as mathematics and numeracy would still find a place.

Appropriate use of personnel, including parents, learning support assistants, and allied professionals such as therapists, is critical to optimizing the learning in inclusive settings. A large number of people can be involved in educating learners with Down syndrome and all should contribute to meetings that develop Inclusive Education Plans. Given adequate training and knowledge, teaching assistants and parents have been found to be effective in supporting the development of literacy and numeracy skills. There is a clear need to identify the "big ideas" of learning so that all involved, and particularly parents, are able to focus and rehearse learning that matters. With many personnel in a variety of roles interacting with learners with Down syndrome across their lifespan, parents often take on the role of "case manager". In most circumstances, they are the only constant member of the team. They know the past experiences and may have a sense of future plans and goals for their child. Partnerships where this "case manager" knowledge is shared with professionals and paraprofessional members can be very effective.

Appropriate use of interventions can be a valuable part of supporting inclusive practices. Intensive, targeted support can enable a learner to acquire or consolidate behaviour patterns or essential academic skills. What is required is a form of supported inclusion—opportunities for exclusive practices alongside genuine inclusive classroom experiences. Timing of the interventions must be carefully considered. Timetabling a young child to work on literacy skills while the other preschoolers are having outside play time might appear sensible—the other children are away, the academic programme is not being interrupted—but hardly likely to be enthusiastically embraced by the child. Similarly, taking the child off to work on number facts while the other students are learning science is inappropriate as the child misses an important aspect of the curriculum and cannot participate in the conversations of the classroom on their return as they have not been involved.

It is important to acknowledge the need for adequate training of personnel in order for them to support learners with targeted interventions. In many countries, "Early Intervention" is available and training begins with families and begins early. This frequently dissipates by the time the child reaches school age. To be effective, it must also be an on-going process for interventionists (teachers, assistants, other therapists, etc.), though can move into community settings for specific skill development (e.g. dance for movement patterns). Expertise and training is important to avoid the very real danger of inadvertently reinforcing challenging behaviour. The cute party tricks that Wishart (1993) described are too easy to be successful, resulting in the child with Down syndrome gaining attention and escaping whatever demands were placed.

The advent of **new technologies** opens up new possibilities for education, including literacy development, and a wide range of instructional resources are now available on the internet. These types of resources are often very motivating for children and offer a useful addition to traditional teaching. However, computers do not do the teaching! As for all technology, they do not take the place of thorough planning of learning and expert teaching. Well-designed computer programs or tablet apps can support learning and teaching by being a vehicle for consolidation and practice.

Assessment

As mentioned in the introduction, assessment serves a range of purposes and practices. In Chapters 5, 6, and 7, the use of one-to-one, task-based interviews are advocated as research tools but also as assessment tools for educators. Such flexible approaches maximized the chances of children with Down syndrome showing what they knew and could do mathematically. Clear assessment and/or measurement should be put into place to ensure that the small steps of progress that may be made are not overlooked by general classroom measures.

There is a need for the development of an expanded set of measurement techniques across a range of areas, including motivation. It is important that these can be applied in a variety of contexts and that they capture the contexts in more mature forms for older children and adolescents. Such methodological advancements would allow longitudinal investigations of individual and group trajectories, and the influences on these, including classroom practices. This could shed light on changes that occur in behaviour and have an impact on education. We are aware of a school system that has reported to us that most challenges faced by their schools concern children with Down syndrome in the early years. The children take time to learn how to behave appropriately in school and this can involve reducing the avoid-learning behaviour patterns. It would seem that, as the children grow older, they learn to adopt more positive learning behaviours.

In the context of inclusion, it is relevant to consider the role of school-based assessment of learning that is undertaken by class teachers as well as state-wide and systemic assessments and the impact of these. In some jurisdictions students with intellectual disabilities are excluded. Is this appropriate? Some argue without inclusion in these testing regimes, accountability for learning and teaching is lost. Others would refute this with a preference for less invasive and stressful assessment proceeds, especially where the only information gained is what the child cannot do, rather than providing data on what they can.

Assessment of learning needs to take a variety of approaches and formal measures such as examinations and tests may not provide the best information. It is known that learners with Down syndrome find difficulty in responding to questions and so strategies that elicit what a child knows or can do may need to be implemented. This might involve observations and anecdotal records. For example, rather than asking a child what a colour is, a teacher might observe a child painting and ask them what colour they would like. If they ask for red and correctly select the red paint brush, it can be noted the child knows the colour red.

Evidence-based practice

The chapters in this book provide considerable evidence on which to build appropriate practices. Clearly, research is on-going and practice will change in the future based on new evidence. We are also appreciating the value that practice gives to evidence. Through informed, reflective practice, evidence accumulates that can be folded into theory, which can then be researched and then turned back into practice: a continuous cycle of improvement of our understanding of teaching and learning. This form of evidence is critical in small populations, such as learners with Down syndrome.

Chapter 4 focuses on the "**how**" of realizing potential for learners with Down syndrome through interventions. Intervention needs to be based on solid science. For practitioners, this means ensuring the practices we engage in have an empirical evidence base. That evidence base may come from learners with other disabilities. Intervention strategies can be adapted to suit the needs of learners with Down syndrome, but the strategies still need to be based on empirical evidence. As researchers, this need for evidence-based strategies should spur us to more research. Improving outcomes and realizing the potential for learners with Down syndrome requires the integration of fields, at least two of which are behaviour analysis and the examination of the Down syndrome behavioural phenotype.

For teachers and other professionals, there are implications of evidence-based practice that include the need for educators to use research, and to read further. Professional practice involves applying what they read to the specific context, studying its impact, and adapting. This implies they need to be researchers of their own practices.

Hopefully, this is undertaken within an environment of reflection and collegial support. Researchers also need to accept responsibility for articulating their results in professional forms that are accessible to practitioners.

Expectations

In Chapter 8, we are reminded of Billie Shepperdson's challenge from 1994 that, until learners with Down syndrome continue to be taught throughout their school years and into adulthood, we cannot know what levels of attainment they may achieve and maintain. In order to make this a reality, we must have high expectations and strive to remove barriers that hinder progress. Timely and appropriate medical care, such as regular checks of hearing, vision, and endocrine function, can minimize the effects of preventable impediments to learning. More pernicious barriers exist, though, that are harder to minimize or overcome. In the classic study from 1968, Rosenthal and Jacobson demonstrated the education equivalent of medicine's placebo effect. Medical research acknowledges the power of placebo to the point where double-blind trials are required to demonstrate the effectiveness or otherwise of new treatments, where neither researcher nor subject knows whether they are receiving the treatment or the control. Rosenthal and Jacobson demonstrated the power of teacher expectations on the subsequent performance of their students. As Roy Brown writes in Chapter 1, high expectations are critical for all involved—parents, teachers, learning support assistants, professionals, and indeed the learners themselves. Over the decades, we have seen so many occasions where learners with Down syndrome have surprised us.

A discussion of expectations needs to consider the consequences when expectations are not realized. Not all children grow up to be astronauts or brain surgeons. As children move through their school years, they along with those who care for them become aware of their particular gifts and talents and also what are not strengths. This is true for young people with Down syndrome as well. Some will enjoy public speaking, where others cringe with embarrassment. Still others would like to have their voice heard and opinions noted but find limitations with speech hold them back. A similar range will be found across most other fields of endeavour. Those supporting people with Down syndrome need to examine the limitations impeding desired accomplishment and systematically work to remove or circumvent the barriers. Learning is lifelong, especially for people with Down syndrome, but they need to be taught.

The future beckons

Education of learners with Down syndrome is an exciting field of research, with much more needed. There are many constructive suggestions provided throughout the book. As we move to a new era of improved health outcomes and enhanced schooling opportunities, a greater emphasis on identifying successful interventions in realistic contexts is needed. Longitudinal studies which clearly identify the intervention children receive from an early age (and amount/duration/frequency) and the impact of this on development longer term would be valuable. Longitudinal studies into the secondary schooling years and beyond would also provide sorely-needed insights.

While our focus for this book has been on the years of formal schooling, significant learning will need to occur in the years beyond formal school for learners with Down syndrome. Much of the research has relevance in such circumstances but the context is likely to change. Innovations in technology are already occurring, which are removing or changing the need for skills once thought to be fundamental. These include handwriting, accessing information, and financial skills (see Chapter 8). There is a need to reconceptualize the purpose of functional education and "life skills" to more accurately reflect the needs of a rapidly changing adulthood. A rich education can involve functional skills but this will not be sufficient—studies from a range of disciplines will be required.

Extending research around the world

A great deal of research is undertaken and promulgated in medium- or high-income countries. Extrapolating research findings to other countries is not necessarily a direct process. With contexts being so different, it cannot be assumed teaching and learning in one culture will transfer automatically. There is a further consideration of whether transfer would even be desirable. A better approach, in our view, is to have researchers in local contexts undertaking research and making the connections between international findings. Chapters 7 and 11 in our book engage in this approach. We look forward to other researchers joining the worldwide conversation and sharing their results for the benefit of all.

Opportunities and possibilities

Educating learners with Down syndrome is full of challenges but also considerable joy. Parents and teachers who are aware of each child's strengths, interests, curiosities, and talents can experience the consummate pleasure of nurturing these gifts. It is a rare privilege to have the opportunity to make a difference in the life of a child.

What more do we need? There is so much we do not know, but this book is a start to consolidate our current understandings and point to future developments. Will you join us in this journey?

References

Boyle, C., Scriven, B., Durning, S., & Downes, C. (2011). Facilitating the learning of all students: The "professional positive" of inclusive practice in Australian primary schools. *British Journal of Learning Support, 26*, 72–78.

Rosenthal, R., & Jacobson, L. (1968). *Pygmalion in the classroom: Teacher expectation and pupils' intellectual development.* New York: Holt, Reinhart and Winston.

Shepperdson, B. (1994). Attainments in reading and number of teenagers and adults with Down's syndrome. *Down Syndrome Research and Practice, 2*, 97–101.

Wishart, J. (1993). Learning the hard way: Avoidance strategies in young children with Down's syndrome. *Down Syndrome Research and Practice, 1*, 47–55.

Epilogue

We began this book with comments from young people with Down syndrome. The authors of this book acknowledge the responsibility we have of writing about Down syndrome and the privilege we are afforded in sharing some part of the story. We conclude with the words of our friends with Down syndrome who inspire us and demand that research continue.

What research should be done?

> Knowing how to help children with Down syndrome to want to go to school. My friend does not want to go to school.
>
> (Ruth)

> Kathleen's brother is going to meet me for lunch to tell me about the [Down syndrome] association. He wants to take her to things to take a bit of the load off of us. So I think more research should be done on the siblings of children with Down syndrome. How does it affect their lives? How does it affect what they do and how they do it? I would really love to see some research on that.
>
> (Kathleen's mother)

What would you like teachers to know about teaching kids with Down syndrome?

> Teachers have to put maths work on a whiteboard and the kids can copy it down in their note books. I copy things down from the board.
>
> (Ruth)

Are there things about school that we could improve?

> Give me work to do in booklets.
>
> (Ruth)

Is there anything else you want to tell other people?

> I've been working on that question for some time. We should let our people know not to be afraid to express your feelings. We are human. Down syndrome and other types of disabilities should not be mistreated. Drop the "R" word now! And

drop the disability down as well. What I mean by that is that people with disability should have the right of what they want, where to live and also we must have the right to live, the right to stay at school, the right to vote! That's what makes us human. We're no different from each other. We all know what's right and wrong. And what I mean by that is that we should stay on right, not wrong and the most important thing is that disability or not, we're as human as we are.

(Dylan)

I think most people know of Down syndrome but they don't really understand the degrees. The different degrees of disability that's entailed within it and what that means. People sometimes think when they talk about Down syndrome it means that they can't do anything. Some think it means they can do what other people can do. There's not that real understanding about the differences. I think it would be really good to educate people in that.

Kathleen's an absolute delight. When she was little the doctors said to us: "If she goes into heart failure, should we just not resuscitate her or do you want us to do something?" We said, "Of course we want you to do something because she is our child!" But if people think that children with Down syndrome can't achieve and don't give as much as they receive, then there is a problem. People often think that we are the ones who do all the caring, the bathing, everything. They don't see all the things they give you. You know it would be great to see some research on that. What do parents see are the positive things that their children or even the siblings see are the positive things that they receive from the child or person or brother or sister with Down's?

(Kathleen's mother)

Subject index

Page numbers in *italics* denote tables, those in **bold** denote figures.

Author index